BROKEN SUNSHINE

A Case Study of Elder Abuse and Exploitation in Florida

CARL R. BAKER

Carl R. Baker

BROKEN SUNSHINE: A Case Study of Elder Abuse and Exploitation in Florida.

Copyright © 2022 Carl R. Baker.

All rights reserved. No part of this book may be reproduced or used in any manner without written permission of the copyright owner except for the use of quotations in a book review.

Published by Hallard Press LLC.
www.HallardPress.com   Info@HallardPress.com   352-234-6099
Bulk copies of this book can be ordered at Info@HallardPress.com

Publisher's Cataloging-in-Publication data

Names: Baker, Carl R., author.
Title: Broken sunshine : a case study of elder abuse and exploitation in Florida / Carl R. Baker.
Description: The Villages, FL: Hallard Press, 2022.
Identifiers: LCCN: 2022906542 | ISBN: 978-1-951188-53-5 (paperback) | 978-1-951188-54-2 (ebook)
Subjects: LCSH Older people--Abuse of--Florida. | Older people--Abuse of--United States. | Abused elderly--Florida. | Frail elderly--Abuse of--Florida. | People with disabilities--Abuse of--Florida. | BISAC FAMILY & RELATIONSHIPS / Abuse / Elder Abuse | MEDICAL / Geriatrics | MEDICAL / Nursing / Gerontology | MEDICAL / Public Health
Classification: LCC HV6626.3 .B35 2022 | DDC 362.6/820973--dc23

Printed in the United States of America   1 2

ISBN: 978-1-951188-53-5 (Paperback)
ISBN: 978-1-951188-56-6 (EBook)

A Case Study Of Elder Abuse And Exploitation In Florida

DISCLAIMER

The conclusions and opinions expressed in this case study are those of the Baker family unless otherwise stated.

A Case Study Of Elder Abuse And Exploitation In Florida

CONTENTS

Chapter 1	Introduction	1
Chapter 2	Florida Overview	7
Chapter 3	A Brief Family History	11
Chapter 4	Sandra Treolo Hine Kaniewski Baker	17
Chapter 5	Profile of a Sociopath	31
Chapter 6	Loving Relationship or Trap	37
Chapter 7	The Marriage	47
Chapter 8	The Quest for Paul's Money	51
Chapter 9	The Day Everything Changed	65
Chapter 10	Court Proceedings	95
Chapter 11	Eldercaring Coordination	129
Chapter 12	The Investigations	195
Chapter 13	A Most Unusual Hearing	297
Chapter 14	Resolution or Turmoil	429
Chapter 15	Postscript	477
Appendix A	Complete Timeline	487
Appendix B	Trust Spreadsheet	503
Appendix C	Antenuptial Agreement	507

A Case Study Of Elder Abuse And Exploitation In Florida

WHO'S WHO

John Paul Baker – Father of Mark and Allyne; brother to Bruce, Carl, Lynn, and Carol; married Sandra on 6/28/16.

Sandra Treolo Hine Kaniewski Baker – Paul's third wife; previously married to Ralph Kaniewski; stepmother to Christine Van Buren.

Bruce Baker –Paul's brother. Lives in The Villages.

Gail Baker – Bruce's wife.

Carl Baker – Paul's brother. Lives in The Villages.

Katherine Baker – Carl's wife.

Mark Baker – Paul's son. Lives in NY State.

Allyne Baker – Paul's daughter. Lives in NY State.

Kaila Baker – Paul's granddaughter. Lives in NY State.

Ralph Kaniewski - Sandra's second husband. Died October 10, 2014.

Christine Van Buren – Ralph's daughter. Sandra's stepdaughter.

Jack and Kathy Warner – Friends of Paul, Bruce, and Carl for over 50 years. Live in The Villages.

Hisham "Sham" Shanaway – Paul's trust attorney.

Michelle T. Morley – Circuit Judge – Sumter County.

Merideth Nagel - Paul's court appointed attorney.

Harry Hackney – Carl's attorney for guardianship.

Cher Myers – Eldercaring Coordinator (Mediator).

Amanda Ritter – Paul's court appointed guardian.

Carl R. Baker

Commendations

There are some people that will be introduced in this book that are true professionals and represented their respective agencies or offices with honor and distinction. I thank and commend the following for their efforts and commitment to the safety of the public and their tireless efforts to do their best for Paul:

The Sumter County Deputies who Sandy sent frequently to our home alleging Paul was kidnapped and mistreated or to deliver a few personal items to Paul.

Detective Larry Thompson, Sumter County Sheriff's Office.

Harry T. Hackney, Attorney at Law.

Robin Steinman, Campione and Hackney Law Office.

Hisham "Sham" Shanawany, Attorney at Law, Millhorn & Shanaway Law Firm. Paul's trust attorney.

Herman Hale, RN, Court appointed examiner for Paul.

Kimberly Mummey, Adult Protective Services Investigator, Department of Children and Families.

Lisa Jacobs, Adult Protective Services Investigator, Department of Children and Families.

Jensey Heding, Counsel's Office, Department of Children and Families.

Pati Kersey, S.A.D.L.E.S. Office Manager (Eldercare).

A Case Study Of Elder Abuse And Exploitation In Florida

JOHN PAUL BAKER

Paul in Vietnam in 1970.

Paul—Lieutenant Colonel in 1984.

**Rescue the poor and helpless;
deliver them from the grasp of evil people."
— Psalm 82:4**

> "It is not good to be partial to the wicked or
> to deprive the innocent of justice."
> — *Proverbs 18:5*

CHAPTER 1

Introduction

Our brother Paul has Alzheimer's. It is a sad, painful situation that thousands of families have experienced. Paul is also a crime victim because someone who was supposed to love him, did not. And then Paul became a victim again when the government stepped in and had more say in his life than his family of 70+ years.

This is a true story that wrote itself. However, from the very beginning it was predictable and we thought that we, his family, had the safeguards in place to prevent it from becoming a reality. We were wrong.

On August 22, 2018, Sandy gained complete control of

Paul's life and mind, and consequently, all his actions as well. Her isolation of Paul from his family was complete and the final impediment in her quest for Paul's money had been eliminated; or so she thought.

There are heroes and zeroes in this saga and once you see how it unfolds, you will easily be able to identify them. Some are individuals and some are government agencies. But the only real safeguard anyone has in exploitation cases like this one, is a loving family.

There is no hidden agenda here. Paul's entire family came together to ensure that the remainder of Paul's life would be the best it could possibly be. We would do whatever needed to be done to protect Paul. We really tried to work with Sandy by constantly offering our assistance, scheduling family meetings, and taking care of Paul when she was away, which was frequent. Unfortunately, it became evident that Sandy did not want anyone who cared about Paul to interfere with her control of him.

This is not one individual's recollection of what transpired over the last several years. Throughout this case study you will read actual correspondence between family members documenting what was happening to Paul before our very eyes. There is no denying the truth of this story and we are grateful that the Lord brought Paul back to the family that has always loved him unconditionally.

What makes this story so tragic, in my opinion, is that the Sunshine State of Florida's probate court is horribly broken. This is not a statement I make lightly and I am not alone in this conclusion. A significant number of professionals who have worked these cases for years, agree with me and have actually told me so. Remember, the Baker family's view is from the outside looking in as victims. To be blunt, we were the payers and not the payees. Our bills for the guardian and legal fees in this case have already totaled well over $60,000. Add all the money spent for Paul's care, and the total is over $300,000. Obviously, those who believe the probate court system works well and is not broken, are largely the parochial players who are on the inside and do very well financially.

To all the government officials, you need to take a long hard look at how you are treating the senior population who you are entrusted to protect here in Florida. There are changes that absolutely need to be made and perhaps this case study will help.

The Baker family is a strong team. We were always taught that it is important to take care of each other. Words cannot express how fortunate I have been to have my wife, Katherine, at my side during this entire ordeal. Any doubts I faced regarding this nightmare, during these past several years, were brushed aside by my wife's love, strength, and strong faith. To my twin brother Bruce and sister-in-law Gail, who also live in The Villages, thank you for all the help and the guidance you gave us during some exceedingly difficult decisions. We could not have done this without you. To our sisters, Lynn and Carol thank you for your help with Sandy's Facebook and your encouragement and suggestions. As you will learn as you read this story, Paul's daughter Allyne spent a great deal of time and effort documenting her interactions with Sandy which truly made a difference. And although Paul's son Mark, had little interaction with Sandy, he documented some key conversations which further revealed Sandy's true goal – control of Paul's non-marital assets.

Jack Warner has been a friend of ours for years and as teenagers we lived in the same neighborhood in upstate New York. In fact, Bruce and I served as ushers in his wedding to Kathy. When Paul, Bruce, and I all moved to the Villages, we learned that Jack and Kathy also lived here and our close friendship was renewed. Jack and Kathy often spent time with Paul and Sandy and their insight of her true motives further reinforced our concern for Paul. We cannot thank Jack and Kathy enough for all the assistance and support they gave our family throughout this ordeal.

Documenting a case like this one was certainly more difficult than writing a police report. Events were occurring daily and many of them would not be discovered for weeks. Attempting to give the reader a chronological story was a challenge and hopefully, was made easier with the interjection of timelines. Appendix A is a complete timeline.

There are so many bureaucratic failures in this case by multiple agencies, that I decided that I would do everything within my power to try to change and improve the probate court system in Florida. Since I needed to document every aspect of the case, there will be some repetition, especially in my letters and complaints, where I am explaining the events that occurred in the past and providing my personal opinion as well. All of this complicates the editing process; however, I was fortunate to have three wonderful editors: my wife Katherine and my brother Bruce, who both know the case as well as I do, and a wonderful friend, Dr. Teri Melton. Thank you for all your hard work.

As you read this story, you will understand the frustration we encountered in dealing with the myriad of government agencies charged with the protection of senior citizens, the prevention of elder abuse, and the enforcement of the Florida statutes. In addition, you will be able to see how the court operates and understand how, in my opinion, a relatively simple process, can be made complex and expensive by the insertion of the eldercaring coordinator. Hopefully, you will learn from our experiences.

I must admit that my passion in life has been law and order, which we all know is a requirement for a civilized society. Otherwise, why would I have spent almost my entire adult life in law enforcement. According to Dr. David Jeremiah, passion is not something you develop as much as something you discover and it is given to you by God. Further, that passion gives you the boldness, integrity and obedience to do what is right.

Two framed sayings have hung on my home and office walls for the past fifty years. Throughout all the trials and tribulations in my life, I would find comfort in reading them and find the strength to do what I needed to do. As you read this sad and sometimes, unbelievable story, you may want to come back and reread these to put some events in their proper perspective. Additionally, there are some people who you will be introduced to in this story who could gain much wisdom and direction by reading these same words:

THE LAW

"Not only life, but living with others is possible because of law. Without law, no man can be assured of the fruits

of his labors. Without law, brute force would prevail, the weak would be destroyed by the strong and the strong would destroy themselves in their ascendancy. Without law there would be no peace or privacy, no protection of persons or property, public or private, no foreseeable future. No assurance of anything we could count on."
— *Aristotle 321 B.C.*

If you think you are beaten, you are;
If you think you dare not, you don't.
If you'd like to win, but think you can't,
It's almost a cinch you won't.

If you think you'll lose, you're lost,
For out in the world we find
Success begins with a fellow's will;
It's all in the state of mind.

Life's battles don't always go to
The stronger or faster man;
But sooner or later the man who wins
Is the one who thinks he can.

— *Author unknown*

"Statistics are the triumph of the quantitative method, and the quantitative method is the victory of sterility and death."
— *Hilaire Belloc,*
The Silence of the Sea

CHAPTER 2

Florida Overview

Florida has a large and growing adult population. The State has a population approaching 20 million with 23% being age 60 or over. That makes the senior population at about 4.6 million and growing. The United States Census Bureau projects that the senior population in Florida will double by the year 2030.

The Florida Department of Children and Families reports the following elderly abuse cases for the years 2014 through 2018, which was the most current data available at this time:

Florida Elder Abuse Cases

Year	Reports	Reports Verified	Reports Not Verified	Referred for Protective Supervision
2014	34,083	3,932	30,151	1,123
2015	35,507	5,393	30,114	1,180
2016	38,592	5,658	32,934	980
2017	38,084	5,429	32,655	908
2018	36,580	5,765	30,815	1,041
Total	182,846	26,177	156,669	5,232

Of the 182,846 cases reported, only 14.3% were verified as elder abuse, which is questionably low. It is even more difficult to comprehend that of the 26,177 cases verified, only 5,232 or 20% were referred for additional supervision. Overall, in a five-year period, less than 3% of all reported cases of elder abuse were referred for protective supervision.

Following is the number of felony arrests and convictions for violation of the Florida Statute, Section 825 (Abuse, Neglect, and Exploitation of Elderly Persons and Disabled Adults) for the years 2014 through 2018 as reported by the Florida Department of Law Enforcement (FDLE):

Exploitation of Elderly Persons

Year	Arrest Charges	Convictions
2014	579	122
2015	615	101
2016	556	120
2017	612	177
2018	597	91
Total	**2,959**	**611**

The number of arrests and convictions when compared with verified reports seems quite low, 11.3% for arrests and 2.3% for convictions. If these figures are accurate, Florida most certainly has a problem. The data here begs the question: Is the State of Florida truly protecting its senior population?

Given the history and documentation of Paul's case, I question what standards Florida uses in deciding to arrest and prosecute a person who commits felony elder abuse. As you will see, this case was well documented and the Florida Department of Children and Families initially did not verify the abuse complaint and did not initiate protective supervision. I appealed their decision and they reinvestigated the case. This time they verified the complaint and forwarded it to law enforcement.

Likewise, the State Attorney elected not to seek prosecution since he first labelled it a civil case and then a "circumstantial case". Obviously, I adamantly disagreed, but I will let the reader review the facts and determine if the State Attorney made the correct decision. When the State Attorney was notified that the Department of Children and Families verified both inadequate supervision and exploitation by Sandy, he stated that it did not change his earlier decision and he would not prosecute the case. That was not the final answer for me and I took it to the next level. Unfortunately, Governor DeSantis never responded to my original certified letter. I waited two and a half months and sent a second follow-up certified letter. Again, he did not respond, nor did his office acknowledge the letter was received. However, I tracked the second letter and his office did receive it five days after I mailed it. What would justify the Governor's Office refusing to respond to my concerns? This should be troubling to every senior citizen in Florida.

"So much of what is best in us is bound up in our love of family, that it remains the measure of our stability because it measures our sense of loyalty. All other pacts of love or fear derive from it and are modeled upon it."
— *Haniel Long*

CHAPTER 3

A Brief Baker Family History

Our brother, John Paul Baker was born on June 6, 1946, exactly two years after D-Day. This was ironic since our father was a well-decorated World War II veteran and retired as a Major General after 40 years of military service. And Paul, following in our father's footsteps, retired as a Colonel after 32 years of service and received a brevet promotion to Brigadier General, for outstanding service in the New York Army National Guard.

Our father and mother were married on November 1, 1941. A

little over a month later, Pearl Harbor was attacked on December 7th, and within days, our father, Captain Baker was off to war. He returned home in 1945 as a war hero. He was awarded a Silver Star for gallantry in action on Saipan while serving in the 105th Infantry Division for halting an attack on his unit. His other awards include the Distinguished Service Medal, Legion of Merit, Bronze Star, Purple Heart with Oak Leaf Cluster, Presidential Unit Citation and Combat Infantryman's Badge.

It did not take long for our parents to start a family. Paul was born in 1946, Bruce and I (twins) were born in 1947, Lynn was born in 1950, and the youngest of the family, Carol, was born in 1952.

It was a typical military family. Our father was strict, and we always answered our parents with either a "Yes Sir" or a "Yes Maam". Since our dad spent a lot of time away from home, our mom was the one who raised us, and she was just as strict as our father.

As adults, all of us entered public service. Paul had a career in the military; Bruce spent 33 years in state service, mostly in the Department of Corrections, retiring as an Assistant Commissioner; l worked in state and local law enforcement for 40 years; and both Lynn and Carol served for years as Court Clerks. Even though we all went our separate ways, our family would get together four or five times a year and we always called each other on holidays and birthdays.

Upon graduation from college in 1969, both Paul and I were commissioned as Second Lieutenants in the United States Army through the Reserve Officer's Training Corps (ROTC) program.

We were very fortunate to have our father present to pin our gold bars on our uniforms.

Paul did his tour in Vietnam in 1970-71 where he served as a forward observer in an artillery company. Like so many other Vietnam veterans, Paul was exposed to Agent Orange and receives a disability from the Veteran's Administration. In November of 2015, Paul's diagnosis of Alzheimer's Dementia was confirmed.

Interestingly, this was after Paul started dating Sandy, but about eight months prior to their marriage on June 28, 2016. Sandy is Paul's third wife and Paul is Sandy's third husband. Ironically, as Paul looked back on his life, there are many times when he told me that divorcing his first wife, Linda, was the "biggest mistake in my life". If so, and I believe he is correct, his third marriage is the "second biggest mistake of his life."

In 2018, Paul was one of the combat veterans included in The Villages Honor Flight. Perhaps the letter I sent Paul for this event summarizes how we developed our close relationship that has lasted until this day.

BG (Ret.) J. Paul Baker
The Villages, FL 32163

Dear Paul,
Remember when we were growing up, like most brothers we fought, perhaps more than most. That all changed in the summer of 1968. We both went off to ROTC summer camp at Fort Indian Town Gap. You started a week earlier than I did, and I wondered how you were doing and what it was like. I arrived and while running to my

barracks on my first day of basic, carrying an armful of just issued uniforms and equipment, I heard someone call my name. I turned around and there you were saying, "Don't worry Carl, it's not bad, we can get through this." I stopped running, turned around and we shook hands. That was the moment we started to be best friends.

On June 1, 1969, we got commissioned together and were very fortunate to have Major General John C. Baker, our father, pin our bars on our uniform. Shortly thereafter, you reported for active duty and I got a six-month delay, so I could complete the New York State Police Basic School.

Shortly after Mark was born, I flew out to Fort Sill to see you and your growing family. I knew that this would be the last time I would see you before you were sent to Viet Nam. It turned out to be quite a trip since the military flight I hopped on to get back to New York crashed landed on an ice-covered runway.

We were all concerned when you started your assignment in Viet Nam. We wrote each other frequently at first and then I left for active duty at Fort Belvoir. The letters were less frequent, but they did continue. When you came home from Viet Nam, I managed to get time off and Dad, Bruce and I met you at the airport. What a relief to see you home and safe. I will never forget that day.

When we were both on active duty, I decided to drive up to Fort Dix from Fort Belvoir to spend a day with you. I do remember our long conversation and closing the bar in the officer's club. That was a great night!

After we both got off active duty, we went our separate ways. I went back to the State Police and you continued your military career in the National Guard. But we remained as close as ever.

It was not long, and we were together again. I was the XO of the

105th Military Police Company and ready to meet my new Company Commander, Captain J. Paul Baker. Several months later (1972), our company was ordered to active duty as Hurricane Agnes flooded Elmira and Corning. I handled the day-to-day operations, and you took care of everything else. This is where we began a phrase that we continue today and describes our friendship and respect for each other: "I got your back." Paul, I still got your back!

    The next ten years we again went down separate paths. I chose to put all my effort in my State Police career and left the military and you started your ascension up through the ranks. In the mid 80's we both ended up in the same headquarters building – you were a Colonel in the Army National Guard and I was a Colonel in the State Police. Occasionally, we had lunch together and we even ran the 5K race together, although I couldn't keep up with my Airborne Ranger brother.

    Even outside our careers we stayed close. We each purchased a condo in the Naples area of Florida. When Katherine and I decided to relocate to the Villages, we finally convinced you to move here as well and the three "Baker boys" were together again for the first time in many years.

    THANK YOU FOR ALL YOUR SACRIFICES AND YOUR 30+ YEARS OF SERVICE.

    WELCOME HOME.

    Love,

    /signed/CARL.

Paul said he never saw this letter until I showed it to him when he came to live with us. In July of 2020, when Sandy was moving, she delivered all of Paul's Honor Flight letters to the staff at Trinity Springs to give to him. My letter was **not** in the package. I believe that, for whatever reason, she intercepted my letter and destroyed it so Paul would not be able to read it.

So this close relationship did continue throughout our lives. After seeing how Paul was treated by Sandy and seeing Sandy's overt actions to take all of Paul's assets, there was only one choice —protect Paul. And that is exactly what Paul's family did.

However, by filing a petition with the court to determine incapacity of Paul, Sandy took all of Paul's rights away from him and replaced family control with government control. Evidently, she thought the court would return the control of Paul to her. Here again, Sandy underestimated the strength of a loving family. There is no way the Baker family was going to allow her to ever put Paul in danger again.

CHAPTER 4

Sandra Treolo Hine Kaniewski Baker

> "First they give themselves to indulgence and then they begin to justify their behavior and proclaim what they do is right and lawful."
> (*Count It All Joy,* David Jeremiah, p. 186)

Unfortunately, this statement accurately describes Paul's third wife.

No one in our family or any of our friends had ever met Sandy until Paul had been dating her for several months. We knew nothing about her past and had no idea she was still married to Ralph until Paul let it slip one day in the fall of 2014. As you would expect, all of us, including Paul's children, started questioning Paul out of our concern for him and what we saw as the start of an unusual and troubling relationship for many reasons. However, when we met Sandy, we were kind and sincere and welcomed her into our homes. We started going to dinner with them and when it came time for the Baker family Florida get together in August, Sandy met Paul's children and grandchildren. Sandy's conversations about Paul with our family always included comments about Paul's trust and his assets. Needless to say, this raised a red flag and none of us ever witnessed any conduct which would have us believe that Sandy genuinely loved Paul.

We also were so fortunate to have the support of Christine S. Van Buren, Ralph's daughter and Sandy's stepdaughter. She not only confirmed our suspicions about Sandy, but she also gave us information which proved invaluable for our case. Paul's daughter, Allyne, initiated the contact with Christine, so what better way to present this than in their own words:

"I first looked up Ralph's obit to see who his children were. Then I started trying to search for each of them online, google and social media. I knew it would be easiest to contact someone that you are not directly connected to through Facebook or Linked In. Christine Kaniewski Van Buren was who I found through Facebook. I sent her a message on September 18th, 2018:

" Hi, my name is Allyne Baker. First, I know this is weird, but I would like the opportunity to speak to you about a personal matter involving my father's wife. If you would be so kind, I would so appreciate a few minutes of your time. Thank you."

I checked every day after that to see if she (Christine) had "read" my message. She didn't read it until October 2nd but responded immediately.

"Nope, not weird at all. Was kind of expecting this. I am traveling today but will call you (later) today."

We spoke that day for my entire lunch hour. We both started out treading lightly, feeling each other out, each of us not wanting to sound too harsh. But as we got into the reason for my call and the situation our family was in, (how she was isolating Dad, was controlling him, not caring for him properly, was evil to me and had changed all intentions of Dad's estate planning), then Christine did not hold back. She told me all about how horrible Sandy was to Ralph for years and wanting to divorce him 10 years into their marriage. Sandy ended up staying with him when she realized she couldn't get any money from his pension if she divorced him. She said frankly Sandy was a money grabbing bitch!!! She also treated her father poorly, and they knew that she started seeing dad (Paul) before Ralph was even gone. That's when she told me her family felt that the car accident was not an accident at all. Why would she take him out of the rehab facility the day before he would be getting discharged? She said she didn't even visit Ralph daily. When the other car T-boned Ralph's door, that was the beginning of the end for Ralph. He never came home after that. Which is what they believe she wanted because she had already moved on to Dad (her next victim). Ralph went from rehab to a memory care facility all while Sandy was dating dad. I apologized to her for my dad's behavior, but I asked her to forgive him as he did have the beginnings of Alzheimer's. She said she didn't hold any hard feeling toward anyone but Sandy because she is the one who was married to her father and supposed to be loyal and faithful to him. I remember her telling me that she and her sisters wanted to investigate the accident further, but their uncle asked her not to. He just wanted Ralph to live out his remaining time in peace without turmoil. She now felt that was a mistake.

(Note: Sandy and Ralph's accident occurred on February 8, 2014, and we believe that Paul started seeing Sandy in July 2014 but cannot confirm it. To determine if Paul or any another person was in Sandy's life at the time of the accident, I asked my attorney and the State Attorney to subpoena Sandy's phone records, which could be very telling. Unfortunately, no subpoena was ever issued.)

Needless to say, we started keeping in contact on a more regular basis after that initial phone call. Christine had a real interest in helping us and said she felt a bit of guilt over not following through on her feeling to warn the family of "Sandy's next victim" when she first learned of their relationship (which was when Sandy brought Dad to Ralph's memorial service). Christine kept saying "you have a friend in Pennsylvania." And that her sisters and she would help us with anything having to do with getting my father to be free of Sandy."

And Christine, we sincerely thank you for all you have done to help us through this. We will be forever grateful.

Sandy's February 8, 2014 Motor Vehicle Accident

The day before Ralph was going to be released from the Rehabilitation Center which he had been in since October 2013, Sandy picked up Ralph to go see a movie. It seemed strange that they did not wait until he came home the next day. Driving westbound on CR 466 (the accident report mistakenly reported her going eastbound), Sandy made a left turn at Morse Boulevard, failing to yield to an eastbound SUV, which struck Sandy's passenger door, severely injuring Ralph.

On the day after the accident, Sandy posted the following message on her Facebook page:

"Ralph was doing so much better that he wanted to go see a movie yesterday...he is still in the rehab center. On the way there we were t-boned, air bags deployed, on star emergency came on and we were rushed to the hospital. I was driving and did not see it coming. What I think happened I was going to make a left and as the light was turning yellow out of nowhere a car hit Ralph's side. I think we were hit from behind because the car that was behind me was going to make a left also. Ralph was pinned in the car and was taken to the trauma center in Ocala and is in ICU with a lacerated kidney and broken ribs. I have cracked ribs but was released. I don't know when this nightmare that started October 26 is going to end and I am begging for prayers again for Ralph. I am positive our car is totaled and now we will need another car. With hospital bills and all, things are starting to get really tough. Love you all."

The Florida Traffic Crash Report and corrected description for Sandy's accident on February 8, 2014 at 11:45 AM follow:

Vehicle 1 (V01) was traveling westbound on CR466 in the left turn lane. Vehicle 2 (V02) was traveling eastbound in the outside lane. Vehicle 3 (V03) was stopped facing north in the inside lane of Morse Blvd. Vehicle 4 (V04) was stopped facing north on Morse Blvd in the outside lane. V01 made a left turn directly into the path of V02. The front of V02 struck the right side of V01. V01 rotated counterclockwise striking the front of V03 and V04 with the rear of V01. V01 came to final rest facing north in the intersection. V02 came to final rest facing south in the intersection. V03 came to final rest at the point of impact. V04 came to final rest at point of impact. V01 driver stated she had yellow light and didn't see anyone coming as she proceeded through the intersection. V02 driver stated when he was going through the intersection the light was yellow.

(Traffic Crash Report follows.)

A Case Study Of Elder Abuse And Exploitation In Florida

FLORIDA TRAFFIC CRASH REPORT

LONG FORM [ ] SHORT FORM [X] UPDATE [ ]
(Electronic Version)

**HIGHWAY SAFETY & MOTOR VEHICLES,
TRAFFIC CRASH RECORDS
NEIL KIRKMAN BUILDING, TALLAHASSEE, FL 32399-0537**

Date of Crash	Time of Crash	Date of Report	Invest. Agency Report Number	HSMV Crash Report Number
08/Feb/2014 11:45 AM	08/Feb/2014 11:45 AM	08/Feb/2014 01:18 PM	FHPC14OFF011707	83671072

CRASH IDENTIFIERS

County Code	City Code	County of Crash	Place or City of Crash	Within City Limits	Time Reported	Time Dispatched
44		SUMTER	LADY LAKE	No	08/Feb/2014 11:51 AM	08/Feb/2014 11:55 AM

Time on Scene	Time Cleared Scene	Completed	Reason (if Investigation NOT Completed)	Notified By
08/Feb/2014 01:03 PM	08/Feb/2014 03:00 PM	Yes		Law Enforcement

ROADWAY INFORMATION

Crash Occured On Street, Road, Highway	At Street Address#	At Latitude	and Longitude
CR466		28.920159999999999	-81.96886000000006

At Feet	Or Miles	Direction	From Intersection With Street, Road, Highway	Or From Milepost #
			MORSE BLVD	

Road System Identifier	Type Of Shoulder	Type Of Intersection
4 County	3 Curb	2 Four-Way Intersection

CRASH INFORMATION (Check if Pictures Taken) [ ]

Light Condition	Weather Condition	Roadway Surface Condition	School Bus Related	Manner Of Collision
1 Daylight	3 Rain	2 Wet	1 No	3 Angle

First Harmful Event Type	First Harmful Event	First Harmful Event Location	Within Interchange	First Harmful Event Relation to Junction
	14	1 On Roadway	No	2 Intersection

Contributing Circumstances: Road	Contributing Circumstances: Road	Contributing Circumstances: Road
1 None		

Contributing Circumstances: Environment	Contributing Circumstances: Environment	Contributing Circumstances: Environment
1 None		

Work Zone Related	Crash In Work Zone	Type Of Work Zone	Workers In Work Zone	Law Enforcement in Work Zone
1 No				

VEHICLE (Check if Commercial) [ ]

Vehicle	Motor Vehicle Type	Hit and Run	Veh License Number	State	Reg. Expires	Permanent Reg.	VIN
2	1 Vehicle in Transport	1 No	5080CG	FL	15/May/2014	No	1GKEC13V04R214535

Year	Make	Model	Style	Color	Extent of Damage	Est. Damage	Towed Due To Damage	Vehicle Removed By	Rotation
2004	GMC	SUBURBAN	SW	MAR	Disabling	8000	Yes	WILDWOOD 352-748-171	Rotation

Insurance Company	Insurance Policy Number
GEICO	4072712030

Name of Vehicle Owner (Check Box If Business) [ ]	Current Address (Number and Street)	City and State	Zip Code
BRENT LEE WICKHAM	9981 COUNTY RD 114A	WILDWOOD FL	34785-9500

Trailer One:	License Number	State	Reg. Expires	Permanent Reg.	VIN	Year	Make	Length	Axles

Trailer Two:	License Number	State	Reg. Expires	Permanent Reg.	VIN	Year	Make	Length	Axles

Vehicle Traveling:	Direction	On Street, Road, Highway	At Est. Speed	Posted Speed	Total Lanes
	East	CR466	45	45	4

CMV Configuration	Cargo Body Type	Area of Initial Impact	Most Damaged Area

Comm GVWR/GCWR	Trailer Type (trailer one)	Trailer Type (trailer two)		

Haz Mat Release	Haz Mat Placard	Number	Class

Motor Carrier Name	US DOT Number

	Motor Carrier Address	City and State	Zip Code	Phone Number

Comm/Non-Commercial	Vehicle Body Type	Vehicle Defects (one)	Vehicle Defects (two)	Emergency Vehicle Use	Special Function of MV
	1 Passenger Car	1 None		1 No	1 No Special Function

Vehicle Maneuver Action	Trafficway	Roadway Grade	Roadway Alignment	Most Harmful Event	Most Harmful Event Detail
1 Straight Ahead	4 Two-Way, Divided, Positive Median Barrier	1 Level	1 Straight	2 Collision with Non-Fixed Object	14 Motor Vehicle in Transport

Traffic Control Device For This Vehicle	First (1) Sequence of Events	Second (2) Sequence of Events	Third (3) Sequence of Events	Fourth (4) Sequence of Events
5 Traffic Control Signal	2 Collision with Non-Fixed Object			
	14 Motor Vehicle in Transport			

VEHICLE (Check if Commercial) [ ]

Vehicle	Motor Vehicle Type	Hit and Run	Veh License Number	State	Reg. Expires	Permanent Reg.	VIN
4	1 Vehicle in Transport	1 No	BVNH40	FL	09/Mar/2015	No	2CNFLNEYXA6339088

Year	Make	Model	Style	Color	Extent of Damage	Est. Damage	Towed Due To Damage	Vehicle Removed By	Rotation
2010	CHEV	SPECTRUM	UT	GLD	Functional	2000	No		

Insurance Company	Insurance Policy Number
PROGRESSIVE	48691763

23

Carl R. Baker

Date of Crash	Date of Report	Invest. Agency Report Number		
08/Feb/2014 11:45 AM	08/Feb/2014 11:45 AM	FHPC14OFF011707		83671072

Name of Vehicle Owner (Check Box if Business)	Current Address (Number and Street)	City and State	Zip Code
DAVID LYNN SWEENEY	2969 BURNETT TER	THE VILLAGES FL	32163-0000

Trailer One	License Number	State	Reg. Expires	Permanent Reg.	VIN	Year	Make	Length	Axles
Trailer Two	License Number	State	Reg. Expires	Permanent Reg.	VIN	Year	Make	Length	Axles

Vehicle Traveling	Direction North	On Street, Road, Highway MORSE BLVD	At Est. Speed	Posted Speed 30	Total Lanes 4

CMV Configuration	Cargo Body Type	Area of Initial Impact	Most Damaged Area
Comm GVWR/GCWR	Trailer Type (trailer one)	Trailer Type (trailer two)	7. Undercarriage / 18. Overturn / 20. Windshield / 21. Trailer
Haz Mat Release	Haz Mat Placard	Number	Class

Motor Carrier Name	US DOT Number		
Motor Carrier Address		City and State	Zip Code	Phone Number

Comm/Non-Commercial	Vehicle Body Type 1 Passenger Car	Vehicle Defects (one) 1 None	Vehicle Defects (two)	Emergency Vehicle Use 1 No	Special Function of MV 1 No Special Function
Vehicle Maneuver Action 1 Straight Ahead	Trafficway 4 Two-Way, Divided, Positive Median Barrier	Roadway Grade 1 Level	Roadway Alignment 1 Straight	Most Harmful Event 2 Collision with Non-Fixed Object	Most Harmful Event Detail 14 Motor Vehicle in Transport
Traffic Control Device For This Vehicle 5 Traffic Control Signal	First (1) Sequence of Events 2 Collision with Non-Fixed Object 14 Motor Vehicle in Transport	Second (2) Sequence of Events	Third (3) Sequence of Events	Fourth (4) Sequence of Events	

VEHICLE (Check if Commercial)

Vehicle 1	Motor Vehicle Type 1 Vehicle in Transport	Hit and Run 1 No	Veh License Number 2194JS	State FL	Reg. Expires 08/Jul/2014	Permanent Reg. No	VIN 3G5DA03L97S577348
Year 2007	Make BUICK	Model RENDEZVOUS	Style UT	Color SGE	Extent of Damage Disabling	Est. Damage 8000	Towed Due To Damage Yes	Vehicle Removed By WILDWOOD 352-748-171	Rotation Rotation

Insurance Company GARRISON PROPERTY AND CASUALTY INSURANCE	Insurance Policy Number 026101218R71011

Name of Vehicle Owner (Check Box if Business) SANDRA JOAN KANIEWSKI	Current Address (Number and Street) 825 PICKETT ROAD	City and State THE VILLAGES FL	Zip Code 32163-2340

Trailer One	License Number	State	Reg. Expires	Permanent Reg.	VIN	Year	Make	Length	Axles
Trailer Two	License Number	State	Reg. Expires	Permanent Reg.	VIN	Year	Make	Length	Axles

Vehicle Traveling	Direction West	On Street, Road, Highway CR466	At Est. Speed 10	Posted Speed 45	Total Lanes 4

CMV Configuration	Cargo Body Type	Area of Initial Impact	Most Damaged Area
Comm GVWR/GCWR	Trailer Type (trailer one)	Trailer Type (trailer two)	
Haz Mat Release	Haz Mat Placard	Number	Class

Motor Carrier Name	US DOT Number		
Motor Carrier Address	City and State	Zip Code	Phone Number

Comm/Non-Commercial	Vehicle Body Type 1 Passenger Car	Vehicle Defects (one) 1 None	Vehicle Defects (two)	Emergency Vehicle Use 1 No	Special Function of MV 1 No Special Function
Vehicle Maneuver Action 3 Turning Left	Trafficway 4 Two-Way, Divided, Positive Median Barrier	Roadway Grade 1 Level	Roadway Alignment 1 Straight	Most Harmful Event 2 Collision with Non-Fixed Object	Most Harmful Event Detail 14 Motor Vehicle in Transport
Traffic Control Device For This Vehicle 5 Traffic Control Signal	First (1) Sequence of Events 2 Collision with Non-Fixed Object 14 Motor Vehicle in Transport	Second (2) Sequence of Events	Third (3) Sequence of Events	Fourth (4) Sequence of Events	

VEHICLE (Check if Commercial)

Vehicle 3	Motor Vehicle Type 1 Vehicle in Transport	Hit and Run 1 No	Veh License Number BZAF43	State FL	Reg. Expires 20/Jun/2014	Permanent Reg. No	VIN WAUAFAFL3EN006179
Year 2014	Make AUDI	Model A4	Style 4D	Color BLK	Extent of Damage Minor	Est. Damage 1500	Towed Due To Damage No	Vehicle Removed By	Rotation

Insurance Company XL INSURANCE AMERICA	Insurance Policy Number RAD943756401

Name of Vehicle Owner (Check Box if Business) ANNE SUSAN HENRY	Current Address (Number and Street) 1831 CLINTON CT	City and State THE VILLAGES FL	Zip Code 32162-0000

Trailer One	License Number	State	Reg. Expires	Permanent Reg.	VIN	Year	Make	Length	Axles

A Case Study Of Elder Abuse And Exploitation In Florida

Date of Crash 08/Feb/2014 11:45 AM	Date of Report 08/Feb/2014 11:45 AM	Invest Agency Report Number FHPC14OFF011707		83671072

Trailer Two	License Number	State	Reg. Expires	Permanent Reg.	VIN	Year	Make	Length	Axles
Vehicle Traveling	Direction North	On Street, Road, Highway MORSE BLVD					At Est. Speed	Posted Speed 30	Total Lanes 4
CMV Configuration		Cargo Body Type				Area of Initial Impact		Most Damaged Area	
Comm GVWR/GCWR		Trailer Type (trailer one)		Trailer Type (trailer two)		18. Undercarriage 19. Overturn 20. Windshield 21. Trailer		18. Undercarriage 19. Overturn 20. Windshield 21. Trailer	
Haz Mat. Release	Haz Mat. Placard	Number		Class					
Motor Carrier Name				US DOT Number					
	Motor Carrier Address				City and State		Zip Code		Phone Number

Comm/Non-Commercial	Vehicle Body Type 1 Passenger Car	Vehicle Defects (one) 1 None	Vehicle Defects (two)	Emergency Vehicle Use 1 No	Special Function of MV 1 No Special Function
Vehicle Maneuver Action 1 Straight Ahead	Trafficway 4 Two-Way, Divided, Positive Median Barrier	Roadway Grade 1 Level	Roadway Alignment 1 Straight	Most Harmful Event 2 Collision with Non-Fixed Object	Most Harmful Event Detail 14 Motor Vehicle in Transport
Traffic Control Device For This Vehicle 1 No Controls	First (1) Sequence of Events 2 Collision with Non-Fixed Object 14 Motor Vehicle in Transport		Second (2) Sequence of Events	Third (3) Sequence of Events	Fourth (4) Sequence of Events

PERSON RECORD

Person# 1	Description 1 Driver	Vehicle # 1	Name SANDRA JOAN KANIEWSKI		Date of Birth 08/Jul/1949	Sex 2 Female	Phone Number	Re-Exam No
Address 825 PICKETT ROAD		City THE VILLAGES		State FL			Zip Code 32163	
Driver License Number K520790497480	State FL		Expires 08/Jul/2020	DL Type 5 E/Operator	Req. End. 3 No Req Endorsement	Injury Severity 4 Incapacitating	Ejection 1 Not Ejected	
Restraint System 3 Shoulder and Lap Belt Used	Air Bag Deployed 2 Not Deployed	Helmet Use	Eye Protection 3 Not Applicable		Seating Location Seat 1 Left	Seating Location Row 1 Front	Seating Location Other 1 Not Applicable	
Drivers Actions at Time of Crash (first) 3 Failed to Yield Right of Way			Drivers Actions at Time of Crash (second)			Driver Distracted By 1 Not Distracted	Vision Obstruction 3 Parked/Stopped Vehicle	
Drivers Actions at Time of Crash (third)			Drivers Actions at Time of Crash (fourth)			Drivers Condition at Time of Crash 1 Apparently Normal		
Suspected Alcohol Use 1 No	Alcohol Tested 1 Test Not Given	Alcohol Test Type	Alcohol Test Result	BAC	Suspected Drug Use 1 No	Drug Tested 1 Test Not Given	Drug Test Type	Drug Test Result
Source of Transport to Medical Facility 2 EMS		EMS Agency Name or ID RARUL METRO		EMS Run Number		Medical Facility Transported To VILLAGES HOSPITAL		

PERSON RECORD

Person# 2	Description 3 Passenger	Vehicle # 1	Name RALPH STANLEY KANIEWSKI		Date of Birth 19/Apr/1937	Sex 1 Male	Injury Severity 4 Incapacitating	Ejection 1 Not Ejected
Address 825 PICKETT ROAD		City THE VILLAGES				State FL	Zip Code 32163	
Restraint System 3 Shoulder and Lap Belt Used	Air Bag Deployed 3 Deployed-Front	Helmet Use	Eye Protection 3 Not Applicable		Seating Location Seat 3	Seating Location Row 1	Seating Location Other 1	
Source of Transport to Medical Facility 2 EMS		EMS Agency Name or ID RARUL METRO		EMS Run Number		Medical Facility Transported To VILLAGE HOSPITAL		

PERSON RECORD

Person# 3	Description 1 Driver	Vehicle # 2	Name BRENT LEE WICKHAM		Date of Birth 15/May/1963	Sex 1 Male	Phone Number	Re-Exam No
Address 9981 COUNTY RD 114A		City WILDWOOD		State FL			Zip Code 34785	
Driver License Number W250072631750	State FL		Expires 15/May/2021	DL Type 5 E/Operator	Req. End. 3 No Req Endorsement	Injury Severity 1 None	Ejection 1 Not Ejected	
Restraint System 3 Shoulder and Lap Belt Used	Air Bag Deployed 3 Deployed-Front	Helmet Use	Eye Protection 3 Not Applicable		Seating Location Seat 1 Left	Seating Location Row 1 Front	Seating Location Other 1 Not Applicable	
Drivers Actions at Time of Crash (first) 1 No Contributing Action			Drivers Actions at Time of Crash (second)			Driver Distracted By 1 Not Distracted	Vision Obstruction 1 Vision Not Obscured	
Drivers Actions at Time of Crash (third)			Drivers Actions at Time of Crash (fourth)			Drivers Condition at Time of Crash 1 Apparently Normal		
Suspected Alcohol Use 1 No	Alcohol Tested 1 Test Not Given	Alcohol Test Type	Alcohol Test Result	BAC	Suspected Drug Use 1 No	Drug Tested 1 Test Not Given	Drug Test Type	Drug Test Result

Carl R. Baker

Date of Crash	Date of Report	Invest. Agency Report Number		
08/Feb/2014 11:45 AM	08/Feb/2014 11:45 AM	FHPC14OFF011707		83671072

Source of Transport to Medical Facility	EMS Agency Name or ID	EMS Run Number	Medical Facility Transported To
1 Not Transported			

PERSON RECORD

Person#	Description	Vehicle #	Name	Date of Birth	Sex	Phone Number	Re-Exam
5	1 Driver	4	DAVID LYNN SWEENEY	06/Mar/1952	1 Male		No

Address	City	State	Zip Code
2989 BURNETT TER	THE VILLAGES	FL	32163

Driver License Number	State	Expires	DL Type	Req. End.	Injury Severity	Ejection
S500172520660	FL	06/Mar/2021	5 E/Operator	3 No Req Endorsement	1 None	1 Not Ejected

Restraint System	Air Bag Deployed	Helmet Use	Eye Protection	Seating Location Seat	Seating Location Row	Seating Location Other
1 Not Applicable (non-motorist)	1 Not Applicable		3 Not Applicable	1 Left	1 Front	1 Not Applicable

Drivers Actions at Time of Crash (first)	Drivers Actions at Time of Crash (second)	Driver Distracted By	Vision Obstruction
2 Operated MV in Careless or Negligent Manner		1 Not Distracted	1 Vision Not Obscured

Drivers Actions at Time of Crash (third)	Drivers Actions at Time of Crash (fourth)	Drivers Condition at Time of Crash
		1 Apparently Normal

Suspected Alcohol Use	Alcohol Tested	Alcohol Test Type	Alcohol Test Result	BAC	Suspected Drug Use	Drug Tested	Drug Test Type	Drug Test Result
1 No	1 Test Not Given				1 No	1 Test Not Given		

Source of Transport to Medical Facility	EMS Agency Name or ID	EMS Run Number	Medical Facility Transported To
1 Not Transported			

PERSON RECORD

Person#	Description	Vehicle #	Name	Date of Birth	Sex	Phone Number	Re-Exam
4	1 Driver	3	THOMAS F HENRY	01/Jun/1941	1 Male		No

Address	City	State	Zip Code
1831 CLINTON CT	THE VILLAGES	FL	32162

Driver License Number	State	Expires	DL Type	Req. End.	Injury Severity	Ejection
H560626412010	FL	01/Jun/2017	5 E/Operator	3 No Req Endorsement	1 None	1 Not Ejected

Restraint System	Air Bag Deployed	Helmet Use	Eye Protection	Seating Location Seat	Seating Location Row	Seating Location Other
3 Shoulder and Lap Belt Used	2 Not Deployed		3 Not Applicable	1 Left	1 Front	1 Not Applicable

Drivers Actions at Time of Crash (first)	Drivers Actions at Time of Crash (second)	Driver Distracted By	Vision Obstruction
1 No Contributing Action		1 Not Distracted	1 Vision Not Obscured

Drivers Actions at Time of Crash (third)	Drivers Actions at Time of Crash (fourth)	Drivers Condition at Time of Crash
		1 Apparently Normal

Suspected Alcohol Use	Alcohol Tested	Alcohol Test Type	Alcohol Test Result	BAC	Suspected Drug Use	Drug Tested	Drug Test Type	Drug Test Result
1 No	1 Test Not Given				1 No	1 Test Not Given		

Source of Transport to Medical Facility	EMS Agency Name or ID	EMS Run Number	Medical Facility Transported To
1 Not Transported			

WITNESSES

Name	Address	City	State	Zip Code
GARY DAVIS	1116 LAKEVIEW LANE	VILLAGES	FL	32163

WITNESSES

Name	Address	City	State	Zip Code
JOE GENTILE	126 LINCOLN	ST KANE	PA	16735

VIOLATIONS

Person#	Name	Florida Statute Number	Charge	Citation
1	SANDRA JOAN KANIEWSKI	316.122	FAIL TO YIELD - TO ONCOMING TRAFFIC/VEHICLE PASSING ON LEFT	A11B46E

NARRATIVE

ID Number	Rank	Name	Troop / Post	Officer Agency	Phone Number	Date Created
115	TROOPER	R.T. FRIESEN	C	FLORIDA HIGHWAY PATROL	352-754-6767	Feb 17, 2014

Vehicle 1 (V01) was traveling eastbound on CR466 in the left turn lane. Vehicle 2 (V02) was traveling eastbound in the outside lane. Vehicle 3 (V03) was stopped facing north in the inside lane of Morse Blvd. Vehicle 2 (V03) was stopped facing north on Morse Blvd in the outside lane. V01 made a left turn directly into the path of V02. The front of V02 struck the right side of V01. V01 rotated counterclockwise striking the front of V03 and V04 with the rear of V01. V01 came to final rest facing north in the intersection. V02 came to final rest facing south in the intersection. V03 was came to final rest at point of impact. V04 came to final rest at point of impact. V01 driver stated she had yellow light and didn't see anyone coming so she proceeded through the intersection. V02 driver stated when he was going through the intersection the light was yellow.

REPORTING OFFICER

ID/Badge #	Rank and Name	Department	Type of Department
2115	TROOPER R.T. FRIESEN	FLORIDA HIGHWAY PATROL	FHP

A Case Study Of Elder Abuse And Exploitation In Florida

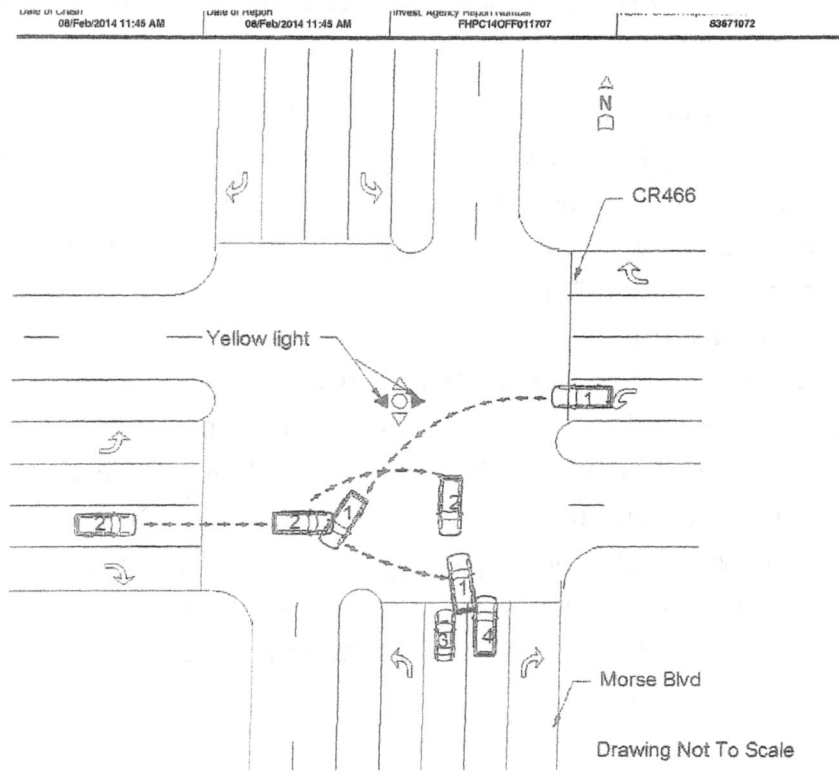

Note: The Florida Traffic Crash Report refutes Sandy's description of the accident.

I really do not know if this was an accident or an attempted murder of Ralph. However, based on the police report, the information from Ralph's family, and Sandy's behavior while Ralph was away from home in a medical facility, I do know that it does not pass the "smell test" and deserves a second look. I did discuss this with the State Attorney's Office and suggested some leads they could pursue, but it appears they were not interested. Given my experience with his office, I am not surprised.

However, I was not comfortable doing nothing, so I submitted a freedom of information request with the Florida Department of Highway Safety and Motor Vehicles to see if there was any additional information available other than the Florida Traffic Crash Report. The following documents that correspondence:

From: "crbaker"
To: "RobertFriesen"
Sent: Friday, July 26, 2019 1:17:55 PM
Subject: Fwd: Traffic Crash Report FHPC140FF01707, CR# 83671072 02/08/4

CONFIDENTIAL

Corporal Friesen

FYI, I spent 40 years in law enforcement. I retired as a State Police Colonel from NY and then served as Superintendent (Colonel) of the State Police in Virginia. The reason that I am sending this email is that you investigated the above accident in February of 2014. The driver of vehicle 1 in that accident was SANDRA JOAN KANIEWSKI.

To make an exceptionally long story short, Sandy's husband, Ralph never recovered from that accident and died in October 2014. Sandy and my brother, J. Paul Baker, a retired Brigadier General, were married in 2016. Unfortunately, he was exposed to Agent Orange in Viet Nam and now has numerous medical problems including Alzheimer's dementia. Sandy had his trust, will and various legal documents changed in an attempt to take all of his non-marital assets. In preparation for court, we contacted Ralph's family and learned some of the details of the accident. Ralph's family believes that it was not an accident and that Sandy intentionally turned in front of the oncoming traffic. After hearing their story and some of the events on the days before February 8th and looking at the accident report, I do understand their concerns.

I know that this accident was years ago and you have most likely investigated hundreds of accidents over the years. However, I thought the least I should do is ask you if you remember anything unusual about this accident or have any information beyond the report. You can call me or email me with your reply, or if you have any questions.

Thank you and stay safe.
Carl R. Baker

I received the following reply from Corporal Friesen on August 16th, and thanked him for his response:

From: "RobertFriesen"
To: "crbaker"
Sent: Friday, August 16, 2019 2:30:41 PM
Subject: RE: Traffic Crash Report FHPC14OFF01707, CR# 83671072 02/08/4

I just found the report the case number is FHPC14OFF011707. I don't have any independent recollection of the crash other than the crash report. I would have notated anything strange in the crash report.

Thank You
Corporal Robert T. Friesen

From my experience, I do understand that homicide or attempted homicide cases by intentional crashes are rare and risky, but they do happen. They are also difficult to prove and near impossible to document years after the alleged incident occurred. The lesson here is that if there is ever any indication that an accident may have been intentional, it needs to be reported to the police immediately.

"From the deepest desires often come the deadliest hate."
—*Socrates*

"The inability to cope with truth is a form of mental illness."
(*Count It All Joy* by David Jeremiah)

CHAPTER 5

Profile of a Sociopath

"*Antisocial personality disorder is characterized by the lack of regard for the moral or legal standards in the local culture. There is a marked inability to get along with others or to abide by societal rules. Individuals with this disorder are sometimes called psychopaths or sociopaths.*" *(DMS-IV Definition).*

I am not alone in my opinion, that Sandy has many of the characteristics of a sociopath. I am not a psychologist or a psychiatrist. However, in both New York and Virginia, I was responsible for the unit that screened individuals for a purchase and/or a permit for concealed carry of a weapon. I have always strongly believed that mental health records should be checked for both. When a person was classified a psychopath, a weapon purchase and/or a weapon carry permit was routinely denied. However, when the classification was a sociopath, there was no automatic denial. I have found that there is a mighty fine line between the two and I spent an extended period of time researching both classifications. Like the above definition, I see no difference between the two.

Sociopaths don't view people as people. They view them as objects to be manipulated and used. They only care about one person – themselves. If any person, a relative or friend, becomes a threat to them, sociopaths will do whatever it takes to eliminate that person from their lives.

Following is a list of some of the common traits or behaviors of sociopaths so the reader will be able to make his or her own determination of Sandy's mental state:

Pathological lying (Even when it serves no purpose.)
No guilt, remorse, or shame
Egocentric; Constantly bragging about themselves
Superficial charm
Manipulative and cunning
Shallow or false emotions
Promiscuous sexual behavior/ Infidelity
Frequent verbal outbursts
Callousness/Lack of empathy toward their victims
Rage and abuse
Parasitic nature (Exploits others)
Criminal conduct (Changes their image as needed to avoid prosecution.)

There is another way to look at Sandy's behavior. Most of us have a very difficult time discerning between an evil heart and an ordinary sinner who isn't perfect and messes up. Some find it difficult to believe that evil people actually exist. After forty years in law enforcement, I never had that problem. I have met many evil people in my life.

Leslie Vernick of the Association of Biblical Counselors wrote a wonderful article in 2015, titled "5 Indicators of an Evil and Wicked Heart". The following delineates those indictors from her article and the reader can draw his or her own conclusions:

1. Evil hearts are experts at creating confusion and contention.
> *They twist the facts, mislead, lie, avoid taking responsibility, deny reality, make up stories, and withhold information.*

2. Evil hearts are experts at fooling others with their smooth speech and flattering words.
> *But if you look at the fruit of their lives or the follow through of their words, you will find no real evidence of Godly growth or change. It's all smoke and mirrors.*

3. Evil hearts crave and demand control, and their highest authority is their own self-reference.
> *They reject feedback, real accountability, and make up their own rules to live by.*

4. Evil hearts play on the sympathies of good-willed people, often trumping the grace card.
> *They demand mercy but give none themselves.*

5. Evil hearts have no conscience, no remorse.

They do not struggle against sin or evil—they delight in it – all the time while masquerading as someone of noble character.

There are those "... who are loaded down with sins and are swayed by all kinds of evil desires, always learning but never able to acknowledge the truth."
— 2 Timothy 3:6-7

Sociopaths are generally narcissists with evil and selfish motives. There is an article written by Jen Grice titled, "8 Reasons Why It's Hard to Separate from a Narcissist" (Crosswalk, February 8, 2021). There are many points in this article that accurately describe the situation with Sandy and Paul. For example:

"Narcissists use a tactic called 'love bombing' to entice and ensnarl their new dating partners. He/She [Sandy] often discard previous relationships to make room on the pedestal for a brand-new relationship. The narcissist's new victim is the best thing that ever happened to him/her—a 'soulmate'—although he/she may have stated this in all past relationships as well. The relationship moves along very quickly so the victim doesn't have time to see the red flags or assert boundaries."

Paul did not see the red flags, most likely because of his dementia. However, his family did, but Paul, as you will learn, ignored the warnings.

I also read a book written by Texe Marrs published in 2020. His book, *Psychopaths—Yesterday, Today and Tomorrow*, is excellent and I highly recommend it. The book also confirms many of the thoughts and concerns many of us have with Sandy's mental state.

In his book, Marrs (2020) lists the 15 characteristics of psychopaths:

1. Lack of Empathy
2. Lack of Conscience
3. Lack of Remorse
4. Glib and Superficial
5. Double-minded
6. Deceitful and Manipulative
7. Grandiose Ego
8. Invented Personas
9. Failure to Accept Responsibility
10. Shallow Emotions
11. Poor Behavioral Controls
12. Parasitic Lifestyle
13. Power Seeker
14. Invokes Pity
15. Morally Debauched

As you read this story, remember the common traits and behaviors of a sociopath/psychopath/narcissist in the preceding paragraphs. If you pause and look at all of Sandy's behavior, do you see any common characteristics? For those who have lived through this saga, there is no doubt in our minds that there are numerous similarities. We never saw any signs that she is remorseful for her actions, she has never apologized to Paul or anyone else, and she continues demonstrating her tremendous ego and arrogance. She is a narcissist and given the fact that the Florida court system is horribly broken, she has never been held responsible for any of her crimes or abusive and exploitative actions and will eventually move on to her next victim. She only cares about herself, her public image, and her future.

I became a threat to Sandy because I was the one that stood in the way of her total exploitation of Paul. Sociopaths often get rid of anyone in their way and Sandy used isolation in her attempt to get what she wanted. That did not work for her since Paul decided to leave her and come live with us. What would be her next action in her attempt to reach her goal? Only time would tell.

In his book, Marrs (2020) also gives his readers some outstanding advice on dealing with psychopaths who may be in your life:

"... whether that psychopath is a lover, a supposed friend, a boss, a co-worker, a neighbor, or even a member of your family. Here's my advice:
Flee! Do so now, immediately. And in the future, have absolutely nothing to do with him or her ...or it!"

I know it would have been wise to heed his advice, but we could not abandon Paul.

My real hope is that someone in Sandy's family suggests that she receive some needed mental health treatment.

"Love does not delight in evil but rejoices with the truth. It always trusts, always hopes, always perseveres."
— *1 Corinthians 13: 6-7*

"The secret to unity and love is integrity."
— *Author unknown*

CHAPTER 6

Loving Relationship Or Trap?

Since my wife, Katherine and I were not living in the Villages full time in the summer of 2014, we do not know exactly when Paul and Sandy met. Our brother Bruce places it sometime in July. The story is that they were both getting gas at a Shell station and Sandy dropped something under her car. Paul was quick to the rescue and the story begins. Sandy was still married to Ralph and at this time; he was a patient in the Villages Rehab Center as a result of Sandy's accident in February of 2014.

Sandy owns several timeshares and at the end of August, Sandy secretly took Paul to one of her timeshares in Naples for several days. Further, we are not sure exactly when it started, but Sandy, knowing that her neighbors knew she was still married to Ralph. began sneaking Paul into her (and Ralph's) bed almost every night and taking him home in the morning so his car would not be parked in her driveway. What we found very strange and shocking was at the next Baker family party here in the Villages with all of us, including Mark, Allyne and all the grandchildren, Sandy told us about sneaking Paul into the house and how he laid down on the seat so none of Sandy's neighbors would see him. And later, not in the presence of Paul and Sandy, our family discussed her comments and we all thought she was bragging about it or just letting us know how much control she had over Paul. In any case, it was very strange and not something a normal person would do. However, a sociopath's poor conduct is supported by a belief that endorses what he or she is doing. Sandy's sense of values appears perverted so she seeks glory in the things she should be ashamed of.

Let's be frank and up front about all this. Paul may have had dementia at this time, but no one in his family condoned his behavior. Paul was a member of Promise Keepers in his church in New York, and to have an intimate relationship with a married woman whose husband is dying, is not the Paul of years ago.

On October 10, 2014, Sandy's husband Ralph died after eight

difficult months trying to recover from the accident. Sandy planned *five* memorial services for Ralph, and Paul attended all of them with her. Needless to say, and rightfully so, Ralph's family was quite upset that Sandy would bring her boyfriend to a service for her late husband and their father. It is truly unclear exactly what message Sandy was trying to send to Ralph's family, our family and her friends by bringing Paul and overtly introducing him at these events? I do not know why Paul allowed himself to be put in this position, but it tells us that Paul's thought process was declining much more rapidly than we realized.

On October 11, 2014, Sandy posted the following on her Facebook:

"It is with a heavy heart that I say a fond farewell to my beloved husband, Ralph. He will be missed as a sweet loving man, father, grandfather and friend. He fought a vigilant year-long fight and God called him home yesterday at 3:45 PM with me, Chris, and two friends, Willie and Jimmy at his side. There will be a memorial mass said at St. Timothy's Catholic Community in The Villages and a veteran's service at the Florida National Cemetery. I plan on a life celebration for our family and friends in Shreveport when I visit Brent and family at Christmastime, an intimate celebration in the Chiricahua Mountains near Tucson, AZ after the first of the year and finally a life celebration in Michigan for relatives and friends in the spring. All the dates and times have to be worked out yet. He is now at peace in the gentle and loving arms of our Savior. Goodbye, Dear Ralph."

A year later, on October 10, 2015, Sandy posted the following on her Facebook with a picture of Ralph's headstone:

"Today was a year ago that God called my beloved husband of 25 years to his heavenly home. Ralph, you have touched many people on this earth. You made them smile and they were blessed by your kindness and gentle ways. God (hold) him in the palm of your hand until we meet again. I miss you dearly. Love, Sandy"

A friend who is very familiar with this entire story sent me the following email:

"Being popular on Facebook is like sitting at the cool table in the cafeteria of a mental hospital."

Seeing all the controversy surrounding Facebook, I am sure that many people would agree.

In my opinion, all this is nothing but "show and tell." It is difficult to believe that this comes from the heart of a woman who cheated on her husband at least twice and is sleeping with another man in her husband's bed while he is in hospice and dying. Let me say unequivocally, that Sandy's public persona is not the real Sandy. The Sandy on Facebook (or Fakebook as we often label it) is not the same Sandy that we have witnessed. If Sandy treated Ralph and his family and Paul and his family the way she treats her Facebook friends, there would not have been a problem. But the person that Sandy pretends to be is, in fact, not the person she really is. And if anyone thinks otherwise, then they would have to believe that Ralph's daughters and friends are lying and that the Baker family spent the last several years emailing each other with events that were made up and never occurred.

In October 2015, Paul announced to his family that he and Sandy have decided to sell their individual homes and purchase a new home jointly, even though they were not married. No one in the Baker family thought this was a good idea or supported it. Allyne sent an email to Bruce explaining how upset she was. In her own words, she wrote:

"My dad and I had a huge argument over the phone because I told him that buying a house with her [Sandy] was ridiculous. And if they wanted to live together, they could live in one house and sell the other. There was no reason for the two of them to be building a bigger house at this point in his life. My dad and I had harsh words for about an hour and the next morning he called me and told me he was going to cancel the contract for the house and keep the things the way they are. And he wanted me to know that he loves me. Two hours after that, Sandy sent me a text:

"I am not going to come between you and your dad. That was never my intention. I am in love with him and love you and Kayla. We have lost $10,000.00 in earnest deposit (Lie) over this house and that is a nonissue [sic]. Your dad loves you so much that he is willing to lose that and me. I am more concerned about the relationship between you and your dad than a house. It is just stuff. I am struggling for him and you and pray that you can mend the hurt. He is hurting more than you know. I cannot sit back and watch this happen. Please, please do not shut him out of your life. He does not know I am writing this. I am praying that love and happiness will envelope both you and Kayla. I care deeply. I lost my husband a year ago tomorrow and now???"

Allyne added the following comments and emailed it to me:

"If my dad backed out of the house, then that meant he lost her!!??? That's what I read between those lines. And that's when dad didn't talk to me for quite a while. Wouldn't answer any calls because this bitch talked him back into the big house and she certainly did not care about my relationship with my dad. She was doing anything she could to isolate him to accomplish her agenda.

In May of 2015, the first time Sandy met me, she suggested that dad needed to be in a facility sometime soon and when I fly to the Villages in the fall, I should plan something with my uncles and her and get my dad on board to go into a facility.

My response to her at that time was, "You must not know my father very well... because an intervention the way you speak of would not go over very well! And my uncles and I will discuss this when the time is right." When I told dad about this conversation a couple weeks later on the phone while I was home, he was very upset and a few hours later both Sandy and he called me back and she was screaming at me calling me a liar. She denied the whole thing! I had no reason to lie and unfortunately my dad believed her.

She has been conniving since day one and has been wreaking havoc on our family ever since."

At this time, Sandy and Paul were already living together and this was long before Paul and Sandy got married. We believe that her first plan was to buy a larger home and then several months later, have Paul committed to a memory facility and then live as an unattached woman in her new home in hope that when Paul died, she would get the home. It is not that different than the lifestyle she had while Ralph was living and in the nursing home? Does this woman have any moral or ethical compass at all?"

Interestingly, in September 2018, Sandy reduced the percentage that Allyne would receive from Paul's estate upon his death, from 65% to 15%. That is how much she "loved" Allyne.

On November 6, 2015, Paul and Sandy did go ahead and buy a new house together on Mango Court and fortunately, both their former houses sold quickly. They each paid half the costs based on their individual trusts and the antenuptial agreement which states that when the house is sold, one-half of the funds received are to be deposited in each of their individual trust accounts.

When discussing how they would handle the bills pertaining to the new home, Bruce suggested that together they open a joint checking account for shared expenses. He told them that they should always deposit the same amount of money into the joint account on a monthly basis, and use the account exclusively for shared expenses (i.e.: groceries, cleaning supplies, utilities, cable, amenity fees, property taxes, lawn service, home improvements and repairs, etc.). They both said it was a good idea, but it was never done. Bruce questioned Paul on this several times and he finally admitted that Sandy did not want to do it. Consequently, there was never any documentation, and obviously no proof that Sandy ever paid her fair share of these expenses. In Paul's confused state, especially pertaining to numbers and money, it was evident that he was paying significantly more than half of the shared costs. This single, deliberate decision created an accounting nightmare and resulted in Sandy's claim that she put more money into the home than Paul and she should receive more than half the funds from the sale. Fortunately, we kept records to refute Sandy's claim.

We all chipped in and assisted Paul and Sandy with getting their new home ready for the move from their current homes. On the first two weeks of December, with the help of our friends, we moved Paul and Sandy to their new home. For whatever reason, Sandy had a breakdown as we were moving Paul's belongings into the house and screamed. She ran to the lanai crying. We all looked at each other in amazement and I went out to the lanai to talk to Sandy to see what was wrong. She never responded, so I went back into the house and told our friends that we were done for the day and we all left. I never learned the reason for Sandy's outburst, but was embarrassed for Paul. However, I later learned that Sandy could make herself the victim no matter what is going on in her life and this behavior has been repeated by her many times, especially in front of an audience.

Paul always told us that "Sandy has a lust for travel." He was correct. Paul and Sandy traveled a lot – visiting family, using Sandy's timeshares, touring Europe, Israel and Hawaii and other locations. There came a time when Paul's doctor told Sandy that Paul needed routine in his life and that he should not be traveling. Sandy general ignored the doctor's orders. But what the entire Baker family found most unusual was the number of times that Sandy did travel without Paul. Sandy will tell you that she traveled alone because the doctor told her that Paul should not travel. But the following travel record of Sandy's trips with and without Paul does not support that statement:

2017

February 11-15   Sandy goes away (location unknown) – Paul is left home without all his prescriptions. I had to go to Walgreens and pick up his medicine.

February 17-21   Sandy travels to Las Vegas. Paul had no flight schedule or hotel reservations. Sandy stated that she was visiting a sick friend.

February 23   I went to the doctor with Paul and Sandy. The doctor stated that Paul should not be left alone, and he needs routine, so travel should be at a minimum.

April 11-23   Paul and Sandy travel to Louisiana to visit her family.

May 19-23   Sandy traveled alone in Louisiana for her grandchild's graduation.

June 9-21   Paul and Sandy traveled to NY and Virginia to visit his family.

June 22-26   Sandy traveled alone to Ohio for a high school reunion.

October 20   We had a family meeting with Carl, Katherine, Bruce, Gail, Paul, and Sandy. Sandy was reminded of the doctor's order that Paul needed routine and should not travel or be left alone. She promised she would not travel anymore with Paul, but the trip to Israel was already scheduled and booked.

November 6 -15 Paul and Sandy travel to Israel.

2018

May 19-Jun 1 Paul and Sandy go to Hawaii.

July 3-14 Sandy traveled to Alaska to visit her daughter and left Paul alone in the house. We checked on him every morning and evening. He ate most of his dinners with us and we sent food home with him. I also took Paul to his VA appointment.

Numerous trips to visit Sandy's family in 2018.

The frequency and the number of days Sandy spent traveling without Paul certainly raised our family's suspicion as to her love for Paul and quite candidly whether she remained faithful to him. Let us just say that this was just another example when Sandy's actions did not "pass the smell test."

Interestingly, after one of Sandy's trips, we picked up Paul and Sandy and had dinner with them at a local restaurant. On the way back to their home, we needed to stop to pick up some milk. Paul and I went into the store leaving Sandy and Katherine in the car. Sandy complained to Katherine about Paul's anger. Sandy got mad when Katherine told her that Paul showed no signs of anger while she was away. I won't say never, but neither Katherine nor I recall Sandy ever saying something pleasant about or complimenting Paul the entire time they were married.

When she complained about Paul, which was frequent, Katherine would ask her what we could do to help her. Sandy only asked for help when she would leave Paul alone while she was away.

"Where love rules, there is no will to power; and where power predominates, there love is lacking."
— C. G. Jung

CHAPTER 7

The Marriage

To say that Paul's and Sandy's wedding ceremonies were unconventional, is probably an understatement. Yes, just like there were multiple services to put Ralph to rest, there were three marriage ceremonies for Paul and Sandy. Rest assured; their marriage was not without controversy.

Both Paul and Sandy were married twice before. This would be a late in life marriage for both of them and one that ended in two and one-half years when Paul left and they both stated that they wanted a divorce.

After Paul and Sandy began discussing marriage, Sandy expressed several concerns to us. She said she was afraid that Paul's daughter, Allyne, would contest their marriage on the grounds that Paul was incompetent. Katherine did not want to get into the whole issue of Paul's competency with Sandy as she knew it would not go well; she also knew she could not honestly say that Paul was competent. Katherine responded to Sandy by saying she did not think Allyne would do that. But it was very disconcerting that Sandy would even broach the topic. Most people would not want to marry someone they thought was not capable of making such a decision if they genuinely loved the person. But that certainly was never the case here and there were many other motivations in play. But Katherine was curious about what was going on in Sandy's mind. Katherine asked Sandy directly, "Why would you say that?" Sandy said that Allyne did not want them to marry and that since Allyne worked for a legal firm, she thought that Allyne would use her firm to try to contest the marriage.

Sandy said she knew there was something wrong with Paul the first time she met him. So, she knew Paul was not competent at the time to be making a decision to marry anyone, as we all did, yet she was determined to consummate the marriage anyway. A psychologically normal person would never have proceeded in the manner that she did. Obviously, Sandy seemed to simply be trying to put out feelers as to whether she should expect any legal push back from Allyne. And perhaps she was just trying to further alienate Paul from his daughter by saying such things.

Before a wedding date was set for Paul and Sandy, Bruce and

I took him to lunch and had a long conversation with him about his pending marriage. Paul and Sandy were already fighting and she had mentioned several times that there were times when "she could not stand being around Paul" and would have to leave the house. Additionally, she was frequently travelling without Paul. He expressed some doubts and seemed more comfortable in the present living situation. However, Paul was so easily swayed by Sandy, that we left lunch feeling that it did not matter what we said, Paul and Sandy would be married.

> *Note: Knowing that Paul and Sandy would be married, we decided that we would not make or participate in any derogatory remarks about Sandy because that was what Sandy was doing to Paul and we really wanted him to have a good marriage. Further, Paul already had too many issues to deal with.*

Sandy planned everything for their wedding and made all the arrangements for them to be married on June 28, 2016 at Gasparilla Island in southern Florida. In an earlier visit with Sandy's son, Sandy told Paul that her son would not allow them to sleep together, so they needed to get married now. No one from the Baker side of the family was invited to the wedding. Access to the Island was by boat only, but that was not a problem since Sandy's children and their families were invited and her son brought his boat to Florida. How convenient!

Although Allyne never had any intention of interfering with her father's wedding, Sandy planned it so no one could stop her from marrying Paul. If love was such a strong, driving emotion for this marriage, why did she later fight for court approval to visit Paul at Trinity Springs, only to walk away from him after three visits, and move to Louisiana? Oh, by the way, on her way out the door she illegally took all of Paul's furniture, all his wall hangings and accessories, the golf cart, and much of Paul's personal property.

> "**For the love of money is a root of all kinds of evil.**
> — *1 Timothy 6:10*

CHAPTER 8

The Quest for Paul's Money

Unfortunately, shortly after Paul and Sandy started dating, it became quite apparent to all of Paul's family that one of Sandy's primary interests in Paul was a desire for her to benefit from Paul's assets - both marital and non-marital. We had hoped this was not true because we really wished that Paul would find a good Christian woman who would love and take care of him for the remainder of his life. It became more and more obvious by Sandy's words and actions that our initial thoughts were correct and we started documenting events which were relevant.

We never really spoke to Paul about all our suspicions until

January 9th of 2019 when I mailed Paul a letter outlining our concerns about Sandy. That was five (5) days before Paul decided to leave Sandy and move in with us.

Paul's Trusts

In August of 2014, Paul had established his first trust naming his daughter, Allyne, Bruce and I as successor trustees, power of attorney and health care surrogates. He also distributed his estate to his two children – 65% to Allyne and 35% to Mark. Paul felt that Mark did very well in his job and since Allyne was a single mother working two jobs, he gave two-thirds to her and one-third to Mark. At the same time, he moved his home and his BB&T bank accounts to the John Paul Baker Trust. Paul also had a life insurance policy with his daughter, Allyne as beneficiary.

In anticipation of his marriage to Sandy, Paul made several changes to his trust on June 5, 2016. He knew that Sandy and Allyne did not like each other, so he removed Allyne's name as successor trustee, power of attorney and health care surrogate which left Bruce and I filling those positions. However, he did add Sandy as another health care surrogate. The distribution of the assets remained the same except for the marital home that was purchased by both Paul and Sandy. The trust now stated that upon the death of either Paul or Sandy, the survivor shall have up to twelve (12) months to either sell the residence or to buy out the other spouse's interest in the residence and the net proceeds shall be divided equally between their trusts.

But most importantly, on the advice of Paul's attorney, Sham Shanawany, of Millhorn and Shanawany Law Firm, Paul and

Sandy signed an Antenuptial Agreement that should have been beneficial to Paul, ensuring that his children received his estate's assets on his death. Unfortunately, the State Attorney and the court appointed guardian were well aware of the agreement but ignored it.

Once Sandy isolated Paul from his family, she changed Paul's trust twice. ***Appendix B*** is a summary of Paul's four trusts with notes. By reviewing it, you will be better able to understand Sandy's abuse and exploitation of Paul and the importance of the Antenuptial Agreement which is ***Appendix C.***

Following is a timeline with documented events that occurred from the time Paul and Sandy started dating, until September of 2018 when $220,000.00 was withdrawn from Paul's non-marital trust account. You can draw your own conclusions as to the validity of our concerns.

TIMELINE OF SANDY'S QUEST TO TAKE PAUL'S MONEY

2014

June/July - Paul and Sandy met at a gas station. Sandy gave Paul her phone number.

Note: Sandy was married to Ralph at this time and he was in Hospice Care.

August 18 – ***The John Paul Baker Trust*** was finalized.

August 30 – Sandy takes Paul to Naples to stay with her in her timeshare for three days.

September – Paul and Sandy continued to date, and Paul hid the fact that he frequently stayed overnight at Ralph and Sandy's house.

October 10 – Ralph died, and Paul went to all the memorial services with Sandy and "helped her spread Ralph's ashes." Ralph's family was not happy that Sandy brought her boyfriend to their father's memorial services.

November – Paul and Sandy each had their own home, but Paul spent most nights over at Sandy's.

2015

May – Allyne came to Florida to visit her dad and this was the first time she actually met Sandy. Allyne already knew that her dad was planning to sell his home and buy a home together with Sandy and Allyne was not happy about it. It became even more bizarre when during this visit, Sandy stated that Paul needed to be in a facility sometime soon and suggested that Allyne fly down in the fall and plan something with Bruce, Carl and her to get Paul to agree to go into a facility. (Note – This would be after Paul and Sandy bought the house together, but before they were married.)

October – Paul and Sandy completed the sale of both their homes and bought one home together.

December – Paul and Sandy moved into their newly purchased home at 3723 Mango Court, each paying half. (The house was sold in December 2020.)

December – Bruce (our brother) suggested that they open a joint checking account for shared expenses and each deposit the same amount of money each month. They both said it was a good idea, but it was never done. After questioning Paul on this several times, he finally admitted that Sandy did not want to do it. Consequently, there was never any documentation, and obviously no proof that Sandy ever paid her fair share of these expenses. In Paul's confused state, especially pertaining to numbers and money, it was evident that he was paying significantly more than half of the shared costs.

2016

June 15 – Paul updated his trust to reflect the new home and his marriage to Sandy. Sandy updated her trust also. They both named their children as beneficiaries as had previously been the case. They also signed an Antenuptial Agreement.

(Note: This turned out to be a very smart move for Paul and shows how much Paul's attorney, Sham Shanawany (Millhorn & Shanawany) protected Paul, Paul's children, and Paul's non-marital assets. He is an outstanding Attorney.)

June 28 - Paul and Sandy were married. Although Sandy's son and family were present, no one from the Baker family was invited. Sandy probably knew that Paul's children already figured out that she was after Paul's assets and she was concerned that Allyne may try to stop the wedding. In retrospect, given Paul's medical condition, the wedding should have never happened. Paul's doctor told Paul that he had wished that he spoke to him before getting married and stated he was against it.

July 11- Paul asked me how he can leave his military pension to Sandy. I told him he could not change the retirement option he chose and, therefore, could not do it. Paul told me that this was a request from Sandy. In fact, Sandy had already told Katherine that she was going to receive Paul's pension.

2017

March – Paul called me and stated that Sandy told him he needed to start taking his money from his IRA. I told him that I have been handling his finances for years and he does not have an IRA. Evidently, Sandy did not believe me, and had Paul call Bruce and ask him about the IRA. Bruce always did Paul's taxes and he also told Paul that he did not have an IRA. About 10 days later, Paul called me again and with Sandy standing right next to him, said "Sandy says I have an IRA." I replied, "Sandy is wrong. You do not have an IRA." Sandy immediately shouted, "I want to know where your f---king money is." The phone then went dead. Obviously, they were having an argument.

This is interesting for several reasons. Sandy has a long-term male friend who lost his wife and frequently visits Sandy and Paul and stays overnight. This friend is a CPA and had offered to do Paul's and Sandy's taxes, which Sandy agreed to. I believed Sandy was getting direction from him, but to what extent, I do not know.

April 24 – While working over at Paul's house, Paul told me that Sandy has had a difficult life and that he wants to do something for her. I told him he should buy her a nice gift. He told me wanted to give her one of his pensions. Again, I told him that was not possible. I suggested that he put her on his Tri-care (military health insurance). He later did get her health insurance.

June – According to Paul's financial adviser in Albany,

New York, Paul called him and told him he wanted to change the beneficiary on his $100,000 life insurance policy from his daughter, Allyne, to his new wife, Sandra. The advisor reminded Paul that he started this policy years ago because Allyne was a single mother and he (Paul) wanted to leave something extra for Allyne. The advisor could hear a woman in the background telling Paul what to say. Paul again stated that he wanted the policy changed. The financial advisor told Paul that since he had Alzheimer's, Paul should talk this over with his family. The woman (Sandy) told Paul to just tell him to mail them the change of beneficiary forms, which Paul did. The advisor later told me he knew exactly what was going on. Sandy wanted the change and Paul was not sure, so the agent never sent the change of beneficiary forms. Fortunately, the agent made the right choice. However, it is most unfortunate that the lawyer who later changed Paul's trust twice, after Sandy isolated him from his family, wasn't as perceptive as Paul's financial advisor.

2018

June 22 – I received a call from Paul and he told me that he had someone coming to his house in less than an hour to give them an estimate on expanding and enclosing the lanai and asked if I could be there. Although it was a short notice, I went. When I got to their house the contractor was already there. He stated the estimate would be done on Tuesday and I asked Sandy and Paul to make me a copy. I also told them to get two more estimates from two other contractors that I recommended. They agreed to do that.

When I was leaving, Sandy told me she would not be available on Tuesday because her friend had asked her "to go on a bus tour" with her. After I asked a few follow-up questions, because she was so evasive, she told me that she was going on a $20 bus tour of all the local assisted living facilities for Paul. She thought it was worth the money and time for her to "see what was available". I told her I thought that this may be premature and that we had agreed that was a decision we would make collectively. As usual, Sandy took offense to my statement saying, "I'm his wife!" However, according to Paul's trust, making that decision includes both Bruce and me.

July 7 – After he was scammed out of money by a landscaper, Paul realized that he could no longer handle his daily personal finances. He asked me what he should do. This is a transcript of a conversation that I had with Paul in response to his question:

C: *Who do you trust more with your Trust Account – me or Sandy?*

P: *I trust you more.*

C: *Given what happened, how do you want to handle your checking account?*

P: *I want you to take it and make sure I have money if I need it. But don't tell Sandy, she will get mad at me.*

C: *Until I figure out how we can do this, do not sign any checks unless I ask you to. Do you understand?*

P: *What if I need money?*

C: *Call me. I live right up the street. Most times I can have a check to you in five minutes.*

P: *Can we keep this between us?*

C: *I do not know what you are talking about. (This has always been the way we kidded when we did not want anything repeated. It meant that it was between us only.)*

Paul then gave me his checkbook and checks. This was Paul's trust account and was not a joint account. Unfortunately, what I did not know at this time, was that Sandy had taken two different pads of Paul's numbered checks and began using them to access Paul's money. Paul continued to sign any check that Sandy put in front of him.

Aug 10 – Mark and Allyne, Paul's children came to Florida to see their dad. Sandy immediately brought up the trust and stated she was going to the attorney to see what changes should be made. The following emails document their conversation with Sandy:

From: Allyne
To: Carl Baker
Subject: Hi, it's Allyne
Aug 12, 2018

Uncle Carl-
We had such a nice time seeing you this past week. Kaila and I really enjoyed our visit with Dad. I could tell he was so happy to have us around for a few days!
   I wanted to thank you and Katherine for planning and cooking such a nice family dinner Friday night, it was so much fun catching up with all of you.
   I hate to bring a dim light to what was supposed to be just a nice

thank you email, but I feel this needs to be addressed. As we've talked about in the past, I don't feel Sandy is very loving toward my father. And furthermore, it sometimes feels like we are living a dateline episode. She swooped in on dad before her other husband was even gone, and I just don't trust her whatsoever.

She claims she is taking dad to see an attorney this week to "check and make sure ALL of his funds are secure for Mark and me". Sandy has been nothing short of nasty to me so I find it hard to believe that all of a sudden, she would have mine or Mark's (or even my Dad's for that matter) best interests at heart.

Can you please help dad and us to make sure she doesn't change his "Family Trust" in any way? Dad trusts you with his whole heart! I know he will listen to what you have to say. When she told Mark and I about this appointment we asked her not to do anything without checking in with us first. My father still had all his faculties when that trust was established before he ever met her.

My father and his trust
From: Mark Baker
Sun, Aug 12, 2018 08:51 PM
To: crbaker
Uncle Carl,

I want to follow up our conversation tonight with something in writing in light of my father's new wife's comments to Katherine today. Based on those comments and how some of my words were being twisted, I thought it important to clearly convey my thoughts.

Sandy abruptly brought up my father's trust this past Friday, August 10th. She asked about five random questions. None of which amounted to anything. I expressed our desire not to have anything changed with that trust, although I don't think she listened to that because it doesn't align with what I believe to be her goal. She asked if it was irrevocable and I responded, I don't think so. She asked doesn't it need to be. I answered "yes" to be exempted from paying facility costs but it would have to be for 5 years. And I stated at this point it's too late, so we want it to stay as it is. We ended the three-minute conversation because I was distracted with watching my 5-year-old with a simple statement. I want her to call me before she takes any action with the trust because that money is there for the care of my father. I said this because it was obvious that she wants to change it, and that's before she's had any meeting by the way.

This woman is not even nice to my father for the two days we were in town. I firmly believe she doesn't have Dad's best interest in mind.

Uncle Carl, my request is that you become responsible for Dad's medical and financial well- being. I am worried for my father because his new wife's singular focus seems to be on his trust, not whether he is taking his medications or making sure she is organizing his life to make routine a priority. Also, I want to clearly state that I would like you to be present at all meetings where my father's long term medical or financial future is being discussed.

Please show this to an attorney. Not for any other reason but for the well-being of my father J. Paul Baker.

-Mark Baker

August 15 - Paul called me at 7:46 AM, terribly upset because Sandy is refusing to go to see the attorney with him (the meeting she set up) because I was going also. He said she is all cranked up because she thinks I do not care for her. I assured Paul that it isn't that I don't like her; I just have some questions about the power of attorney. I asked him what is the sense of going to the meeting since she is the one that wanted it. She told Paul she doesn't want me to know anything about her money. I told him that I do not care about her money, I care about his money and Paul said he knows that. We both agreed that Sandy is over-reacting and Paul said she is having a meltdown. We talked about the Medicaid trust and why Paul does not need one. Paul told me that it is his opinion that he doesn't need to change his trust and that Sandy talked to both of his children and they both do not want him to change his trust. We decided to go to the meeting and get copies of all Paul's documents because he does not know where his copies are. I asked him to get the attorney's address from Sandy and Paul said he didn't know if she would give it to him.

Paul told me that Sandy just doesn't understand how close he and I are, and always have been. He said maybe she is having a break-down, he doesn't know. I told Paul that maybe Sandy could benefit from some counseling and reminded him that Paul's doctor told Sandy that she needed counseling. I agreed to pick Paul up at 12:00. Paul said he is so shaken, he cannot function. He said he wishes Sandy would come to her senses.

At 1:00 PM, Paul, Sandy and I attended the meeting with Attorney Sham Shanawany (Millhorn & Shanawany.

This meeting was set up by Sandy to go over their individual trusts because of Paul's Alzheimer condition and to make sure "all their ducks were in a row". Sandy started the meeting by stating that they were now married, and Paul's Alzheimer was progressing. She explained that she did not know that Bruce and I had Paul's power of attorney and since she was his wife, she wanted sole financial and health care power of attorney to include Paul's trust.

I objected to her having POA over Paul's trust account since he does not have POA for hers and the trust money goes directly to his children. Sandy stated that she is treated like a "second class citizen" and as his wife she should have sole POA. After a lengthy discussion, Sandy threw up her arms and said she wants nothing to do with Paul's finances so no one in Paul's family can say she took Paul's money.

The following decisions were made during the meeting:

Decision: No change to the Durable Power of Attorney

Sandy then stated that Paul's children wanted the trust changed to an irrevocable medical trust and that she be made the trustee. I stated that was false. Paul asked how I knew that, and I stated I had emails from his children stating that fact.

Decision: The J. Paul Baker Trust will not be amended.

Sandy then stated that she wanted Health Care Power of Attorney. I explained that she already had that along with Bruce and me. I told everyone that it states that we could act on his behalf either jointly or independently.

Decision: The Health Care Power of Attorney will not be changed. The attorney recommended that we always act jointly.

Decision: Paul will not sign any documents prepared by the Attorney without Carl's approval.

When we were finished with our discussion on Paul's trust, Sandy asked Paul and me to leave the room so she could discuss her trust with Attorney Shanawany. As we left the room, I told Paul he should stay in the room. Sandy was present when your trust was discussed so there is no reason you should not be present when her trust is discussed. Paul responded that he really does not care about her trust because that is her money. Unfortunately, Sandy did not feel the same about Paul's money and all our lives were about to undergo a dramatic change.

A Case Study Of Elder Abuse And Exploitation In Florida

> "Isolation is the number one tactic used in elder abuse."
> — *Robin McGraw (Dr. Phil TV Show)*

CHAPTER 9

The Day Everything Changed

August 22, 2018 was a Wednesday and exactly one week after the attorney refused to make the changes in Paul's trust that Sandy requested. The day started off like most days at this stage in my life. Paul called me almost daily requesting help with a repair or a project or with a question about a piece of mail or a financial matter. He usually waited to Sandy left the house before he called and wanted me to leave before she returned home. And I usually dropped whatever I was doing and drove to their house. Many of my waking hours were spent helping Paul and Sandy and I knew that he counted on me, very much like he has his entire life.

When our father had Alzheimer's in the 1990's, I was living in Virginia and was unable to help my family in New York with my father's care. My brother, Bruce, lived closest to my dad, so it mostly fell on him to do there what I was doing for Paul here in Florida. Quite honestly, I had always felt bad about not being there to help with my dad and now God was calling on me to help Paul and I wasn't about to disappoint either of them.

9:10 AM - Paul called me and told me he didn't trust Sandy and wanted me to ensure his trust was protected. I met with Dawn Machado, Assistant Vice President, BB&T to discuss Paul's bank accounts and to ascertain what I needed to do to protect him. I told her that Paul had asked me to take over the accounts and help him with the bookkeeping. I explained that Sandy had tried to get exclusive power of attorney, however, I attended the meeting with the attorney and Bruce and I retained POA. I explained the problems with Sandy taking several books of checks (out of sequence) and asking Paul to sign them without my knowing it and providing no accounting for the money. Paul also suddenly stopped using his BB&T credit card.

> Note: I handled that account for Paul and saw all the credit card transactions. I assume that Sandy was behind this because she did not get power of attorney. When I asked why they were not using the BB&T credit card, Sandy told me that the card had split, and they had not yet received the new ones they ordered. Actually, Sandy was trying to block me from any knowledge of her and Paul's spending.

I also explained that Sandy was on a $10,000 spending spree on the house for crown molding, trim, hardwood floors and new rugs. The agreement was to each pay half. One payment had been made to date, but I had not seen any bills. I had asked Sandy to see them.

I gave Dawn copies of the August 18, 2014 JOHN PAUL BAKER TRUST and the Durable Power of Attorney. I also asked Dawn to check into the status of Paul's BB&T credit cards.

Note: When I was in another BB&T bank one day to make a deposit, one of the teller's pulled me aside and asked if I was Paul Baker's brother. She told me that no one in the bank liked the fact that Sandy was always with Paul when he withdraws cash and then she would take the money. She was happy to see me taking control of Paul's account.

12:50 PM - Paul called me again and asked if I would come down to his house, so we could talk about the argument that he had with Sandy yesterday. Paul called from his house phone since he could not use his new smart phone which was Sandy's old phone and needed a password to make a call. Paul usually called when Sandy was not at home because he knew Sandy did not like Paul talking to me when she was not present to hear and control the conversation.

I started the conversation by asking Paul what happened yesterday morning that made him so upset. He said that he didn't remember too much but that Sandy was always "bossing him around." Paul said that he got angry and they were yelling at each other. I told Paul that he has to control his anger and learn to walk away and let things calm down. I also stated that he needs to call me when he gets angry (I have told Sandy the same thing) so I can help both of them.

5:15 PM - Dawn Machado called to tell me that she would get back to me on Friday on Paul's accounts and the Trust. I asked about Paul's new credit cards, and she stated that there were no new credit cards ordered. I was not surprised. Sandy lied about the "split credit card."

Throughout this entire ordeal, Sandy would lie constantly and do whatever was necessary to get control of Paul's trust. She also lied in the documents she submitted to the court.

6:15 PM - Sandy called me and told me that she and Paul had an argument over a Sam's Club bill. Paul said they (he and Sandy) needed to talk to Carl and Sandy started yelling at him. Paul told Sandy that he was leaving to go talk to me. He wanted to take the car and Sandy wouldn't let him (which was a good move on her part), so he was walking to our house. Note: Paul was doing exactly what I suggested. He walked away from the argument.

I picked up Paul on Hillsborough and brought him back to our house. Paul told me that Sandy told him that he better hire an attorney because she was getting a divorce.

6:42 M - After picking up Paul on Hillsboro Trail, I called Sandy to let her know Paul was safe and I would bring him home later. I also explained to Sandy about my earlier conversation with Paul regarding his anger yesterday morning. I told him that he needs to calm it down and if he and Sandy get into an argument, he needs to walk away.

Sandy stated, "I feel side-stepped here." For the next 10 minutes, Sandy "went off" on both Katherine and me about never notifying her when we talk to Paul and went back to the time Paul got lost (See page 69) and stated that we never called her. That is a lie. We called her twice to keep her up-to-date and told Paul he needed to call her. Her desire to be notified whenever we talk to Paul is another indication of her need to control Paul's contact with his family. Basically, Sandy does not want Paul talking to his family without her being present. Every time Allyne, Mark, Bruce or I call Paul, Sandy listens in and you can hear her in the background telling Paul what to say.

8:27 PM - After Paul had dinner with us, we told Paul that he needed to call Sandy. He was trying to work his phone to call her, but did not know the pass code, so he used my cell phone. The call lasted for about 50 minutes, so what follows are only exerts from the call from the notes we wrote. The speaker phone was on, so we heard the entire call.

When Sandy answered the phone, she became confused and kept asking who she was talking to—Carl or Paul. Paul said, "It's Paul your husband." She responded that she didn't know how much of a husband he is anymore—that he left her and that it wasn't the first time he had done that. Paul then asked if she was okay with just ending it, referring to her earlier comment about divorcing him. Sandy said she didn't know and that she was so confused and that she didn't appreciate that he had betrayed her. Sandy said that she does not betray their trust. She told him that there is no trust anywhere in this whole mess and that they are not husband and wife and haven't been ever since day one.

Sandy again went back to the day Paul got lost and claims she never heard from anyone for five hours. In that instance, Paul had left the house again due to an argument they had and Sandy had waited two hours to even let anyone know he was gone. I called Paul and told him to call Sandy. Katherine and I worked to locate him which was not easy since he did not know the area. We finally figured it all out and drove to his location, retrieved him and I drove his car back to his house and Katherine followed. Upon arriving, Sandy berated both of us, in front of her neighbor, for not calling her sooner, even though Paul called her again when we started home. Sandy never showed any relief that her husband had been found and was safely home. Sandy still denies the phone calls and said I had the audacity to call her a liar. It is important to note that Sandy never once showed any sign of gratitude that Paul was safely home or any affection toward Paul. However, the next day, she sent an email with an apology.

As their phone conversation continued, Sandy told Paul that there are a lot of things about his finances that she believes are being withheld from her. Sandy added, "You have not shared where you went with Carl while I was in Alaska. You have not shared that Carl talked to Bill, her neighbor. You have not shared that you talked to Carl today." Evidently, Sandy expects Paul to tell her every time he talks to anyone, especially his own family.

Sandy then told Paul that she can't trust him anymore "because I am your wife and we do not have a husband-and-wife relationship because you have been going behind my back." She then said she was probably on speaker so that Carl and Katherine can hear this, stating, "So if you have me on speaker, which I think you do, and I think this whole conversation is being heard, that's fine."

Sandy then told Paul that he has a whole lot more money than he ever let her know about and she can't believe all of this.

(Note: This is false. All of Paul's financial assets are in his trust account.)

She then said that with everything she heard tonight, that "their whole marriage was a sham." Sandy then told Paul, "... you're better off without me. You're better off with your family who, you know, you guys trust each other." Sandy then told Paul she would leave him and fight to get everything and every penny that is hers.

Paul asked, "What does this mean?"

Sandy replied that she made a big mistake by marrying him and Paul had the audacity to walk away from her and go to Carl's house. Sandy called Paul "nuts" and asked, "What the f—k is wrong with you?"

Sandy continued saying that Paul "crossed the line" and that she was going to put the house on the market. They have not been living as a married couple because she has been totally deceived and she can't trust Paul anymore.

Sandy told Paul that "you go around and tell the neighbors you don't know where I am and yet there is a white board *(Which we asked her to get for Paul and it took a month)* and I have told you over and over again where I am. I explain it 4 or 5 times before I leave. And you go to the neighbors and ask like you don't know where I am."

Then Sandy lied to Paul and tried to taunt him by saying," Your brothers don't include you in golf anymore. I wonder why? You have not played golf in months. You have been totally left out of playing golf with your brothers. I don't really know why this is. Maybe it's because you have Alzheimer's and they just don't want to deal with it. Have you noticed that?"

The truth of the matter was that Sandy was well aware that Paul got dizzy on the golf course and decided to stop playing until the fall when it would be cooler. And it was not months since Paul played golf, it was weeks. That was a horrible thing to say to Paul. It was cruel and an example of how she treated Paul when she did not get exactly what she wanted. It is also an example of her brainwashing Paul. In my mind, Sandy definitely has a need for mental health treatment.

When the conversation got back on track, Paul asked her, "So you're going to end it." Sandy responded with, "I'm pretty close. But you know, you don't have to worry you've got Carl to take care of you. You've got Carl to come and make sure that you get every fricking little dirty dime that you've been holding onto and haven't told me about."

The conversation on money and finances continued with Sandy stating that she has been open with Paul on her financial assets, but Paul has not, which was absolutely not true.

Paul responded, "I have no idea what your finances are."

Sandy yelled, "Oh my God. You know what, your Alzheimer's sure kicks in when it's convenient for you, doesn't it?" Paul got terribly upset by this and replied, "No, it doesn't go away. My Alzheimer's doesn't go away! "

Sandy constantly pitted herself against Carl and Katherine and told him he was making an irrevocable choice the result of which would be divorce, implying that this was all his doing and that it is all his fault.

The phone call continued for several more minutes and ended

with the following dialogue:

Paul: "You obviously don't want me."

Sandy: "I can't live with a liar. Are you freaking kidding me? What kind of fool do you think I am? *(Laughs.)* You are so twisted. *(Laughs.)*

Paul: I'm glad you think that's funny. Thank you.

The call ended.

We asked Paul what he wanted to do. We encouraged him to go in the other room and pray about it. After about 15 minutes, Paul came back to the kitchen and said he wanted to go home. I drove him home and he asked that I drop him off where Sandy would not see him. I asked him "Why?" He never gave me an answer. I dropped him off a short distance down the street.

The next day everything was different. Sandy basically prevented Bruce, Gail, Katherine, and me from having any contact with Paul. Exactly one week after Sandy fails in her attempt to change Paul's trust to give her full control of his assets, she begins to isolate Paul from his family fully realizing that she will never have control of his money if we are still in Paul's life. As you will see, this would become a textbook case of elder abuse and exploitation.

Despite all our efforts, we were never able to have a substantive conversation with Paul for the next eleven weeks.

I still had Paul's checking account and checks, but Sandy was having Paul sign checks from another numbered series which she took from Paul. I tried to return Paul's checkbook and checks to him in person, but neither the phone nor the door was answered. Bruce and I both tried to contact Paul numerous times.

We heard nothing from Paul or Sandy for several weeks. Paul and Sandy were scheduled to return home on September 13, 2018 from a week at a timeshare in Orlando, so Bruce called to see if Paul was still available for lunch on Friday. The call immediately went to voice mail and the call was never returned.

The following day, Bruce and I drove to Paul's house at 11:30 AM to see if he was available for lunch. No one was home. Bill (neighbor) stated that he saw the car leave at 8:15 that morning. Both Bruce and I called Paul's cell. Both calls went immediately to voice mail and we both left messages. Since he was not home, I did not leave the package (BB&T checkbook) that I have been trying to give him since September 6th.

Again, Bruce and I drove to Paul's house at 11:00 AM. Again, no one was home. I called Paul on his cell. This time it did not go directly to voice mail and I left another message for Paul. I then called Sandy's cell and left a message that I have a package for Paul and would she please call me when Paul is home so I can deliver the package.

I again called Paul's cell at 6:15 PM. Left voice mail. "Paul, how about giving me the courtesy of a return call!

Bruce sent the following email at 8:33PM:

Paul/Sandy,

Over the past few days, Carl & I have made several attempts to communicate with Paul. We've made several telephone calls that rolled over to voice mail and left several messages to return our calls.

Our initial call was to ask Paul to lunch on Friday (yesterday) with myself, Carl and Jack Warner. Obviously, that didn't happen.

We stopped by the house both yesterday and today, but no one was at home. Carl called Sandy's telephone number yesterday and left a message to call when you were home. Also didn't happen.

Sandy, in your email response to me last Sunday about Paul's availability for golf, you were going to let me know Thursday when you got home. Also did not happen. It may be too late for next Tuesday, but I will need to know by Monday night, September 17th if Paul is available for golf on Tuesday, September 25th.

Thanks!
Bruce

At 8:47PM, Bruce received the following text from Sandy using Paul's phone:

"I will not be playing on Tuesday. Paul"

Bruce received the following email from Sandy at 5:05 PM in response to his 9/15/18 email to Sandy about Paul playing golf:

"Paul said he is not playing on the 25th due to the heat. There is a lot that needs to be discussed for inaccuracies in the above e-mail. But we don't feel like dealing with it at this time."
Paul and Sandy

Sandy texted me at 9:47 PM on September 15, 2018 from Paul's phone pretending to be him:

"Sandy said you have a package for us. Who is the package from and what is the delivery address? How did you get the package? Paul"

I replied at 6:51 AM, the next day:

"Paul, I know Sandy sent this message, but the package is for you and I can drop it off this afternoon any time after 1PM. Let me know when you are home."

Sandy replied on Paul's phone at 9:26 AM:

"We have plans all day. Please put the package on the porch. Thanks."

I am not going to leave a checkbook with blank signed checks on the porch! I decided that I will not respond and I will mail Paul his checkbook by registered mail, return receipt requested. I cannot be responsible for their mishandlings and of course, Sandy will never accept responsibility and will blame me.

I sent the following text at 7:10 AM on September 17, 2018:

"What time today will Paul be there so I can drop off the package?"

Sandy/Paul responded at 11:35 AM.

"This is Paul, not Sandy. We are out doing errands. Please leave with Bill next door."

I wanted to get the checkbook back to Paul, so I mailed the package to Paul, registered mail, with the following letter and accounting:

Paul

"I have been helping you with your checking account and bills long before you were married. In July after your fraud case with the landscaper, you asked me to take over your checking account so that you would have a more accurate accounting. You have never had a complete check register and often made out checks to cash and many times it was impossible to tell where the cash was going.

I am returning your checkbook and checks to you along with a spread sheet that you should continue. Without your cooperation and with you and Sandy writing checks from two different numbered series (1140's and 1240's) from the checks you gave me (1360 series), it is obvious you no longer desire my help and it is impossible for me to keep an accurate accounting. You also asked that I keep your large JPB Trust Account at an even thousand-dollar amount. I have done that. I have also been able to increase this account by $3000 each month for a current balance of $233,000.

I recommend that you continue to maintain an accurate ledger and keep all costs for home improvement documented by check. For example, check #1146 mixes the cost of your flooring with termite prevention which is not a deductible expense when the house is sold. Keep a separate file for *all home improvement expenditures.*"

Love,
Carl

FINAL ACCOUNTING OF J PAUL BAKER CHECKING ACCOUNT

Check Number	Date	Amount	Unverified Amount	Paid To	Purpose[1]
1350	01/05/18	$700.00		J Paul Baker	January house expense
1351	02/10/18		$115.00	Sandra J Baker	House expense
1352	02/10/18	$150.00		J Paul Baker	February house expense
1353	02/27/18		$1,150.00	J Paul Baker	March house expense
1354	03/03/18	$100.00		Mark Baker	birthday
1355	03/23/18		$21.99	Sam's Club MC	
1356		VOID	VOID	VOID	
1357	03/30/18	$700.00		J Paul Baker	April house expense
1358	03/30/18	$250.00		Sandra J Baker	ruby ring for Sandra
1359	03/30/18	$200.00		Allyne Baker	birthday
1360	04/09/18		$635.00	Sandra J Baker	2017 income tax[2]
1361	04/09/18		$750.00	J Paul Baker	2018 quarterly income tax[2]
1362	05/03/18	$800.00		J Paul Baker	May house expense
1363	05/15/18	$800.00		J Paul Baker	June house expense
1364	06/07/18		$750.00	J Paul Baker	tax payment[2]
1365	06/25/18	$800.00		J Paul Baker	July house expense
auto deduction	07/03/18	$35.00		Verizon	phone bill
1366	07/03/18	$520.00		Manny Martinez	fraudulent lawn care
1367	07/07/18	$10,000.00		Allyne Baker	gift
1368		VOID		VOID	
1369	07/07/18	$10,000.00		Mark Baker	gift
auto deduction	07/17/18	$1,850.52		BB&T Credit Card	
auto deduction	07/17/18	$201.96		Mass Mutual	life insurance policy
1370	07/27/18	$800.00		Sandra J Baker	August house expense
1371	08/01/18	$500.00		Joss Baker	HS graduation gift
auto deduction	08/03/18	$35.00		Verizon	phone bill
1372	08/08/18	$300.00		Cash	Paul (uncashed)
1246	08/08/18		$2,351.00	Trim Works	half of crown molding etc
auto deduction	08/17/18	$2,453.85		BB&T Credit Card	
1128	08/17/18	$400.00		Kaila Baker	gift
auto deduction	08/20/18	$201.96		Mass Mutual	life insurance policy
1374	08/27/18	$800.00		Sandra J Baker	September house expenses
1249	08/29/18		$1,168.29	Trim Works	half of flooring
1146	08/31/18		$1,355.54	Sandra J Baker	termite protection & flooring
auto deduction	09/04/18		$33.75	Sam's Club MC	
Totals		$32,598.29	$8,330.57		

Footnotes:
[1] Information based solely on information written on check
[2] Property taxes should be split 50-50. Income taxes should be prorated based on total individual taxable income, less individual taxes withheld and individual quarterly payments made.

A Case Study Of Elder Abuse And Exploitation In Florida

We later learned that on September 21st, Paul and Sandy went to the BB&T Bank in the Villages to withdraw money from Paul's trust account. A cashier's check for **$220,000** removed most of Paul's money from his account. At that time, we had no idea where it went, but we knew Sandy had control of Paul's life savings.

On October 20th at 2:30 PM, I called Paul's cell phone. Much to my surprise, he answered the phone. This is the first time in almost two months that I was able to speak to him. The text of the call follows:

P: *Hello*
C: *Paul this is your brother Carl.*
P: *(Long pause)*
C: *Paul, when are we going to sit down and talk.*
P: *We are on our way home, so not now. (Sandy was in the car with him. He probably answered the phone because Sandy most likely removed my number and he did not know who was calling him.)*
C: *I will drive down to your house right now so we can talk.*
P: *No.*
C: *Paul why did you stop talking to your family?*
P: *I talk to Allyne and Mark.*
C: *You haven't spoken to me or Bruce in almost two months. The two people who have helped you the most in life.*
P: *You told me 5 times that my wife was a liar.*
C: *Let's sit down man to man and talk about it.*
P: *I don't want to talk to you.*

C: *Paul, the truth is your wife is a liar. She is filling you with bullshit to keep you away from your family so she can steal your money.*
P: *(Hung up the phone.)*

There is no doubt in my mind that for whatever reason, Paul feared Sandy. I have no idea what she has told him. What I do know is that Paul's actions are the result of Sandy's taking advantage of his confused mind.

On Friday, November 9th, we were meeting friends from church for dinner at Carrabba's Italian Grill. I dropped Katherine off to get us on the wait list and parked the car. When I entered the restaurant, Katherine was in the waiting area talking to Paul and Sandy.

I walked over to Paul to shake hands and he refused. I told Paul there was no reason for us not to talk. I could see that he was actually scared to talk to me in front of Sandy. Knowing Veteran's Day was on Sunday, I said, Paul. Happy Veteran's Day. Thank you for your service," That broke the ice and when I put out my hand, he shook it. I told him that I understood that he was going on the Veteran's Honor Flight and I wanted to come to the ceremony even though I was not invited. I asked him if he wanted me to attend. He looked over to Sandy and said, "No."

I then asked Paul if both he and I could have lunch together and see if we could talk and work out our differences. He said he would like to do that. Sandy immediately stated," I have a problem with that." Katherine then told Sandy there is no reason we shouldn't all be able to talk. Sandy again stated she "had a problem with Paul talking to Carl", even though Paul stated he wanted to meet Carl for lunch. I went ahead and continued the conversation with Paul and told him I would call him and set a day and time for lunch and pick him up. Paul said that would be fine.

The following day (Saturday), Bruce, Gail, Katherine and I drove to the Ocala Theater to see a play. I am not sure what the odds are here, but we ran into Sandy and Paul again. Paul waved to Bruce, but Paul and Sandy made no attempt to talk to any of us.

The next week, on November 20th, I tried to call Paul several times by phone but was unsuccessful. So, I sent him the following text message on November 20th and we had the following exchange:

11:31 AM:

Paul
Did you read my letter? (Honor Flight) We need to talk.
Carl

2:21 PM - Response
(Again, Paul has never texted in his life. This was sent by Sandy pretending to be Paul.)

We have nothing to talk about.

On December 1, 2018, I tried to reach out to Paul once again and at 3:09 PM sent the following text: "I know Sandy does not want you talking to any of us, but I have some information that you really need to know. Let's have that lunch you promised me. Carl." The response, obviously sent by Sandy, did not come until December 4 at 9:01 PM:

"I promised nothing."

In mid-December, when Allyne was sending me an email outlining the difficulty she had in trying to communicate with her dad, she began the email with the following:

"I wish I could retell these events without sounding like a little girl fighting to keep my dad in my life and competing against the wicked step-mother. There should be no competition whatsoever. But when someone has an agenda to control my dad and his money, I guess she'll stop at nothing to achieve it. Including isolating him from his loved ones."

This says it all. The heartache that Sandy has caused our family in the past several years cannot be measured and has taken a toll on all of us.

Time continued to pass with no communication with Paul. On January 7, 2019, at about 10:00 AM, while running some errands (bank and cleaners), I decided to go by Paul's house and knock on the door to see if I could talk to him. The house was dark, and all the blinds were drawn, but I rang the bell anyway. Much to my surprise, he came to the door and paused. I told him we needed to talk, and he opened the door. Obviously, he had just gotten up since the unused breakfast dishes were still on the table. He looked pale and lethargic.

I told Paul that we needed to talk and started by asking him what he thought I did wrong to cause him to stop talking to me. I added that everything I did for him was at his request. After a brief silence, he told me that I said Sandy was a liar. I told him that I have and always will tell him the truth and that Sandy is a liar and she has been lying to him as well. I cited the time that Sandy told him that Bruce and I would not play golf with him because he has Alzheimer's. He seemed to understand.

I told him that he cut four people that loved him, out of his life - Bruce, Gail, Katherine and me. He did not say a word. I asked him why he had done this. He could not give me an answer; however, he did say he loved us.

I asked him how he was doing and if he was feeling OK. He told me that Sandy had heard that "they" found a cure for his sickness (Alzheimer's) and she was researching it for him. I told him I thought they had some promising studies, but as far as I knew, nothing new has been made available yet. I asked him if Sandy was giving him any extra pills. He said," She always gives me two pills when I have a headache." I asked how often he has a headache. He said that they are "more now." He added that the pills make him sleep more.

I asked to see his phone. I took out my phone and called his. His phone did not ring, and my call immediately went to voice mail. I then took his phone and could not find my name in his contacts. I then tried to dial my cell phone from his and I could not make an outgoing call. He told me that his cell is useless since he does not know how to use it. *(As stated before, Sandy put a pass code in his phone, so she could control his calls.)*

I told him that we were concerned that Sandy removed the money from his trust account and we have no idea what is going on. If Sandy has control of his money, there is no telling what she will do. Sandy had already told us she wants to move him to a VA facility in St. Augustine, which is over 100 miles and over two hours away and would certainly limit the number of times he would get visits from his family.

He appeared confused again and I asked him if he knew where the $235,000 from the original trust was now. He said in an account in Sandy's bank. I asked, "Chase?" He told me he thought so. I asked him if all of it was there. He did not know. I asked him if Allyne was still the beneficiary on his $100,000 life insurance policy. He said," I am paying it now." *(I was paying it for him until September, because he fell behind in payments.)* I told him I knew that but asked if Sandy is the beneficiary now. He couldn't answer that.

I then asked him about his new trust. He had no clue what I was talking about. I reminded him that both he and Sandy had trust accounts and when it came time to sell their home, the proceeds were to be evenly split between the trusts. He asked me if that was still the case. I told him I did not know, but if he let me see the trust, I could tell him. He told me that he does not know where it is because Sandy takes care of all that.

I told him that one of his children should oversee his finances and he told me that Mark should do it.

I also told him that unless we get to the bottom of this,

Sandy could have very well stolen over $500,000 from him. He was silent for about a minute. Then he asked me, "Can we get it back?" I told him that we could, but the longer this goes on the more difficult it could be. I told him that I had filed a criminal complaint against Sandy.

I could see that he was getting nervous and he said, "You better leave before Sandy comes home." I asked him if he feared her. He said "no", but Sandy would not be happy if she found out I was there. I told him that I would not say a word about it and he said he also would not. He then said something that I thought was promising. How can we keep in touch? I told him that Sandy never lets my calls through. *(He acted surprised that I had called.)* I told him that Sandy has probably fixed his cell phone, so he cannot call me. I suggested that I send a letter directly to him stating that I filed a criminal complaint against Sandy and if we all sat down perhaps, we can work something out. He said, "Send the letter!" I told him I would think it through more thoroughly.

Since it is near my home, I pass by the street leading to Paul's house three or four times a week. I really do not know what made me turn down his street on that day and ring his doorbell, especially since I tried so many times before without success. I view it as an answer to all our prayers. And this split-second decision to turn down that street on that day, changed everything and perhaps, even saved Paul's life.

At this stage, I still did not know exactly what happened to the money from Paul's account, nor did I know what changes Sandy made to Paul's trust. Additionally, I had no idea if the life insurance beneficiary was changed to Sandy. So, I mailed the following letter to Paul in hope that he would realize that he was being exploited:

PERSONAL AND CONFIDENTIAL
Paul
Let me start by saying that I really wish that this were not necessary, but with your refusal to speak to any of us, I was left with no other choice. *I have filed a felony complaint against Sandy and it is currently under investigation.*

Sandy has no right to your non-marital assets any more than you have a right to hers. That is why when your thinking was clear, you both established trusts and a prenuptial agreement. I personally do not gain anything by doing this. You, Mark and Allyne are the victims here, and as your brother and Trustee, I feel I must do everything in my power to protect you and prevent this. Remember, you are the one that asked me to protect your trust and that is exactly what I am doing.

Paul, I do not know if you knew this, but I have made hundreds of arrests in my career of almost 40 years, and I have never lost a trial. My rule in life is always do your homework and that is what we are doing here.

1. We have a complete background review of Sandy Treolo Hine Kaniewski Baker. Paul, you would find this most interesting. Unfortunately, we know your wife better than you do. Past performance is a good indicator of present and future performance.

2. With the help of many people, I have about a hundred pages of documentation on Sandy's past actions concentrating largely on

the last two to three years. Basically, it goes from the time Sandy was sneaking you into her house to sleep together in Ralph's bed while he was in Hospice, until today. Much of this outlines Sandy's quest to get your trust money even before you were married. When you do a timeline on the facts, a definite pattern emerges. She was after your money!

3. We have a number of people who stated that they would be willing to testify at Sandy's trial. In fact, we have more than we need.

4. I have researched the Florida Code for an appropriate charge. Chapter 825 - Abuse, Neglect, and Exploitation of Elderly Person and Disabled Adults is perfect for many reasons. If you read the Code, and I encourage you to do that, pay close attention to the definitions. Note that the "Position of trust and confidence" includes the spouse. Sandy was always telling me, "I am his wife". Yes, she is, however, she has crossed the line and needs to be held accountable.

5. My recommendation to the prosecutor is to charge Sandy with Section 825.103, *Exploitation of an elderly person or disabled adult.* If you look at Section (2)(a) it states that if the funds involved in the exploitation of the disabled adult are valued at $100,000 or more, the offender commits a felony of the first degree. This is the highest felony and punishable to up to *30 years in prison.* A felony crime of this nature calls for a much more thorough investigation. This will take at least another month or so.

6. I have gone through the statute in much detail and identified the elements we would need for a conviction. I then took those

elements and compared them to our documentation and what we can prove in court. There are several unknowns here. Where did the $220,000 go? Was the $100,000 life insurance changed from Allyne to Sandy? What happens to the funds when the house is sold? That means the actual exploitation could go as high as *$550,000* or more. I have recommended that a law enforcement forensic accountant review all of this to include both of your financial records for the past several years, your new trust and other documents.

7. Indications are that Sandy did not do all of this on her own and was receiving advice and council from another person. There will be an electronic trail on this which cannot be erased, so we will determine if this is true and confirm the identity of that person. If true, that person may be subject to arrest also.

All these questions will be answered by the investigation. And let me assure you of one thing. *No stone will be left unturned.*

Paul, I have asked you many times to sit down and talk to me about all of this, just the two of us. You agreed to it the night we ran into you at Carrabba's (Nov 9). Sandy was against it because she can't take the chance that our conversation may bring you back to your senses. You later told me, "We have nothing to talk about." If she loved you, she never would have separated you from your family or taken your life savings. You are the victim of exploitation and that is why Sandy needs to be arrested. This is my last communication to you on this. Talk to me about this one on one or I will see you in court. Your choice!

Signed/Carl

Katherine and I returned to Paul's home at the same time on the following Monday. Katherine parked down the street and I again rang the doorbell. Paul answered the door and invited me in. I stated that I told him I would be back and it was time for him to make a decision. I asked him if he wanted to stay there with Sandy and continue living like he is now or does he want to leave and live with Katherine and me. He did not hesitate at all. He replied, "Get me out of here!" I called Katherine on her cell and she pulled into the driveway and came in. We talked for several minutes. I wrote a note on the whiteboard on the refrigerator stating that I took Paul to lunch. We left and drove back to our house.

We spent the next 30 to 40 minutes talking to Paul to make sure he was comfortable with his decision. Paul was adamant that he was not happy being separated from his (the Baker) family and further stated that Sandy was always leaving him alone in the house. We asked how often this happened and he said, "Almost every day." Since we have only had one contact with him since August, we had no way of knowing how often he was left alone, but we do know she left him alone more than she should.

We then drove to Chase Bank to put a hold on Paul's trust account, so Sandy would not be able to access it. While we were in the Bank's Vice-President's office, Sandy, her next-door neighbors, Bill and Lil, and another neighbor burst into the office and Sandy started screaming, "What are you doing with my husband?" Bill and Lil began yelling as well making accusations that Paul hated us and we kidnapped him and should be arrested.

Sandy stated that she wanted a divorce. Paul replied that he did too. Sandy was shocked! She immediately blamed Katherine and me and stated, "What did you do to my husband?" Sandy was always threatening Paul with divorce, but this is the first time he agreed. My guess is that by Sandy leaving him alone so often, separating him from his family, and their constant fighting, Paul finally had had enough and told Sandy that he wanted to end their marriage. Sandy responded with more accusations against all of us and said that she would divorce him. The four of them continued to scream all types of threats and the bank Vice President told them to leave the bank. On the way out, Sandy said she would be calling the police and evidently, she did.

Once we left the bank, we went to the Verizon store to have them examine Paul's phone (which was Sandy's phone that she gave Paul). Just as we thought, they told us the phone could not be used by Paul since it was programmed so Sandy was the only one that could use it and it was either password or fingerprint protected. We purchased a flip phone for Paul, like the one he previously used for years, since he could not use smart phone that Sandy gave him. We then took Sandy's old phone as evidence of her abuse (isolation).

The next several days were very telling. Sandy has always made herself the victim and Facebook gave her the public stage to play the poor grieving, loving wife she is not. And many of her friends fell "hook, line, and sinker" for her lies and posted horrible comments about me and Katherine. Several samples of her Facebook or more accurately, her "Fakebook" follow:

"Sandy Kaniewski is feeling sad.

Paul's brother, Carl, and sister-in-law, Katherine stole my husband who has Alzheimer's and whom I am deeply in love with out of our home while I was playing golf yesterday. They have ruined our marriage and I will never be the same without him. Prayers for my dear Paul and myself please."

From SC: "Sandy, I am praying that this comes to a speedy resolution. This is clearly kidnapping and if they crossed state lines. [sic] Brother has no legal standing. You are his wife. I know how very much the two of you love each other. I pray that he keeps asking for his Sandy and makes them feel guilty enough to bring him back to you."

From CL: "Sandy, you are legally his next of kin. Please file a police report ASAP. What they are doing is illegal. Only you have the authority to make decisions for him. Please contact an attorney to see what your options are."

Sandy: "I contacted the police, talk to a lawyer tomorrow. Thanks for your concern. I can't fight them. They are evil horrible people."

Of note, Sandy did send the police to our home. The police questioned Paul thoroughly. He told them that he left her and wanted a divorce because he was abused and left alone in the house all the time. The police closed Sandy's complaint of kidnapping as unfounded. *(Note that Sandy states she "can't fight" us. She said that because she knows her story is not true.)*

From LM: "I can't understand how twisted someone must be to be able to take their ailing brother from the love of his life and rob him if as much love and happiness as he can have for the good days that are left for him! "

"To shatter Sandy and Paul's love because you have hate and revenge in your soul and call this "having you brother's back" is evil and sick. You will have your judgement day, buddy!"

From GSS: "What a wonderful photo of you and Paul. You should take this and a photo album to share with Elder Care Rep when you meet. It is criminal that Carl has taken Paul from you, your marriage and home. It is beyond my imagination how Carl has been permitted to fill Paul's head with lies to cause him this confusion. Hopefully, you will have the same judge when this goes before the court again. I think she was spot on to assign an Elder Care Arty [sic] on Paul's behalf. However, I think it was a mistake, knowing Paul is not competent, that he was left in Carl's care. It was quite obvious, to all who knew/know you and Paul as a loving, caring couple, that Carl has filled Paul's mind with lies and confusion. I fear for Paul in Carl's care."

From LM: "Right on, GSS! Carl is nuts and evil!"

From GSS: "Sandy, we are SOOOO sorry that you AND Paul are having the HORRIFIC experience. Carl Kaniewski [sic] has to be a very dangerous, controlling individual and I cannot imagine the pain he has inflicted on you or the unimaginable terror he will add to Paul's thoughts. Remember that a monster named Adolf Hitler separated families once. HITLER was a very selfish, deranged, individual, a sociopath. The action of Paul's brother Carl (and his wife) is terribly frightening.

In the name of GOD, perhaps his brother Carl is more ill than Paul. Obviously, Carl is evil and wicked to commit the "crime" against Paul AND you [sic]."

For those who are void of integrity, social media sites have become weaponized with disinformation and out-and-out lies in an attempt to destroy people's reputation and change truth to propaganda to further one's cause and destroy opposing views. There is a fierce continuing battle for the soul of the internet.

However, the most interesting and telling post on Sandy's Facebook occurred on March 4, 2019:

From YL: "Good morning Sandy, our whole family is thinking of you. We hope paul [sic] has found his home and that happiness has returned to your home. Lots of kisses from all of you."

Sandy responded: "No, I have not seen Paul in two months. His Alzheimer's is much worse according to incompetency assessments. I made the decision today to let him stay with his brother after much expense with the judicial system."

(Note: On the next day, March 5th, Sandy cancelled the March 7th court appearance, withdrew the petition she filed and her attorneys petitioned the court to be released from representing her. We had no idea what caused her to do this. However, she hired new attorneys and refiled her petition. Eventually, her new lawyers petitioned the court to be released also.)

There were some very sincere responses on Sandy's Facebook showing concern for Sandy and the situation. The problem is that many of these people only know the personality that Sandy displays in public. My hope is that this book will allow them to have a better understanding of the abuse and exploitation that Paul experienced from Sandy. He is the only real victim in this saga!

"Nothing is more destructive of respect for the government and the law of the land than passing laws which cannot be {or are not} enforced." {Emphasis added.}
— *Albert Einstein*

CHAPTER 10

Court Proceedings

There were numerous court orders and petitions filed throughout this process and throughout this book, some of these were referenced in the text when necessary. In this chapter, I did not attempt to list all of them. However, the brief summary of the petitions and orders that follow, are here to show the irrational actions of Sandy which perhaps made this case much more difficult than it needed to be.

The following petition was filed in the Circuit Court for Sumter County on January 31, 2019:

PETITION TO DETERMINE INCAPACITY

On January 31, 2019, Sandy filed the following petition with the court:

PETITION TO DETERMINE INCAPACITY
Petitioner, Sandra J. Baker, alleges:

1. Petitioner, Sandra J. Baker, whose address is 3723 Mango Court, The Villages,
FL 32163, and whose relationship to the named alleged incapacitated person is spouse.

2. Petitioner believes John Paul Baker ("Person"), whose date of birth is June 6, 1946, who is 72 years of age, whose primary spoken language is English, and who resides at 3723 Mango Court, The Villages, FL 32163 but was taken to 1816 Wading Heron, The Villages, FL 32163 by his brother, Carl R. Baker, to be incapacitated, based upon the following factual information:

Petitioner/wife of AIP was concerned about the AIP after he was taken from their marital home to Carl Baker's home on January 14, 2019 (Carl Baker is brother of the AIP). She called the Sumter County Sheriff's Office to seek their assistance and was informed this is a civil matter and she needed to contact an attorney. Petitioner states person is a 72-year-old vulnerable adult who after extensive testing by neurologist Dr. Pedro Geliga approximately three years ago was diagnosed with Alzheimer's. Over time person's condition has progressed with person's spouse/petitioner ensuring the care and health needs are met. Although person needs only occasional cueing to accomplish his ADL's, petitioner handles most IADLs, including medication management, cooking, shopping, maintaining the home, scheduling and attending medical appointments, and managing household finances. The AlP's driver's license was revoked in November 2018 after the AlP was getting lost and unable to find his way home. He no longer plays golf. In church, the AlP was having difficulty keeping up with the reading and verses in hymns. Petitioner quit the choir to sit by him so he could stay engaged and enjoy church. Petitioner feels the AlP's symptoms associated with Alzheimer's have been exacerbated due to continual efforts of the AlP's brother, Carl Baker, to break up their marriage. Those efforts include calls to DCF and the Sumter County Sheriff's Office (SCSO) suggesting petitioner was taking the AlP's money and isolating him from his family. A SCSO report dated October 15, 2018 called in by the AlP's brother, Carl Baker, accused the petitioner of isolating the AlP and stealing his trust funds. This resulted in an officer going to the AlP's residence and questioning him. The officer found the AlP in good spirits, not depressed and stated he did not meet Baker Act criteria. When the AlP asked who filed the report and the officer refused to tell him, he stated it must be his brother

(Carl Baker). (See attached SCSO report marked Exhibit "A") Petitioner states two weeks later a DCF investigator showed up at their home questioning she and the AlP on the same issues reported in the SCSO report. On January 9, 2019 petitioner and the AlP received a letter from DCF stating the investigation was closed with a recommendation for the AlP to continue with appropriate medical care and assistance with affairs from wife/petitioner. (See attached Letter from DCF closing their investigation marked Exhibit "B"). On January 14, 2019, Carl Baker picked up the AlP under the auspices of taking him to lunch and immediately went to the bank with the AlP to check into his accounts and then took the AlP to Carl Baker's home where he has remained since that time. Petitioner is confident Carl Baker has continued his verbal attacks of her and that the AlP, in his condition, is easily influenced. Should the Court find that the AlP is determined to be incapacitated and that an alternative to guardianship is in place, Petitioner requests that the AlP be able to reside at home, with the recommendation of his doctors, and that an injunction be issued against Carl Baker so that the Petitioner and AlP may resume their marriage in harmony. 3. The names and addresses of all persons known to petitioner who have knowledge of such facts through personal observations are:

*Bill & Lillian Monty, 3715 Mango Court, The Villages, FL 32163 - neighbor - 413-218-8663
*Neal & Mary Hicks, 3726 Mango Court, The Villages, FL 32163 - neighbor - 248-366-7842

Terry and Mike Reed, 3081 Maginn Drive, Beavercreek, OH 45434-friends-937-231-0941

Brent Hine, 102 Sunny Trail, Benton, LA 71006 - Sandra's son - 318-349-7276

Angelique Mock, 1361 Normandy Court, Ft. Wainwright, AK 99703 - Sandra's daughter- 601-550-0509

Rev. Janice Barnes - Holy Trinity Episcopal Church, Fruitland Park, FL - 352-633-8735

Mary Beth Eason, 1223 Old State Rd, Wilmington, OH, 45177-Sandra's sister - 937-72S-1983

Joe and Bette Pascucci, 3000 Burbank Lane, The Villages, FL 32162, -friends-401-S9S-8420

*Most familiar with current situation

7. The alleged incapacitated person's attending or family physicians are:

Dr. Pedro Geliga - 601 Medical Plaza, Ste 601, Leesburg, FL 34748 - 352-787-7611- neurologist

Dr. Win - Psychiatrist, The Villages Outpatient Clinic, 8900 SE 165th Mulberry Lane, The Villages, FL 32162- 352-674-5000

Dr. Mark Rothschild - 8575 NE 138th Lane, Ste 203, Lady Lake, FL 32159 - 352-674-2080 - Cardiologist

Dr. Rochelle Knowles- The Villages Outpatient Clinic, 8900 SE 165th Mulberry Lane, The Villages, FL 32162 - 352-674-5000 - primary

Dr. David J. Casper - 8620 E. County Road 466, The Villages, FL 32162 - 352-399-7295- Dermatology

Petitioner requests that an examination be made as to the mental and physical condition of the alleged incapacitated person as provided by law, and that an order be entered determining the mental and physical capacity of said person. Under penalties of perjury, I declare that I have read the foregoing, and the facts alleged are true, to the best of my knowledge and belief.
Signed on January]0, 2019.

    Sandra J. Baker, Petitioner

/s/Michael C. Norvell
Co-Counsel for Petitioner

/s/Suzanne 1. Przystawski
  Co-Counsel for Petitioner

MOTION TO WITHDRAW AS COUNSEL

On March 6, 2019, attorneys Michael C. Norvell and Suzanne L. Przystawski, who represented Sandra J. Baker, filed a motion with the court to withdraw from representing her. Although the real reason for the motion is unknown, I know Sandy asked that Paul "return" home to live with her. Paul does not want that and I doubt that Paul's attorney would allow that. The motion was approved by the court, and Sandy currently has no legal representation.

The Court granted a motion to postpone the hearing on the pending Petitions until April 29, 2019.

After the above attorneys, at their request, were permitted by the court to be released from representing Sandy, a second petition for guardianship was filed by Sandy's new attorneys:

IN THE CIRCUIT COURT OF THE FIFTH JUDICIAL CIRCUIT, IN AND FOR SUMTER COUNTY, FLORIDA PROBATE DIVISION

IN RE: GUARDIANSHIP OF
JOHN PAUL BAKER,
Ward and Alleged Incapacitated Person.
-------------------------~/
File No. 2019 MH 89
File No. 2019 GA 158

PETITION FOR APPOINTMENT OF PLENARY GUARDIAN
(Incapacity - person and property)
Petitioner, SANDRA J. BAKER, alleges:

1. Sandra J. Baker, Petitioner (hereinafter "Sandy"), residence is 3723 Mango Court, The Villages, Florida 32163, and Petitioner's post office address is the same.

2. JOHN PAUL BAKER, is an alleged incapacitated person

(hereinafter "Paul" or "Ward") whose date of birth is June 6, 1946 and who is age 72.

3. Sandra and Paul have been married since June 28, 2016 and, from and after this date, lived together continuously as husband and wife until January 14, 2019 when Paul was removed from the marital home by his brother, Carl R. Baker (hereinafter "Carl"). Paul is currently residing with Carl in his home located at 1816 Wading Heron Way, The Villages, Florida.

4. The nature of the Ward's alleged incapacity is cognitive impairment related to Alzheimer's Disease.

5. There is a known alternative to guardianship that would sufficiently address the problems of the alleged incapacitated person in whole or in part.

6. On September 20, 2018, Paul executed a Durable Power of Attorney prepared by Michael Hollander, Esq., Hollander Law, LLC, 225 NE 8th Avenue, Ocala, Florida 34470 naming Sandra as his attorney in fact, and naming his son, Mark E. Baker, as his successor attorney in fact, as well as a Last Will and Testament, and a Health Care Power of Attorney which names Petitioner, Sandra J. Baker, as Paul's Health Care Agent.
I. Michael Hollander confirmed that John Paul Baker had capacity to execute his estate planning documents, including but not limited to his Durable Power of Attorney, Last Will and Testament, and Health Care Power of

A Case Study Of Elder Abuse And Exploitation In Florida

1. Petition for Appointment of Plenary Guardian; In re Guardianship of John Paul Baker; Case No. 2019 HM 89 and 2019 GA 58

7. Pursuant to the terms of the September 20, 2018 Health Care Directive, a true and correct copy of which is attached hereto as Exhibit" A", Sandra is designated as Paul's Health Care Agent with the power to make decisions with regard to his health care if he is unable to make his own health care decisions. Paul's son, Mark, is named as Paul's successor Health Care Agent.

8. Although Paul was allegedly diagnosed with Alzheimer's Disease in 2015, until very recently he remained healthy, active, and outgoing.

9. An August 15, 2018 report from Florida Heart & Vascular, a copy of which is attached as Exhibit "B", does not reflect any symptoms of dementia. In fact, the report states that,
"Patient is independent in all activities of daily living, such as bathing, eating and dressing ... using the telephone, shopping, preparing meals, housework, laundry, medications and managing finances."
Page 2 of the Report states under the heading "Psychiatric: **Awake and alert. Mood and affect appropriate. Recent and remote memory intact. Able to give personal history.** " *[emphasis added*

10. While Sandra may have married Paul after his initial *diagnosis* with Alzheimer's Disease, no evidence has been

introduced that reflects the fact that Sandra had a nefarious or alternative motive or intent behind the marriage and, at the time of their marriage in June 2016, Paul was exhibiting few symptoms. Until Paul was physically removed from the marital home by Carl, the parties were affectionate, very much in love, and Sandra cared for Paul on a daily basis.

11. Sandra is the wife of Paul and is sui juris and otherwise qualified under the laws of Florida to act as plenary guardian of her husband, John Paul Baker.

12. Sandra was named as Paul's Health Care Agent (See Exhibit "A") to serve in the event that Paul is unable to make his own health care decisions and to: " ... take whatever steps are necessary or advisable to enable me to remain in my personal residence as long as it is reasonable under the circumstances. I realize that my health may deteriorate so that it becomes necessary to have round-the-clock nursing care if I am to remain in my personal residence, and I direct my Health Care Agent to obtain that care, including any equipment that might assist in my care, as is reasonable under the circumstances. Specifically, I do not want to be hospitalized or put in a convalescent or similar home as long as it is reasonable to maintain me in my personal residence." [See Section 2.03, Exhibit "0"]

13. Likewise, Section 3.02 of the Health Care Power of Attorney (**Exhibit "A"**) entitled Attorney, on September 20, 2019.

2 - Petition for Appointment of Plenary Guardian; In re Guardianship of John Paul Baker; Case No. 2019 HM 89 and 2019 GA 58

"Guardian" states: "My Health Care Agent's authority precludes the need for appointment of a Guardian. But if any proceeding is commenced for the appointment of a Guardian, **I nominate my Realty Care Agent** to serve as Guardian. " [emphasis added]

14. As the wife of John Paul Baker, Sandra is not required to comply with the registration requirements of §744.1 083 of the Florida Statutes. The relationship and previous association of the proposed guardian to the Ward is SPOUSE/WIFE.

15. Sandra, as the proposed guardian, should be appointed because she is the spouse of the Ward and is able to provide a loving, caring environment for the Ward. Sandra and Paul have been married since June 2016 and have resided together as a couple. Sandra has an appropriate home with special provisions made for Paul, and Sandra is able to provide 24 hour skilled nursing care for Paul, and Paul has more than sufficient assets to pay for the same. The proposed guardian is not a professional guardian.

16. Sandra requests that, pursuant to the Florida Statutes, as well as the terms of the attached Health Care Power of Attorney, she be appointed the Plenary Guardian of the person

and property of her husband and Ward, John Paul Baker, and allowed to exercise all delegable rights of the Ward including the immediate return of Paul to the marital home.

17. The names and addresses of the next of kin of the Ward are:

NAME	ADDRESS	RELATIONSHIP
Sandra J. Baker	3723 Mango Court The Villages, FL 32163	Spouse
Mark Baker	Saratoga Springs, NY 12866	Son
Allyne Baker	Watervliet, NY 12189	Daughter
Carl R. Baker	The Villages, FL 32163	Brother
Bruce W. Baker	The Villages, FL 32162	Brother
Lynn Meyer	Saratoga Springs, NY 12866	Sister
Carol O'Brien	Clifton Park, NY 12065	Sister

18. Reasonable search has been made for all the information required by Florida law and by the applicable Florida Probate Rules. Any such information that is not set forth in the above

cannot be ascertained without delay that would adversely affect the Ward. Petitioner, Sandra J. Baker, requests she be appointed Plenary Guardian of the person and property of her husband, John Paul Baker, and that John Paul Baker be immediately returned to the marital home to be cared for by Petitioner under any terms and conditions this Court deems just and proper.

Under penalties of perjury, I declare that I have read the foregoing and the facts alleged are true, to the best of knowledge and belief.

Signed on the 28th day of March 2019

HUNT LAW FIRM, P.A.

There were so many lies and untruths in this petition, I could not ignore it and I sent an email to my attorney making the following observations:

On the application for guardianship, Sandy responded that when Paul left her in January, she sought mental health assistance because she was so distraught. This is not true. A year earlier, Paul's doctor (Dr. Geliga) told Sandy, in my presence, that she should seek mental health assistance. Sandy asked counseling or psychiatric? He replied "both". Also, Sandy told my wife, probably a year ago (long before Paul chose to leave her), that she had gone to a doctor to get a prescription for herself to calm her down due to the stress of trying to take care of Paul and complained about how difficult it was for her.

Sandy also stated in the application that she had experience caring for Alzheimer patients since her second husband, Ralph had Lewy Body disease. I am not sure this is true. Christine Van Buren, Sandy's stepdaughter remembers it this way: " After their car accident Sandy moved my father to a nursing home. At that point I recall Sandy saying she "thought" my Dad may have Lewy Body and/or Sundown Syndrome. However, to my knowledge, there was no "official" diagnosis from a doctor and I would be willing to bet that if his medical records were subpoenaed there would be no such diagnosis. Sandy's "diagnosis" was AFTER she moved him to the nursing home. At no time while my Dad lived with her, did he exhibit any signs of Lewy Body/Sundown Syndrome, nor was she a full time care giver of him with said condition(s). My Dad was in complete control of his faculties and was able to fully care for himself the entire time they lived together."

The petition had the following false information:

Paragraph 3 - Paul wasn't "removed". He decided to leave after I gave him a week to think about it.

Paragraph 6 - The September 20, 2018 Trust and Power of

Attorney is no longer valid. Paul generally changed everything back to his 08/18/2014 Trust (when he was of sound mind) in a Restated Trust dated 01/23/19. Further, Sandy herself had Paul's trust changed a second time in December 2018. So, it is not even the most recent trust she was instrumental in creating.

Paragraph 7 - Sandy is no longer Health Care Surrogate. Mark (son), Allyne (daughter), and Bruce and Carl (brothers) are designated as of 01/23/19.

Paragraph 9 - Exhibit "B" - There is so much that is untrue in this report that I do not know where to start. Note the date (08/15/2018) is one week before Paul was isolated from his family. The functional assessment states Paul "is independent in all activities of daily living, such as bathing, eating and dressing. This is generally true, but Paul needs to be reminded to shower and his clothes are normally laid out for him.

The next line in the report states: " Patient is also independent with all instrumental activities of daily living, such as using the telephone, shopping, preparing meals, housework, laundry, medications, and managing finances." This is absolutely false and he needs assistance in all these areas and has for some time. I have helped him with his finances for years. I am not sure what the source was for this conclusion, but it would be a good question to ask. My best guess is that it was a questionnaire filled out by Sandy to justify that she left Paul alone daily, according to Paul. The report also states that Paul's hearing is screened and is negative. He has had a hearing loss since Viet Nam. And finally, the report states Paul was screened for dementia which was negative.

(Note: At Paul's next appointment with this doctor (GP), I showed him the report that Sandy included with her petition to the court. He acknowledged that this information was totally incorrect and that the questionnaire was completed by Sandy. So, Sandy includes the report with the petition as Exhibit B and "under penalties of perjury, and declares "the facts alleged are true." It appears to me that Sandy lied on the medical questionnaire in order to cover her exploitation of Paul by changing Paul's trust on September 23, 2018.)

Paragraph 10 - I have pages and pages of documentation from a number of sources to refute this. Also, Sandy told Katherine that she could tell that something was wrong with Paul the first time she met him, long before they were married.

Paragraph 12 - Not true.

Paragraph 13 - Paul states that he never knowingly did this.

Paragraph 15 - After our evidence is presented the Judge can determine if Sandy ever provided Paul with a "loving, caring environment."

A Case Study Of Elder Abuse And Exploitation In Florida

ORDER APPOINTING ATTORNEY AND ELISOR FOR ALLEGED INCAPACITATED PERSON

On February 5, 2019, the court appointed Merideth C. Nagal, Esq. as attorney for John Paul Baker and as elisor to serve on and read to the alleged incapacitated person the Notice of Petition to Determine Incapacity and all other pleadings required to be served on the incapacitated person. This was necessary so that Paul fully understands what is happening in court. But it is not without its problems. For example, I sent the following email to Merideth's office to seek guidance on how to handle filing Paul's 2018 income taxes:

From: Carl Baker
To: Joshua Rosenberg (Paralegal)
Sent: Friday, March 29, 2019 3:03:49 PM
Subject: Fwd: Taxes

Josh

Paul has all his information to file his income taxes and we are unsure how to handle this. I believe that he and Sandy paid additional quarterly payments for 2018 of $3000 each. Perhaps an extension is the best solution for now.
Looking for some guidance on this.

Thank you.

I never received a reply to this email. However, I received the following email from my attorney regarding my email to Paul's attorney concerning his taxes:

From: Harry Hackney
To: Carl Baker
SENT: Friday, March 8, 2019

Now that you're represented by counsel you really shouldn't be communicating with Merideth and her staff directly. Merideth has an ethical obligation to NOT discuss the case with you. She's under no obligation to take direction from you as she is not your lawyer. It would be better for you to communicate with me.

Comment: But Merideth does have an ethical obligation to communicate with Paul who she represents. But Paul has Alzheimer's and has difficulty comprehending conversations and his short-term memory is failing. Every time Merideth's law office needed anything from Paul, they called me. And if a question arose, I called them. Paul lives with my wife and me and I have his power of attorney. So, let me see if I have this correct. Paul has an attorney, Merideth Nagel, who had an initial meeting with Paul and me. I have an attorney, Harry Hackney, who I hired to represent me because Merideth thought it would be wise for me to apply to be Paul's guardian to prevent Sandy from being his guardian and she recommended Harry Hackney. Paul is incapacitated, but still knows what is going on and has concerns. But I cannot email those concerns to Paul's attorney because I have an attorney to represent me on my application for guardianship, so I need to give Paul's concerns to my attorney so that he can give them to Paul's attorney and since she cannot talk to me, she must give the information to my attorney and he will give it back to me and I will give Paul the information he is seeking. And normally both attorneys will bill their clients for the time it took to answer Paul's question. Could anyone in their right mind think this system is not broken? I certainly understand that in criminal cases, it is best to go through your own attorney. But in this case, Paul has difficulty comprehending any legal matter and the four of us are all on the same side. Merideth knows that Paul wants me to be his guardian and obviously agrees with him or she would not have asked that I apply for guardianship. If Merideth was appointed by the court to be Paul's attorney and both she and Paul want me to be Paul's guardian, why can't we all work together? There must be a better way when dealing with Alzheimer's victims.

I had many conversations with my attorney, Harry Hackney. I did not always agree with his response. However, since I was not familiar with probate court, I had to rely on his experience and he explained most everything completely. He is an excellent attorney, but we certainly had a different perspective than his on certain actions. Unfortunately, the court procedures are making something that was rather simplistic to something far more complex.

ORDER APPOINTING EXAMINING COMMITTEE

On February 5, 2019, on the petition of Sandra J. Baker, Circuit Court Judge Michelle T. Morley issued an order appointing an examining committee to determine Paul's alleged incapacity. The following three persons were named to the committee:

Cesar Sarmiento, M.D.

Herman Hale, R.N.

Barbara Preiss, R.N.

On February 12, 2019, Herman Hale, R.N. was the first to examine Paul. He called and made an appointment that was convenient for all of us. When he came to the house, he sat down and explained the procedure to Paul, Katherine and me and stated that after examining Paul, he would like to talk to the two of us. Mr. Hale was excellent in communicating with Paul and after the examination, he was honest with us and thanked us for the care we were giving Paul.

Herman Hale, R.N. was one of the few true professionals that we encountered during this entire experience and most certainly was the best examiner of the three.

Barbara Priess, R. N. was the second one to examine Paul. On February 18, 2019, she came to the door of our home unannounced with her brother, who drove the vehicle. When they first came, Katherine was not home, but arrived during the examination. Barbara was no longer able to drive, so her brother was with her. They are truly kind Christians who treated Paul with the upmost respect. Unfortunately, I thought Barbara may have mild dementia. She could not take his blood pressure, so I did. She seemed much more interested in telling us her stories and in the end, she told me that she forgot to fill out some of the forms, but she could take care of that later. She seemed somewhat confused during the entire examination.

Cesar F. Sarmiento, M.D. was the third and final person to examine Paul. On February 27, 2019, Dr. Sarmiento called me in the morning while Paul and I were at his doctor's appointment. Evidently, Dr. Sarmiento mistakenly went to Paul and Sandy's home on Mango Court. Obviously, Paul was not there and he evidently listened to Sandy's story and then drove to our home.

Since we were at the doctor's office, no one answered the door and when he spoke to me, he was upset that he had to drive from Leesburg a second time to examine Paul. I told him that he should have called and set up an appointment rather than just showing up unannounced at the house.

Dr. Sarmiento came back to our home that afternoon at 1:00 PM and was present for only 15 to 20 minutes. I quickly detected that he had an "attitude" and he did not speak with us, nor did he ask us any questions like the other two examiners. From reading his report, it is clear that he wrote a very bias report using Sandy's lies as facts. His report states, "Considering that the AIP (alleged incapacitated person) had been removed from his residence with his wife to the brother's home, AIP should be placed in an assisted living facility with 24-hour custodial care and supervision, till (sic) conflict is resolved." Personally, I have a problem with Dr. Sarmiento making a recommendation to remove Paul from his family and placing him in an assisted living facility based on Sandy's lies and never attempting to learn or consider what really happened. I would hope that the court does not use Dr. Sarmiento as an examiner in future cases since his objectivity is certainly questionable.

All three examiners recommended to the court that Paul be found incapacitated. Paul's family agreed with the recommendations. However, it breaks your heart to see your father or your brother, a proud, well decorated, combat military veteran, go down this road. Alzheimer's is a horrible, debilitating disease for families to endure.

As expected, the court issued the following order based on

the examination of Paul:

ORDER DETERMINING TOTAL INCAPACITY

On April 29, 2019, the court ordered that JOHN PAUL BAKER is hereby determined to be totally incapacitated and a plenary guardian should be appointed to provide for the welfare and safety of the Ward.

It was recommended by both Paul's attorney and my attorney that I fill out an application and file a petition to be Paul's guardian. The petition was filed with the court on February 27, 2019, for Carl R. Baker to act as plenary guardian for his brother, John Paul Baker.

PETITION FOR APPOINTMENT OF PLENARY GUARDIAN

IN THE CIRCUIT COURT OF THE FIFTH JUDICIAL CIRCUIT, IN AND FOR SUMTER COUNTY, FLORIDA

PROBATE DIVISION

IN RE: GUARDIANSHIP OF JOHN PAUL BAKER

File Number: 2019-MH-_____
_____/

PETITION FOR APPOINTMENT OF PLENARY GUARDIAN

Petitioner, CARL R. BAKER, alleges:

1. Petitioner's residence 1816 Wading Heron Way, The Villages, Florida and his mailing address is the same.

2. JOHN PAUL BAKER is an alleged incapacitated person whose date of birth was June 6, 1946 and who is 72 years of age. The current location of the alleged incapacitated person is The Villages, Florida, and his permanent residence address is 3723 Mango Court, The Villages, Florida. The nature of the alleged incapacitated person's alleged incapacity is: Dementia of the Alzheimer's type with loss of short-term memory and serious cognitive deficits. He requires assistance with his finances, health, and other matters.

3. JOHN PAUL BAKER is currently the subject of incapacity proceedings filed by his spouse, Sandra J. Baker. The incapacity case is captioned In re: Guardianship [sic] of John Paul Baker, case number 2019-MH-89 and is pending in the Circuit Court of the Fifth Judicial Circuit in and for Sumter County, Florida.

4. In her petition for incapacity, Sandra J. Baker, alleges that JOHN PAUL BAKER is a vulnerable adult who was diagnosed with Alzheimer's approximately three years ago after extensive testing by Doctor Pedro Geliga, a neurologist located in Leesburg. It should be noted that Sandra J. Baker married JOHN PAUL BAKER six months after his diagnosis of Alzheimer's.

5. There are no alternatives to guardianship known to petitioner that would sufficiently address the problems of the alleged incapacitated person in whole or in part, thus, it is necessary that a plenary guardian of the person and property be appointed to exercise all delegable rights of the Ward.

6. The names and addresses of the next of kin of the alleged incapacitated person are:

NAME	ADDRESS	RELATIONSHIP
Carl R. Baker	The Villages, FL 32163	Brother
Bruce W. Baker	The Villages, FL 32162	Brother
Lynn Meyer	Saratoga Springs, NY 12866	Sister
Carol O'Brien	Clifton Park, NY 12065	Sister

Mark Baker	Saratoga Springs, NY 12866	Son
Allyne Baker	Watervliet, NY 12189	Daughter
Sandra J. Baker	The Villages, FL 32163	Spouse

7. The proposed guardian CARL R. BAKER, whose residence is 1816 Wading Heron Way, the Villages, Florida 32163; whose post office address is the same, is sui juris and otherwise qualified under the laws of Florida to act as plenary guardian of the alleged incapacitated person.

8. The proposed guardian is a brother of JOHN PAUL BAKER and as such is a family guardian not required to comply with the registration requirements of §744.1083, Florida Statutes. The relationship and previous association of the proposed guardian to the Ward is BROTHER.

9. Alternatively, if the Court declines to appoint Petitioner, CARL R. BAKER, then he petitions for the Court to appoint VIVIAN QUATTLEBAUM, a professional guardian who has no previous relationship with any interested party and is otherwise qualified under the laws of Florida to act as Plenary Guardian of the person and property of the ward. As a professional guardian, VIVIAN QUATTLEBAUM has complied with the registration requirements of §744.1083.

10. Reasonable search has been made for all the information required by Florida law and by the applicable Florida Probate Rules. Any such information that is not set forth in full above cannot be ascertained without delay that would adversely affect the Ward.

WHEREFORE, Petitioner requests that CARL R. BAKER be appointed plenary guardian of the person and property of the Ward or, if the Court should determine that CARL R. BAKER is not a suitable guardian, that VIVIAN QUATTLEBAUM be appointed plenary guardian of the person and property of the Ward instead.

Under penalties of perjury, I declare that I have read the foregoing, and the facts alleged are true, to the best of my knowledge and belief.

Signed on February _____, 2019.

Carl R. Baker, Petitioner

CAMPIONE & HACKNEY, P.A.
Attorneys for Petitioner

NOTICE OF HEARING

IN THE CIRCUIT COURT OF THE FIFTH JUDICAL CIRCUIT IN AND FOR SUMTER COUNTY, FLORIDA PROBATE DIVISION IN RE: GUARDIANSHIP OF JOHN

PAUL BAKER FILE NO.: 2019-GA-158 _____
_____/ NOTICE OF HEARING YOU ARE NOTIFIED that a hearing in this action on the "Motion for Continuance of Hearing for Determination of Incapacity" has been set as follows: JUDGE: Michelle T. Morley PLACE: Sumter County Judicial Center 215 E. McCollum Street Bushnell, FL 33513
TIME: 9:30 a.m. (30 minutes) DATE: March 5, 2019.

CERTIFICATE OF SERVICE

I HEREBY CERTIFY that a true and correct copy of the foregoing has been furnished via electronic mail to: Merideth C. Nagel at merideth.nagel@mnagellaw.com and Joshua.rosenberg@mnagellaw.com; Michael C. Norvell at lakelawmcn@aol.com and cherly.kilgore@gmail.com; and Suzanne L. Przystawski at suzanne@greenlawfl.com on this 28th day of February, 2019. CAMPIONE & HACKNEY, P.A. Attorneys for Plenary Guardian /s/ Harry T. Hackney Harry T. Hackney, B.C.S. Board Certified Specialist Florida Bar No. 602442 2750 Dora Avenue Tavares, Florida 32778 Telephone: 352-343-4561 Telefacsimile: 352-343-7456 Primary E-mail: hhackney@campionehackney.com Secondary E-mail: rsteinman@campionehackney.com

ORDER APPOINTING PLENARY GUARDIAN OF PERSON AND PROPERTY

On October 4, 2019, Judge Morley stated that Amanda A. Ritter is qualified and appointed plenary guardian of the person and property of John Paul Baker. Amanda immediately hired Judge Morley's former law partner, Michael Rogers as her Attorney. This is generally referred to as a quid pro quo which is simply defined as a favor or advantage granted or expected in return for something, which in this case was Amanda being appointed Paul's guardian by the judge.

Needless to say, the entire Baker family had a problem with this order. In my mind, this is the major crux of what is wrong with the entire probate process in the State of Florida. The problem has nothing to do with Amanda Ritter. The problem is that the court routinely takes control of the Ward from his family and gives him or her to a complete stranger when the court artificially claims, "family conflict". This was not a family conflict; it was elder abuse and exploitation of Paul by his wife. Unlike many of the abused and exploited elderly, Paul was fortunate to have a loving family who watched out for him. As far as I know, Judge Morley never made the effort or took the time to actually learn the facts of the case, or if she did, she ignored them.

Section 744.331(6)(b) of the Florida Guardian Statutes states:

"When an order determines that a person is incapable of exercising delegable rights, the court must (emphasis added) consider and find whether there is an alternative to guardianship that will sufficiently address the problems of the incapacitated person. A guardian may not be appointed if the court finds there is an alternative to guardianship which will sufficiently address the problems of the incapacitated

> *person. If the court finds there is not an alternative to guardianship that sufficiently addresses the problems of the incapacitated person, a guardian must be appointed to exercise the incapacitated person's rights."*

Therefore, I filed a petition to be Paul's guardian and since Paul was now living in our home, which is exactly what I was doing, acting as Paul's guardian.

Again, our question to the court is, "What did the Baker family do that removed them from any consideration for guardianship? All we did was try to protect Paul from the elder abuse he was experiencing. We filed an elder abuse complaint, filed two police reports, filed a bar complaint, and sent documented evidence of Sandy's abuse to Ms. Nagel, Ms. Myers, and Ms. Ritter. In addition, the Judge actually heard Harry Hackney's summary of Sandy's abuse in Court. Yet, the issue was never raised again. Unfortunately, the judge chose the easy way to end this case, by claiming this was a "family conflict" rather than an abuse and exploitation of Paul by his wife, and then appointed a professional guardian rather than a willing and qualified family member. As a result, the court never held Sandy accountable for her illegal behavior, and if fact, rewarded it by allowing Sandy to take most of Paul's premarital property.

I sent the following email to my attorney on April 12, 2019:

I hope you understand that I did not hire you and file for guardianship to "throw in the towel." No professional will have the long-term understanding of who Paul is or was or have his best interests at heart more than his family who have demonstrated their love for him his entire life. All of Paul's family agrees, guardianship needs to stay in the family, and we are willing to make whatever sacrifices are necessary to make sure that Paul's remaining time is the best it can possibly be. He and I have been together for over 70 years, went into the military together and have been close friends our entire life. We fully understood Paul had dementia and were handling it quite well. I handled his finances and Bruce handled his taxes and we both assisted him in all major decisions. Even after Paul married Sandy, he continued to trust and rely on us on an almost daily basis until Sandy isolated him in order to gain control of his trust account. Before Sandy entered the picture, our family had no problems in dealing with Paul's Alzheimer's.

Since Paul came to live with us in January, we have made Paul our priority, providing 24/7 supervision. Paul has never been left alone and he loves the companionship. We love being able to encourage and support him to stay active physically and mentally. He is playing golf again and he does 5 to 6 puzzles a day on his Kindle.

Katherine and I were able to locate a caregivers training course specifically designed for caregivers of Alzheimer's patients and are currently enrolled in the seven-week program.

Further, as a family, we have developed a plan for taking care of Paul for the remainder of his life. We have visited memory care facilities (for the future when needed) in New York and Florida looking at location, activity schedules, medical care, food service and visiting hours. We also want a place where Paul could join his family and friends for activities outside the facility. We have talked to management and patients and their families in several places. We have narrowed it to two facilities and have received written two-year quotes from each facility. When the time comes, we want to let Paul visit both and see which one he is more comfortable with.

In summary, subjecting Paul to a stranger who will make decisions for him and determine his future will destroy Paul. Sandy has already destroyed the trust he had hoped for in his marriage. We all recognize that regardless of the progression of this disease, our brother still has a comfort level with his siblings and many memories that he happily shares with us. Familiarity with family, surroundings, personal items, and family activities are an integral part of his happiness and contentment during his remaining years.

There is no better care than a loving family that is willing to step up to the plate and do all that is humanly possible for Paul. It's called agape - unconditional love!

My attorney's response follows:

"I hope you understand that I did not hire you and file for guardianship to "throw in the towel." (He quoted this sentence from my email to him.)

[Harry Hackney:]
"Perhaps not. However, I thought you hired me and filed for guardianship seeking what is best for your brother. I've been doing this since 1998 and the most common outcome in a case like this is a professional guardian. [Emphasis added.] We discussed pleading for

a professional in the alternative for that reason and that's what I did with your agreement. Nothing has changed. In fact, the Examining Committee consistently recommended that outcome due to the "family conflict." That is consistent with what I've been advising from the beginning. That ought to demonstrate to you that I'm familiar with how this usually goes where there is "family conflict." I'm using quotes because I'm sure you don't consider his Johnny-come-lately" wife to be "family." I'm very sympathetic to that position. I see far too many people in these situations causing no end of problems by "marrying" late in life."

(Note: I added the emphasis above to support my opinion, that I was never even considered for guardian. My attorney has had many cases before Judge Morley and obvious he believed that she would appoint a professional guardian, and he was correct. However, the judge never spoke to me, ignored all the evidence of Sandy's abuse and exploitation and ignored the wording in Section 744 of the statute.)

I hired my attorney on the advice of Merideth Nagel, Paul's court appointed attorney. She told me that my applying for guardian would give the court an alternative to appointing Paul's wife, Sandy, as guardian. That was an easy decision for all of us. Sandy becoming Paul's guardian would be a worst-case scenario and as a loving family, we could not allow that to happen. So, after paying an attorney $ 17,500 in fees, I now realize that the court never actually considered letting Paul stay with his family. And if the court states they did consider my petition for guardianship, we deserve to know why the court felt it necessary to make Paul a ward of the state and remove him from a loving family. It appears that the court has a "boiler plate solution" for "family conflict" which triggers the appointment of a professional guardian. It is the easy way out of a situation that the court does not want to deal with. However, this was not a family conflict. It was an outright abuse and exploitation criminal case and everyone involved was well aware of it.

Again, I must raise the question. How can any logical person review this entire case and believe that Florida's probate court is not broken?

There are many events that occurred in this case, which were ignored or disregarded by the court in determining guardianship.

If you look at the petitions, orders and the judicial emails on this case, you will find numerous references stating that Paul "was taken from his house by his brother." As this is an out-and-out lie, one must ask if this is a biased statement by the court which appears to take Sandy's alleged kidnapping as fact? Or was it just an extremely poor choice of words that most certainly had a detrimental effect on our case for guardianship? The truth is that Paul was isolated from his family by Sandy. She gave him her smart phone which she controlled and he could not use unless she was present. She blocked our numbers, so Paul could not call his brothers and she texted us on Paul's phone pretending to be him. Interestingly, isolation from family members is the number one tactic used in elder abuse according to the experts. After my second visit with Paul in January of 2019, Paul told Katherine and me that he was always left alone by Sandy and he wanted to leave her. He later asked if he could live with us and we agreed. Sandy then called the Sheriff's Office and claimed we took Paul against his will. The Deputy interviewed Paul and us and closed the case as unfounded.

Further, during the first hearing on April 29, 2019, my attorney's opening statement included a short, but detailed synopsis of Sandy's abuse and exploitation of Paul. Therefore, it is without a doubt that Judge Morley knew there was another side to the story. Unfortunately, the hearing ended before any witnesses testified because Paul's attorney, Merideth Nagel, made a motion to have the case resolved through mediation using the Eldercaring Coordination Program. Despite the Judge, Paul's attorney, Merideth Nagel, and the Eldercare Coordinator, Cher Myers, all being fully aware of the documented abuse and exploitation of Paul by Sandy, I never heard another word about it from anyone except my attorney.

The total contention seemed to be that because Paul and Sandy were married, she could do anything she wanted including committing crimes, and for whatever reason, she was above the law. If Paul had all his senses, he never would have allowed his situation to continue and he finally did end it. He was easy prey and that did not seem to be a factor. Instead of the court taking action against Sandy for abuse and exploitation, it appears the court considered the marital status to be sacrosanct above all else, despite the wording in the statute that specifically states a spouse can be charged.

In the end, not one government entity held Sandy accountable for any of her actions and, quite candidly, they do not appear to really care.

> "For where you have envy and selfish ambition, there you find disorder and every evil practice."
> — James 3:16

CHAPTER 11

Eldercaring Coordination

The insertion of an Eldercaring Coordinator into the court system changed the entire process dramatically. While I had hoped that the mediation would result in some sort of understanding that would allow both sides to move on, it did not. There was no meaningful mediation and Eldercaring Coordination turned out to be a horrible decision for Paul and the Baker family and a huge waste of money.

At the first court hearing on April 29, 2019, opening statements were given by Sandy's attorney and my attorney,

Harry Hackney, who gave an outstanding summary of Sandy's abuse and exploitation. So, Judge Morley knew there was another side to the story.

The first witness, Sandra Baker, was called to the stand and sworn in. Before the first question was asked, Merideth Nagel, Paul's attorney asked the Judge if she could approach the bench and all the attorneys went with her. Next the attorneys and Sandy and I went to the Judge's chamber for a discussion. Merideth had asked the judge to move this case to mediation (Eldercaring Coordination), which would immediately end today's court proceedings. My attorney told me that this was Judge Morley's pilot project and after a short discussion, the attorneys agreed with Merideth. Quite honestly, I was disappointed that we were not able to present our case, but my attorney stated that if the mediation did not work out, we could return for a court hearing. Court was then adjourned by the Judge and the case was sent for mediation by the Eldercaring Coordinator, Cher Myers.

On May 29th, Paul and I drove to Cher Myers residence and had an hour and half meeting with her where she reviewed the process with us and we signed the agreement. We outlined our goals for mediation and told Cher that Paul would like a divorce or legal separation, the return of his premarital property and that the house be sold and the proceeds split in half.

I told Cher I would pay both my and Paul's part of the cost. I asked her for the amount so I could write the checks and she handed me a piece of paper with all the costs broken down. I paid our part and we left with some optimism that this process may very well work for us.

When I got home, I noticed that the paper Cher gave me with her handwritten amounts of our costs for her services, was actually a memo from Judge Morley to Cher, and it appeared to be the original copy. I sent an email to Cher and told her that I mailed the memo back to her. However, I did read it and thought immediately that I may have made a huge mistake by agreeing to Eldercaring Coordination. The memo in part follows:

"This wife (Sandy) has not seen her husband since January. Brother (Carl) took husband out of the house. They each want to be appointed as Ward's guardian. I found total incapacity today but in the midst of the negative opening statements I convinced them to go to Eldercaring Coordination so I was unable to determine who should be appointed guardian. I hope the family can get in to see an (Eldercaring Coordinator) quickly so some form of visitation between husband and wife and an agreement on who will serve as guardian can be discussed. ... The brother is a retired Chief of Police. Ward is a retired Brigadier General. The wife (married in 2016 a few months after his Alzheimer's diagnosis) retired from GM (General Motors) but no indication what position she held."

After reading this, my mind went in several different directions and what follows are the thoughts and questions that were raised in my mind:

The first sentence appears to me that the Judge has already decided that Sandy is the victim in this case and the second statement reinforces that thought. ***I did not take Paul out of the house.*** As explained earlier, I went to Paul's house and was able to speak with him for the first time in several months. I asked him to think about what he wanted to do and told him I would be back in a week or so. I returned in a week and Paul told me he wanted to leave Sandy.

"I found total incapacity today but in the midst of the negative opening statements I convinced them to go to eldercaring coordination..." The convincing must have been before court. Merideth Nagel was appointed by the Judge as Paul's lawyer and temporary guardian. And it was Merideth who stood and asked to approach the bench after opening statements. Perhaps Sandy's attorneys needed convincing. If so, the Judge must have done that during the short time they were at the bench. My thought was this was all planned before court. Judge Morley, in seeking someone to serve as Elder Coordinator wrote. "...so, I was unable to determine who should be appointed guardian."

How could the Judge determine who should be guardian when she never heard any testimony? My attorney's opening statement briefly summarized Sandy's unethical and immoral behavior, her abuse of Paul, and the exploitation of his non-marital trust assets. Why would the judge immediately state this was negative? The facts of the case were certainly negative for Sandy. What really troubled me here was the Judge chose not to hear any testimony of the case. Did she not want to make a decision? Or did she already decide that Sandy was the victim here and not Paul? From what took place in this case, this was not as far-fetched as it first seems.

And finally, it appears the Judge was in a rush "for some form of visitation between husband and wife....", even though she had heard about Sandy's abuse and exploitation of Paul. The general rule in abuse cases is that you never put the parties back together without counseling and supervision. In fact, Paul's attorney Merideth, had already received pages of documented evidence of abuse and exploitation and had suggested that I should file a criminal complaint with law enforcement, which I did.

Following is the information that I initially received from Cher Myers, the Eldercaring Coordinator assigned by the court to assist in Paul's case:

The Association for Conflict Resolution and Florida Chapter of the Association of Family and Conciliation courts worked together to develop eldercaring coordination in guardianship/probate cases that involve high conflict family dynamics that affect the wellbeing and safety of an older adult, limit filling court orders, hamper court process, or detract from the benefits of guardianship and other appointments by the court.

Over the past several years, twenty United States and Canadian as well as 20 state-wide organizations have worked together to address the needs of elders and their families living in tension. The purpose of the project is to reduce the level of conflict and find solutions to problems that elders and their families are facing.

ELDERCARING COORDINATOR AGREEMENT

John Paul Baker Guardianship, Carl R. Baker, Sandra Baker (the "Parties") agree to purchase Eldercaring Coordinator services from Cher Myers and to follow the following provisions:

1. Eldercaring Coordinator. The Eldercaring Coordinator is an impartial third person whose role is to assist the parties in resolving disputes with high conflict levels in a manner that respects the elder's need for autonomy and safety.

2. Role of the Eldercaring Coordinator. Cher Myers, L.C.S.W. will serve as an Eldercaring Coordinator to the Parties. The Parties understand that Cher Myers will assist them with issues involving John Paul Baker as set forth in the order appointing him/her.

Cher Myers will facilitate the ability of the elder and other eldercaring coordination participants to work collaboratively in a way that respects the safety and autonomy of the elder. The Eldercaring Coordinator shall, for those purposes, initiate referrals for services and investigations if necessary and make recommendations to the parties as he/she deems appropriate.

Cher Myers will not provide therapeutic or evaluative services to the Parties, nor will she offer the Parties legal advice.

3. Duration of Appointment. Cher Myers' appointment does not begin until the signed agreement and required deposit is returned by all Parties and Cher Myers signs the agreement. Cher Myers' appointment will end either two (2)

years from the date of the signed agreement, or in the time frame set forth in the appointing order, whichever is earlier. Cher Myers may also end his/her appointment at his/her sole discretion if any Party is not fully complying with this agreement, or by court order.

4. Scope of Authority. The Eldercaring Coordinator shall be authorized to make limited decisions as set forth in the Order appointing him/her.
With expressed written consent of the elder and parties designated in this court order, the Eldercaring Coordinator may have additional temporary decision-making authority to resolve specific, non-substantive disputes between the parties until such time as a court order is entered modifying the decision; or make recommendations to the court concerning modifications to orders related to the resolution of disputes regarding the care of the elder.

5. Limitation of Authority. The Eldercaring Coordinator shall not have decision making authority to resolve substantive disputes between the parties. A dispute is substantive if it would:
- *Change the determination of capacity or incapacity of the elder;*
- *Change the nature and scope of the existing authority of a legally authorized decision-maker;*
- *Change the residence of the elder; or*
- *Delegate any rights of the elder to another person.*

The Eldercaring Coordinator will not make a substantive recommendation to the Court unless the Court, on its own motion or joint motion of the parties, determines that:

- There is an emergency affecting the safety of the elder;
- The recommendation would be in the best interest of the elder;
- The parties agree that any ElderCaring coordination communications that may be raised to support or challenge the recommendation of the Eldercaring Coordinator will be permitted.

6. Conduct in the Eldercaring Coordinator Process. The Eldercaring Coordination process will be conducted in the manner that Cher Myers believes will best and most quickly permit full understanding, discussion, and resolution of the issues. Cher Myers may meet with the Parties together or separately, in person, by telephone or through electronic means, such as e-mail. She may also request meetings with significant others or other family members on issues related to the Elder.

7. Confidentiality. All information provided to or obtained by Cher Myers is confidential unless otherwise provided in the order appointing him/her. However, the Eldercaring Coordinator has a duty to report any suspected abuse, neglect or exploitation required or permitted by applicable law.

(Note: Cher was notified in writing of Sandy's abuse and exploitation of Paul. I do not know if she reported it to the court or any other agency.)

No meeting may be audibly or visually recorded in any way without written permission of everyone present.

8. Authorizations for Release of Information. The Parties agree that they will sign whatever authorizations for release of information Cher Myers decided is necessary for his/her to fulfill his/her duties.

9. Cancellation Policy. If a Party is unable to keep an appointment, the Party must notify our office two (2) business days in advance. If advance notice is not received, that Party will be responsible for paying for the missed appointment.

10. Payment for Eldercaring Coordinator's Time. The Parties shall pay for all time spent by Cher Myers, at the rate of $250.00 per hour. Time is billed at a minimum of .25-hour increments (15 Minutes). The bill each Party receives will reflect the full hourly rate; however, the amount billed to each party will reflect the percentage of the fee allocated to them as set forth in the order appointing him/her: 30% paid by John Paul Baker Guardianship($75.00), 35% paid by Carl R. Baker ($87.50) and 35% paid by Sandra Baker ($87.50). This fee will be charged for any and all time Cher Myers spends working on this matter, including meetings with the Parties, telephone calls pertaining to the matter, reviewing

and responding to e-mails, reviewing letters and other records and written material, preparation of written reports, round trip travel time and any other time expended in direct association with the duties of the Eldercaring Coordinator. Payments for each face-to-face meeting will be made at the end of each meeting. If Cher Myers decides to hold separate meetings with the Parties, or if there is an order which requires that separate meetings be held, then the party attending the meeting will pay for the entire meeting at that time.

Payment for non-session time and for costs incurred shall be made as follows:

(a)   The Parties shall make a deposit of $3,000.00, with each party paying their percentage share of the deposit according to the allocation schedule in the order appointing him/her, with this signed agreement. 30% by John Paul Baker Guardianship ($900.00), 35% by Carl R. Baker ($1,050.00) and 35% by Sandra Baker ($1,050.00). No appointments will be set, or services provided until this agreement is signed and the deposit received.

(b)   Each party must pay their share of the deposit and return the signed Eldercaring Coordinator Agreement to Cher Myers within ten (10) business days of entry of the Order appointing him/her. Failure to pay the deposit or return the agreement shall result in Cher Myers declining service in this matter.

(c) The Parties shall make an additional deposit when the previous deposit has fallen below a $500.00 balance (per party) or will fall below a $500.00 balance by the non-session work needed before the next face-to-face meeting. This deposit shall be an amount equal to the previous deposit, or a lesser amount if Cher Myers reasonably expects that the remaining non-session fees will be less than the amount of the previous deposit. If the Parties fail to make the deposits as required above and/or any outstanding fees are not paid in full, services will be suspended on the file, and Cher Myers may choose to withdraw.

(d) Cher Myers may assess more than the proportion of the fees and costs allocated to a party if she determines that a party has abused the process or if Cher Myers involvement was unnecessary. If Cher Myers determines that no party has abused the process or if his/her involvement was necessary, then Cher Myers shall divide the costs and fees between the Parties as set forth in the order appointing him/her.

(e) The Parties shall pay any fees and costs not covered by the above deposits within twenty (20) days after billing for same.

(f) Any unused portion of the deposits required above will be refunded to the parties when Cher Myers is assured that the service is no longer needed. In order to be sure that the refund is correctly computed, it will not be paid until completion of the monthly billing statements for the month in which Eldercaring Coordinator services were terminated.

11. Non-Payment.

(a) Absent other agreement, Cher Myers reserves the right to suspend all services, including provision of any written documentation, until payment of any unpaid balance.

(b) In the event one party does not pay his or her share of the retainer, any other party/parties may pay the full retainer requested and bring a motion for contempt of court and/or seeking reimbursement for the non-complying party's share of the retainer.

12. Payment for Administrative Costs. There will be a one-time administrative fee of $100 charged which is divided among the parties. This administrative charge shall be paid with this signed agreement.

13. Complaints Procedure. If a party or participant wants to make a complaint about the Eldercaring Coordinator, s/he shall take the following steps:
(a) submit a written complaint to the Eldercaring Coordinator regarding the Eldercaring Coordinator's conduct.
(b) Review the written complaint with the Eldercaring Coordinator.

(c) If the party is not satisfied with the resolution of the complaint, s/he may file a motion with the court to seek a termination of the Eldercaring Coordinator's services.

(d) The Court may remove the Eldercaring Coordinator from the case and may appoint a substitute Coordinator.

(e) Upon a finding of good cause, the Court may also refer the complaint to the appropriate licensure board or certification organization.

My signature below indicates that I have received, read and understand the information in this agreement, and that I agree to retain Cher Myers, L.C.S.W. as Eldercaring Coordinator under the conditions described in this agreement.

{Signed by all participants.}
Cher Myers – Eldercaring Coordinator

I received the following emails from the Eldercare office manager:

Sent: Tuesday, April 30, 2019 3:53 PM
Subject: 2019 GA 158, John Paul Baker

Good Afternoon Ladies and Gentlemen,

Cher Myers has asked that I please send this to each of you as her acceptance to the Eldercaring Coordinator position for the John Paul Baker case.

As soon as I speak with Sandra Baker and Carl Baker and receive their email addresses, I will also send this to them unless their counsel can provide me with that information.

If you should have any questions or concerns please do not hesitate to call me or by email to the address highlighted below and I will be happy to help in any way possible.

Sincerely,
Sadles Office Manager

From: Eldercare Office Manager
To: "crbaker
Sent: Monday, May 13, 2019 12:43:54 PM
Subject: FW: Baker Eldercaring Case 2019 GA 158

Good Afternoon Mr. Baker,

There are several attachments in this email which will include the Eldercaring Agreement Form that will need to be signed by you as well as the intake survey (Elder intake Survey Form for Mr. John Paul Baker and a Participant Intake Survey form for Carl Baker) forms that I have to send to everyone to fill out (Judge and Counsel included!). The Eldercaring process is still considered a pilot program and with the information provided by the participants it is then used to make the process better. There are some questions that might be perceived to be of personal or intrusive in nature, we do not expect anyone to put their personal information into a survey if they are not comfortable with it and I apologize beforehand. These surveys are not generated by us but if you will fill it out to what you are comfortable in writing, I would appreciate it. I will then send it to the Pilot Administrator office for their use. Please be advised that no names are ever associated with the information that you provide as they are coded by numbers only describing what state, district, number of Eldercaring cases, etc... If you would also have your brother, Mr. John Paul Baker fill out what he can or with your help his intake form that would be greatly appreciated.

I have also attached the Response by Eldercaring Coordinator (Cher Myers) accepting this case which I sent to Judge Morley yesterday afternoon. There is the last attachment that is a note from Mrs. Myers explaining what her goals are toward this process and some information about the Eldercaring process.

I would like for you to please call our office at your earliest convenience so that I can set up an appointment time to meet with Cher and at that time you can either bring all of these forms with you or you can send them back to me via email. Our phone number is xxx-xxx-xxxx and if I am away from the phone, please leave a message and I will call you back. I will be out of the office tomorrow, Tuesday, May 14, 2019 but will return on Wednesday. I would like to apologize for the delay in you receiving this email but have been trying to send it to you since May 1, 2019 but the email provided to our office was typed incorrectly. If you could send me a quick email stating that you did receive this email along with the attachments, I would appreciate it very much.

From: officemanager
To: "crbaker

Sent: Wednesday, May 15, 2019 2:42:49 PM
Subject: Appointment with Cher Myers
Mr. Baker,

I did speak with Cher and she advised that Paul is more than welcome to attend the meeting on May 29, 2019 at 3:30 if he is able to.

If you have any questions or concerns, please let me know and I will be happy to help in any way I can.

Thank You,

From: "crbaker
To: "Cher Myers
Sent: Wednesday, May 29, 2019 6:44:21 PM
Subject: Emails with Documentation

Cher
Please acknowledge this email so I can make sure you get all the documents.

You will start seeing emails with attachments. When it is complete, I will send you the list of all the files.

Cher - I mistakenly picked up the paper with the fees listed. I already mailed it back to you.

Thank you,
Carl Baker
From: "crbaker501
To: "Cher Myers"

A Case Study Of Elder Abuse And Exploitation In Florida

Sent: Wednesday, May 29, 2019 10:31:32 PM
Subject: Eldercare Documents Provided

Cher

This is a list of the documents that you will be receiving. I still need to send the original trust dated 08/18/14.

Please call if you have any questions or need any additional information. I have a lot more documentation on almost every aspect of this saga if you need to see it.

Thank you for everything.
Carl Baker

The following documents were provided to Cher Myers so that she would have a background on the case and an understanding of Sandy's abuse of Paul:

The John Paul Baker Trust - 08/18/14
Signed copy of Antenuptial Agreement
Abuse Report - 10/8/18
Letter to Paul on Trust Account with Final Accounting – 09/06/18
Copy of Teller Cashed Check for $220,000 - 09/21/18
Timeline on Quest for Money w/ Emails from Mark & Allyne
John Paul Baker Trust Timeline
Text Messages to and from Paul's Phone
Email from Allyne outlining calls with her dad 8/20 – 8/23/18

Email from Allyne 12/27/18
Trust Certification w/ Changes 9/20/18
Trust Certification w/ Changes 12/03/18
Memo documenting my 01/07/19 meeting w/ Paul

From: "crbaker
To: "Cher Myers"
Sent: Monday, June 3, 2019 9:03:53 AM
Subject: Fwd: Guardianship of John Paul Baker - Email 1 of 2

Cher
I discussed this with my attorney, and both of us agree that you should have a copy.

(Note: Letter from Sandy's attorney filled with nothing but lies.)

Thank you.
Carl Baker

From: "Harry Hackney"
To: "crbaker501"
Cc: "rsteinman"
Sent: Wednesday, May 29, 2019 4:36:39 PM
Subject: FW: Guardianship of John Paul Baker

Please see the attached from Cara Singeltary. I haven't replied yet and see no rush to do so. Generally, my reply would be that you have a privilege to report suspected elder abuse and the report of a suspected crime to law enforcement isn't actionable. As for everything else, you didn't claim they were divorced. You didn't see any need for Paul to be paying insurance when he couldn't drive and Sandy refused to get her own insurance. Let me know if you have any other suggestions or comments.

Following is a copy of the letter from Sandy's attorney and my response to my attorney:

Hunt Law Firm, P. A.

May 16, 2019
VIA ELECTRONIC MAIL ONLY

Hhackl1ey@campionehacklley.com

RE: Guardianship of John Paul Baker

Dear Harry,

I wanted to bring to your attention a series of recent activities undertaken by your client, Carl Baker, which I believe are intended to intimidate and harass my client, Sandy Baker, wife of John Paul Baker above-referenced.

The most recent event occurred yesterday, May 15, 2019, when our client was contacted by Detective Cohen with the Sumter County Sheriff's Office. Apparently, Carl initiated an investigation against Sandy for unknown allegations related to Paul's trust which Det.

Cohen would not disclose. In addition to yesterday's false allegations against Sandy, Carl has done the following:

1. Contacted the Sumter County Sheriff's Office on or about October 15, 2018 because "Carl believes Sandy is trying to take all of Paul's money since she married him two years ago". Please see a copy of the attached report.

2. Contacted the Sumter County Sheriff's Office on January 17, 2019 (after Carl had removed Paul from the family home) because "brother is going thru divorce and he needed advice on how to do the S54". Please see a copy of the attached report.

3. Contacted USAA on March 7, 2019 and removed Sandy from the auto insurance policy, listing her instead as an "ex-wife". Please see the attached confirmation from USAA of a "change in your household" dated March 7, 2019.

4. Contacted Tammy Dunseath, a broker associate/realtor with Re/Max, on March 12, 2019 and provided Tammy with Sandy's email address. Apparently, Carl advised Tammy, either by email or verbally, that Sandy was interested in selling the marital home on Mango Court. Please see the attached email dated March 12, 2019 from Tammy Dunseath to Sandy, as well as the March 13, 2019 email to Sandy wherein Tammy advises that "I have your request for your home value and the report is nearly completed based on public records ... ". At no time did Sandy contact Re/Max regarding the sale of the Mango Court home, or any other realtor or broker.

Obviously, the above statements regarding an ex-spouse

and divorce are completely fabricated as Paul has not filed for a divorce, nor could any divorce be initiated at this time due to the guardianship proceedings. *Fla. Stat. Am.* §744.32] 5 and the decision of *Vaughan v. Guardianship of Vaughan*, 648 So.2d 193 (Fla. DCA 1994).

Over and above the foregoing, Carl has cancelled Paul and Sandy's joint bank account and, in all likelihood, has changed all of Paul's estate planning documents to remove Sandy's name as trustee, personal representative and/or beneficiary.

These types of vigilante actions against our client need to stop. Carl closed the parties' joint bank account to which Paul and Sandy contributed equally for the payment of the household expenses, and then refused to contribute on Paul's behalf to any of the monthly expenses despite the fact that he is a co-owner of the home, leaving Sandy to bear the sole cost of maintaining the marital home. Despite the fact that Sandy has not seen Paul in over 4 months, and it is our understanding and belief that Carl has had exclusive and uninterrupted access to Paul and all of his financial and estate planning documents, Carl is now accusing Sandy of tampering with Paul's trust to which she has had no access.

If Carl does not immediately cease and desist from attempting to intimidate, manipulate, and harass Sandy by filing false allegations and interfering with her accounts, we will have no choice but to bring this situation to the attention of the Court. Should you wish to discuss this matter, or anything contained in this letter, please do not hesitate to contact me at your earliest opportunity.

Sincerely,
signed/ Cara Singeltary

I sent the following reply to my attorney on May 30, 2019:

Harry

I will reply by paragraph. It does not surprise me that Sandy would make these allegations. But then again, she is a sociopath who believes she can do no wrong. What did somewhat surprise me is the letter from her attorney. What did she think this would resolve? I guess she just expected me to go away. Trust me, that is not going to happen. If anyone wants to see false allegations and lies, they should look at Sandy's court petitions and the hate speech Sandy has generated and fueled on her Facebook page.

Number 1

The fact that $220,000 was taken from Paul's trust account on 9/21/18, the day after she changed Paul's trust, more than justifies notifying the police. But the true concern that day was the location of Paul's three pistols, which Sandy claimed she has no idea where they are. FYI, Cher Myers (Eldercare) has put this on the top of her list.

If the guns are not located shortly, I will report them missing so they can be entered in the federal and local stolen weapons database.

Number 2

Sandy sent a Deputy Sheriff to our home that week to see if Paul was being held against his will. The Deputy found that Paul chose to be here, he listed Sandy's complaint as unfounded. On the way out the door, he suggested that when we go to pick up Paul's clothes and items, that we call and ask a Deputy to meet us there (Mango Court).

I called on Thursday and they were busy and asked if we could do it early Friday. I called early Friday morning and the Deputy met us at Mango court. Sandy refused to let me on the property, refused to let Paul enter HIS home, and walked out with several articles of clothing and gave them to Paul. To this day, in spite of requests, Paul has never received any more clothes or personal items. Cher Myers has this on her list as well.

Number 3

On May 1, 2018, Sandy and Paul brought their 2016 Buick Enclave in for service. They left with a newly leased 2018 Buick Enclave, the same color (white) as the 2016. Sandy probably thought we would not realize that she exploited Paul by convincing him to spend $28,784 on a new car they did not need. The real problem with this is that Paul got lost several weeks before this and Sandy would not let him drive anymore and turned in his license. So, in reality she got herself a new car. There is no way that Paul should pay for the lease or insurance on this car that he cannot drive or even be transported in now that he chooses to no longer live with Sandy.

Number 4

I do not know Tammy Dunseath, nor have I even heard her name before. I did not call her, email her, or contact her in any way. This is nothing but another lie.

General Comments

I have never said that Paul is divorced from his wife. Paul did meet with a divorce attorney last January but was told he could not proceed until after the competency hearing. I have, however, told people on occasion that Paul is separated.

I have never attempted to intimidate, manipulate, or harass Sandy by filing false allegations. I have however filed criminal charges against Sandy based on facts, her actions, and out of our concern for Paul's physical and financial well-being. The criminal case is proceeding and still pending.

Perhaps we should bring all of this to the attention of the court.

Thank you.

My attorney and I agreed that we would just ignore this letter and not reply since none of it was true. As far as I know, Attorney Singeltary never again raised any of this with my attorney.
Note: On December 27, the Hunt Law Firm filed a Motion to Withdraw as Counsels for Sandra J. Baker. To date, I do not know the reason for the motion.

I received the following email from Cher's office manager acknowledging that they received all the documentation I sent outlining Sandy's abuse and exploitation of Paul:

From: officemanager
To: "crbaker

Sent: Tuesday, June 11, 2019 4:26:35 PM
Subject: RE: Emails with Documentation

Mr. Baker,

We are good to go as I did receive everything. On a personal note, I applaud you for your detail record keeping. I get excited when I can locate the light bill at my house!!! Just kidding on that part but am impressed.

Talk to you soon.
Pati

From: "crbaker>
To: "Cher Myers
Cc:Officemanager
Sent: Wednesday, June 19, 2019 7:01:43 AM
Subject: Thank you

Cher

When I went out to get the paper this morning, I found three bags in the driveway containing Paul's underwear, socks, pajamas and t-shirts.

Thank you!
Carl and Paul

From: "Cher Myers"
To: "crbaker" >
Sent: Wednesday, June 19, 2019 11:34:51 AM
Subject: Re: Thank you

You are welcome when Sandy left my office yesterday our plan was for me to go over to her house Monday and to get those things and bring them over to you but I guess she took care of it anyway.

From: "crbaker"
To: "Cher Myers"
Sent: Wednesday, June 19, 2019 12:23:52 PM
Subject: Re: Thank you

Thanks again. Will Paul's pants, shirts, jackets, shoes, etc and toiletries be coming also?

From: crbaker
To: Cher
Sent: Thursday, June 20, 2019 9:51:29 AM
Subject: Email from Sandy

Cher
I am taking the high road and will ignore this:

From: "Sandy"
To: "crbaker501"
Sent: Wednesday, June 19, 2019 12:46:40 PM
Subject: My Beloved Paul

LOVE IS THE ANSWER, Paul's and my Anniversary is next week.

You have destroyed him to a mind of a three year old who doesn't remember me or our lives together, but you will never vengefully destroy the remarkable, incredible love and memories we shared etched in my heart. It was the best time of my life and I am blessed and thankful for that. Still praying for the Baker family. I know Paul will see the truth when we are souls together in heaven.

Since Sandy only gave Paul his underwear, socks and pajamas, are you still planning to go to Paul and Sandy's home on Mango Court on Monday. I want to make sure I am available if and when the clothes are delivered.

Thank you again for everything.

Carl

From: "Cher Myers"
To: "crbaker"
Sent: Sunday, June 23, 2019 8:55:19 PM
Subject: Re: Email from Sandy

Thank you Carl for forwarding this email to me. Yes, I am still planning on going over tomorrow. It would be easiest if I could go straight to your home after I meet her at 2 PM I will be in touch tomorrow.

Cher Myers

6/24 - Cher changed the date for Paul's clothes delivery to July 3rd due to an emergency on her ranch. It would have been sooner, but Sandy told her she would be out of town until then.???

7/03 – Pati and her husband picked up some of Paul's clothes, shoes, caps and toiletries from Sandy and brought them over to our house. Cher did not meet with Sandy.

(Note: Pati told me she asked Sandy about getting Paul's three pistols and Sandy immediately burst into tears and went to another room. Since Sandy would not assist them, Pati and her husband went ahead and took what they thought Paul needed and left.)

From: "crbaker
To: "Cher Myers
Sent: Monday, July 15, 2019 10:05:43 AM
Subject: Status

Cher

I was hoping to speak to you last week, but realize you had another commitment. I enjoyed meeting Pati and her husband - nice people.

Paul and I appreciate their help and with what they brought over; we will be fine for now. However, I am concerned about the three pistols in light of Sandy's reaction when Pati asked about them.

I would like a telephone update on the case if that is appropriate. The only time I am tied up is today until 2:00 PM. On Tuesday and Friday morning, Paul and I are playing golf from 7:30 AM to 11:00 AM, weather permitting.

Thank you,
Carl Baker

A Case Study Of Elder Abuse And Exploitation In Florida

From: "Cher Myers
To: "crbaker Thursday, July 18, 2019 4:43:20 PM
Subject: Re: Status

Hi Carl, I am at a training in Atlanta and will not return until Sunday. I would be happy to meet via phone next week. PATI has my schedule so if you would please call the office on Monday, we can arrange a convenient time.
Cher Myers

On July 24, 2019, Katherine and I had a conference call with Cher Myers. The following items were discussed:

We thanked her for her efforts to get some of Paul's personal items but shared with her that we needed to get a date and time where we could go to Paul's house and remove all items that belong to him. She said that Sandy is too emotional for that now and she wants to have a meeting with Paul. We stated that was totally up to Paul to make that decision. Cher suggested that we wait until the August 8th court hearing.

We told her our goal was still an annulment for Paul and to ensure that they both retain their own assets. She told us that she thinks Sandy wants to sell the Mango Court home. We agreed.

Bruce, Gail, Allyne, Katherine and I have all been working to find a suitable memory care facility for Paul for the past six weeks. We have three facilities that we found that would meet Paul's needs—The Willows, Brookdale and Mission Oaks. Cher commented that she had looked at Brookdale for her mother and was very impressed by what she saw. We told her that we need to move forward and she agreed and said she would help.

We talked about getting Paul's pistols. She told us that after the court hearing on August 8th, she would talk to Sandy about them and get back to us.

We also discussed the fact that Cher has only met with us once and she still has not spoken to Paul's daughter Allyne. She told us that she would schedule both and let her know the dates of Allyne's next visit with her dad. Allyne called Cher and spoke with her directly.

On September 3, 2019, Paul moved to his room in the memory care unit of Trinity Springs. He was in great spirit and actually looking forward to the move.

From: "Carl Baker
To: "Cher Myers"
Cc: "Bruce Baker" "amanda a ritter"
Sent: Monday, September 9, 2019 11:38:14 AM
Subject: Paul's Pistols

Cher

Have you followed up with Sandy on locating Paul's three pistols? As a reminder, the pistols are:

.32 Auto Military Semi-automatic - This was my father's weapon that is going to be passed down to Paul's son.

.38 Spec S&W six-shot revolver with a 4" barrel

9mm Glock - Model G19 - Serial NLP120

It is important that these weapons be found and returned or reported as stolen or missing.

Thank you.
Carl

On September 20, 2019, at 9:28, I called Cher Myers since I had not received any response from Cher on the above email on Paul's three handguns. I left a voice mail message to return my call. Cher returned my call at 10:09 AM on September 26. She stated that she just received my voice mail. I told her that I also sent her an email on September 9th. She stated that she was having a problem with her internet also. Additionally, Cher stated that she is a caretaker for a relative which is taking more of her time.

I then explained that the Eldercaring Program is not working. I am contacting her on every issue, yet Sandy is going through her attorney, who contacts my attorney, who contacts me. A good example of this is the sale of the Mango Court house. So, what is actually taking place is we are paying for the Eldercaring coordinator who is accomplishing very little because Sandy is not participating and I am still paying attorney fees for events that should have been handled by the Coordinator. I did tell Cher that the system is broken resulting in increased frustration. For whatever reason, Cher wanted to again wait on approaching Sandy about the three pistols.

On September 28, Allyne was in town with Rick visiting her dad. According to Allyne, Cher was supposed to meet her at Trinity Springs and from there go to Paul's house on Mango Court and pick up some of Paul's personal items. Cher did not show up.

On October 9, I received a call from Pati Kersey from Saddles. She asked if Paul's appointment with Dr. Win (VA Clinic) was still on for tomorrow. I told her it was and I planned on picking Paul up at about 8:00 AM. Pati told me that both Meredith Nagel and Cher Myers were planning on meeting us at the VA Clinic at 8:45 AM.

The next day, Bruce and I picked up Paul from Trinity Springs and brought him to the VA Clinic for his 9:00 AM appointment with Dr. Win. Merideth Nagel and Cher Myers arrived shortly before 9:00 AM. Cher and Merideth meet privately with Dr. Win first for a short time. My understanding is that Dr. Win declined to get involved in Paul's court case because if he did, he would be unable to continue as Paul's psychiatrist. He did recommend that Paul have an examination by another neutral psychiatrist who could testify at future court hearings.

Note: This visit was initiated by a directive from the court to establish visitation by Sandy. Further, Amanda Ritter, Paul's guardian, had already arranged an evaluation by another psychiatrist and it was completed several weeks ago.

Dr. Win then asked Paul, Bruce, and I to come to his office for his scheduled visit. Cher Meyers was also present. After leaving Dr. Win's office, we had a short discussion with Cher. She did not know that Paul had already had his examination with another psychiatrist, so I told her that she needed to talk to Amanda. Cher then told us that she and Amanda were going to meet with Sandy on Monday the 14th. We reminded her that there were several items that are pending and needed to be resolved: the procedure for the sale of the home, return of Paul's three pistols, Paul's social security statement so we could file his taxes by October 15th, and a time when we could pick up all of Paul's personal property to include our father's flag from his burial and other memorabilia.

Note: Amanda already has a list.

From: Carl Baker
To: Cher Myers, Amanda Ritter
Re: Meeting with Sandy
Date: October 14, 2019
Cher
How did you make out with your meeting with Sandy today? Did you retrieve any of Paul's personal items? We do need Paul's SS statement. His taxes are due this week.
Carl

From: "Carl Baker
To: "amanda a ritter"
Sent: Thursday, October 17, 2019 7:35:56 AM
Subject: Eldercaring Program

Amanda
Can you give me a call sometime this morning? The only time I am not available is between 10:30 and 11:15 AM.
As you probably know, Cher Myers told us that she would be talking to Sandy on Monday about a number of important items - guns, sale of home, Paul's personal property, income taxes and more.

As far as I know, she did not follow up on this. I have everything documented.

    I would like to talk to you before I take my next step.

Thank you.
Carl

From: "amanda a ritter"
To: "Carl Baker"
Cc: "Cher Myers"
Sent: Thursday, October 17, 2019 7:50:37 AM
Subject: Re: Eldercaring Program

Carl,
    I will do my best to call during that small window but I also have a day full of appts. (Note: Evidently Amanda read my email wrong. The "small window" is when I was NOT available.) Cher and I met with Sandy yesterday at her house and we have a plan to retrieve Paul's things as soon as I have my guardianship papers. I have spoken with Cher and her office multiple times since last week and now that I'm finally almost official we just need time to act on some of these things we have been tasked with and also some items the Judge is inquiring on.
    Sandy says she does not have Paul's Social Security statement. The current guardian would have been able to go to social security and get a copy but since that was not done, as soon as I have my guardianship papers I will be going to social security to reroute the benefits and can get a copy then. I'm hoping to have my certified Letters of Guardianship by early next week pending Judge Morley. I

have copied Cher on this correspondence for transparency and so that she can also respond.

Thank you,
Amanda Ritter
Professional Guardian and VA Fiduciary

From: "Carl Baker"
To: "Katherine Baker" Bruce Baker "astylin13"Mark Baker"
Sent: Thursday, October 17, 2019 8:57:47 AM
Subject: Fwd: Eldercaring Program

Looks like we are back on track, but the system is broken!

Allyne - Did Amanda or Cher let you know about this?

From: "Carl Baker"
To: "amanda a ritter"
Cc: "Cher Myers"
Sent: Thursday, October 17, 2019 8:54:54 AM
Subject: Re: Eldercaring Program

We had no idea what was going on, so thanks for letting us know. No longer any need to call. Communication is the key and we need to keep each other up to date. Did Sandy say anything about the pistols?

Brenda from Trinity will be sending you a form to have their doctor start seeing Paul replacing Dr. Gegaj. It will make it a lot easier with prescriptions. Paul will still see his primary care doctor at the VA

and his specialists.
   Thank you,
   Carl

   From : Office Manager
   Subject : Information on Paul's guns.
   To : CARL BAKER
   Cc : amanda a ritter
   Tue, Oct 22, 2019 11:25 AM

Dear Carl,
   Cher asked that I please send you this email to let you know that she has found out by Sandy that Paul's guns have been located and found in the safe. Unfortunately, she has placed a lot of his personal effects and such on top of the floor safe located in his study/office. She has reassured Cher that as soon as these items can be picked up and/or moved she will gladly call Cher to come back over to the house and retrieve the guns. Cher and her husband Mike, who is a retired LEO (Law Enforcement Officer), both carry concealed weapons permits and Mike will be with Cher at that time. Once they are in Cher's possession, she will give you a call and then transport them over to your residence. I will call you prior to the day that they actually make the trip over just to make sure that you will be home.
   Hope all of you are doing well and I will speak with you soon.
   Take care and thank you as always,
   Sadles Office Manager

   From: Carl Baker
   Subject: Re: Information on Paul's guns.
   To: officemanager
   Bcc: Katherine Baker

A Case Study Of Elder Abuse And Exploitation In Florida

Bruce Baker
Mark Baker
Allyne

Tue, Oct 22, 2019 03:00 PM

Pati
Thank you very much. If they can, they should also take the safe. Paul had this safe years before he was married. I can help if they need me.
Carl

    I have not to date had an accounting of the $3000 that I paid for Eldercare Coordination, but November 27, 2019, I received the following email and bill. Quite candidly, I was surprised and had many questions.

Dear Carl,
    I have attached a statement of your account to this email for you. As of this date, November 27, 2019, there is an outstanding balance of $831.27 on the account. Cher is anticipating that in addition to the balance that another $500.00 should be enough to cover the future costs in this case. Of course, if more time is needed after that, then I will let you know the amount that MIGHT be needed. If there should be any amount left over in your account, we will send you a check for that amount.
    If you have any questions or concerns please do not hesitate to call me or by email and I will be happy to help in any way that I can.
    Happy Thanksgiving to you and your family.

Sincerely,
Pati
From: "Carl Baker"
To: "Pati Kersey"
Sent: Monday, December 30, 2019 3:37:01 PM
Subject: Statement from S.A.D.L.E.S

Pati

Hope you and your family have a happy New Year.

I apologize for taking a while to respond. I spent some time in the last few days to review and analyze the statement and I do have some questions.

Understand that I am only commenting on the activity outlined in the statement - May 14 to November 20, 2019.

The total that we started with was $3000.00. The total expenditures from your statement are $1,881.27, leaving a balance of $1,118.73. You have listed the amount due as $831.27. This leaves a total expenditure of $1,950.00 that is not included in the statement. I do understand that there may be other expenses, so I would like an accounting for the additional $1,950.00.

The majority of the Cher's time to date was spent with Sandy which, quite candidly, did nothing to help either Paul or me. I was told that by agreeing to the Elder Coordinating program, we would all save attorney expenses and our differences would be worked out through mediation by the Coordinator. From that point forward, I started using Cher rather than my attorney as evidenced by the documentation and the emails that I sent to you and Cher. Sandy, on the other hand, continued to use her attorney and I found myself paying for both an attorney and a Coordinator.

I did an analysis as to how the money was spent. I broke down the statement that you sent me by which one of the three of us - Paul,

Carl or Sandy - benefited by Cher's time. Cher spent by far more time with Sandy than she did with Paul and me. The breakdown from the statement total of $1,881.27 shows $984.38 for meetings with Sandy, $678.13 for court and matters pertaining to Paul and $218.76 for the initial meeting that Paul and I had with Cher on May 29th and two telephone conversations with Katherine and me on July 24th and September 26th.

To be fair and to help me take an objective look at the Eldercaring program, I am also requesting that Cher send me a list of what she sees as the Eldercaring Coordinator accomplishments to date.

Thank you and please feel free to call me should you have any questions or need any additional information.

On Friday, January 10th, 2020, Allyne (Paul's daughter and trustee) had a conversation with Cher Myers and sent me the following email:

> From :Allyne
> Subject :Spoke to Cher
> To :CARL BAKER
> Sat, Jan 11, 2020 09:53 PM

Spoke with Cher Meyers on Friday, January 10, 2020. I was asking AGAIN for her to facilitate getting my dad's belongings. I was abrupt with her as I had tried to contact her several times over this past year and never got any responses. I'm guessing I finally received a phone call because I left a "not so nice" voicemail. While on this phone call I asked her to explain exactly what her role is. She gives extremely evasive, nondescript responses when faced with this question. Especially when I ask "what exactly have you done for this situation with my father?"

I explained our discontent with the fact that Sandy has been allowed to hold my father's belongings hostage for an entire year. And that the only clothes she allowed him to have was some underwear, socks and pajamas that was left in three garbage bags at the end of my uncle's driveway. 'Frankly, I find it shocking that a court appointed mediator is paid to make absolutely no progress in returning a man's meaningful personal property to his own possession. It's been A YEAR!!!!!! And furthermore, I feel my father has been victimized by this system by being forced to be around his abuser that he finally had escaped from.

During my hour-long phone conversation with Cher, she told me that during Sandy's first visit, my dad was telling Sandy about this awful woman who was in his life who had done all of these terrible things to him. Clearly, he didn't know he was speaking to Sandy. His Alzheimer's prevented him from identifying her by sight, but he clearly has a feeling and remembers what he experienced at the hands of this evil woman.

In essence, Cher had the nerve to witness such an encounter and yet her evaluation and report to the court was that the visit "went well". How could anyone in a position like this report such lies to the court. What exactly went well!????? You were able to please the abuser by allowing her in. You were reporting what you thought the judge wanted to hear??? My father was victimized, yet again.

Sandy has repeatedly displayed behavior that should provoke the court and any officer of the court to protect a man in my father's condition from a woman who has nothing but ill intentions. Instead, his condition/ disability was used against him and he has been forced to be unknowingly in the presence of his abuser. This entire situation is an obscene failure by this court system.

What troubles me the most about the conversation is that this is the first time we heard that Paul told the story of how he was abused by Sandy to a woman he did not know was Sandy. Neither Cher nor Amanda ever mentioned that to anyone in our family and as far as I can tell, never put it in her report and never told the court. Nor did they acknowledge that Paul did not know that it was Sandy he was speaking to.

From: "Pati Kersey"
To: "Carl Baker"
Sent: Thursday, January 30, 2020 1:44:14 PM
Subject: STATEMENT FROM SADLES

Dear Carl,
Thank you for responding back to me through email concerning the statement that I had printed out in last month.
The statement that the system prints out can be very confusing to say the least but unfortunately there isn't any way to re-format it. I will try to explain to the best of my ability what you are reading.
You are correct that at the beginning of Cher becoming the Eldercare Coordinator, there was a $3000 retainer placed. This was divided among Paul, Sandy and yourself per the court order that states that you and Sandy will each pay 35% and Paul 30% of the retainer as well as Cher's normal charge of $250 per hour. So as far as the retainer goes, you and Sandy both paid $1050 and Paul paid $900. Each time that Cher worked on the case (phone calls to parties involved in the case, visits to the ranch and/or your homes or to Paul's, etc.) her fee was again divided between all of you per the court order. This fee would be in increments of 15 (.25) minutes each time. So, at the beginning you had a surplus of $1050. Each time that Cher worked

on the case I took off your percentage (35% or $87.50 per hour) from this surplus. I did the same thing for Paul's and Sandy's account on that same day using the same "formula". The "surplus" balance more or less ran out on October 10, 2019 and that is when it then became a deficit balance for each of you.

The court order *did not* state that time expended by Cher in speaking to Sandy would be charged only to Sandy. It *did* state that the Court allocates payment of Cher's fees and costs for ElderCaring Coordination as the 35% for you and Sandy ($87.50 per hour again in 15 minutes increments) and 30% ($75.00 per hour also in 15 minutes increments) for Paul.

Note: The above statement by Pati is not true. Item 10 in the Eldercaring Agreement states the following: "If Cher Meyers decides to hold separate meetings with the Parties, or if there is an order which requires that separate meetings be held, the party attending the meeting will pay for the entire meeting at that time." Why should the Baker family pay 65% of the cost for a covert meeting with Sandy, which by design, we had no idea was taking place?

Since there has been recent activity on the case since December, I have printed out another statement for you that is current as of January 30, 2020 and attached it to this email. I have done the same for Paul and Sandy also.

Please call me if you should have any questions concerning this and my explanation of how the fees came to be.

Sincerely,
Pati

After reviewing Pati's email and the up-to-date Statement

and after much thought on the entire Eldercaring process, I sent the following return email to Cher as this complaint is directed at Cher, not Pati. Pati has always been helpful and easy to work with.

> From: "Carl Baker"
> Sent: Tuesday, February 4, 2020 4:00:46 PM
> Subject: Complaint
>
> Cher
>   Effective immediately, I am terminating my Eldercaring Coordinator services agreement with you.
>   Additionally, I am submitting the following complaint regarding the process and your conduct.

Note that in my December 30, 2020, email to Pati, I made the following request:

"To be fair and to help me take an objective look at the Eldercaring program, I am also requesting that Cher send me a list of what she sees as the Eldercaring Coordinator accomplishments to date."

I never received that list.

When I originally signed this agreement, I was told that Eldercare Coordinating was a program that would allow mediation to assist in conflict resolution and save the parties a substantial amount of money in attorney fees. I had high hopes that we could come to a suitable compromise and put this entire episode behind us. That did not happen and although I used you exclusively, Sandy continued to use her attorney and my attorney bills continued as well.

The first conflict that had to be resolved was to have Sandy permit Paul to take possession of his clothes, personal items and his belongings which we discussed at our initial meeting on May 29th, 2019. Although Paul had some of his clothes returned in July, he did not receive most of his belongings until January 17th, 2020, one year from his initial request to Sandy. (Note: There are still items that were never received.) All of this is well documented. This delay cost Paul several hundred dollars because he had to have some clothes for everyday living and many personal items which he owned had to be purchased again because Sandy would not release them to Paul. So why did we have to pay thousands of dollars to you for Paul to get what was rightfully his when a court order could have resolved this in one day?

Secondly, on October 25th, 2019, Amanda and you brought Sandy into Paul's room at Trinity Springs without notifying Paul or anyone in his family. Both of you knew that Paul had told his attorney, Merideth Nagel, numerous times that he did not want to see Sandy and he wanted her out of his life. It has been stated that you and Amanda made a conscious decision to do this without any coordination with Paul or his family. There was no "mediation" involved, only "coaching" of Sandy as documented by you. From the billing statement, it appears to me that the plan for this visit began the 10th of October. Although Paul and I were not included in any of this, we have each been billed for approximately $765 for something that did not include us nor did we want. Clearly, this was not done for Paul's benefit. You consciously and deliberately ignored Sandy's abuse of Paul and just marched Sandy into his room unannounced without consulting with Paul and his family. In fact, we later learned that Paul did not know who Sandy was and proceeded to tell this woman (Sandy) how his wife abused him. Yet, you said the meeting went extremely well, and, in fact it could not have gone better. I think you both took unfair advantage of Paul's mental state and it is my position that both of you violated the guidelines for professional guardians as outlined in the Florida statutes.

Section 10 [d] of the agreement states, "Cher Myers may assess more than the proportion of the fees and costs allocated to a party if she determines that a party has abused the process...". The entire cost of this "secret visit" should come from Sandy since she is the only one you included in the process and the only one who would benefit.

Your prompt response would be appreciated.

As of February 19th, I had not received any communication regarding my complaint. To make sure that she does receive it, I mailed a certified copy to her with the following note:

Cher:
Since I have not received a reply or acknowledgement from you on my February 4th email, I am sending another copy to you certified mail just In case you did not receive it.
Thank you.
{signed}
Carl R. Baker

After receiving the certified mail, Pati sent me the following response:

From: "Pati Kersey"
To: "crbaker"

Sent: Wednesday,
February 26, 2020 12:44:38 PM
Subject: ElderCaring Case for Paul Baker
Dear Carl,

We received the certified letter yesterday (Tuesday, 2/25/20) and I wanted to let you know that we are auditing your account at this time. Cher does agree with you concerning the first visit to Trinity Springs that you were not aware of and I will delete your portion of the charges and bill to Sandy the majority of the charges. I will then send you a corrected copy of the statement for payment.

At this time, we will notify the court and discharge this case.

I just wanted to touch base with you concerning all of this and Cher did advise me that she will be getting back in touch with you.

Sincerely,
Pati

I thanked Pati for her reply.
Three weeks later, Pati sent me the following email:

From: "Pati Kersey"
To: "crbaker"
Sent: Thursday, March 19, 2020 3:34:35 PM
Subject: Statement of Account for S.A.D.L.E.S. Ranch

Dear Carl,
I have attached the latest statement of your account for

payment. Cher did remove the fee for the first visit to Trinity Springs from this account.

Please remit as soon as possible. We do take cash, check or credit card for your convenience.

If you should have any questions or concerns, please contact me and I will be happy to help in any way possible.

Sincerely,
Pati Kersey

Carl R. Baker

S.A.D.L.E.S., Inc.
41025 Thomas Boat Landing Road
Umatilla, FL 32784
352-669-1012

Statement

Date
1/17/2020

To:
BAKER, CARL EC CASE
1816 Wading Heron Way
The Villages, Fl

Amount Due	Amount Enc.
$1,793.77	

Date	Transaction	Amount	Balance
05/14/2019	Balance forward		0.00
05/15/2019	Initial meeting with Mrs. Sandra Baker on 5/15/19 from 12:45 till 2:15 --- Eldercaring Coordination. 1.5 @ $87.50 = 131.25	131.25	131.25
05/29/2019	Initial meeting with Mr. Carl Baker (brother of elder, Paul Baker) on 5/29/19 from 3 till 4:30 --- Eldercaring Coordination. 1.5 @ $87.50 = 131.25	131.25	262.50
05/29/2019	PMT ##1473. PAID $1050.00 WITH CHECK # 1473 FOR 35% OF RETAINER FEE	-1,050.00	-787.50
06/12/2019	Phone Conference with Meredith Nagel (attorney rep Paul Baker) on 6/12/19 form 1:05 to 1:35 --- Eldercaring Coordination. 0.5 @ $87.50 = 43.75	43.75	-743.75
06/18/2019	Office visit with Sandy Baker and Meredith Nagel on 6/18/19 from 3:30 to 5:15 --- Eldercaring Coordination. 1.5 @ $87.50 = 131.25	131.25	-612.50
07/24/2019	Phone Conference with Carl Baker on 7/24/19 from 12:43 till 1:26 --- Eldercaring Coordination. 0.75 @ $87.50 = 65.63	65.63	-546.87
07/25/2019	Phone conversation with Sandy Baker, her attorney Cara Singletary and Cher from 11 to 12 --- Eldercaring Coordination. 1 @ $87.50 = 87.50	87.50	-459.37
08/07/2019	Case review for court on 8/8/19 --- Eldercaring Coordination. 0.5 @ $87.50 = 43.75	43.75	-415.62
08/08/2019	Court case before Judge Morley in Sumter County from 2 to 3 on 8/8/19 --- Eldercaring Coordination. 1 @ $87.50 = 87.50	87.50	-328.12
09/26/2019	Phone call with Carl and Allyne --- Eldercaring Coordination. 0.25 @ $87.50 = 21.88	21.88	-306.24

CURRENT	1-30 DAYS PAST DUE	31-60 DAYS PAST DUE	61-90 DAYS PAST DUE	OVER 90 DAYS PAST DUE	Amount Due
350.00	1,443.77	0.00	0.00	0.00	$1,793.77

A Case Study Of Elder Abuse And Exploitation In Florida

Statement

S.A.D.L.E.S., Inc.
41025 Thomas Boat Landing Road
Umatilla, FL 32784
352-669-1012

Date: 1/17/2020

To:
BAKER, CARL EC CASE
1816 Wading Heron Way
The Villages, Fl

Amount Due	Amount Enc.
$1,793.77	

Date	Transaction	Amount	Balance
10/09/2019	ELDERCARE CASE REVIEW --- Eldercaring Coordination, 1 @ $87.50 = 87.50	87.50	-218.74
10/09/2019	PHONE CONFERENCE WITH AMANDA RITTER(NEWLY APPOINTED GUARDIAN FOR PAUL BAKER --- Eldercaring Coordination, 0.5 @ $87.50 = 43.75	43.75	-174.99
10/10/2019	MEET WITH PAUL BAKER'S VA PSYCHOLOGIST W/ MEREDITH NAGEL P.A. FROM 8:15 TO 10:15 (TRAVEL TIME INCLUDED) --- Eldercaring Coordination, 2 @ $87.50 = 175.00	175.00	0.01
10/10/2019	PHONE CONFERENCE WITH CARA SINGLETARY (SANDY BAKER'S ATTORNEY) --- Eldercaring Coordination, 0.5 @ $87.50 = 43.75	43.75	43.76
10/16/2019	HOME VISIT TO SANDY BAKER'S FROM 11:30 TO 2:00 (TRAVEL TIME INCLUDED) --- Eldercaring Coordination, 2.5 @ $87.50 = 218.75	218.75	262.51
10/24/2019	PHONE CONFERENCE WITH AMANDA RITTER FROM 12:50 TO 1:20 ON 10/24/19 FOR CASE REVIEW --- Eldercaring Coordination, 0.5 @ $87.50 = 43.75	43.75	306.26
10/25/2019	PHONE CONFERENCE WITH AMANDA RITTER FROM 3:30 TO 4:00 --- Eldercaring Coordination, 0.5 @ $87.50 = 43.75	43.75	350.01
11/01/2019	SUMTER COUNTY COURTHOUSE BEFORE JUDGE MORLEY, ATTORNEYS FOR PARTIES AND AMANDA RITTER FROM 12:00 TO 2:15 (TRAVEL TIME INCLUDED) --- Eldercaring Coordination, 2.25 @ $87.50 = 196.88	196.88	546.89

CURRENT	1-30 DAYS PAST DUE	31-60 DAYS PAST DUE	61-90 DAYS PAST DUE	OVER 90 DAYS PAST DUE	Amount Due
350.00	1,443.77	0.00	0.00	0.00	$1,793.77

Page 2

Carl R. Baker

S.A.D.L.E.S., Inc.
41025 Thomas Boat Landing Road
Umatilla, FL 32784
352-669-1012

Statement

Date
1/17/2020

To:
BAKER, CARL EC CASE
1816 Wading Heron Way
The Villages, Fl

Amount Due	Amount Enc.
$1,793.77	

Date	Transaction	Amount	Balance
11/20/2019	PHONE CONFERENCE WITH AMANDA RITTER FROM 11:30 TO 12 ON 11/20/19 RE TO CASE REVIEW --- Eldercaring Coordination, 0.5 @ $87.50 = 43.75	43.75	590.64
12/06/2019	HOME VISIT WITH CARL BAKER RE TO ELDER PAUL BAKER FROM 1:15 TO 5:00 ON 12/6/19 (TRAVEL TIME INCLUDED) --- Eldercaring Coordination, 4.25 @ $87.50 = 371.88	371.88	962.52
12/09/2019	PHONE CONFERENCE WITH CARL BAKER AND SANDY BAKER --- Eldercaring Coordination, 0.5 @ $87.50 = 43.75	43.75	1,006.27
12/11/2019	VISIT TO TRINITY SPRINGS. VISIT BETWEEN ELDER PAUL BAKER, WIFE SANDY BAKER, BROTHER CARL BAKER AND AMANDA RITTER IN ATTENDENCE.FROM 12:30 TO 5:00 (TRAVEL TIME INCLUDED) --- Eldercaring Coordination, 4.5 @ $87.50 = 393.75	393.75	1,400.02
01/14/2020	PHONE CALL WITH CARL BAKER. PHONE CALL WITH AMANDA RITTER. ALL IN RE TO PAUL BAKER'S PERSONAL BELONGINGS AT FORMER RESIDENCE. --- Eldercaring Coordination, 0.5 @ $87.50 = 43.75	43.75	1,443.77
01/17/2020	HOME VISIT TO SANDY BAKER'S ALONG WITH AMANDA RITTER TO GATHER ELDER PAUL BAKER'S PERSONAL POSSESSIONS --- Eldercaring Coordination, 4 @ $87.50 = 350.00	350.00	1,793.77

CURRENT	1-30 DAYS PAST DUE	31-60 DAYS PAST DUE	61-90 DAYS PAST DUE	OVER 90 DAYS PAST DUE	Amount Due
350.00	1,443.77	0.00	0.00	0.00	$1,793.77

Cher did not send me the list of Eldercaring accomplishments that I requested. I did not think she would, because there aren't any. However, Cher did remove the $393.75 she charged me for the secret visit that she and Amanda orchestrated, but still charged me for all the coaching they gave Sandy and other meetings they had in preparation for the surprise visit on Paul. This was not acceptable.

That afternoon, I sent the following response:

From: "crbaker"
To: "Pati Kersey" Sent: Thursday, March 19, 2020 4:21:58 PM
Subject: Re: Statement of Account for S.A.D.L.E.S. Ranch

Thanks Pati. I did ask Cher to send me a list of what she considers as the Eldercaring Coordinator accomplishments to date. I never received it. If you have anything similar already completed, like progress reports to the judge, that will work. In the meantime, I will look at the bill and get back to you if I have any other questions.

Six days later, I get another email from Pati:

From: "Pati Kersey
To: "crbaker"
Sent: Wednesday, March 25, 2020 4:08:36 PM
Subject: List of accomplishments requests

Dear Carl,

Cher asked that I please let you know that due to the confidentiality of an Eldercaring case she will not be able to provide you with progress reports to the judge, notes that were taken from involved parties, etc. She has petitioned the court today for a Status Conference with Judge Morley concerning this case and requesting to be discharged as the Eldercaring Coordinator which only the Judge can order. You will also be receiving a copy of the request shortly along with everyone involved in the case.

If there is anything else that I can do for you, please let me know.

I did receive a second email, minutes later:

From: "Pati Kersey"
To: "crbaker", "Sandy", "meredith nagel", "joshua rosenberg", "Harry Hackney", "Todd Mazenko", "amanda a ritter", "Allyne C. Baker", "Mark Baker"
Sent: Wednesday, March 25, 2020 4:18:18 PM
Subject: Request for Status Conference on John Paul Baker, 2019 GA 158

Good Afternoon Ladies and Gentlemen,

Attached you will find a request for a Status Conference with Judge Michelle Morley from Cher concerning the Eldercaring case of John Paul Baker, 2019 GA 158.

At this time, Cher is requesting to be discharged from the case as the Eldercare Coordinator and to let the court know that she has not been paid by the parties for her services except for the detainer (sic) that was received in May, 2019.

(Note: I sent an email to Cher on February 4th which she never responded to. So, I sent a certified letter to her on February 19th, and Pati responded to me on February 26th, over three weeks from my original email, telling me Cher would get back to me. As stated, I received that response another three weeks later, on March 19th and replied to her the same day. And now six days later, she sends me a notice that she is requesting a court hearing because she has not been paid. You have got to be kidding me. And they all keep telling me the system isn't broken!)

I sent the following email the next day in response to Cher claiming the progress reports to the judge are confidential.

From: "crbaker"
To: "Pati Kersey" Sent: Thursday, March 26, 2020 2:26:02 PM
Subject: Re: List of accomplishments requests

Pati
That is not a problem. After I did not get a response to my initial request of December 30th, 2019 for a list of what Cher saw as accomplishments, I suggested the progress reports only if it would prevent you from writing another document and perhaps make it easier for you. I am simply asking for a summary of Eldercaring accomplishments. I certainly should be entitled to that and was waiting to see if that answered some questions I had on the bill. Just like any other bill I receive; I need to fully understand it before I pay it and this bill totals $5,487.52 for the Baker family. Secondly, when I compared your statement with my records, I found an error. I am not refusing to pay the bill; I just want to fully understand it. I asked Allyne not to pay Paul's portion, since her statement has the error as well. If for some reason, Cher decides to not send me the Eldercaring accomplishments, please let me know the reason and we will move forward.

I received the following email from Pati Kersey on March 31st:

Subject: Account statement

Dear Carl,

Cher is currently working on your request for what she feels were accomplishments in this case and just as soon as I receive it, I will forward it to you.

I understand your statement concerning wanting to fully understand the bill before paying it. You mentioned an error that you found both on your statement and the one that I sent to Allyne and Mark for Paul's portion while comparing this statement against your records. Can you please advise me what it was? I hate making mistakes especially on someone's bill and if I did make one than I am terribly sorry for it and please know it was not with malice by any means.

I just saw where you responded to Ms. Thompson reference to the remote hearing. I also sent an email to her advising that Cher said that it could wait until the courts re-open which was in mid-April as of last week. If something should change, then I will make sure you are aware as I am sure Ms. Thompson will too.

Hope to hear from you soon. Also, during this time we are experiencing please stay safe and stay well.

Sincerely,
Pati

On April 6th, I sent the following email to Cher regarding the two statements (bills) that both Allyne and I received:

From: "crbaker"
To: "Cher Myers"
Cc: "amanda a ritter"
Sent: Monday, April 6, 2020 10:22:02 AM
Subject: Statement Payment

Cher

You have sent statements for your services to both Paul (Allyne) and me that total $5,487.52, which is a substantial amount of money. This email includes comments on both our bills.

On three different occasions starting on December 30, 2019, I sent you correspondence requesting that you send me a list of what you see as the Eldercaring accomplishments to help us take an objective look at the program and link them with the activities in the statement. This was not an unreasonable request. To date, you have not outlined any of your accomplishments to me. I find that very troubling. In fact, on a number of occasions, my correspondence and/or telephone calls to you went unanswered for days or sometimes weeks (e.g., September 2019).

As I go through our correspondence and my notes and compare it to the statements, there are a number of events that I have no idea what took place or why the meeting did not include anyone from the Baker family. To be perfectly candid, the vast majority of our conversations centered on retrieving Paul's personal property which was rightfully his and could have been easily accomplished with a court order at no cost to us, instead of thousands of dollars. Sandy was unreasonable about returning Paul's property from the beginning and all his property has still not been returned.

A second way to a view the statement is by your time spent with each party. An analysis shows that you spent much more time with Sandy than you spent with Allyne and me combined. Sandy abused and exploited Paul and despite all the documented evidence I sent you, you and others have chosen to ignore that fact. Sandy continued to be abusive throughout the Eldercaring Program and she continues her abuse today. There was little or no real mediation. Sandy laid down the rules, and you did nothing to mediate any compromise. For example, you allowed Sandy to determine what property was to be returned to Paul. Paul was never allowed to enter his own home which he had every right to do. Sandy would not even allow anyone from Paul's family or his friends to move his property from the home at no cost. So, you and Amanda picked up the property and you charged us $650 for four (4) hours to move Paul's items to my garage. And I still have no idea what Amanda will charge Paul's trust for this move. Needless to say, your hourly rates of $250 are much higher than a mover would charge, and certainly more than the free services offered by his family and friends. Again, there was no mediation and Sandy's demands were never questioned.

But most disturbing was your secretly coaching Sandy for the preparation of the surprise visit to Paul. As we expressed at the time, you never consulted with Paul or anyone from his family and you took unfair advantage of Paul's dementia when you knew that he stated time and time again, that he wanted nothing to do with Sandy. In so doing, it is apparent to me that you violated the model standards of conduct for mediators of the Association of Conflict Resolution, the rules for certified and court appointed mediators and the guidelines for professional guardians all of which are outlined in the Florida statutes. By disregarding these rules, I believe that you also abused Paul. Paul summarized it by saying, "I hate being tricked like this!"

Paul still has a right to privacy which was violated. In our opinion, this entire secret meeting episode was just another exploitation of Paul, only this time it was by his guardian and Eldercaring coordinator.

Note the below guidelines for informed consent [as outlined in the Florida statutes]:

(6)(a) "Decisions that Professional Guardians make on behalf of their Wards under guardianship shall be based on the principle of Informed Consent."

(d)(4) "Maximize the participation of Wards in understanding the facts and directing a decision, to the extent possible."

(d)(5) "Determine whether a Ward has previously stated preferences in regard to a decision of this nature."

When Paul's attorney, Merideth Nagel, asked Paul if he wanted to see Sandy, each and every time Paul responded that he did not want to see her, have anything to do with her and he wanted her out of his life. Paul's request at our initial meeting was for an annulment or divorce from Sandy and that is still his request today.

(7)(d)(1) "Professional Guardians should ask their Wards what they want."

Rule 10.060 (Self Determination):

"A mediator must not substitute the judgment of the mediator for the judgment of the parties, coerce or compel a party to make a decision, knowingly allow a participant to make a decision based on misrepresented facts or circumstances, or in any other way impair or interfere with the parties' right of self-determination."

"A line is crossed and ethical standards are violated when any conduct of the mediator serves to compromise the parties' basic right to agree or not to agree."

Standard 1. Self-Determination:

"A mediator shall conduct a mediation based on the principle of party self-determination. Self-determination is the act of coming to a voluntary, uncoerced decision in which each party makes free and informed choices as to process and outcome."

"A mediator shall not undermine party self-determination by any party for reasons such as higher settlement rates, egos, increased fees, or outside pressures from court personnel, program administrators, provider organizations, the media or others."

Furthermore, you told Allyne and later admitted to us that during Sandy's secret visit, Paul was telling Sandy about this awful woman who was in his life and had done all these terrible things to him. Obviously, he did not know he was speaking to that very woman—Sandy. His Alzheimer's prevented him from identifying her by sight, but he remembered the abuse by Sandy. You also stated that you were surprised that Paul remembered these events so clearly. What troubles us about the conversation is that this was the first time we heard that Paul told the story of how he was abused by Sandy to a woman he did not know was Sandy. Neither you nor Amanda ever mentioned that to anyone in our family and as far as I can tell, never put it in your report and never told the court about the conversation before or at the hearing. Nor did you acknowledge that Paul did not know that it was Sandy he was speaking to. In fact, Amanda wrote in her initial email regarding the surprise meeting that you both orchestrated, "there was absolutely not one moment of negativity." That was not true.

In light of all of this, we refuse to pay any of the charges relating to the secret meeting and visit by Sandy since it was never a part of the mediation, we were never notified about it, and it was not in compliance with the procedural rules that you are required to follow.

Additionally, the statement charges us for a conference call with me and Sandy on December 9th. I have no recollection of that call and am quite sure I would have remembered a call with Sandy. But to be sure, I checked and found nothing in my notes or phone records. The first time I saw or spoke to Sandy during this entire process was two days later at Trinity Springs. I have not included the charge for this call in the payments.

I will send you a check for $1,400.02 and Allyne will send you a check for $1,237.50, which brings the amount paid by Paul and me to over $4,500.00. And for the record, we (the Baker family) have tried to list the benefits of the Eldercaring program and that is why I asked for your input. We were not able to identify any.

I look forward to the conference with Judge Morley, so please let me know the time and date and I will definitely be there.

Carl Baker

I also forwarded the same email to Paul's Attorney, Merideth Nagel with the following note:

Merideth

I am sending you a copy of my response to Cher regarding her statement (bill) since I do refer to you regarding your conversations with Paul about speaking to or seeing Sandy.

If you still represent Paul as his attorney, it would be advantageous for both of us to have a conversation. There is a lot going on that you may not know.

Several months ago, I appealed the finding of the Florida Department of Families and Children (Elder Abuse) on Sandy's abuse of Paul. Several weeks ago, I confirmed that the Exploitation and Inadequate Supervision charges have been verified and have been referred to the Sumter County Sheriff's Office and the State Attorney's Office for follow up.

I will again be talking to Brad King [State Attorney] about prosecution and I would appreciate any advice you can give me.

Thank you.

Carl Baker

The first response to my April 6th email to Cher was an email to Allyne and Mark from Amanda Ritter, Paul's guardian on April 9th:

"Good morning. I wanted you to see the email Carl sent to Cher and copied me. I take a few of these lines as threats to myself and my position so I forwarded the email to my attorney also. I just wanted you both to be aware in an abundance of transparency.

I just wanted you to know that my email was more in a response to the threats against myself as guardian. I stand by every action that I have done so far. I'm very concerned that if the trust doesn't separate themselves from Carl's actions it's going to cost your dad a lot of money. And I also wanted you both to be in it completely in the loop with all communication." (sic)

Thank you,
Amanda Ritter

To start, I was expecting a reply from Amanda. However, I do have several comments to place it in the proper perspective. I never threatened Amanda or anyone else in my email. I was simply stating the facts and my concerns. Amanda's "abundance of transparency" was certainly not present when Cher and she snuck Sandy into see Paul. Additionally, she did not need to worry about my transparency since I copied Allyne when I sent the email to Cher.

It has been apparent to me and others that throughout this entire process, no one wants to be held accountable for their own actions and for whatever reason, Amanda is almost always defensive in her response. I see this as huge problem in probate court. It makes no difference what the topic is—choosing a guardian, recovery of Paul's personal property, Sandy's visitation, and others, there is little flexibility and I have been told numerous times "That is the way it is done in probate court." Guiding principles are bent or ignored, the ward's opinion and feelings are not considered and the basic premise that if you question anything, is that you receive a response like the one above from

Amanda. Amanda attempted to create a division in our family because I hold people accountable and she would rather deal with Allyne and Mark. Nice try, but it did not work.

The probate process is horribly broken. The court cannot use template solutions for every case, which is what they tried to do in Paul's situation. We, the Baker family, hope that we will be a catalyst for change and intend to do everything within our power to make it better for the wards and their families. Holding people accountable for their actions would be a good start.

The following response was received from Cher's office on April 4th:

From: "Pati Kersey"
To: "crbaker"
Sent: Tuesday, April 14, 2020 4:06:18 PM
Subject: Receipt from S.A.D.L.E.S. Ranch

Dear Carl,
I received your check (#1557) today for the amount of $1400.02. Cher has wrote(sic) off the $393.77 balance at this time. That was the charge for your visit to Trinity Springs on 12/11/2019.

I will be notifying the court on Thursday, April 16, 2020 that all parties have satisfied their account balances at this time and Cher is only requesting that the court discharge her from this Eldercaring Case. I will be sending a copy of this email to everyone on this day.

The ranch has been closed due to the Covid-19 virus until at least April 20, 2020 but if you need to make contact with me, I do come in on Tuesday and Thursdays for a couple of hours to check the emails and phone messages.

Take care and thank you for the check,
Sadles Ranch

My response:

From: "crbaker"
To: "Pati Kersey"
Sent: Wednesday, April 15, 2020 5:00:04 PM
Subject: Re: Receipt from S.A.D.L.E.S. Ranch

Pati

Thank you for your response. I know it was probably easier for you to deduct the 12/11 transaction (Visit to Trinity Springs) because the amount $393.75 is the difference between the S.A.D.L.E.S. statement of 11/17/2020 and the amount of my check. However, for the record, I paid for that transaction. The ones that I deducted from the bill are the four in relation to the surprise visit to Paul by Sandy, Cher and Amanda and the conference call that did not take place. The transactions in question were as follows:

10/10 Phone Conference with Cara Singletary (Sandy's Attorney)	$ 43.75
10/16 Home Visit to Sandy Baker (Coaching)	218.75
10/24 Phone conference with Amanda Ritter	43.75
10/25 Phone conference with Amanda Ritter	43.75
12/09 Phone Conference with Carl and Sandy	43.75
Total	$393.75

Hope the above clarifies this for you. Again, I am available for the hearing; just let me know the date and time.

Please stay safe.

On April 16th, I received the following email from S.A.D.L.E.S.:

Good Afternoon Ladies and Gentlemen,
This letter is just to advise everyone that as of April 14, 2020 all direct parties involved in this case has (sic) satisfied their monetary obligations with S.A.D.L.E.S. Ranch and Cher Myers.

Cher is still requesting that the court discharge her as the Eldercare Coordinator in this case and advised that it can wait until the court re-opens to be placed on the calendar.

The ranch is closed also but I do come in on Tuesday and Thursday's to check the messages and emails. If you need to contact us, please leave us a message or email and we will contact you back as soon as possible.

Please stay safe and stay well.

I find it deeply troubling that 65% of the cost for the eldercaring coordinator is paid by the Baker family and we are not entitled to any progress reports or a simple list of what the coordinator sees as accomplishments for the case. The coordinator only furnishes reports to the court, who pays not a dime for eldercare coordination. I would very much like to review the reports that Cher furnished to the judge and compare them with all the correspondence that went back and forth between us. My best guess is there would be many differences.

My conclusion, which is well documented, is that Eldercare Coordination provided no care or benefit to Paul and was a waste of time and money. Since Sandy's abuse and exploitation of Paul was totally ignored, my recommendation would be to reject any suggestion to use Eldercare Coordination for an abuse or exploitation case.

"Without prosecution, the law is nothing more than words, on a page, in a book, which sits on the shelf."

CHAPTER 12

The Investigations

There were four different agencies that investigated this case and although they sometimes overlapped, for simplicity, they are summarized separately.

Florida Department of Children and Families Adult Protective Services Program

Concerned for Paul's safety, I filed the following adult abuse/exploitation complaint through the Florida Abuse Hotline on November 1, 2018 naming my brother, John Paul Baker as the victim and his wife, Sandra Kaniewski Baker as the person responsible for the abuse and exploitation:

My brother Paul is a retired Army Colonel and Viet Nam veteran who has a disability (Agent Orange) and now has Alzheimer's with very little short-term memory. He has been married to Sandy for two years.

In early July of this year, Paul wrote out a check to a lawn maintenance contractor for $520.00 for fertilizing three palms. Obviously, he was taken advantage of and I initiated a case with Seniors Against Crime. This has been resolved, but Paul is no longer able to handle financial matters. He had a Trust Account of approximately $235,000 which was for future medical costs and long-term care. Upon his death, the remainder was to go to his two children. Since I have been his Trustee and have been helping him with financial matters for years, Paul asked me to handle his checking account and told me he trusted me more than his wife. Sandy has always been abusive to Paul, but now she was angry and, on a quest, to steal his trust. I was in Law enforcement for almost 40 years, and my wife and I have substantial documentation of her abuse.

Sandy has been trying to get the money from the Trust even before they were married and I have prevented that until last month. She made an appointment with the Trust attorney to replace me as the trustee and make herself the trustee. I attended the meeting at the attorney's office. The attorney recommended no changes to the trust. Since then, Sandy has isolated Paul from his family by taking charge of his phone, screening his calls, and pretending she is Paul and sending text messages on his phone. We know that it is her for many reasons namely, Paul has never texted in his life. Further she is "brainwashing" Paul by telling him lies and turning him against his family. My twin brother Bruce and I have not heard from Paul for over six weeks. Up until then, Paul called me at least once a day.

A Case Study Of Elder Abuse And Exploitation In Florida

Sandy is a narcissist and has never admitted that she has ever done anything wrong. She lies about everything even when it is not necessary. In my opinion, she tends to overestimate her own skills and abilities and believes that she is totally entitled to all of Paul's assets and is willing to eliminate anybody and everybody that gets in her way. That is the reason she had to eliminate both Bruce and me from Paul's life by filling his head with lies. She knows that if we get Paul alone, she may well lose the money that she has exploited from him.

On September 21, $220,000 disappeared out of Paul's trust account and it was taken in cash which required a bank CTR. Sandy did this so that the money could not be easily traced. My guess is that everything Paul has left to his children is now going to Sandy. Note that the trust account is not a marital asset and was created prior to their marriage. Further, the trust is protected by a pre-nuptial agreement. I believe that Florida Code, Chapter 825 comes into play here and I would like to discuss this with you.

Paul is presently receiving mental health care at the VA. Now that she has the money, I believe she will be making false complaints against him so she can place him in a nursing home and move on to her next victim. Paul is her third husband and like her marriage to Ralph Kaniewski (her second husband), money was her main objective. (See the attached statement of Christine S. Van Buren.)

There is so much more to this saga that I am requesting that you have someone sit down with us to get a better explanation of what is going on.

One other issue is very pressing. Paul has a conceal carry permit and owns three guns. We know for a fact that those weapons were in his present home because the gun safe was brought out to the garage by Sandy during a garage sale. Once someone told her what was inside the safe, she returned it to the inside closet. When Paul started failing, I asked Paul where his guns were. He told me he has not seen them for a long time. I searched all the closets and the garage attic and have not been able to find the safe or guns. There are file drawers that are locked and that Sandy has the only key. I sent Sandy an email asking her if she knew where the guns were. She stated she does not know and she would look for them. That was months ago and I have not heard a word about them. Paul is being treated for mental health and the doctor has recommended counseling for Sandy. The guns need to be removed from the home.

The following support statement from Ralph Kaniewski's daughter and Sandy's stepdaughter was sent as an attachment to the original complaint:

"I have known Sandy Treolo Hine Kaniewski Baker for approximately 30 years when she met and married my father. Second marriages for both.
My father had a rough life and most of his family died young and he thought he would too, so he lived "for today", not putting money away for retirement. I'm not exactly sure when Sandy realized my father didn't have any money but once she did, her attitude toward him changed dramatically. She was mean to him, belittling and made him feel like he was a burden. He was clearly afraid of her; afraid she would leave him. There was nothing he could do right and any chance she got to tell us about it, she did. My father told me Sandy had affairs during their marriage, one of which she admitted to me.

A Case Study Of Elder Abuse And Exploitation In Florida

At one point, I believe they were married for about 10 years, Sandy called me and told me she was divorcing my father. When she went to an attorney to file, she was advised that she would have to split her money, including what she had in her retirement savings, with him. She told me because of this, she was not divorcing him. Sandy remained married to my father until his death in 2014 but it was clear she was angry about the continued burden of having to deal with my father. As my father got older Sandy began to claim that my father was developing Alzheimer's. She even went so far to have him tested and the results from the doctor said he had "brain fog", which was perfectly normal for a man his age.

One Saturday afternoon while enjoying a college football game, my father developed chest pains. Sandy had him rushed to the hospital where they ran a battery of tests. The results were that he had a gangrenous gall bladder which was immediately removed. Due to his age, it was a very long recovery from the toxins that had been released into his body. He was released from the hospital but due to his weakened state, he went to a rehab center. My father loved living in the Villages and despite the way Sandy treated him, he loved her and wanted to enjoy the rest of his life with her and all of the friends they made in The Villages.

I don't think I ever saw my father work harder at anything than at his rehabilitation from this illness. He was determined to get better. Dad was there for quite a while and made a full recovery. He was walking on his own and was much stronger. It was a Sunday afternoon and my father was to be released from the rehab facility on the very next day, Monday, when Sandy and he decided to go to a movie, *The Monuments Men*. They were on their way to the theater when Sandy turned left on a yellow (maybe green?) light and an oncoming car "T-boned" theirs on the passenger side where my newly rehabbed father was strapped in by his seat belt. I will never forget Sandy telling me just before the impact my father clearly saw what was about to happen, the car coming right at him, and said, "OH MY GOD." They were both taken to the hospital where my father was admitted and Sandy was treated for minor injuries. I don't recall all of the injuries my father sustained but I do know he had broken ribs. While in the hospital he became confused and sometimes didn't know who we were. He was in the hospital for several weeks and eventually we were told he would need to go to a nursing home/facility. During this time Sandy would call me and angrily complain about having to take care of, and pay, for my father's care. She would make me feel so guilty. At the time I was unemployed and recently divorced and didn't have the means to help, even though I wanted to. What I really wanted to do was to get my Dad away from her. It was truly painful to see and hear the way she treated him.

  Dad was in and out of the hospital for various reasons over the next several months and never fully recovered. The last time Dad was admitted, the doctor said he was not going to get better and we should consider taking him off all meds and putting him in hospice. I personally spoke to the doctor. My father was aware what was happening and he was very sad. He didn't want to die.

  Once Dad was moved to hospice, I went to be with him for the remainder of his days. He was already unconscious when I arrived. I told Sandy if she wanted to stay with him, we could take turns and she said no, she was fine and already said her goodbyes. As he drew nearer to death, I asked her if we should call a priest for last rites and she informed she had already done so, not waiting for me.

  Dad died on October 10, 2014. I helped Sandy with the

obituaries and she planned three memorial services, one in Florida, one in Shreveport LA and one in Michigan. I originally planned to attend the one in Michigan but ended up not attending as I cut all ties with Sandy. Neither of my sisters went, either, but our cousin attended and informed us that her new boyfriend was with her…at my father's memorial service. I couldn't get over the disrespect.

A few days after Dad died, I was getting ready to fly home and Sandy and I went to dinner at one of the restaurants in The Villages. We were sitting outside enjoying the weather, chatting, and she said, "I was talking to one of my friends and she said, "you'll be married again in six months". This was such a bizarre statement for my own stepmother to say to me when my father, her dead husband, only just died 48 hours ago. I looked at her, dumbfounded, and told her she should concern herself with getting this one buried before moving on to the next. The weird thing is, I don't know if it was six months, but it was within a year when I learned she remarried.

As I said earlier, I cut all ties with Sandy upon my return home. I wanted nothing to do with her after the way she treated my Dad. I blocked her on Facebook but my daughter who was still "FB friends" with her told me she had remarried. I felt sick to my stomach. Part of me felt like I should contact her new husband's family and warn them, but I thought perhaps she changed, perhaps her new husband's family will embrace her and they will live happily ever after. Sadly, this was not the case.

I was contacted by Allyne Baker last week over Facebook, who had questions about Sandy. Sadly, I expected it. I KNEW Sandy would continue with her mean, manipulative ways. After discussions with Allyne and Carl, I have learned that Sandy was already in a relationship with Paul, her current husband, while my father was in the hospital. I didn't want to believe it but I do now, firmly believe that Sandy wanted to be rid of my father so she could move on and have a relationship with Paul. Sandy didn't expect my father to recover and when he did, she intentionally turned left with a speeding car coming right at my father, trying to kill him.

Please call me any time to discuss any of the information I have provided."

Christine S. Van Buren

Protective Investigator Antonia D. Vasquez was assigned to investigate my complaint. I never had a face-to-face conversation with Investigator Vasquez, which I thought was unusual, so all our correspondence was either by email or phone.

Following are the emails I sent to Investigator Vasquez when I responded to her questions or provided her with additional information:

A Case Study Of Elder Abuse And Exploitation In Florida

November 14, 2018

Toni

After talking to Allyne and a friend to both Paul and me, I have more than reasonable grounds to believe that Sandy has taken control of all of Paul's lifetime savings most of which were not marital assets and were protected by a trust agreement and an antenuptial agreement. I had thought all along that this was the case. Sandy is now stating publicly that all of Paul's assets are " our assets and we can do anything we want to do with them. I'm his wife." In fact, she threw it in Allyne's face as "a badge of honor " rather than the commission of a felony. The translation of this is Sandy can do anything she wants to do because Paul has no idea what is going on and will do anything Sandy tells him to do.

The assets possibly taken by Sandy are as follows:

1. Paul's trust account (BB&T) had an August closing balance of $235,000. $220,000 in cash was taken from the account on 09/21/18 and the remainder later.
2. Paul has a $100,000 life insurance policy with Mass Mutual naming his daughter, Allyne as beneficiary. I was working with the agent because Paul fell behind in his payments. His payments are up to date through 2018.
3. Both Paul's and Sandy's individual trusts stated that upon the death of either party, the proceeds from the sale of the home were to be split between the two trusts. Paul's trust stated that the proceeds would go to Paul's children, Mark and Allyne. I believe the new trust has it all going to Sandy. Based on the original price of the home and

the capital improvements, the house is worth about $500,000. So, the value of Paul's assets taken would be $250,000.

The total that Sandy has taken from Paul is approximately $585,000. I have copies of most of the documents, trust agreements and accounts to support all of this.

What I do not have is a copy of the new trust agreement. Based on my law enforcement experience, I believe that Sandy should be charged with Section 825.103, Exploitation of an elderly person or disabled adult. I am sure you are aware that since the funds involved in the exploitation are more than $100,000, Sandy has committed a felony in the first degree.

The bottom line is that Sandy has no right to Paul's trust and non-marital assets any more than Paul has a right to hers. The main problem is the safety of Paul. Sandy sees Paul's death as her road to riches. The latest bathroom incident, Sandy ignoring the doctor's instructions (no travel for example) and her doing everything to keep Paul away from his family are all telltale signs of what lies ahead. My best guess is that if Sandy were told to return the funds to their original trust accounts, she would divorce him and leave town. While there does not appear to be a happy ending here, a divorce may well be the best outcome.

Thank you for all you help. Any update you could give me on the case would be appreciated. Please call me if I can assist you on any way.

Carl Baker

On December 4, 2018, Toni Vasquez telephoned Bruce, Allyne and Christine Van Buren to get more information on

A Case Study Of Elder Abuse And Exploitation In Florida

Sandy's abuse of Paul.

Toni

On Monday (January 7, 2019), I took a chance and drove to Paul's house and knocked on the door just like I have done so many times before. This time he opened the door and let me in. Obviously, Sandy was not home. A summary of our 30-minute conversation is attached for your information and whatever actions you deem appropriate.

This is the first time I have spent any real time with him since August. Quite candidly, he was pale, lethargic and confused. He was open to our discussion, but as you can see from my summary, he really has no idea what is going on in his life. All of Paul's family are extremely concerned about Paul's health and care. Obvious concerns that require answers are as follows:

1. Sandy is filling his head with lies. For example, Sandy telling him that she is going to research the recently found cure for Alzheimer's is one of her attempts to make sure that Paul believes that she is the only person in his life that is looking out for him. Instead of filling his head with lies, she should be following the doctor's orders which she ignores.

2. What drug is Sandy giving to Paul. Note that Paul said Sandy gives him two pills when he has a headache which are more frequent. And he stated that he sleeps much more now. With the bathroom incident [Sandy came home and found Paul passed out on the bathroom floor. She said he was sleeping.], we are concerned that there may be a problem with what Sandy is giving him. Have you followed up on this?

3. Note the write-up on Paul's cell phone and now you know why Sandy took his flip phone away and gave him her smart phone

without giving him the pass code to use it. This is without any doubt Sandy's exploitation to isolate and totally control Paul by not allowing him to make calls without her present and it appears that she has blocked me from calling Paul. Allyne and Mark have trouble reaching their Dad and when they do, Sandy is right next to him. If Paul had an emergency while Sandy was away, how would he call for help. This abuse needs to be corrected.

    4. Note that Paul is so confused about his financial assets, that he has no idea that Sandy has taken his non-marital assets. Paul did not even remember that he had a new trust. He did not know where the trust was because "Sandy takes care of all that." *Don't you find it strange that Paul's new trust has not been shared with anyone in his family?* Have you or FDLE even looked at Paul's new trust to see how his assets are dispersed? Have you or FDLE even checked to see if the beneficiary was changed on Paul's life insurance policy? How about Paul's health care decisions? Does Sandy now have sole designation as his Health Care Agent? Paul's past trust included his two brothers in health decisions.

    5. Within 10 minutes of talking to Paul, he began to realize how Sandy is controlling his life. He started crying and told me he was sorry. He even asked me if he could get his money back. We also agreed that Paul's son Mark should control his finances.

    6. The stress this has caused Paul and his family is abhorrent. No one should have to watch a family member being treated this way, exploited and abused. Fortunately, Paul has a devoted, loving family that has always availed themselves to support him. We feel compelled to step in and have all taken many actions to try to correct this horrendous situation, apparently to no avail. I have especially felt this burden as I promised Paul that I would always have his back and

he repeatedly asked me to take care of his trust and finances because we were so close, and he knew he couldn't continue to handle things himself.

    I can only imagine what must happen to those elders that don't have concerned family members willing to go out on a limb to protect and provide for their care. We have been unable to get Sandy to take even the smallest of measures to help Paul and follow his doctor's orders. For example, when she booked a trip to Israel, his doctor said, "Okay, but no more travel after this. Paul needs routine to enable him to be self-sufficient for as long as possible." She then proceeded to book a trip to Hawaii and claimed she did not know his doctor had said that, even though she had promised the entire family there would be no more travel. And now that she has isolated him, she takes him wherever she wants to go, whenever she wants to go – which is frequent short and long trips. I couldn't even get her to buy green tea for him to drink, which is believed to have beneficial effects on Alzheimer's patients.

    The family is at a loss as to where to turn for help. I have reached out to the authorities that should be able to save Paul, but we do not see any concrete action being taken. We are all terrified that she is going to physically harm him. It already appears that he is being drugged in some manner. Sandy told him probably over a year ago that there is a pill he can take to end his life. Who does that??? Instead of suggesting suicide, she should have assured him that she and his family will be there for him every step of the way on whatever his journey with this disease requires.

    I'm sure you can understand the frustration his children experience when they must call 5-10 times to get to talk to him once and the call is NEVER in private. She is always listening in. And

Sandy has blocked all communication with his brothers since August, almost 5 months, and we used to speak daily. Frustration in no way adequately describes the emotions his family has experienced. I can't begin to relay all the tears, broken hearts, emotional turmoil, and sleepless nights that have affected everyone. I want you to put yourself in our shoes and imagine if this was your father or brother.

Both Allyne and I have asked to be updated on your findings. Right now, we have no idea what conclusions or findings you will include in your report. Will you be sharing your findings with us? If not, please explain the reason why you won't or can't. While we certainly appreciate everything you are doing, I am sure that you can also understand the frustration we are feeling knowing the way Paul is being treated by Sandy.

Paul is clearly being abused emotionally, mentally, and perhaps physically. If he were a child, action would have been taken immediately. If fact, he is far more vulnerable than many children. He can no longer think clearly, nor can he even remember the many abuses he has endured. And he is just as dependent on his caretaker, Sandy, as children are on their parents – and similarly afraid of upsetting her. As you can see from the notes of me seeing him this week, he was very concerned that I be out of the house before Sandy returned, due to the ramifications he knew would be coming. He expressed his desire not to continue to live this way. What else can we do to help him?

This case has lingered too long. I see all the elements here for felony Exploitation of a Disabled Adult in the first or at a minimum second degree depending on the wording in the new trust. Let's get a copy of the new trust and compare it with the past trust. I have said this before, and I will say it again. As long as Sandy thinks she can get all of Paul's assets, his life is in danger. How will we all feel if something goes terribly wrong?

I never received a response from Investigator Vasquez. I called Adult Protective Services several times in an attempt to speak to a supervisor and again my calls and messages were ignored. Left with no other alternative, I sent the following letter:

September 24, 2019
Sheri Peterson
Program Administrator
Adult Protective Services
1300 Duncan Drive
Building C
Tavares, Florida 32778
RE: 2018-738264
Dear Ms. Peterson:
I was referred to you by Jensey Heding in the enclosed letter dated August 23, 2019.

On September 16, 2019, I called your office with several questions on the above case. The receptionist I spoke to was very professional and very helpful. Since you were not available, she looked up the case and referred me to Jessica Moreira, Protective Investigator Supervisor, and gave me her cell number. She also explained that she would email Jessica and give her the case number and let her know that I would be calling her.

I waited about 15 minutes to call Jessica. I got her voice mail and left a message with my name and number.

I did not hear back from Jessica, so I called her again on

September 18th at 11:33 AM. To date, I have not received a return call, which is why I am writing this letter.

As the complainant in this case, am I allowed to get any feedback from the case? In Antonia Vasquez's letter of January 9, 2016, she states:

"*Pursuant to s. 415.104(4), Florida Statutes, the following services have been recommended to alleviate the causes or effects of the abuse, neglect, or exploitation.*

The following services have been recommended: V (Paul) needs to continue with appropriate medical care and assistance with affairs from his wife."

After serving almost 40 years in law enforcement, I would like to understand how Ms. Vasquez came to this conclusion. I have documented all the information Paul's family furnished to APS and quite candidly, it is difficult for us to believe that APS, at a minimum, did not recommend some follow up visits. In support of this, I will make the following points:

- There is ample documentation that Sandy was after Paul's non marital assets from the start of their relationship. Much of this information was given to Ms. Vazquez.
- Sandy controlled all of Paul's conversation with his family by putting a code on his cell phone and she blocked me and our brother, Bruce from contacting Paul. She also sent text messages pretending to be Paul. Isolation from family members is common in elderly abuse and exploitation cases. All of this is well documented, and we have Paul's phone as physical evidence.
- Sandy told Paul's daughter, Allyne, that she came home, and she thought Paul was sleeping. After not hearing from Paul for a while, she checked on him and found Paul "asleep" on the bathroom floor.

She was laughing as she told this story to Allyne and we thought this was very strange and made sure that Ms. Vasquez was aware of it. Paul has a history of passing out and we thought he may have had another episode. Allyne asked Sandy to take Paul to a doctor, but she said it was not necessary. We question if Sandy was giving Paul something each time before she left him home alone.

- Paul states he was left alone almost daily in the house. In fact, according to Antonia, someone from APS visited Paul's house one day and found him alone. My understanding is that Paul was very friendly and chatty, until Sandy came home and started yelling at everyone and questioning the presence of the investigator. Paul's demeanor changed immediately and he too appeared angry. Being a retired General, Paul would never admit this, but he feared Sandy probably because she was always telling him that she was the only person he had to take care of him. This was a lie and another common tactic in exploitation cases.

- In mid-January, I found Paul alone in the house twice. Fortunately, he spoke to me and I told him what was going on. He broke down and cried and told me he wanted to leave. I told him to think about it and I would try to see him again. He rushed me out the door, because he was scared that Sandy would come home and find me there. I went back a week later and Paul again said he wanted to leave. He came to live with my wife and me until he went to a memory care facility on September 3rd. All of this is well documented also.

I respectfully request that APS at a minimum provide the reasoning for no follow up supervision. Was all the information we provided included in the report? Did APS question the validity of the information we provided? Did APS place more reliability on Sandy's statements?

No matter what the reason, I believe we have the right to know. I thank you for taking the time to read this and I look forward to your reply.

Sincerely,

Carl R. Baker

I never received a reply to my letter to Sheri Peterson despite my numerous attempts to contact her by phone. Having no other choice, I filed a complaint with the Florida Department of Children and Family Services.

December 20, 2019
Secretary Chad Poppell
Florida Department of Children and Families
1317 Winewood Blvd.
Building 1, Room 202
Tallahassee, FL 32399-0700
Dear Secretary Poppell:

I sent the enclosed letter to Program Administrator Sheri Paterson, Adult Protective Services on September 24, 2019. As you can see from the letter, I sent it because I never received a return call from Ms. Peterson.

I never did receive an acknowledgement from my letter, so I called Ms. Peterson's Office on October 23rd. I spoke to a receptionist and told her that my call was regarding a letter I sent on September 24th. The receptionist stated that Ms. Peterson was out having surgery today and she was not sure when she was returning to work.

I left my phone number telling her there was no rush, and I could certainly wait until she returned to work. I thanked her and she told me to have a nice day.

On November 12th, I called again since I had not heard from Ms. Peterson. I spoke to Shelby who told me she was not in the office, but she would call Ms. Peterson and give her my number to call me.

On December 13th, I called again and got her voicemail, so I left a message with my name and number. I thought I heard someone pick up the phone, so I called again. This time I got a person who told me that she would get in touch with Ms. Peterson and have her return my call. That was a week ago today.

In summary, since August 23, 2019, as suggested by Jensey Heding, I have attempted to contact Ms. Peterson at least seven times by phone and sent a letter on September 24 (almost three months ago) and I have never received any response from the Department. I doubt very much that this would be allowed in the Governor DeSantis administration and I would really like to understand how this could happen in your Department.

I am fully aware that there is some confidentiality in elder abuse cases. However, given the well documented abuse and exploitation of my brother, J. Paul Baker by his wife, Sandra Baker outlined in my September 24th letter, I would simply like to know why Adult Protective Investigator Antonia Vasquez saw no reason for any follow-up whatsoever.

Quite candidly, based on my experience, I find it difficult to believe that if all the documentation that we forwarded to Investigator Vasquez was included in the report, how any review could result in no further supervision.

Should you have any questions, or need any additional

information, please feel free to call me.
Thank you,
Carl R. Baker

On January 22, 2020 at 11:10 AM, exactly one month after Mr. Poppell received my letter, Sheri Peterson left the following telephone message on my cell phone:

"Hey Mr. Baker, this is Sheri Peterson from the Department of Children and Families. I have several calls and a letter that you sent. I have to be honest with you, I never received this letter. My program manager gave it to me. So, I read it and I was shocked when I saw that you called me several times. I don't remember speaking with you or having any messages on you. I actually asked for my cell phone records to see if you did call me.

So, I apologize. I don't know exactly what happened here, but I do have your letter and I am going to look at the case and see what happened and if you need to speak with me this is my direct cell phone number and not the number that you were calling. Shelby is the secretary in another area. My secretary's name is (inaudible).

If you can give me a call back at (phone number), I would be happy to talk to you. I am going to look at the case now and if necessary, I am going to send this to my program manager for further review. Thank you."

I am sorry, but it is extremely difficult for me to believe that after sending a letter and making seven phone calls, no one replied until I sent a complaint to a member of the Governor's staff.

On January 23rd, I returned Ms. Peterson's call. She again told me she did not remember seeing my letter or receiving any messages that I called. However, after reading my letter, she is aware of my concerns. She stated that she will review the case and check with the Department's legal staff to see what information she can share with me.

On January 28th at 12:57 PM, I received a message on my cell phone from Kimberly Mummey, Adult Protective Investigator, Department of Families and Children, asking for me to return her call. She stated that they were again looking into the abuse complaint I filed against Sandy.

I returned her call at 1:52 PM. Kimberly stated that she was assigned to review the entire case and asked for specific information. In accordance with her request, I sent the following email to her:

From: "crbaker
Sent: Tuesday, January 28, 2020 3:42:42 PM
Subject: Per your request

Kimberly
There will be seven additional emails with attachments that follow this one. I will put them in order so it is easier to follow - starting from Antenuptial Agreement to the timeline. I am ready to answer any questions you have either by phone or email. My wife, Katherine and my twin brother, Bruce and his wife, Gail also are also very familiar with all that has taken place.

Paul's court appointed guardian is Amanda Ritter and can be reached at (phone number) should you need to speak to her.

Thank you.

The following documents were sent to Kimberly:

- Paul and Sandy's Antenuptial Agreement.
- Letter from Dr. Geliga stating that Paul was diagnosed with Alzheimer's Dementia in November 2015, months before they were married.
- BB&T Trust Accounting and letter.
- Copy of the $220,000 cashier's check taken from Paul's trust account.
- Outline of the changes made in Paul's trust account by Sandy.
- Email documenting Paul's request to leave Sandy and live with us.
- Timeline on Sandy's quest to take over Paul's non-marital assets.

On February 21, 2020, I called Sheri Peterson to check on the status of the Department of Children and Families review of my abuse complaint. She told me that Kimberly Mummey is still working on the case reviewing medical records. Once that is completed, the Department will give me their findings and determine what information they will make available to me.

On March 5th, I spoke to Kimberly Mummey and she had told me that her review of the case was completed and that the exploitation, lack of supervision, confinement and medical neglect have all been changed to verified and referred to the

Sumter County Sheriff's Office and the State Attorney's Office for follow-up. I should have a copy of the report in a week and Investigator Mummey referred me to Jensey Heding from her Department for follow-up.

I immediately called Ms. Heding and spoke to her. She told me that she would need a copy of my power of attorney for Paul. I emailed it to her that afternoon.

Sumter County Sheriff's Office

10/08/18

On October 8, 2018, I called Sumter County Sheriff's Office (SCSO) Investigative Division and left a message and asked for a return call.

As of October 15, 2018, I did not have a reply from SCSO, so I called the Florida Department of Law Enforcement (FDLE) and reported the $220,000 taken by Sandy. I spoke to SA Don Schrenker and followed up with an email to him outlining the details.

Later that day, Detective Larry Thompson (SCSO) returned my call from October 8th. He told me that the original call went to the desk of a receptionist who was on vacation and he did not get the message until today. He asked me to come to his office and file a report. I also told him about the three (3) pistols in Paul's house. Later that day, Detective Thompson came to my house and took a statement regarding the guns.

On October 22, 2018, I called Detective Larry Thompson, Sumter County Sheriff's Office. Detective Thompson did a safety check on Paul's house. He told Paul that his family was concerned about him and he was just checking on him. Paul immediately assumed that I was the one asking for the check and Paul got angry and immediately went off on me.

Detective Thompson thought that Paul's current condition did not justify removing the weapons from his home at this time, but would check with the court.

(Note: Detective Thompson is an outstanding investigator. As soon he realized that we had a miscommunication, he came to our home and got the information he needed to have a better understanding of the situation. He went to Paul's residence for a safety check and kept me informed. Detective Thompson later called me to tell me the court saw no reason to remove the weapons from Paul's home. I disagree with the court. Neither Paul nor Sandy is of sound mind and I just wanted to prevent a tragedy.)

The Dehumanization of Crime and It's Victims

Unfortunately, in my opinion and based on my experience, the dehumanization of crime and its victims is an unacceptable practice in law enforcement today. The dehumanization of crime and its victims is a process that has been progressing rapidly over the past 10 to 15 years. Dehumanization is defined as the process of depriving a person or group of positive human qualities. Human contact has been replaced with electronic contact. Obviously, as you walk the streets of any city, most people have a cell phone in their hand or pocket and are communicating with someone (another human being) by texting or voice. We have replaced face-to-face conversations by use of inanimate objects (cell phones, computers, digital answering machines, etc.) that are now capable of sending replies to any caller without any human intervention. It makes no difference which side of the encounter you are on; talk has been replaced by keystrokes.

Unfortunately, many law enforcement agencies have fallen into this trap and the result, many believe, is a decrease in the quality of the investigation and further separates the police from the public they are sworn to serve and protect. If this continues, police and community relations will continue to deteriorate.

If you look closely at the next two criminal investigations of this exploitation case, one by the Florida Department of Law Enforcement (FDLE) and the second by the financial crime detective from the Sumter County Sheriff's Office, you will have a better understanding of the impact of the dehumanization of crime and its victims. In the FDLE investigation, neither Paul nor I had a face-to-face conversation with anyone from the Department. In the Detective Cohen investigation, I was unable to find any documentation that he ever left his office. Although we lived only several miles from his office, Detective Cohen never spoke to Paul, and I never actually met him until we had a meeting with the State Attorneys at his office at the conclusion of the investigation. Further, he spoke to Paul's wife, Sandy, who was the subject of the investigation, by phone. In all my years in law enforcement, this was never acceptable, even more so for a felony in the first degree, which is the crime in this case. In my experiences, if we had to interview a suspect or material witness in another part of the country, we would either send a detective to the suspect's location or work with another department to ensure that there was a face-to-face interview or interrogation. You can learn a lot more from a suspect by being physically present than by a phone call, especially for the initial encounter.

Florida Department of Law Enforcement

On October 22, 2018, I again called Special Agent Don Schrenker Florida Department of Law Enforcement and left voice mail asking him to return my call.

On October 24, 2018, SA Don Schrenker returned my call. He stated he discussed the case with his supervisor and that the information submitted was insufficient for the FDLE to adopt a case. I explained the elements of the Florida Code and that there was no way to determine if a felony of a first degree (over $100,000) was committed unless it was determined where the $220,000 went. If it was not available for Paul's use, Sandy committed a felony. I also explained that there was possibly another $100,000 from an insurance policy that was going to Sandy that was intended to go to Paul's daughter. He stated that he would again talk to his supervisor and get back to me.

Note: During our initial conversation, SA Schrenker asked that I just send him a summary for now and not forward any documents.

On October 29, I called SA Don Schrenker (FDLE) for an update and got his voice mail. I left a message.

Since I never received a response from SA Schrenker, I called him again on November 1, and left a second voice message.

After calling a third time on November 5 and not getting an

answer, I sent the following email:

> SA Schrenker
> Re: Exploitation Case
>
> I have left three (3) voice mails for you to get an update on the status of the above case. You may be on vacation or in training. In any case, I would appreciate a call back as soon as you can.
>
> Thank you,
> Carl Baker

The message was read by SA Schrenker 35 minutes after I sent it.

My concern for my brother's safety was growing and I did not understand why my calls to FDLE were being ignored. The general police standard requires a call to be returned in twenty-four hours unless there is an explanation that the detective or agent will be out of the office for an extended period, i.e., vacation or training. So, on November 7, 2018, I sent a second email to SA Schrenker:

> Evidently, we have a misunderstanding. On 10/24/18, you called me and told me you discussed the case with your supervisor and that the information submitted was insufficient for the FDLE to adopt a case. I explained the elements of Florida Code 825.103 and that there was no way to determine if a felony in the first degree (over $100,000) was committed unless it was determined where the $220,000 went. See Code 825.106 2(b). You told me that you would

again speak to your supervisor and get back to me. That is why I have been calling you.

On our initial conversation, you asked that I just send you a summary and not forward any documents. I went through all the elements of this section of the Code and can document everything except where the money went and if Paul is "temporarily or permanently deprived of the use, benefit or possession of the funds." I know that Sandy is using some of the funds to pay bills (probably her bills as well), but where is the remainder of the money? In addition, the original trust (I am the Trustee) that Paul created prior to his marriage and when he was of sound mind, gave his two children everything. With the value of his home, life insurance and cash, the total value is close to $600,000. Paul is in failing health and unless some action is taken, this money will be gone.

If you simply did a credit check on both Paul and his wife, that would give you a good idea if the money is still available to Paul. I have some indication (unconfirmed) that Paul's wife is seeing another man and she may be sending the money to him for their use when Paul passes. I am certain that a review of Sandy's cell phone usage would determine if this were true.

I respectfully request that you again talk to your supervisor and let me know your collective decision.

Thank you.
Carl Baker

The read verification below shows the email was read shortly after I sent it:

To: Schrenker, Don
Subject: Misunderstanding
Sent: Wednesday, November 7, 2018 8:23:12 AM (UTC-05:00) Eastern Time (US & Canada) Your message was read on Wednesday, November 7, 2018 8:23:41 AM (UTC-05:00) Eastern Time (US & Canada).

On November 13, 2018, I received a call from SA Don Schrenker telling me that FDLE would adopt my case and that a SA that handles Sumter County would be calling me in the next several days. He told me he was on vacation last week.

On November 19, 2018, I called Investigator Toni Vasquez, Elder Abuse. I left a voice mail thanking her and letting her know that FDLE notified me that they are adopting a case. I also requested that she return my call should there be anything she could share with me as to her findings.

Toni Vasquez returned my call two days later and told me that the case is still open and that she will return to Paul's residence again. She told me there was a lot of anger but little that they said made sense. I briefly explained the situation to her and she asked that I send her the timeline on Sandy's quest to obtain Paul's money. I emailed it to her shortly after the telephone conversation.

From: CARL BAKER
Subject: Call from Special Agent
To: donschrenker
Mon, Nov 26, 2018 01:44 PM

SA Schrenker:

Tomorrow will be two weeks since you called me and told me that a Special Agent that works in Sumter County was taking my case and he would contact me. FYI, I have not heard from anyone.

Just want to make sure the Agent has the correct contact information. If there is anything else I need to do, please let me know.

Thanks for the help.

Carl Baker

From: "donschrenker"
To: "crbaker"
Sent: Monday, November 26, 2018 2:35:23 PM
Subject: Read: Call from Special Agent
Your message
To: Schrenker, Don
  Subject: Call from Special Agent
  Sent: Monday, November 26, 2018 1:44:18 PM (UTC-05:00) Eastern Time (US & Canada) was read on Monday, November 26, 2018 2:35:23 PM (UTC-05:00) Eastern Time (US & Canada).

12/10/18

December 10, 2018 10:42 AM
From:
crbaker

To:donschrenker
Agent Schrenker

A Case Study Of Elder Abuse And Exploitation In Florida

Tomorrow will be four weeks since your call to me about another agent taking the above case. I have not heard from that Agent. Without the help of FDLE, I have no way of determining what happened to the $220,000 withdrawn from Paul's account. And since his wife went to another attorney to create a new trust, I have reason to believe that the funds and assets involved could easily exceed $500,000 and there may be another person involved. Either way, it is a felony in the first degree.

I have a lot more information that will help with your investigation. Would you or the assigned Agent please give me a call with an update on the case. Any assistance you can provide will be greatly appreciated.

    Thank you,
    Carl Baker

    Re: Exploitation Case December 12, 2018 12:04 PM
    From:
    donschrenker

To:crbaker

Could you please resend the documents you emailed me earlier.

Thank you.

Re: Exploitation Case December 12, 2018 1:33 PM
From: crbaker

To: donschrenker
SA Schrenker

I will go through my files this afternoon and send the documents to you later today.

Thank you for getting back to me.
Carl Baker

SA Schrenker
   Follow-up December 13, 2018 6:14 AM
From: crbaker
To: donschrenker

Yesterday, I sent you three emails with a total of five attachments. If any are missing, please let me know.

FYI, I also have copies of all of my brother's trust documents, nuptial agreements, bank records and a copy of the teller cashed check for $220,000 from his trust account should you need them.

As I mentioned before, the actual value of the exploitation may very well exceed $500,000, which is all of Paul's assets - the $220,000 cash from the trust account, a $100,000 life insurance policy listing Paul's daughter as beneficiary and half the equity of his home which he left to his son and daughter. I have no way of confirming this without your help, so again I appreciate everything you are doing.

Carl Baker

Read: Follow-up December 13, 2018 7:22 AM
From: donschrenker

To:crbaker
Your message
To: Schrenker, Don
 Subject: Follow-up
 Sent: Thursday, December 13, 2018 6:14:26 AM (UTC-05:00) Eastern Time (US & Canada) was read on Thursday, December 13, 2018 7:22:12 AM (UTC-05:00) Eastern Time (US & Canada).

 Fwd: Update on the Sandy Baker Complaint December 27, 2018 2:50 PM
 From: crbaker
 To: donschrenker

SA Schrenker
FYI. This is the email I Sent to Toni Vasquez at Social Services Elder Abuse.
Any update you could give me on the case would very much be appreciated.
Please call me If I can be of any assistance.
Thank you,
Carl Baker

Read: Fwd: Update on the Sandy Baker Complaint   December 27, 2018 3:20 PM
From: donschrenker
To:crbaker

Your message
To: Schrenker, Don
Subject: Fwd: Update on the Sandy Baker Complaint
Sent: Thursday, December 27, 2018 2:50:23 PM (UTC-05:00) Eastern Time (US & Canada) was read on Thursday, December 27, 2018 3:20:07 PM (UTC-05:00) Eastern Time

Update on case
January 8, 2019 9:03 AM
From: crbaker
To:donschrenker

SA Schrenker
I know that SS (Elder Abuse) has been to Paul and Sandy's home twice with law enforcement. Was that someone from FDLE?
I really do not know what is going on from your end. Any update you could give me would greatly be appreciated.

Thank you.
Carl Baker

Read: Update on caseJanuary 8, 2019 9:03 AM
From: donschrenker
To: crbaker was read on Tuesday, January 8, 2019 9:03:46 AM (UTC-05:00) Eastern Time (US & Canada).

I never did understand why I never heard another word from FDLE, despite my calls and emails. On January 15th, 2019, exactly three months after my initial call to report Sandy's abuse and exploitation, it became obvious to me that there was no investigation by FDLE, so I called Special Agent Schrenker and asked him to close the case. Obviously, they have extremely poor customer service.

I sent the following freedom of information request on July 16, 2019 an attempt to find out what actually happened:

Florida Department of Law Enforcement
Attn: Office of the General Counsel
P.O. Box 1489
Tallahassee, FL 32302-1489
Dear Custodian of Records:
Pursuant to Article I, section 24 of the Florida Constitution, and chapter 119, F.S., I am requesting an opportunity to obtain copies of public records, to include all reports and notes regarding a criminal complaint of exploitation that I filed against Sandra Baker on 10/15/18 with Special Agent Don Schrenker and FDLE officially adopted on 11/13/18.
1. If there are any fees for searching or copying these records,

please inform me before filling my request if it is more than $50.00. If you estimate that the fees will exceed this limit, please call me first. However, I do request a waiver of all fees for this request since the disclosure of the information I seek is not primarily in my commercial interest and is likely to contribute significantly to public understanding of the operations or activities of the government, making the disclosure a matter of public interest.

2. Should you deny my request, or any part of the request, please state in writing the basis for the denial, including the exact statutory citation authorizing the denial as required by s.119.07(1)(d), F.S.

If you have any questions in the interim, you may contact me at the below cell phone number or by email.

Thank you,
Carl R. Baker

In response to my request for a copy on the investigative report, I received the following:

FLORIDA DEPARTMENT OF LAW ENFORCEMENT
INVESTIGATIVE REPORT

This report is predicated on activity of Florida Department of Law Enforcement (FDLE) Special Agent (SA) Don Schrenker, who was one of the assigned duty agents for the Tampa Bay.

Regional Operations Center (TBROC) for the week of October 11-October 18, 2018.

10/15/2016

A Case Study Of Elder Abuse And Exploitation In Florida

Carl Baker is a retired Colonel from the NYSP, who currently resides in Sumter County FL, in the Villages. Baker contacted FDLE wanting to report that his brother's, John Paul Baker, wife had stolen approximately $220,000 dollars from a trust account. John Baker has trouble making financial decisions and Carl had taken over his finances. Baker stated that this money was supposed to be protected by a pre-nuptial agreement. Baker sent SA Schrenker an email with further information. The information obtained was reviewed by SAS Rick Tavares who advised that the information did not meet the criminal threshold for an FDLE investigation and was more of a civil matter. Baker was advised of this but has continued to contact FDLE stating his case. SAS Tavares advised that the request would be forwarded to the Brooksville Field Office for follow up. Baker still has continued to call FDLE to make the complaint.

[REDACTED SECTION]

10/16/2018

[REDACTED SECTION]

Case Number: TM-73-5526 Serial #: 79
Author: Schrenker, Donald Isaiah Office: Tampa
Activity Start Date: 10/12/2018 Activity End Date:10/31/2018
Approved By: Scanlan, J Davidson
Description: Duty activities 10/12-10/18/2018

THIS REPORT IS INTENDED ONLY FOR THE USE OF THE AGENCY TO WHICH IT WAS DISSEMINATED AND MAY CONTAIN INFORMATION THAT IS EITHER PRIVILEGED OR CONFIDENTIAL AND EXEMPT FROM DISCLOSURE UNDER APPLICABLE LAW. ITS CONTENTS ARE NOT TO BE DISTRIBUTED OUTSIDE YOUR AGENCY.

Case Number TM-73-5526
IR Number 79
[REDACTED]
10/15/208
[REDACTED]
10/17/208
[REDACTED]
Case Number TM-73-5526
IR Number 79
[REDACTED]
10/18/2018
[REDACTED]

I was shocked that the entire investigative report that I received from the Florida Department of Law Enforcement was ten lines long. What I also did not understand was why so much of the report was redacted.

I made several calls to FDLE and received some information on the redacted material but no information as to the brevity of the report. In order to determine exactly what FDLE handled my original complaint and investigation, I filed the following letter of complaint:

December 9, 2019
Letter of Complaint
Commissioner Richard L. Swearingen
Florida Department of Law Enforcement
P. O. Box 1489

A Case Study Of Elder Abuse And Exploitation In Florida

Tallahassee, FL 32302-1489
RE: Case Number: TM-73-552

Dear Commissioner Swearingen:
Having served in law enforcement for over 40 years, it is with much regret that I send you this letter of complaint. I began my career as a Trooper in the New York State Police, working myself up through the ranks in the uniform force and the Bureau of Criminal Investigation. I retired in 1990 as a Deputy Superintendent (Colonel) and moved to Virginia to take the position of Director of the Bureau of Criminal Investigation (Lt. Colonel) in the Virginia State Police. Two years later, the Governor appointed me to Superintendent (Colonel) of the Virginia State Police. In 1994, when George Allen was elected Governor, he appointed me to serve on his Cabinet as the Deputy Secretary of Public Safety overseeing the operations of 11 agencies to include the State Police and National Guard. I served my last 11 years in public service as Chief of Police in Chesterfield County (Virginia) overseeing a department of 600 employees. I retired in 2007 and started my own company, Public Safety Consulting and was a partner in another consulting firm, Decide Smart. I tell you this to emphasize the vast experience I have in criminal investigations.

My brother, J. Paul Baker, retired from the US Army as a Brigadier General after 32 years of service. He served in Viet Nam and received a partial disability from the VA because of Agent Orange. He was diagnosed with Alzheimer's dementia in 2014 and today, he is in a memory care facility.

Paul had a short-term late life marriage in 2016. His wife abused him and exploited him by isolating him from his family and withdrawing $220,000 from his non-marital trust account. This was the basis for my filing a complaint against his wife, Sandra with FDLE.

Enclosed is eleven pages of a timeline I kept documenting the actions that I took in an attempt to protect Paul and his assets. According to his trust (before his wife changed it), all his assets to include one-half of the value of the marital residence are to be distributed to his two children upon his death.

I have also enclosed a copy of the "Public Records" Response, FDLE Docket No. PRR-2019-2379 which I received on December 3rd.

When you compare the two documents, it appears to me that Special Agent Donald Schrenker's report certainly does not match my notes and documentation. In fact, in all my years of experience, this is by far the worst case of customer service that I have ever seen from a law enforcement agency.

As you review this case and my enclosures, please consider the following:

The report that I received as a result of my FOI request included a 10-line summary and approximately 77 lines of redaction which is 88.5% of the report. On 12/04/2019, I called the number for records (850-410-7676) and spoke to Jason Harrison. He told me that he would check on the reason for the extensive redaction and get back to me by the end of the day. Jason did return my call the following day and explained that the redacted entries were logged in calls at this center and had nothing to do with my case. I asked him if the ten-line summary was the complete report. He told me that is all FDLE had on my complaint.

If this is the only information you have on my complaint, I would say that every other communication I had with FDLE was never recorded and there was never any type of investigation. There is something very strange about this entire experience and someone owes me an explanation.

1. I called SA Schrenker on 10/22 and left a voice mail asking him to return my call. On 10/24 he returned my call and told me that the information I submitted was insufficient for the FDLE to adopt a case. After our discussion in which I relayed many more facts about the case, he stated he would again talk to his supervisor and get back to me. (Note in my enclosure that SA Schrenker did not want me to send him all the documents that I had at this time.)

2. I called SA Schrenker on 10/29, 11/01, 11/05 and sent him an email on 11/05 which he read shortly after he received it. He did not respond to any of the calls or the email.

3. I sent a lengthy email to SA Schrenker on 11/07 outlining why I was expecting a return call from him. Just as a reminder, I am sitting at home, unable to contact my brother, seeing $220,000 disappear from his non-marital trust fund and wondering if he is safe, given his wife's past actions. For many reasons, I believed it was extremely important to include law enforcement in this matter. SA Schrenker read my email within a minute of receiving it.

4. On 11/13/18 at 11:38 AM, I received a restricted call on my cell phone from SA Don Schrenker. He told me that FDLE would adopt my case and that a SA that handles Sumter County would be calling me in the next several days. He also told me he was on vacation last week. You can follow along on the enclosure and see that no one ever contacted me. After several weeks, I began to wonder what was really going on here. Did FDLE just write me off as a senile old, retired cop and not take my correspondence as creditable. Trust me, I am of sound mind and body and based on my years of experience, I believe that I had enough evidence for a conviction.

5. Since I had no real documentation of the November 13th call, I went back and photocopied my restricted phone call even though

my neighbor witnessed the call. I was certainly pleased that FDLE was finally going to look at this case. Obviously, I was wrong. Was FDLE just "playing a game" with me? Was SA Schrenker really on vacation and if so, why was my email opened so rapidly?

6. Note that SA Schrenker sent me an email on December 12, 2018 asking me to resend the documents that I had emailed earlier. I sent him the documents that afternoon. The report you sent me in no way matches what actually happened. Obviously, SA Schrenker was not including our communications or his activities in the report. What is going on here? If the only report is the ten lines you sent me, we have a problem.

7. If SA Schrenker closed the case, why didn't he just send me an email and tell me that after a second review, they were not going to adopt a case? Why did he string me along for such a long period of time? Why did he tell me that the Special Agent that worked in Sumter County would call me? I figured that FDLE was not doing anything with the case and I could not get a straight answer from FDLE. SA Schrenker had to know that our entire family was extremely concerned about Paul's safety. How did something like this actually occur in a law enforcement agency like FDLE?

I have everything that occurred in this fiasco with Paul and his wife well documented. I have much more information than SA Schrenker ever requested. I was alleging that Sandra Baker had committed a felony in the first degree, yet FDLE did not ask for additional information nor, according to the report you sent me, did they do any investigation whatsoever.

By making this complaint, I am again just asking that you tell me the truth as to what happened and explain all the concerns that I have raised.

Thank you,
Carl R. Baker

I received the following response from the Florida Department of Law Enforcement: (see following page)

So, after three months (October 15, 2018 to January 15, 2019) and all my efforts and emails, the Florida Department of Law Enforcement never even started an investigation. Having worked years in state investigative agencies, I cannot tell you how disappointed I was with FDLE. Evidently, it is much more difficult to get a law enforcement agency to investigate a case of elder abuse in Florida than I ever would have imagined. This should be totally unacceptable to all of Florida's elected officials.

The Sumter County Sheriff's Office was my last and only hope for a criminal investigation of Sandy's abuse and exploitation.

Carl R. Baker

Florida Department of Law Enforcement	**Criminal Investigations and Forensic Science** Tampa Bay Regional Operations Center 4211 North Lois Avenue	Ron DeSantis, *Governor* Ashley Moody, *Attorney General* Jimmy Patronis, *Chief Financial Officer*
Richard L. Swearingen *Commissioner*	Tampa, FL 33614 (800) 226-1140 www.fdle.state.fl.us	Nikki Fried, *Commissioner of Agriculture*

December 23, 2019

Mr. Carl R. Baker
1816 Wading Heron Way
The Villages, FL 32163

Dear Mr. Baker,

The Florida Department of Law Enforcement (FDLE) was in receipt of your correspondence dated December 9, 2019, regarding service provided to you by Special Agents in the Tampa Bay Regional Operations Center (TBROC). A thorough review of all electronic communications was conducted by Assistant Special Agent in Charge Sharon Feola.

Additional electronic correspondence was located and the following was determined. On December 13, 2019, your complaint as well as all the associated documents you provided were forwarded from TBROC Special Agent (SA) Donald Schrenker to Brooksville Field Office (BFO) Resident Agent in Charge (RAC) Edith Neal for evaluation and follow-up. Subsequently, RAC Neal assigned your complaint to BFO SA Christopher Ludlow to contact you and determine if a criminal investigation was warranted. On January 15, 2019, SA Schrenker forwarded correspondence from you to BFO SA Ludlow advising that the situation seemed to have been resolved and thanking SA Schrenker for his assistance.

Regrettably, SA Ludlow failed to contact or follow up with you in a timely manner. The timeliness of RAC Neal's and SA Ludlow's response to your request has been addressed. Lastly, during our conversations you have indicated that your complaint was investigated by the Sumter County Sheriff's Office. The Office of the State Attorney, Fifth Judicial Circuit, determined that criminal prosecution would not be sought.

If in the future you should need assistance from the FDLE Tampa Office or any of our offices statewide please do not hesitate to contact me.

Sincerely,

Sharon Feola
Assistant Special Agent in Charge
Tampa Bay Regional Operations Center

SF/ces

Sumter County Sheriff's Office

March 25, 2019

When Paul's attorney, Merideth Nagel, suggested that I file charges with the State Attorney's Office, I called their office and they referred me to the Sumter County Sheriff's Office Sheriff's Office (SCSO) for investigation. Since FDLE never investigated my criminal complaint, I again contacted Detective Larry Thompson (SCSO) and he suggested I call and have a Deputy come to my home and take the initial report and then it would be assigned to a financial crime detective for investigation.

Later that afternoon, I filed the criminal complaint with Deputy J. Bolling, who came to my home. The case was assigned to Detective Jeff Cohen for investigation.

March 27, 2019 5:05 PM

I received a call from Detective Jeff Cohen (SCSO) regarding my criminal complaint of exploitation by Paul's wife Sandy. Detective Cohen wanted to explain how he was going to proceed with my complaint.

He asked if Paul was still alive and I replied he was and living with us in our home. He went on to explain that charging a wife in this type of complaint was difficult. We talked about the fact that Chapter 825 of the Florida Code specifically states that a spouse can be charged. He agreed and stated that the letter from Paul's doctor greatly helped since the $220,000 was withdrawn from the bank after the date on the letter.

His next step was to see if the bank had any video of the money being withdrawn from the bank. He would then call his contact at the State Attorney's Office and discuss the case with him. He advised me that if they did not think they could get a conviction, they would not proceed with the case. Why did Detective Cohen make a statement like this so early in the case? Normally, if the prosecutor thinks he cannot get a conviction, he will explain what is lacking to see if the case can be strengthened.

I explained that I had a lot more documentation that he has not reviewed, and he replied that he has enough to talk to the attorney. I told him that if a decision were made not to take the case forward for prosecution, I would like a written explanation with the reasons for his conclusion.

I went on to explain that the exploitation involved Paul's non- marital assets and that they each had their own trust. Once Sandy isolated Paul from his family, Sandy changed Paul's trust and made herself power of attorney and changed the trust denying Paul's children the equity of his half of the home until she died instead of when Paul died. Detective Cohen then asked the location of the attorney who changed Paul's trust. I told him Ocala and he stated that he could not include that in the case since it was not in his jurisdiction and we would have to handle that in civil court. Not sure I understand what he is saying here. The exploitation took place in Sumter County by Sandy and currently, I am not seeking charges against any of the attorneys involved in creating Paul's trusts. However, I did plan on filing a bar complaint.

I went on to explain that there may be a third party involved and that I would like for him to subpoena Sandy's phone records to determine if this is true. He told me that he could not subpoena the phone records for this case. I told Detective Cohen that the prosecutor could subpoena the phone records if he thought it would help.

Detective Cohen asked me what I wanted out of the prosecution—the money returned or for Sandy to go to jail. I explained that although Paul did not get all his money back, we were able to secure most of it when we met with the Vice President at the bank. I further explained that the exploitation statute only required intent. Further, Paul was Sandy's second victim and that she needed to be held accountable to prevent any more victims. Detective Cohen told me he would get back to me after he spoke to the State Attorney.

Thursday March 28, 2019 4:33 PM

Detective Cohen called me and told me that he spoke to the State Attorney's Office and the SA would like to see Paul's antenuptial agreement before making a final decision on the case. He asked that I fax him a copy.

When I got home, I called Detective Cohen back and told him that my copy of the agreement was unsigned, and I would contact Paul's attorney and get a signed copy.

I sent Sham Shanawany, Paul's attorney, an email and asked him to call me. Later that evening, I received a text message from Sham that he was out of town and would call me either tomorrow or Monday.

Friday, March 29, 2019 9:04 AM

Detective Jeff Cohen called to tell me that he did talk to his contact in the State Attorney's Office again. In addition to a signed copy of the antenuptial agreement, he is requesting copies of the trusts that Paul signed prior to his marriage. I let him know that Paul's attorney was out of town and I would follow up with him on Monday to get a signed copy of the agreement and the trusts.

Monday, April 1, 2019 10:06 AM

Called Sham Shanawany regarding getting signed copies of Paul's 2016 Trust Reinstatement and the antenuptial agreement. He sent the 2016 Trust immediately. However, he did not have a copy of the signed antenuptial agreement since that was created when he was with another law firm. He told me that I would have to call that firm.

10:13 AM

Called Eric Millhorn's law firm and spoke to a receptionist. She transferred me to the person who handles records. I got a recording and left a message explaining exactly what I needed. The conversation ended by the recording stating someone would get back to me in 24 hours. I relayed this information to Detective Cohen.

A Case Study Of Elder Abuse And Exploitation In Florida

From: CARL BAKER
Sent: Thursday, April 04, 2019 11:40 AM
To: Jeffrey Cohen
Subject: Fwd: Antenuptial Agreement

Detective Cohen:

Signed copy attached. I also sent a copy to the State Attorney's Office. Paul's financial affidavit shows $178,000 in the bank which was his trust account and when he sold his home, the amount increased to over $200,000. This is a non-marital asset protected by the trust and the Antenuptial Agreement from which Sandra withdrew the $220,000.

FYI, I asked Millhorn Law if there was a financial affidavit from Sandra that was also attached to this agreement. I am awaiting a reply and I will let you know.

Please let me know if you need any additional information.

Carl Baker

State Attorney's Office

Brad King began his legal career as an assistant state attorney under State Attorneys Gordon Oldham and Ray Gill. He worked in every division and became a mentor and supervisor to other prosecutors before winning election to State Attorney in 1988. Since having been sworn into office in January of 1989, he has remained the elected State Attorney serving the Fifth Judicial Circuit which includes Marion, Citrus, Lake, Sumter, and Hernando counties.

The following statement of State Attorney King was taken from his Fifth Judicial Circuit website:

"As your State Attorney, I am committed to ensuring public safety and promoting respect for government through the prompt, effective, and compassionate prosecution of cases. This must be done in a manner that advocates for the interests of all victims, respects law enforcement agencies, and holds offenders accountable at the same time as protecting the constitutional and legal rights of the accused."

After reviewing the State Attorney's website for the Fifth Judicial Circuit, I was impressed and honestly believed that Sandy was finally going to be held accountable for her actions. I was pleased that he had spent some time as a Deputy Sheriff for several years. I always believed that having experience as a "street cop" made for a better prosecutor.

On the website, I took the time to review the mission, vision and values for the State Attorney's Office. It was obvious to me that the State Attorney's Office has a "Total Quality Management" program and recognizes the importance of publishing their mission, vision and values for the public to see.

| About Us | Prosecution | Victim/Witness | General Info | Publications/Forms |

State Attorney, 18th Judicial Circuit's

Mission, Vision, Values

Mission

To pursue vigorous and fair prosecution of criminal cases, with a commitment to serve as an advocate for the rights of all victims, and promote the safety and well-being of the public.

Vision

To excel and be acknowledged as a leader in providing quality prosecution, exceptional service to victims, and for our work in partnership with the community in providing early intervention and preventive education programs for juveniles, consistent with the safety and well-being of the public.

Values

We are dedicated to:

L eading the way toward a productive partnership with the community and other agencies to prevent and suppress crime.

E stablishing honesty and integrity in fulfilling the responsibilities of this office.

A fair and objective judicial process for all persons.

> **D** efending the rights of victims and witnesses with concern, compassion, and respect for their dignity.
>
> **E** ffective communication with all involved in the criminal justice system.
>
> **R** ecognizing our employees as our most valuable asset by empowering them individually and as a team.
>
> **S** haring the belief that the best opportunity we have to steer a person away from crime is in their youth.
>
> **H** ighly responsible utilization of public resources.
>
> **I** nsuring professional and effective representation of the people.
>
> **P** ride in excellence.

Note: Unfortunately, in my opinion and others, State Attorney King's Mission, Vision and Values statements were only words since apparently, he did not emulate them. I had high hopes that perhaps this unbelievable nightmare that we (the Baker family) have been living for close to a year, would finally come to a successful conclusion. Sadly, I was wrong and what I thought was a very professional prosecutor's office turned out to be, in my opinion, one of the worst prosecutor's offices that I have ever dealt with in a forty-year law enforcement career. But do not take my word for it, review everything that follows and draw your own conclusions.

04/11/19

11:21 AM Email to Detective Cohen requesting an update on the date for a meeting with the State Attorney which he was trying to schedule.

04/18/19

Email to Detective Cohen outlining my available dates for meeting with State Attorney. Reply "…he is still reviewing the documents, so no tentative appointment set yet."

04/30/19

Email to Detective Cohen telling him that the court ruled Paul incapacitated yesterday and the court accepted the letter from Paul's doctor that Paul's diagnosis of Alzheimer's Dementia was confirmed in November 2015 (before they married).

Reply—Information passed to State Attorney. (I am waiting for him to set up the appointment."

05/06/19

11:13 AM Received call from Detective Cohen who told me that the Assistant State Attorney Eric Rauba did not believe that he had enough to charge Sandy with a crime. I told him that was not acceptable to me until he at least sits down with me and reviews the documentation. He told me the prosecutor would call me. I asked him to please leave the case open until we spoke.

05/08/19

9:07 AM Call from Erik Rauba. Had some questions for me. Unfortunately, I missed the call.

9:47 AM I returned his call and the receptionist said he was on the phone and she would let him know I returned his call.

05/09/19

9:04 AM Again called State Attorney's Office. Eric in court and would return call.

05/10/19

9:45 AM Sent update email to Detective Cohen.

1:29 PM Called State Attorney's Office. Left message with Kimberly to have Eric return my call.

05/14/19

9:12 AM Called State Attorney's Office again. Erik was on the phone. Left message with receptionist to have him return the call.

12:38 PM Received a call from Detective Cohen asking if I had talked to Eric Rauba from the State Attorney's Office. I told him that he called me last Wednesday and left a message that he had several questions for me. I told him that I had called him back four times, but I have not heard back from him yet. He told me that he would give him a call and try to set up a meeting. He also told me again that Erik was not sure that he could win this case and was not sure he would charge Sandy. I again stated that I would like a chance to present all my documentation to both of them before a final decision is made. Detective Cohen stated he would call me back once he spoke to Eric.

05/16/19

State AttorneyMay 16, 2019 11:53 AM
From: crbaker

A Case Study Of Elder Abuse And Exploitation In Florida

To:jcohen
Detective Cohen
Were you able to talk to Erik about a meeting? I did not want to call his office again until I touched base with you.
Thank you,
Carl

Jeffrey Cohen
Subject: State Attorney
Sent: Thursday, May 16, 2019 11:53:30 AM (UTC-05:00) Eastern Time (US & Canada) was read on Thursday, May 16, 2019 12:02:20 PM (UTC-05:00) Eastern Time (US & Canada).

State AttorneyMay 16, 2019 2:55 PM
From: jcohen
To:crbaker

It is still in the works.

05/23/19

From: CARL BAKER
Sent: Thursday, May 23, 2019 12:11 PM
To: Jeffrey Cohen
Subject: Update

Detective Cohen

Do we have a meeting date yet? I know you are probably frustrated as well since you are carrying an open case. I fully realize that Erik certainly has higher priorities than meeting with us, but this meeting has been pending for over a month and a half. I am requesting only 30 minutes of his time. There are some aspects to this case that both of you need to know before deciding on prosecution.

As an alternative, I would be happy to sit down with you and then at least you would have all the information for your report. If that works for you, just let me know.

Again, I want to thank you for all your help and keeping me up to date.

Carl Baker

RE: UpdateMay 23, 2019 5:22 PM
From: jcohen
To:crbaker
He was in court all day today and couldn't be reached. I would prefer to meet with you in the company of the attorney.

From: CARL BAKER
Sent: 8:50 AM
To: Jeffrey Cohen
Subject: Fwd: Baker Trusts

Detective Cohen
The enclosed chart hopefully simplifies the changes that Paul's

wife (Sandy) made in his trust. I thought this may simplify our discussion with Erik. Please feel free to forward a copy to him.
(Note to reader: See Appendix B.)

Three things to remember:

Paul's trust was created two years before they were married and was not a marital asset.

The only valid trust is the 2014 trust which was dated when Paul's thoughts were quite clear. The 2019 trust is generally the same as the 2014 trust with one notable change of successor trustees to Paul's children.

None of the changes that Sandy made in the 09/20/18 and the 12/03/18 trusts were in compliance with the antenuptial agreement.

There are several other items not related to the trust that we need to discuss at our meeting.

Thank you.
Carl Baker

Baker Trusts
June 3, 2019 9:56 AM
From: jcohen
To: crbaker

I have passed it along to him...he isn't in today. I have added your document to the case file.

State Attorney's Office

06/10/19

9:20 AM—Called Erik Rauba and spoke to Kimberly. Eric was not available, and Kimberly took all the case information and the reason for my call (meeting) and stated she would give him my message and he would return the call.

Note: For the record, Erik Rauba never returned any of the numerous calls I made to his office. Customer service is obviously not a high priority at the State Attorney's Office.

06/17/19

9:30 AM Finally met with Detective Jeff Cohen, Assistant State Attorney Erik Rauba and his supervisor Mark Simpson at the SCSO Building in Wildwood.

In retrospect, I was not really encouraged after this morning's meeting which lasted two hours. The good news is that they have not yet made a final decision on prosecution. The State Attorney said he would like more time to review all the new information he got today and check some additional information before he decided. He did state that he would check her phone records.

Basically, the supervising attorney said that he thought Sandy's actions were morally and ethically wrong, but he did not see a violation of the exploitation statute because Sandy had not used any of Paul's Trust funds to benefit herself. He does not deny that this was the direction she was taking, but our intervention prevented the crime from being committed. FYI, I disagree with this and told him that the change in successor trustee and the change in the residence (she can live there as long as she wants instead of 12 months) temporarily deprives Mark and Allyne of 1/2 the property or funds of a sale. This matches the wording of the statute which states, "Knowingly obtaining or using, or endeavoring to obtain or use, an elderly person's or disabled adult's funds… ". That is like saying if you steal a car and do not drive it, you cannot be held accountable.

My next argument was Sandy buying herself a brand-new car after Paul got lost and Sandy later turning in his driver's license. Their response was that it was in both their names and Paul signed the contract. Again, Sandy knew Paul would sign anything Sandy put in front of him.

Several months ago, I asked Paul if he remembered signing for a new car. He did not.

I also brought up Sandy's accident on 02/08/14. Sandy's husband, Ralph was coming home from the nursing home on next day, Sunday, February 9th. Sandy states that she picked up Ralph on Saturday morning from the Villages Rehab and Nursing Center on Route 466 to "go see a movie". At the first major intersection (Morse Boulevard), Sandy made a left-hand turn to go south on Morse Blvd., failing to yield to the traffic and a GMC Suburban struck Ralph's door. He had severe injuries, never again returned home, and died in the rehab center. Ralph's family had always believed that Sandy's actions were intentional and she was responsible for his death. Basically, they (State Attorneys) were not interested.

Update July 1, 2019 9:09 AM
From: crbaker
To: jcohen

Detective Cohen

Just checking to see if you had heard anything from Erik regarding phone records or his review of the case.

Thank you.
Carl Baker

From: "jcohen" <jcohen@sumtercountysheriff.org>
To: "crbaker501" <crbaker501@centurylink.net>
Sent: Monday, July 1, 2019 9:33:47 AM
Subject: RE: Update

He still said the case is not criminal and is still working on the things he told you about the day of the meeting.

Status
July 15, 2019 9:48 AM
From: crbaker
To: jcohen

Detective Cohen
Just my biweekly check on the case. Anything from Erik?

Thank you.
Carl Baker

From: "jcohen"
To: "crbaker501"
Sent: Monday, July 15, 2019 10:18:20 AM
Subject: RE: Status

The case has been closed out as being civil in nature.

Note: Without prosecution, the law is nothing but words on a page, in a book, which sits on a shelf.

This decision was appealed.

Following is Detective Cohen's investigative report:

Carl R. Baker

Incident Report

SUMTER COUNTY SO
7361 POWELL RD. WILDWOOD FL 34785

Report Date / Time	Report Number	Report Case/CAD Number	Reporting Officer Rank / ID	Reporting Officer Name
03/25/2019 12:25:12	SCSO19OFF001495 (07)	SCSO19OFF001495 / SCSO19CAD028093	DEPUTY / 60342	BOLLING, JAMES CODY
Originating Agency ORI	Reported to Agency Date	Occur Date Range	Jurisdiction	Status: CLOSED
FL0600000	03/25/2019 09:49:41	08/01/2018 09:49:41 - 03/25/2019 11:00:00	WITHIN JURISDICTION	Clearance:
Offense Description				
4402 INFORMATION/INTELLIGENCE, OTHER				

LOCATION(S)

County	Location Type	Location Description						
SUMTER	INCIDENT LOCATION							
Street Number	Street		Apt/Lot/Bldg	City		State	Zip Code	Phone Number	Ext.
1816	WADING HERON WAY			WILDWOOD		FL	34785		

Person: OTHER PERSON

First Name	Middle Name	Last Name	Suffix	Race	Sex	Height	Weight	Hair	Eyes
JOHN	PAUL	BAKER		WHITE	MALE	602	190	BAL	BRO
MNI #	SSN	Date of Birth	Age	Place of Birth		Drivers License or other ID		State	ID Type
SCSO19MNI006569		08/06/1946	72	NEW YORK, NY, USA		B260475462060		FL	E

Addresses
• Residence / 3723 MANGO CT, FL 32163 /

Person: OTHER PERSON

First Name	Middle Name	Last Name	Suffix	Race	Sex	Height	Weight	Hair	Eyes
CARL	ROBERT	BAKER		WHITE	MALE	601	200	GRY	BRO
MNI #	SSN	Date of Birth	Age	Place of Birth		Drivers License or other ID		State	ID Type
SCSO19MNI007176		07/14/1947	71	NEW YORK, NY, USA		B260136472540		FL	E

Addresses
• Residence / 1816 WADING HERON WAY, THE VILLAGES, FL 32162 / 352-674-0340

Person: OTHER PERSON

First Name	Middle Name	Last Name	Suffix	Race	Sex	Height	Weight	Hair	Eyes
SANDY		BAKER							
MNI #	SSN	Date of Birth	Age	Place of Birth		Drivers License or other ID		State	ID Type
SCSO19MNI007177									

Addresses
• Residence / 3723 MANGO CT, THE VILLAGES, FL 32163 / 517-974-2494

Business: OTHER

Business Name	MBI #	Phone Number 1	Ext 1	Phone Number 2	Ext 2
BB&T BANK	SCSO15MBI001972	352-561-3026			

A Case Study Of Elder Abuse And Exploitation In Florida

Report Date / Time 03/25/2019 12:25:12	Report Number SCSO19OFF001495 (07)	Report Case/CAD Number SCSO19OFF001495 / SCSO19CAD028093	Reporting Officer Rank / ID DEPUTY / 60342	Reporting Officer Name BOLLING, JAMES CODY
Originating Agency ORI FL0600000	Reported to Agency Date 03/25/2019 09:49:41	Occur Date Range 08/01/2018 09:49:41 - 03/25/2019 11:00:00	Jurisdiction WITHIN JURISDICTION	Status: CLOSED Clearance:
Offense Description 4402 INFORMATION/INTELLIGENCE, OTHER			

County SUMTER	Street Number 3340	Address WEDGEWOOD LANE	Apt/Lot/Bldg	City THE VILLAGES	State FL	Zip Code 32162
Other Information						

Narrative: INITIAL

Narrative Date/Time 03/25/2019 15:01:48	Narrative Synopsis DEPUTY BOLLING #172		
Reporting Officer BRALEY, VICKI	Officer Rank CIVILIAN	Officer ID No 60539	Officer Org/Unit
Officer Signature	Officer Agency SUMTER COUNTY SO		

On 3/25/2017, at approximately 9:57 A.M., I responded to 1816 Heron Way, The Villages, Florida, located in Sumter County, in reference to a possible theft.

Upon arrival, I made contact with the complainant, Mr. Carl Baker. Mr. Baker stated his brother, Mr. John Baker, had been taken advantage of by his wife and she stole $220,000.00 from his bank account. Mr. Carl Baker advised me both verbally and in a written sworn statement that his brother, John Baker, had been married to Ms. Sandy Baker for approximately two years. The two met while she was still married to her former husband. Mr. Carl Baker said that his brother, John Baker, was deemed incapacitated to handle any financial or legal matters as of 8/27/2018. Mr. Carl Baker also advised that he held a power of attorney for John Baker's estate and finances since 8/18/2018 and that Sandy had no rights to his finances.

Mr. Carl Baker provided me with a copy of the cashier's check #8539977 in the amount of $220,000.00 from BB&T bank that was cashed on 9/21/2018. The check was written and signed by Mr. John Baker.

Mr. Carl Baker believes given the circumstances of his brother's mental status, along with Sandy's actions and the short time they've been married, she is taking advantage of his brother and is exploiting him. Mr. Carl Baker is adamant about prosecution on Ms. Baker stating she is guilty of exploiting the elderly regardless if the two are married or not.

Mr. Carl Baker signed an intent to prosecute and was explained and signed for a Victim's Right's Pamphlet. Mr. Carl Baker also provided paperwork to include a pre-typed statement as well as several documents substantiating Ms. Baker's character and ill intent.

This case will be forwarded to the Sumter County Sheriff's Office Criminal Investigation Division for further review.

This report was transcribed for Deputy Bolling by STAR Reporter Vicki Braley.

Incident Report

Carl R. Baker

Report Date / Time	Report Number	Report Case/CAD Number	Reporting Officer Rank / ID	Reporting Officer Name
03/25/2019 12:25:12	SCSO19OFF001495 (07)	SCSO19OFF001495 / SCSO19CAD028093	DEPUTY / 60342	BOLLING, JAMES CODY
Originating Agency ORI	Reported to Agency Date	Occur Date Range	Jurisdiction	Status: CLOSED
FL0600000	03/25/2019 09:49:41	08/01/2018 09:49:41 - 03/25/2019 11:00:00	WITHIN JURISDICTION	Clearance:
Offense Description				
4402 INFORMATION/INTELLIGENCE, OTHER				

Narrative: INVESTIGATIVE

Narrative Date/Time	Narrative Synopsis			
03/27/2019 17:27:21				
Reporting Officer		Officer Rank	Officer ID No	Officer Org/Unit
COHEN, JEFFREY A		DEPUTY	60134	SCSOINVESTIGATIONS
Officer Signature	*Jeffrey A. Cohen*	Officer Agency		
		SUMTER COUNTY SO		

On Wednesday, March 27, 2019, I received this case for review. Carl Baker reported that his brother was being financially exploited by his wife. Robert Baker has been diagnosed with dementia and deemed by a physician to make any financial decisions for himself. Carl contends that his brother's wife has visited an attorney in Ocala and changed legal documents regarding her husband's finances as well as Power of Attorney. A check in the amount of $220,000 was allegedly cashed by Ms. Baker after her husband had been deemed incompetent.

I called Carl and he stated that his brother now resides with him, but his brother's wife is still residing in the residence. Carl has gotten all but $12,000 of the $220,000 back and is currently involved with civil litigation with his brother's wife. he told me that the check had been cashed at the BB&T branch in Colony Plaza. I informed him that I would contact the bank to try and obtain video surveillance footage and that I would discuss this case with the State Attorney's Public Interest Unit in Ocala. This case is still active at this time.

DETECTIVE JEFFREY COHEN #60134

Narrative: INVESTIGATIVE

Narrative Date/Time	Narrative Synopsis			
03/29/2019 09:23:08				
Reporting Officer		Officer Rank	Officer ID No	Officer Org/Unit
COHEN, JEFFREY A		DEPUTY	60134	SCSOINVESTIGATIONS
Officer Signature	*Jeffrey A. Cohen*	Officer Agency		
		SUMTER COUNTY SO		

On Friday, March 29, 2019, I called the complainant and advised him that based on my conversation with the State Attorney's Public Interest Unit, he needed to provide notarized copies of his brother's pre-nuptial agreement as well as any documents discussing the allocation of his brother's assets that were decided prior to his marriage to his current wife. The attorney with the PIU Unit noted the intricacies in this case due to the victim being married

A Case Study Of Elder Abuse And Exploitation In Florida

Report Date / Time 03/25/2019 12:25:12	Report Number SCSO19OFF001495 (07)	Report Case/CAD Number SCSO19OFF001495 / SCSO19CAD028093	Reporting Officer Rank / ID DEPUTY / 60342	Reporting Officer Name BOLLING, JAMES CODY
Originating Agency ORI FL0600000	Reported to Agency Date 03/25/2019 09:49:41	Occur Date Range 08/01/2018 09:49:41 - 03/25/2019 11:00:00	Jurisdiction WITHIN JURISDICTION	Status: CLOSED Clearance:
Offense Description 4402 INFORMATION/INTELLIGENCE, OTHER				

to the person accused of exploiting him. I will try and arrange a meeting with the State Attorney and complainant once the required legal documents are obtained in order to see how best to proceed. This case is still active at this time.

DETECTIVE JEFFREY COHEN #60134

Narrative: INVESTIGATIVE

Narrative Date/Time 05/06/2019 11:19:59	Narrative Synopsis			
Reporting Officer COHEN, JEFFREY A		Officer Rank DEPUTY	Officer ID No 60134	Officer Org/Unit SCSOINVESTIGATIONS
Officer Signature *Jeffrey A. Cohen*		Officer Agency SUMTER COUNTY SO		

I have continuously been in contact with both the complainant, Carl Baker, and the State Attorney's Public Interest Unit regarding this case. As it stands now, the State Attorney's Office does not see this as a criminal case based on their review of all submitted documents and facts. The attorney will contact the complainant to discuss with them their decision and I am leaving this case open until that happens, but will most likely be closing this case at that time.

DETECTIVE JEFFREY COHEN #60134

Narrative: INVESTIGATIVE

Narrative Date/Time 06/03/2019 09:57:42	Narrative Synopsis			
Reporting Officer COHEN, JEFFREY A		Officer Rank DEPUTY	Officer ID No 60134	Officer Org/Unit SCSOINVESTIGATIONS
Officer Signature *Jeffrey A. Cohen*		Officer Agency SUMTER COUNTY SO		

On Monday, June 3, 2019, I received an e-mail from Carl Baker in reference to this case. I included the document contained in his e-mail as a report attachment and forwarded it to the State Attorney currently reviewing

Carl R. Baker

Report Date / Time	Report Number	Report Case/CAD Number	Reporting Officer Rank / ID	Reporting Officer Name
03/25/2019 12:25:12	SCSO19OFF001495 (07)	SCSO19OFF001495 / SCSO19CAD028093	DEPUTY / 60342	BOLLING, JAMES CODY
Originating Agency ORI	Reported to Agency Date	Occur Date Range	Jurisdiction	Status: CLOSED
FL0600000	03/25/2019 09:49:41	08/01/2018 09:49:41 - 03/25/2019 11:00:00	WITHIN JURISDICTION	Clearance:
Offense Description				
4402 INFORMATION/INTELLIGENCE, OTHER				

all the other documents provided. This case is still active at this time.

DETECTIVE JEFFREY COHEN #60134

Narrative: INVESTIGATIVE

Narrative Date/Time	Narrative Synopsis			
06/14/2019 11:03:01				
Reporting Officer		Officer Rank	Officer ID No	Officer Org/Unit
COHEN, JEFFREY A		DEPUTY	60134	SCSO\INVESTIGATIONS
Officer Signature	*Jeffrey A. Cohen*	Officer Agency		
		SUMTER COUNTY SO		

On Friday, June 14, 2019, I was contacted by the State Attorney's Public Interest Unit in Ocala and advised they would be responding to our agency's Main Office on Monday, June 17th @9:30am to meet with Carl Baker. I called him and advised him of the appointment. The goal is to have the SAO speak with Carl about his allegations and their decision as to the case being civil or criminal.

DETECTIVE JEFFREY COHEN #60134

Narrative: INVESTIGATIVE

Narrative Date/Time	Narrative Synopsis			
06/17/2019 13:18:39				
Reporting Officer		Officer Rank	Officer ID No	Officer Org/Unit
COHEN, JEFFREY A		DEPUTY	60134	SCSO\INVESTIGATIONS
Officer Signature	*Jeffrey A. Cohen*	Officer Agency		
		SUMTER COUNTY SO		

On Monday, June 17, 2019, I met with Carl Baker and Assistant State Attorneys Eric Rauba and Mark Simpson at our agency's Main Office to discuss this case. Mr. Baker mentioned to the SAO's his belief that his brother's wife is financially exploiting him and presented his case to them to support his belief. Mr. Baker also presented additional paperwork which I included as a report attachment.

A Case Study Of Elder Abuse And Exploitation In Florida

Report Date / Time 03/25/2019 12:25:12	Report Number SCSO19OFF001495 (07)	Report Case/CAD Number SCSO19OFF001495 / SCSO19CAD028093	Reporting Officer Rank / ID DEPUTY / 60342	Reporting Officer Name BOLLING, JAMES CODY
Originating Agency ORI FL0600000	Reported to Agency Date 03/25/2019 09:49:41	Occur Date Range 08/01/2018 09:49:41 - 03/25/2019 11:00:00	Jurisdiction WITHIN JURISDICTION	Status: CLOSED Clearance:
Offense Description 4402 INFORMATION/INTELLIGENCE, OTHER				

The SAO's advised Mr. Baker that money was never put in the wife's control and Mr. Baker confirmed that she never spent any of the money. Another troubling occurrence is that although Mr. Baker presented a letter from a physician stating that his brother lacks all mental capacity to make any decisions for himself, he has taken his brother to an attorney to make financial changes, which would go against the doctor's letter.

At this time, the attorneys are considering Mr. Baker's allegations to be civil and not criminal in nature and they advised him of such. They have to look at a couple of more things so this case is still active at this time.

DETECTIVE JEFFREY COHEN #60134

Narrative: INVESTIGATIVE

Narrative Date/Time 06/27/2019 16:27:55	Narrative Synopsis		
Reporting Officer COHEN, JEFFREY A		Officer Rank DEPUTY	Officer ID No 60134	Officer Org/Unit SCSO/INVESTIGATIONS
Officer Signature	*Jeffrey A. Cohen*	Officer Agency SUMTER COUNTY SO	

The State Attorney's Office has made a definitive decision that this case is not criminal and no crimes have occurred. As a result, I will be closing and clearing it.

DETECTIVE JEFFREY COHEN #60134

Officer: Approving Supervisor (Supplement 07)

Officer Name HAVENS, ELMER L	Officer Rank SERGEANT	Officer ID No 60017	Officer Agency SUMTER COUNTY SO
Approval Date / Time 06/28/2019 09:14:57	Officer Signature	*Elmer Havens*	

Incident Report

Carl R. Baker

Report Date / Time	Report Number	Report Case/CAD Number	Reporting Officer Rank / ID	Reporting Officer Name
03/25/2019 12:25:12	SCSO19OFF001495 (07)	SCSO19OFF001495 / SCSO19CAD028093	DEPUTY / 60342	BOLLING, JAMES CODY
Originating Agency ORI	Reported to Agency Date	Occur Date Range	Jurisdiction	Status: CLOSED
FL0600000	03/25/2019 09:49:41	08/01/2018 09:49:41 - 03/25/2019 11:00:00	WITHIN JURISDICTION	Clearance:

Offense Description
4402 INFORMATION/INTELLIGENCE, OTHER

Sup #	Officer Name Rank / ID #	Involvement On Report / Reporting Role	Officer Agency Org/Unit
01	BOLLING, JAMES CODY DEPUTY 60342		SUMTER COUNTY SO SCSO\PATROL
01	COHEN, JEFFREY A DEPUTY 60134	REPORTING OFFICER	SUMTER COUNTY SO SCSO\INVESTIGATIONS
04	MULLINS, JOEL A SERGEANT 60122		SUMTER COUNTY SO SCSO\INVESTIGATIONS
01	SMITH, WILLIAM DEAN SERGEANT 60074		SUMTER COUNTY SO SCSO\PATROL
02	HAVENS, ELMER L SERGEANT 60017	APPROVING SUPERVISOR	SUMTER COUNTY SO SCSO\INVESTIGATIONS

The undersigned certifies and swears that he/she has just and reasonable grounds to believe that the above named Defendant, committed violation(s), of law, on the below date(s) and time(s), as listed in the narratives associated with this report:
Officer: Reporting Officer (Supplement07)

Officer Name	Office Rank	Officer ID No	Sworn and subscribed before me, the undersigned authority
BOLLING, JAMES CODY	DEPUTY	60342	This the _____ day of _____, _____
Officer Agency			DEPUTY OF THE COURT, NOTARY OR LAW ENFORCEMENT OFFICER
SUMTER COUNTY SO			

Officer Signature: *bCyRl.*

A Case Study Of Elder Abuse And Exploitation In Florida

Over my career, I have reviewed hundreds of investigative reports and I found myself doing it again when I received a copy of Detective Cohen's report. Remember, the crime alleged here is a felony of the first degree with a possibility of up to thirty years in prison. I am not nor would I advocate any sentence close to that. I mention it to show the reader the seriousness that Florida has placed on exploitation of elderly or disabled adults by making it the highest felony. Given the seriousness of the crime, I make the following points after reviewing Detective Cohen's report:

• *Detective Cohen never interviewed Paul who is the victim of this crime. Yes, Paul has Alzheimer's and during the period of this investigation the court found him incapacitated. I still believe in the long-standing rule that every victim be interviewed face to face during the investigation. Paul can still carry on a conversation, tell you how he feels about the situation and may actually provide some information. It is always better for an investigator to put a face with a name, especially a victim. Otherwise, they are dehumanizing crime and its victims.*

• *Even though my home, where Paul lives with my wife and me, is only several miles and 5 minutes from his office, I never met Detective Cohen until June when I went to his office to meet with the State Attorney. Detective Cohen did all his communicating by phone or email. Additionally, he never spoke to my wife or my brother Bruce, who have been as much involved in this case as I have.*

- Although it was not in the report, Detective Cohen told me that he attempted to interview Sandy by phone and she referred him to her attorney. Interviewing a suspect in a felony case by phone was never allowed in all my years of policing. Naturally, she would not talk to him and he missed his chance to look her in the face and watch her reaction and gestures. If the suspect were 1000 miles away, we would not ever consider making a phone call. We would either send an investigator or contact the nearest agency and brief them on the case and have one of their detectives interview the suspect and send us a report. I truly hope this is not an acceptable practice in the Sumter County Sheriff's Office.

- On page 3 of the report, Detective Cohen wrote, "Robert Baker has been diagnosed with dementia...". My brother's name is John Paul Baker. Robert is my middle name. Detective Cohen probably would not have made this mistake if he had taken the time to speak to my brother.

- On page 6 of the report, Detective Cohen wrote the following: "Another troubling occurrence is that although Mr. Baker presented a letter from a physician stating that his brother lacks all mental capacity to make a decision for himself, he has taken his brother to make financial changes, which would go against the doctor's letter." First, I told Detective Cohen that I did not get a copy of this letter until after Paul's trust was returned to the original language he used before he was incapacitated. This is all explained in detail in my September 19th memorandum *to State Attorney Brad King. Secondly, it appears that from the beginning of this entire process, Detective Cohen and the State Attorney's Office ignored the wording in the statute, were negative about prosecuting this case, were quick to criticize my actions and defend Sandy's actions. Again, no one is holding Sandy accountable.*

In conclusion, I did not see evidence in the report that Detective Cohen ever left his office to do any investigation for this case. If this is the new policing in America, the police departments will lose the support of the citizens they have been sworn to protect and serve.

On the other hand, as previously stated, I believe that Detective Larry Thompson is a good cop. The same goes for all the officers that Sandy sent to our home to see if Paul was kidnapped or not being fed or whatever. She also had them deliver Paul's medicine and other necessities. All those officers that came to our home were very professional and a credit to the Sumter County Sheriff's Office. Thank you for your service!

There is no way that I could not appeal their decision that this case was civil and not criminal. For whatever reason, the State Attorney's Office just wanted the case and me to go away and their response was not acceptable to me. At a minimum, I deserved some sort of reasoning for their decision. I sent the following letter to Mr. King:

July 17, 2019
Mr. Brad King

Carl R. Baker

State Attorney
Fifth Judicial Circuit
State Attorney's Office
110 NW 1st Avenue, Suite 500
Ocala, Florida 34475
RE: Case Number SCSO19OFF001495
Dear State Attorney King:

On March 25, 2019, I filed a criminal complaint with the Sumter County Sheriff's Office against Sandra Baker, who married my brother, John Paul Baker three years ago. They have been separated, living apart since January of 2019. Paul has Alzheimer's and his wife has exploited him several times. The final straw was last August when she blocked him from all contact with his family and removed $220,000 from his trust account which was established years before they were married and is a non-marital asset protected by Paul's trust and an antenuptial agreement.

Detective Jeff Cohen was assigned to the case and he has been working with Erik Rauba from your office. I have been providing them with any requested information and /or documents throughout the investigation.

On June 14, 2019, Erik Rauba and Mark Simpson were kind enough to meet with both Detective Cohen and me to go over the case. In the end, your office "considered the allegations to be civil and not criminal in nature" and the case was closed.

With all due respect, I disagree with this decision. After spending 40 years of my life in law enforcement and witnessing and documenting all that has transpired, I find it hard to believe that all of Sandra Baker's actions were civil and not criminal.

I researched the statutes and I believe the facts of this case meet all the of elements of Section 825.103, Exploitation of an elderly person or disabled adult. During our meeting, Mark Simpson stated that although he agreed that what Sandra did was wrong, but since she had not yet taken any money for herself, there was no crime. He also stated that there was no doubt as to Sandra's motives, but because Paul's family intervened before Sandra used Paul's assets to benefit herself, she couldn't be charged. Note that the statute states "or endeavoring to obtain or use." Webster's dictionary defines endeavor as "to try to do" or 'to make an earnest attempt", which explains her conduct perfectly. The statute seems very clear to me that Sandra can and should be charged. This is one of the better exploitation statutes in the country and by adding the wording stated above, the legislature eliminated an obvious loophole. Also, Sandra changed Paul's trust where she would have complete control of his non-marital assets once he was found incapacitated and she also changed the trust to allow her to live in the residence for as long as she chooses which was different than the original trust and antenuptial agreement and would "temporarily deprive" Paul's children of the funds when the house was sold within one year of Paul's death.

In Paul's trusts prior to the September 18, 2018 trust (created by Sandra), all of Paul's residue of his estate would be distributed to his children, Mark and Allyne, in accordance with the provisions of the trust. When Sandra changed Paul's trust, she also had Paul change his last Will and Testament to state that if Paul's trust agreement is not in existence on the date of his death, Paul "gives, devises and bequeaths all tangible property and all the residue of his estate" to Sandra if she survives him. Clearly there would be no need for such a change unless she intended to have Paul's trust revoked prior to his death.

So, in summary, you have a woman who dates a man with Alzheimer's dementia while she is still married to her second husband, who is in hospice as the result of injuries from a car accident in which she was charged for failing to yield the right of way. Before they even marry, she starts plotting to take his non-marital assets. After a blatant attempt to change his trust for her benefit failed due to objections from his family, she shops for another attorney who will change Paul's trust making her the successor trustee, gives her power of attorney and distributes the property differently than stated in the antenuptial agreement. She then isolates Paul from his family by taking his phone from him giving him her iPhone with a pass code that only she knows so she can control his calls. Then she blocks some family members from calling him. Next, she takes $220,000 out of his saving trust account and moves it to her bank and links it to her checking account so that she can move money between accounts. (By the way, Paul is totally computer illiterate.) From my years of experience, this is a textbook case of exploitation. The fact that your office sees this as a civil matter, quite candidly, makes no sense to me.

I respectfully request that you review this case to include all the documents that I provided to your office. We can win this case. I have witnesses that are more than willing to testify and during my career I have made hundreds of arrests and testified in over a hundred trials. With no prosecution, Sandra will just move on to her next victim.

Should you decide that you are comfortable with the decision to not prosecute, please make any recommendation for changes in the statute that may help another family find justice in a similar situation. If changes need to be made, I will contact Attorney General Ashley Moody and be a very strong advocate to amend the statute.

Thank you.
signed
Carl R. Baker

For the reader's convenience, a copy of Florida Statute 825.103 follows:

2018 Florida Statutes
Title XLVI CRIMES
Chapter 825 ABUSE, NEGLECT, AND EXPLOITATION OF ELDERLY PERSONS AND DISABLED ADULTS
Entire Chapter

SECTION 103
Exploitation of an elderly person or disabled adult; penalties.
825.103 Exploitation of an elderly person or disabled adult; penalties.—

(1) "Exploitation of an elderly person or disabled adult" means:
(a) Knowingly obtaining or using, or endeavoring to obtain or use, an elderly person's or disabled adult's funds, assets, or property with the intent to temporarily or permanently deprive the elderly person or disabled adult of the use, benefit, or possession of the funds, assets, or property, or to benefit someone other than the elderly person or disabled

adult, by a person who:

1. Stands in a position of trust and confidence with the elderly person or disabled adult; or
2. Has a business relationship with the elderly person or disabled adult;

(b) Obtaining or using, endeavoring to obtain or use, or conspiring with another to obtain or use an elderly person's or disabled adult's funds, assets, or property with the intent to temporarily or permanently deprive the elderly person or disabled adult of the use, benefit, or possession of the funds, assets, or property, or to benefit someone other than the elderly person or disabled adult, by a person who knows or reasonably should know that the elderly person or disabled adult lacks the capacity to consent;

(c) Breach of a fiduciary duty to an elderly person or disabled adult by the person's guardian, trustee who is an individual, or agent under a power of attorney which results in an unauthorized appropriation, sale, or transfer of property. An unauthorized appropriation under this paragraph occurs when the elderly person or disabled adult does not receive the reasonably equivalent financial value in goods or services, or when the fiduciary violates any of these duties:

1. For agents appointed under chapter 709:
a. Committing fraud in obtaining their appointments;
b. Abusing their powers;
c. Wasting, embezzling, or intentionally mismanaging the assets of the principal or beneficiary; or

d. Acting contrary to the principal's sole benefit or best interest; or

2. For guardians and trustees who are individuals and who are appointed under chapter 736 or chapter 744:

a. Committing fraud in obtaining their appointments;

b. Abusing their powers; or

c. Wasting, embezzling, or intentionally mismanaging the assets of the ward or beneficiary of the trust;

(d) Misappropriating, misusing, or transferring without authorization money belonging to an elderly person or disabled adult from an account in which the elderly person or disabled adult placed the funds, owned the funds, and was the sole contributor or payee of the funds before the misappropriation, misuse, or unauthorized transfer. This paragraph only applies to the following types of accounts:

1. Personal accounts;

2. Joint accounts created with the intent that only the elderly person or disabled adult enjoys all rights, interests, and claims to moneys deposited into such account; or

3. Convenience accounts created in accordance with s. 655.80; or

(e) Intentionally or negligently failing to effectively use an elderly person's or disabled adult's income and assets for the necessities required for that person's support and maintenance, by a caregiver or a person who stands in a position of trust and confidence with the elderly person or disabled adult.

(2) Any inter vivos transfer of money or property valued

in excess of $10,000 at the time of the transfer, whether in a single transaction or multiple transactions, by a person age 65 or older to a nonrelative whom the transferor knew for fewer than 2 years before the first transfer and for which the transferor did not receive the reasonably equivalent financial value in goods or services creates a permissive presumption that the transfer was the result of exploitation.

(a) This subsection applies regardless of whether the transfer or transfers are denoted by the parties as a gift or loan, except that it does not apply to a valid loan evidenced in writing that includes definite repayment dates. However, if repayment of any such loan is in default, in whole or in part, for more than 65 days, the presumption of this subsection applies.

(b) This subsection does not apply to:

1. Persons who are in the business of making loans.

2. Bona fide charitable donations to nonprofit organizations that qualify for tax exempt status under the Internal Revenue Code.

(c) In a criminal case to which this subsection applies, if the trial is by jury, jurors shall be instructed that they may, but are not required to, draw an inference of exploitation upon proof beyond a reasonable doubt of the facts listed in this subsection. The presumption of this subsection imposes no burden of proof on the defendant.

(3)(a) If the funds, assets, or property involved in the exploitation of the elderly person or disabled adult is valued at $50,000 or more, the offender commits a felony of the first *degree, punishable as provided in s. 775.082, s. 775.083, or s. 775.084.*

(b) If the funds, assets, or property involved in the exploitation of the elderly person or disabled adult is valued at $10,000 or more, but less than $50,000, the offender commits a felony of the second degree, punishable as provided in s. 775.082, s. 775.083, or s. 775.084.

(c) If the funds, assets, or property involved in the exploitation of an elderly person or disabled adult is valued at less than $10,000, the offender commits a felony of the third degree, punishable as provided in s. 775.082, s. 775.083, or s. 775.084.

(4) If a person is charged with financial exploitation of an elderly person or disabled adult that involves the taking of or loss of property valued at more than $5,000 and property belonging to a victim is seized from the defendant pursuant to a search warrant, the court shall hold an evidentiary hearing and determine, by a preponderance of the evidence, whether the defendant unlawfully obtained the victim's property. If the court finds that the property was unlawfully obtained, the court may order it returned to the victim for restitution purposes before trial on the charge. This determination is inadmissible in evidence at trial on the charge and does not give rise to any inference that the defendant has committed an offense under this section.

History.—s. 4, ch. 95-158; s. 5, ch. 96-322; s. 1, ch. 97-78; s. 29, ch. 2009-223; s. 4, ch. 2014-200.

I waited three weeks and sent an email to Brad King as a follow-up on August 13th:

Sent: Tuesday, August 13, 2019 2:34 PM
To: Brad King
Subject: Fwd: Recent Correspondence

Mr. King
 My records show that you received my July 17th letter on July 22nd. Would you give me a time frame when I can expect a reply?
Thank you.
Carl R. Baker

Mr. King's reply:

From: "BKING"
To: "crbaker"
Sent: Friday, August 16, 2019 5:01:39 PM
Subject: RE: Recent Correspondence

Your letter went to Mark Simpson and he reviewed it with my chief assistant. I am in a capital homicide trial for the next three weeks, so I will not be reviewing it any time soon.

From: "crbaker
To: "BKING"
Sent: Saturday, August 17, 2019 9:36:35 AM

Subject: Re: Recent Correspondence

Thank you.

Brad King sent a response to my initial July 17th letter by email on August 26th:

From: "BKING"
To: "crbaker"
Sent: Monday, August 26, 2019 1:34:23 PM
Subject: RE: Recent Correspondence

Mr. Baker,
 Attached is a memo written by ASA Rauba who reviewed this case and spoke to you. I have read it and agree with the legal premise that it states. Assuming the facts are as stated, we cannot prove a criminal offense given Florida case law.

MEMORANDUM

DATE: August 16, 2019
TO: Mark Simpson
FROM: Erik Rauba
RE: Sandra Kaniewski S-2019-16863

This case was referred for review from Detective Cohen in Sumter County. The complainant, Carl Baker, reported his brother, Paul Baker, had been exploited by Paul's wife Sandra Kaniewski. The broad allegations were that Sandra cut off Paul's communication with his family and had him change his trust when he lacked capacity to do so. As a background, Sandra and Paul started dating in 2015 after Sandra's husband passed away. They both sold their individual houses and purchased a home together. Both their names are on the deed and each used their own money to buy half of the house. They decided to marry in 2016 and they executed an antenuptial agreement indicating that they would keep their preexisting bank accounts, property and most of their individual wealth separate. Paul had already established a trust in 2014 devising his wealth to his children Allyne Baker and Mark Baker. His power of attorney was Carl Baker. After his marriage to Sandra in 2016, he amended his existing trust to include the language that Sandra may continue to utilize the shared residence for up to 12 months following Paul's death. After that point, Sandra may buy out Paul's half if she wished to stay in the house. Otherwise, the house would be sold and Paul's half would be placed in the trust and dispersed to his beneficiaries.

Paul had been diagnosed with Alzheimer's Dementia in November of 2015 by Dr. Geliga. Although diagnosed with early onset dementia, it did not affect his capacity to make legal and fiscal decisions until 2018. On September 20, 2018, Paul Baker amended his trust again and changed the disbursement amounts to his beneficiaries and added a grandchild beneficiary Kayla Baker. He also changed the language in the trust allowing Sandra to stay in the residence for as long as she chooses upon his death. However, if she moves or dies, his 50% interest in the property would be distributed in accordance with his trust, which would go to his kids and grandchild. He also made Sandra successor trustee removing Carl Baker as trustee and making Bruce Baker a secondary successor trustee.

A Case Study Of Elder Abuse And Exploitation In Florida

In the fall of 2018, Carl Baker concerned over the way Sandra was isolating his brother from the family. He stated he went to the residence one day and Paul asked for help. He then took Paul to his house and refused to allow Sandra to see him anymore. Carl began managing Paul's affairs with his designated Power of Attorney and found the amended trust from September and that Sandra had moved his trust savings account from one bank to another. Carl then went to Dr. Geliga to request a letter stating Paul lacked capacity to handle his affairs and finances. With this letter, he was able to locate Carl's money. He then took Carl to his attorney and had him amend the trust language back to the original 2014 version. He received power of attorney and contacted law enforcement. A guardianship proceeding was initiated and the Court has ruled that Carl lacks capacity and appointed a temporary third-party guardian as Carl and Sandra are litigating against each other.

On June 17, 2019 Mark Simpson and myself met with Carl Baker to discuss the case with him. Carl reiterated that Sandra had stolen $220,000 from his brother. Upon further questioning it was revealed that Paul's money was moved from one bank to another. However, the new account that was opened only had Carl's name on it. Therefore, the money never left his possession. Sandra had no right or control over the money. Moreover, she never spent any of the money on herself. Carl was convinced that she was going to take the money in the future. Mr. Simpson explained to him that was a condition precedent and we had no evidence that she was going to take his money and or exploit him. A conviction cannot be sustained unless the evidence is inconsistent with any reasonable hypothesis of innocence. See State v. Law 559 So.2d 187 (Fla.1989)·, Dupree v. state, 705 So.2d 90, 94 (Fla. 4th DCA 1998). A motion for judgment of acquittal should be granted in a circumstantial evidence case if the state fails to present evidence from which the jury can exclude every reasonable hypothesis except that of guilt. It was represented that Sandra was not happy with BB&T and that is why she moved the money.

Importantly, the controlling trust document did not make Sandra a beneficiary. She was named as a trustee but if she failed to act in the best interest of Paul or the beneficiaries, then she would be in breach of her duties as trustee and would be removed. At this point Carl Baker informed us that he had taken his brother back to his attorney on January 23, 2019 and had Paul amend his trust again removing Sandra as successor trustee and removing the language about her remaining in the house until her death.

This was extremely concerning for Mr. Simpson and myself as he had been telling us and Detective Cohen that his brother had lacked capacity to change his trust since September of 2018 but had him change it in January of 2019. In addition, Carl was in possession of the letter from Paul's doctor dated August 27, 2018, stating Paul was incapacitated to handle any financial, legal or fiscal matters because of his dementia. He did exactly what he is accusing Sandra of doing.

We explained that the language giving Sandra a life estate would be difficult to prosecute. She paid for half of the house herself. They were married. Her benefit was simply a place to live. Paul's half would still be devised to his children. Moreover, the parties filed and received a homestead exemption for the property. Pursuant to Florida Statute 732.401, the homestead provision protects a spouse in several ways. First, it restrains the homeowner from conveying the property without the approval of their spouse, even if the property is entirely in the name of one spouse or was purchased entirely from funds of one spouse. The provision also prohibits a spouse from devising the property by will, if the homeowner is survived by a spouse or a minor child. If such a devise is made, it is deemed invalid, and the surviving spouse will enjoy a life estate with the remainder to the decedent's children.

Upon hearing that the allegations were not criminal, Carl Baker then informed us that Sandra had leased a new vehicle with the help of Paul. We explained the lease predated any medical conclusion that Paul lacked capacity. In addition, she had been leasing a vehicle for the last several years and that her leasing a new vehicle was consistent with prior purchases Paul and Sandra had made. Carl then insinuated that Sandra had intentionally killed her prior husband. We explained that was well outside of our investigation and we would not be able to help with that. We again reiterated the State could not go forward with prosecution.

On July 17, 2019, the State Attorney's Office received a letter from Mr. Carl requesting Mr. King review the case again. His main contention was that under Florida Statute 825.103 it includes the language "endeavoring to obtain to use." As noted at the meeting, there is a lack of evidence to prove Sandra intentionally endeavored to obtain Paul Bakers funds, assets or property. The facts are she moved his money from one bank to another. However, she did not comingle the funds, she did not spend the funds on herself and she is not named on the bank account. She has no control over his money. The next allegation is that Sandra temporarily deprived Paul's children of an inheritance by giving herself a life estate in the marital property. Pursuant to Florida law, if the home is homesteaded as a marital home, she is given a life estate in the home and no trust agreement can change her rights. Lastly, Carl states that when Paul changed his Last Will and Testament to include the language that if there is no trust in place upon Paul's death his estate would be given to Sandra. However, if someone dies without a trust in place or will devising the assets to other people, it would go to the surviving spouse under Florida law. This language is nothing different then reiterating the per stirpes inheritance law.

In conclusion, based on the evidence provided at this time, the State will not be going forward with prosecution.

It needs to be noted here that this memorandum in response to my letter, was written by Erik Rauba, the attorney assigned to the case. It appears to have been forwarded to his supervisor, Mark Simpson who approved it and forwarded it to Brad King who I assume read it and then emailed it to me. So, three attorneys reviewed and approved it before it was emailed. As you will see there were so many mistakes in this email that it is shocking that they cannot even get the names right, much less the facts. It is difficult to believe that any one of the three spent much time reviewing it. What troubles me the most is they missed the fact that the homestead exemption was waived by both Paul and Sandra in the antenuptial agreement, which they had in the papers I provided. Yet they mistakenly used the homestead exemption to justify not prosecuting the case.

Given all the mistakes and misinformation in their reply, there is no way that I could accept their memorandum as even being close to factual and I sent a second response to Brad King on September 19th.

Memorandum

A Case Study Of Elder Abuse And Exploitation In Florida

Date: September 19, 2019
To: Brad King, State Attorney
From: Carl R. Baker
RE: Sandra Kaniewski S-2019-16863

While you have already made your decision not to pursue any criminal action in this case, I thought it was necessary to point out errors in Erik Rauba's memorandum of August 16, 2019 to Mark Simpson in order to accurately portray what actually occurred.

Please note the following:

First paragraph, line 5—**"...Sandra and Paul started dating in 2015 after Sandra's husband passed away."**
This is not true. Paul and Sandy started dating in the summer of 2014 while Sandy's husband, Ralph was in rehab. In September 2014, they traveled together to Sandy's timeshare for several days and she was frequently sneaking Paul into her home to spend the night. Ralph died on October 10, 2014 and Paul attended the memorial services with her which was extremely upsetting to Ralph's family.

Second Paragraph, line 1—**"Paul had been diagnosed with Alzheimer's Dementia in November of 2015 by Dr. Geliga. Although diagnosed with early onset dementia, it did not affect his capacity to make legal and fiscal decisions until 2018."**
I am not sure how you came to this conclusion. What is the factual basis for this statement?

Second Paragraph, line 7—**"He also made Sandra successor trustee removing Carl Baker as trustee and making Bruce Baker a** *secondary successor trustee."*

This is not true. Mark Baker (Paul's son) was made a secondary successor trustee.

Third Paragraph, line 2—**"He then took Paul to his house and refused to allow Sandra to see him anymore."**

This is not true. On the first night Paul spent with us, Sandy called him several times at 2:30 AM saying she "needed to talk to Paul." In the morning, I told Paul that Sandy called, and he told me that he did not want to talk to her. Several days later when we went to Mango Court to pick up some clothes for Paul, she refused to let him in his own home. Sandy never stopped by our home and we never received a call or an email from Sandy asking to see Paul. She never asked to see Paul until she hired an attorney and all requests from her attorney went to Paul's attorney and we had nothing to do with it.

Third Paragraph, line 5—**"Carl then went to Dr. Geliga to request a letter stating Paul lacked capacity to handle his affairs and finances. With this letter, he was able to locate Carl's money."**

This is not true. To begin, Erik evidently got the names confused and had my name in place of Paul's name in four places. Unfortunately, no one caught the error before it was sent out.

Additionally, the timeline here is wrong. In August, Paul wrote a check for over $500 for some yard work that should not have been more than $150. When I spoke to Paul about this, he asked me to take over all his finances because, as he stated, "he trusted me more than he trusted Sandy." Doctor Geliga's letter is dated August 27, 2018, more than four months before Paul came to live with us and weeks before Sandy withdrew the $220,000 from Paul's non-marital trust account. The letter was required by BB&T Bank to allow me as his POA, to handle his account. Unfortunately, BB&T said they never received the letter that Doctor Geliga sent. I never saw the letter or knew it existed until my brother Bruce, and I took Paul to his next appointment with Dr. Geliga in late January 2019. At that time, Dr. Geliga gave me a copy of the letter.

Fourth Paragraph, line 4—*"However, the new account that was opened only had Carl's name on it. Therefore, the money never left his possession."*
The new account had Paul's name on it, not Carl's name.

Fourth Paragraph, line 11—*"It was represented that Sandra was not happy with BB&T and that is why she moved the money."*
This is absolutely true, and your wording is interesting. Sandy, not Paul, moved the money and she had total control over Paul. He feared her. Sandy was unhappy with Paul's account in BB&T because I could review all of Paul's transactions and there were a number of transactions which I questioned. There were far too many teller checks made out to cash. So, Sandy moved Paul's non-marital trust accounts to her bank (Chase) and opened a joint account. Paul is computer illiterate, so all the money being moved to the joint account was done by her and all checks were written by her and placed in front of Paul to sign, which he never questioned. This is exactly what she wanted.

By the way, before Sandy went through all this trouble and waste of Paul's money to change Paul's trusts twice and move his money to her bank, I decided that with all the craziness and Sandy writing out checks from different number series, I felt I could not and would not take responsibility for something that I had no control over. On September 6th, I returned Paul's BB&T checkbook with a full accounting by registered mail, return receipt requested. So, there was no real reason for Sandy to move Paul's money. Fifteen days later, $220,000 was withdrawn from his account.

Fifth Paragraph, line 3—*"At this point Carl Baker informed us that he had taken his brother back to his attorney on January 23, 2019 and had Paul amend his trust again removing Sandra as successor trustee and removing the language about her remaining in the house until her death."*

This was extremely concerning for Mr. Simpson and myself as he had been telling us and Detective Cohen that his brother had lacked capacity to change his trust since September of 2018 but had him change it in January of 2019. In addition, Carl was in possession of the letter from Paul's doctor dated August 27, 2018, stating Paul was incapacitated to handle any financial, legal or fiscal matters because of his dementia. He did exactly what he is accusing Sandra of doing."

To start, I never knew the letter ever existed until after the papers were signed by Paul. As stated earlier, BB&T never received the letter and my brother Bruce, and I got a copy of the letter at Paul's appointment with Dr. Geliga after the trust papers were signed.

I take offense to your statement that I "did exactly what I am accusing Sandy of doing." Detective Cohen had it in his report as well and you had it your response.

Several facts were omitted on this statement. First, I was never listed as a beneficiary to any of Paul's assets, nor did I ever want anything from Paul. His estate rightfully belongs to his children. Once Paul realized how much his trust and will had been altered, he wanted to revert to his original 2014 trust. All of Paul's family agreed because that is when Paul knew exactly what he wanted to do with his estate. On the advice of Paul's original trust attorney, everything was changed back to the 2014 trust with one exception. Mark, Paul's son, and Allyne, Paul's daughter, were made successor trustees. So, it was a family decision, not my decision.

Let me ask you, if this were your brother what would you have done? If we did nothing, we would not have been able to protect Paul's life earnings. I only wish that Sandy's actions were as "extremely concerning" to you as my actions apparently were. Paul is now in a memory care facility. We did our best to protect our brother and seek justice and we would have certainly been remiss in protecting him had we let the 2018 trust stand.

Ninth Paragraph, line 7—*"The next allegation is that Sandra temporarily deprived Paul's children of an inheritance by giving herself a life estate in the marital property. Pursuant to Florida law, if the home is homesteaded as a marital home, she is given a life estate in the home and no trust agreement can change her rights."*

This statement is true. However, you asked for and I sent you a copy of the antenuptial agreement, dated June 17, 2016. Section 18 is a waiver of homestead, property, estate and other rights. Sandy waived her rights, so she was not given a life estate in the home. My response to your memorandum was delayed because I took the time to have this confirmed by an attorney. So, under the statute, she could be charged with Exploitation.

I admit that circumstantial evidence cases are difficult at times, but with enough documented overt acts in furtherance of the crime, juries will return a guilty verdict. I still strongly believe that we have documented enough of Sandy's actions to get a conviction here especially with the "endeavoring to obtain or use" wording in the statute and the corrections outlined in this memo. But that is not my call; it is totally up to you.

Unfortunately, the winners in this saga are the "Dirty Johns" and "Dirty Janes" who prey on the disabled seniors throughout Florida. The losers are the 4.5 million seniors who decided to spend their final years in the Sunshine State, including those living in *Florida's Friendliest Hometown*.

State Attorney Brad King never responded to my September 19th email in response to his email.

Now I ask you. Given all the mistakes in the State Attorney's memorandum which were overlooked in two reviews, their failure to realize the homestead exemption was waived, which negates one of their main reasons for not prosecuting and their disregard of the "endeavoring to obtain or use" wording in the statute, how would you rate the professionalism of this office?

From the very beginning of the investigation, both Detective Cohen and Erik Rauba were indicating to me that they were not going to prosecute this case. They first stated that the case was civil in nature. Since that is obviously not true, they changed their reason to not prosecute to, "based on the evidence provided at this time, the State will not be going forward with prosecution."

From all the cases I have had in my career, I never encountered so much negativity at the investigative stage of a case. In all my experiences, if the prosecutor did not think they had everything needed to prosecute, he or she would specifically tell me what was lacking and I would continue the investigation to try and obtain the needed information. We worked as a team. I never saw any of that team work here. Instead of being treated as a complainant who was concerned about my brother's well-being, they acted like I was a pain in their side (I am being polite here), and they never had any intention of taking this case.

From: Carl Baker
April 8, 2020 at 9:43:54 AM EDT
To: Brad King
Subject: Update on Criminal Referral - Sandra Kaniewski S-2019-16863

Mr. King
    Several months ago, I appealed the finding of the Florida Department of Families and Children (Elder Abuse) on Sandy's abuse of Paul and they assigned another investigator to look at the case. Several weeks ago, I confirmed that the exploitation and inadequate supervision charges have been verified and were sent to the Sumter County Sheriff's Office and the State Attorney's Office for follow up on or about March 3rd. I have a copy of the DFC report. Detective Cohen has not received the referral.
    I am checking to see if you have received this recent referral. If not, I will send a copy to both of you.
    Thank you.
    Carl Baker

From: "BKING"
To: "crbaker"

Cc: "Mark Simpson"
Sent: Thursday, April 9, 2020 9:06:30 AM
Subject: RE: Update on Criminal Referral - Sandra Kaniewski S-2019-16863

Regardless of a new or amended finding by DCF, our position still remains as stated in the memo sent to you on 08/26/2019 which is attached. I understand that you do not agree, but your disagreement will not change the decision.

Now ask yourself. Do they really care about the abuse and exploitation of seniors? So far, I am only able to find a few that truly do.

(Note: See the April 22 letter to the Governor and Attorney General for my comments on Mr. King's response.)

Bar Complaint

Reference is made to the chart on pages 55 -66 titled, "THE JOHN PAUL BAKER TRUSTS". The first trust (2014) was created by Paul before he was experiencing any real signs of Alzheimer's dementia. Quite candidly, this should be the determining trust since he was of "sound mind and body" at this time. The second trust (2016) was created by Paul as an update because of his marriage to Sandy. All his assets were still going to his two children and both he and Sandy signed an Antenuptial agreement which turned out to be one of the smartest decisions by Paul in his entire relationship with Sandy.

The next two trusts (September 2018 and December 2018) were created after Sandy isolated Paul from his family and controlled all his actions and communications. This is classic exploitation. Although Paul signed these two trusts, Sandy determined what changes were to be made and how his assets would be distrusted. Sandy hated Allyne and note that her distribution was reduced by Sandy from 65% to 15%. When I asked Paul about these changes in January 2018, he had no idea what I was talking about.

The last trust (2019) was created upon the recommendation of Paul's attorney. To protect Paul and his non-marital assets from being controlled by Sandy, everything was returned to the language in the 2014 trust except the successor trustees were changed to Mark and Allyne Baker, Paul's children.

The Florida Bar
Inquiry/Complaint Form

Attorney: Michael A. Hollander Florida Bar No. 85973

Background
My brother, J. Paul Baker is a retired Army Colonel and Vietnam veteran who has a disability (Agent Orange) and now has Alzheimer's with very little short-term memory. He had been married to Sandy Kaniewski for about two and a half years before they separated in January 2019. He is now in a memory care facility.

In early July of 2018, Paul wrote out a check to a lawn

maintenance contractor for $520.00 for fertilizing three palms. Obviously, he was taken advantage of and I initiated a case with Seniors Against Crime. This has been resolved, but Paul was no longer able to handle financial matters. At that time, he had a Trust Account of approximately $235,000 which was for future medical costs and long-term care. Upon his death, the remainder was to go to his two children. Since I had been his Trustee and have been helping him with financial matters for years, Paul asked me to handle his checking account and told me he trusted me more than his wife.

On August 10, 2018, Mark and Allyne, Paul's children came to Florida to see their dad. Sandy immediately brought up the trust and stated she was going to the attorney to see what changes should be made. Both of Paul's children told Sandy that they did not want the trust changed.

On August 15, 2018, Paul and Sandy met with Attorney Sham Shanawany (Millhorn & Shanawany). I also attended the meeting at Paul's request.

This meeting was set up by Sandy to go over their individual non – marital trusts because of Paul's Alzheimer condition and to make sure "all their ducks were in a row." Sandy started the meeting by stating that they were now married, and Paul's Alzheimer was progressing. She explained that she did not know that Bruce and I had Paul's power of attorney (POA) and since she was his wife, she wanted sole financial and health care power of attorney to include Paul's trust.

I objected to her having POA over Paul's trust account since he does not have POA for hers and the trust money goes directly to his children. Sandy became furious and stated that she is treated like a "second class citizen" and as his wife she should have sole POA. After a lengthy discussion, Sandy threw up her arms and said she wants nothing to do with Paul's finances so no one in Paul's family can say she took Paul's money. **Decision: No change to the Durable Power of Attorney.**

Sandy then stated that Paul's children wanted the trust changed to an irrevocable medical trust and that she be made the trustee. I stated that was false. Paul asked how I knew that, and I stated I had emails from his children stating that fact. **Decision: The J. Paul Baker Trust will not be amended.**

Sandy then stated that she wanted Health Care Power of Attorney. I explained that she already had that along with Bruce and me. I told everyone that it states that we could act on his behalf either jointly or independently. **Decision: The Health Care Power of Attorney will not be changed. The attorney recommended that we always act jointly.**

Additional Decision: Paul will not sign any documents prepared by the Attorney that change the trust without my approval.

In less than two weeks after meeting with the attorney, Sandy isolated Paul from his family by taking his simple flip cell phone away from him and replacing it with a smart phone with a pass code that only she knew. This confused Paul and he had to depend on Sandy to use his phone and she took charge, screening his calls and voice mails, listening in on every conversation and even going so far as pretending she was Paul by sending text messages from his phone. We know that it was her for many reasons namely, Paul has never texted in his life. Further she had "brainwashed" Paul by telling him lies and turning him against his family. She also blocked me from contacting Paul. Despite all our attempts, my twin brother Bruce and I had not heard from Paul from August of 2018 until January 2019 when he came to live with me and my wife. Up until then, Paul called me at least once a day.

Sandy's behavior clearly showed signs of a sociopath in addition to elder abuse, and she has never admitted that she had done anything wrong. She lies about everything even when it is not necessary. In my opinion, she tends to overestimate her own skills and abilities and believes that she is totally entitled to all of Paul's assets and the scariest issue at hand was there was little doubt she was willing to eliminate anybody and everybody that got in her way. That is the reason she had to eliminate both Bruce and me from Paul's life by filling his head with lies. She knew that if we got Paul alone and helped him understand what is really going on, she would never gain control of his trust.

Subsequently, Sandy contacted another attorney, Michael Hollander. This resulted in a new trust agreement that was signed by Sandy and Paul in Mr. Hollander's office on September 20, 2018. On the very next day, September 21, $220,000 was withdrawn from Paul's Family Trust Account at BB&T Bank and it was taken in a cashier's check.

It is abundantly clear that Paul was not the decision maker here. This was orchestrated by Sandy without notifying any member of Paul's family. She had abused him and exploited him to get to this day when she took control of all of Paul's non-marital assets, even though Paul had protected himself by setting up the trust in 2014 and an antenuptial agreement in 2016.

Sandy made herself the successor trustee, power of attorney, health care surrogate and changed the trust to give her the home as long as she lives. By the way, Sandy signed a waiver of homestead, property, estate, and other rights in the antenuptial agreement, dated June 17, 2016.

To say Sandy disliked Paul's daughter is probably an understatement. From the beginning we all saw that Sandy was after Paul's assets and Allyne questioned her often about some of her actions and statements. As a result, Sandy reduced Allyne's distribution of her father's assets from 65 % to 15%.

On December 3, 2018, Sandy and Paul were again in Attorney Michael Hollander's office signing yet another trust. This time, the distribution of Paul's assets was split 50/50 between his two children. Sandy could still live in the home as long as she lives. I have no idea why this change was made. When I later asked Paul about all of this, he was extremely upset that Allyne was treated so poorly by Sandy.

I do not know Michael Hollander personally, but I would think that he is quite intelligent. In your own rules of professional conduct (Chapter 4), you state, "The Rules of Professional Conduct are rules of reason." I am not sure what Sandy told Mr. Hollander as to why the trust was being changed so dramatically from the 2014 and 2016 trusts, but it most certainly did not pass the "smell test" and had to raise some questions for Mr. Hollander. If Mr. Hollander had any conversation with Paul, he must have detected his Alzheimer's. And then to return to the office several months later to again make changes to the trust should raise a red flag. Knowing this was a late in life marriage of short duration, did Mr. Hollander ask any questions that would have to be answered before the new trust papers were signed? Did Mr. Hollander check with Paul's attorney or any of Paul's family to get a better understanding as to the reason for the trust changes? Evidently not. Otherwise, it is sign the papers, collect your fee, send them out the door and let someone else worry about it.

Florida has approximately 4.6 million seniors. I would assume there must be some training programs for lawyers on recognizing senior abuse and exploitation. Did Mr. Hollander ever take such a course?

If this complaint is unfounded, I ask that at least you tell me what was said or done that allowed Mr. Hollander to believe that proceeding and changing Paul's trust twice was in Paul's best interest. My goal is to make some changes in a system that is broken, so feel free to make suggestions and perhaps we can prevent other families from going through the turmoil we experienced.

Thank you.

Carl R. Baker

The Florida Bar
651 East Jefferson Street
Tallahassee, FL 32399-2300
Joshua-E. Doyle850/561-5600
Executive Directorwww.FLORIDABAR.org
October 4, 2019

Mr. Carl R. Baker
1816 Wading Heron way
The Villages, FL 32163
Re: Mr. Michael Alfred Hollander; REA No.: 20-4354

Dear Mr. Baker:

All documentation submitted in this matter has been carefully reviewed. The Florida Bar is the licensing agency for all attorneys admitted to practice law in the State of Florida. In cases where discipline is indicated, the disciplinary action is taken against the attorney's licensure, and will not affect or overturn the outcome of any proceeding.

Your complaint primarily stated that Mr. Hollander provided legal representation to the listed individuals and then alleged that this was somehow improper since you and others disagree with this action having been done. There were no allegations of misconduct and certainly no supporting documentation for same was submitted.

While I understand that you believe the attorney acted unethically, I must conclude that your complaint constitutes a civil dispute which is best resolved through the civil system. The Supreme Court of Florida has ruled that the disciplinary process and proceedings are not to be used as a substitute for civil proceedings and remedies. In the event that a court of competent jurisdiction makes findings in your case which suggest misconduct by the attorney you may re-file your complaint at that time, enclosing the relevant findings.

Consequently, I have closed our record in this matter. Pursuant to the Bar's records retention schedule, the computer record and file will be disposed of one year from the date of closing.

Sincerely,

Charles Hughes, Bar Counsel

Attorney Consumer Assistance Program ACAP Hotline 866-352-0707

cc:Mr. Michael Alfred Hollander

This is hard to believe that there are no safeguards in Florida to prevent this type of exploitation. Additionally, from what I have experienced in this case, it appears that state holds no one responsible for mistakes or poor customer service. I feel the need to do something to correct this and will send this case study to Florida Governor Ronald DeSantis and Florida Attorney General Ashly Moody. I will make a suggestion that they review this case and introduce legislation to put safeguards that will prevent "lawyer shopping" where a disabled elder is the victim. The chance of passing this type of legislation in a legislature full of lawyers is extremely difficult without a major push by the Governor and the support of Florida's 4.6 million seniors.

> Deceiving someone for his own good is a responsibility which should be shouldered only by God."
> —*Anonymous*

Chapter 13

A Most Unusual Hearing

This must be one of the most bizarre episodes ever to occur as a result of a petition in a probate court. The only thought that comes to mind is, "You can't make this stuff up." And just so there is no mistake about this, I was generous in using the word "stuff" rather than what it really is.

I received the following email on August 12:

From: Harry Hackney
To: crbaker
Sent: Monday, August 12, 2019 6:29:00 PM

Subject: FW: Proposed Order / Guardianship of Paul Baker

FYI Merideth and I spoke after the hearing and agreed that we could only think of one guardian that we would want and that is Amanda Ritter. I called and spoke to Amanda and she agreed to serve. Today Cara asked whether we had any suggestions and I said only one --- Amanda Ritter. They have agreed to Amanda. See the email below.

Subject: Proposed Order / Guardianship of Paul Baker

Hello Harry,
I have confirmed with my client that she is agreeable with Amanda Ritter being appointed as the professional plenary guardian. Do you want us to prepare the proposed order to that effect?

Thank you,
Cara C. Singeltary, Esq.

On October 4, 2019, Judge Morley stated that Amanda A. Ritter is qualified and appointed plenary guardian of the person and property of John Paul Baker.

Within the next several days, I sent the following email to Paul's new guardian:

From: crbaker
To:amanda a ritter
Bcc:Katherine Baker Bruce Baker

Good morning,

You will be receiving seven emails this morning with documents attached that should give you a better understanding of what happened over the last few years. It has been frustrating for our entire family and we have done our best to protect Paul. FYI, I have much more documentation, so if you should have a question or need any additional information, please do not hesitate to call or email me.

And finally, will you reply to me once you have all the documents so I know you have everything.

Thank you and we look forward to working with you.

Carl Baker

On August 28, 2019, Paul and I were at Trinity Springs Memory Care to start the admission procedure. While we were there, Merideth Nagel, Paul's attorney and temporary guardian had to sign the contact, so Trinity Spring's staff called Merideth to discuss how best to send the forms for signature.

Merideth asked to speak to Paul and the staff member and Paul went to another room for some privacy. When they returned, Paul told me that he told Merideth that he did not want to ever see Sandy again, he wanted nothing to do with her and he wanted her out of his life. The staff member told me that Merideth was going to forward a picture of Sandy to be placed at the front desk and Sandy was not allowed in the building.

A short time later, at approximately 1:00 PM, the staff member got a phone call and told us that Paul's wife, Sandy was in the front lobby demanding to see Paul and the staff immediately went down to the first- floor lobby.

Amanda Ritter, Paul's soon to be permanent guardian called my cell phone at 1:44 PM and asked me if I knew what was going on downstairs. I told her that I did, and she explained to me that it was her fault that Sandy learned that Paul was at Trinity Springs and apologized. Evidently, Amanda sent a reply email to bring Paul's attorney (Merideth) and my Attorney (Harry Hackney) up to date on Paul's memory care and did not realize that Sandy's attorney was also included in the original email. Amanda stated that she talked to Sandy by phone and Sandy agreed to be escorted off the premises.

> Note: This was the first of several questionable decisions and mistakes that Amanda made as guardian. However, at this time, we did not make a big deal of it and it never was mentioned again.

When the staff member came back upstairs, she told us that Sandy was telling everyone that she was Paul's wife and demanded to see him. She then called her attorney crying and shaking and told her that all she wanted was a tour. The staff member said that was not true. I told her that Sandy lies all the time and what she witnessed was another one of Sandy's "Show and Tell" episodes which she often uses when she has an audience.

They gave Sandy a brief tour showing her the front hallway and fitness room and then escorted her off the property.

Given all that happened, we were hoping that this would show how unstable Sandy really was and we were ready for the hearing on October 11th.

On September 6, 2019, Judge Morley scheduled a hearing for October 11th at 9:00 AM for an oral hearing on Sandy's petition for visitation with Paul. Unfortunately, some of the other participants had conflicts and a new date had to be set. The Motion to Continue was granted, but I do not think the judge was happy about it. It is my understanding that her Judicial Assistant sent an email to all parties outlining the information she wanted available for the hearing, now scheduled for November 1st.

Paul was settling into his new home at Trinity Springs and was doing quite well. He was getting more and more involved in group activities. The facility had asked us not to visit Paul initially to facilitate his acclimation to his new home. The picture of Sandy was at the front desk and the staff was doing an excellent job of screening Paul's visitors. After several weeks, we started signing Paul out and taking him to lunch with his family and friends.

On October 22, Bruce, Jack Warner, Walt Kelly and I played golf at one of the Executive Courses. After golf, Bruce and I picked up Paul from Trinity Springs so he could have lunch at Steak and Shake with his golfing buddies.

During lunch, Paul looked at me and stated, "I can't believe what that bitch (Sandy) did to me. She took away my life." I could see the tears streaming down his face. I comforted him by reminding him that he was having lunch with his family and friends and that we would be doing this more often.

Jack Warner began visiting Paul every Friday. Jack told our golf group that every week Paul states, "I can't believe what that bitch has done to me." Jack also told us that he can see the anger in Paul whenever Paul talks about Sandy.

Paul does have times when he knows exactly what is going

on and realizes how his life has changed. And when he does, he blames Sandy for his situation. Over the last several months, Paul has actually apologized to family members for giving her the Baker name. But all in all, it was going as best as could be expected for Paul.

However, that all changed on the afternoon of October 25th, exactly one week before the hearing on Sandy's request for visitation. My first indication that there was a problem was a text message from Paul's daughter Allyne that stated, *"Check your email. It's obscene."*

I immediately went to my computer and found the following message from Amanda Ritter, Paul's newly appointed guardian:

From: Amanda Ritter
Sent: Friday, October 25, 2019 2:43:15 PM
Subject: Baker Visit

Carl and Allyne,

Good afternoon. I wanted to let you both know that Cher (Court Eldercaring Coordinator) and I facilitated a supervised visit with Sandy this afternoon. She brought Paul a few personal items what (sic) Cher's suggestion and it went very well. There are a few items I'm having maintenance put on the walls. I submitted a ticket to have this done at the front desk. As for the other personal items I will take care of getting them all soon.

I know you both have very strong feelings about this and Cher and I would like to have a conference call with one or both of you early next week to debrief. Cher and I are handling this as a united front so it is important we are both on the phone when it is discussed going into us testifying to the judge next week. It also was important to facilitate this quickly as we have a hearing coming up next Friday. Let us know by replying all to this email with some days/times that work well and we can work with our schedules to make the call happen.

Paul was very happy the entire short visit and was in excellent spirits when we left.

I ask that you please support this positive spirit by not bringing up anything negative to him while I wade through all of this. It is very apparent where Paul is Im [sic]is memory now as much of the conversation revolves around speaking about his father and early days in the service. Sandy will not be visiting without the supervision of Cher and/or myself **at this time.** (Emphasis added.)

Thank you,
Amanda Ritter
Professional Guardian and VA Fiduciary

I was dumbfounded. My first thought was what would make these two professional women bring Paul's wife, who has been barred from seeing Paul at his and his attorney's request, to visit him unannounced and without notifying any of his family. They knew how Sandy exploited and abused Paul and they knew he never wanted to be in the same room with her again. Further, we were getting ready to go to court to determine visitation. Why would they force visitation on Paul just one week before the hearing? How, in their minds, did they think this would benefit Paul? And to me, the last line in Amanda's email indicates that they eventually plan to let Sandy visit Paul without one of them being present.

My wife and I immediately left our home and drove to Trinity Springs to see Paul. As we signed in on the visitor's log, the first thing I checked was if Sandy had signed in when she visited Paul earlier. She did not. Amanda and Cher signed in, but Sandy did not. Why?

We went to Paul's room and he immediately started the conversation about the visit. He told us that three women came into Trinity Springs (the Memory Care Unit) and he was with his group and they took him away from the activity room and took him to his bedroom.

(Note: We totally disagree with taking him to his bedroom. There is a sunroom at the end of the hallway where they could have privacy and that is where they should have taken him.)

He told us that he had no idea who these women were and one of them (Sandy) kept asking him questions about events and asking if he remembered them. He stated that he remembered some of them. Sandy then told Paul that she was with him and that she had loved him forever. That confused Paul even more. When Paul learned it was Sandy, he asked, "Can anyone come in here? I feel like I am being tricked."

When we returned home, I immediately sent an email to Amanda and Cher with one simple question:

Why would you do this?

Likewise, Allyne sent the following email to Amanda, Cher and

Amanda's attorney:

> From: Allyne Baker
> To: amanda a ritter
> Cc: Cher Myers, Mike Rogers,
> Sent: Friday, October 25, 2019 3:56:55 PM
> Subject: Re: Baker Visit
>
> To all involved:
> Frankly, this approach is appalling!!!
>
> Allyne Baker"

As you can clearly see, the Baker family was not at all pleased and obviously, we were not off to a good start on our relationship with Paul's newly court appointed guardian. In our opinion, Amanda and Cher took advantage of Paul's Alzheimer's condition and deceived him by not starting their conversation be telling Paul who Sandy was. They knew immediately that Paul did not know Sandy and they let this charade continue. In our opinion, both Amanda and Cher actions were unprofessional and abusive.

As the day was ending, Cher Myers sent the following email in support of hers and Amanda's actions:

> From: Cher Myers
> To: Allyne
> Cc: amanda a ritter, crbaker, Mike Rogers, Pati Kersey
> Sent: Friday, October 25, 2019 5:11:46 PM
> Subject: Re: Baker Visit

Hello all, speaking from a clinical perspective with 30 years experience in mental health, today's visit was a positive for Paul! He needs "Happy in his world" and Sandy was coached and followed the protocol that Amanda and I established. We are both available after 12 noon on Monday for a conference call. We want to all be on the same page for Paul. Please let us know if you are interested in talking to us together. Amanda and I truly have Paul's best interest in mind.
Cher Myers
S.A.D.L.E.S.

After reading this, my first thought was great, now we have more questions that need answers. What does, "He (Paul) needs "Happy in his world" mean? Neither of these people have ever spent any real time with Paul. They do not know him nor do they have any idea what makes Paul happy. In fact, if they did know Paul, they would realize that Sandy makes Paul very unhappy. Let's review the next statement... *and Sandy was coached and followed the protocol that Amanda and I established.* Evidently, the protocol was 'let's not be honest and up front with Paul and see how much further we can confuse him.' Perhaps this wasn't what they wanted, but that is certainly what they accomplished. And no one in the Baker family believed they had "Paul's best interest in mind."

We thought that it would be best to sleep on all and see what it looked like in the morning. We know that God is in control and we needed to give it all to Him. Unfortunately, at times, that is much easier said than done.

None of us slept very well that night. Saturday, I woke up

exceedingly early thinking that Amanda and Cher could easily pass off my one question response as a rhetorical question and never respond. So, I sent another email to make sure everyone knew I was expecting an answer:

Amanda and Cher

FYI, my email was not a rhetorical question. Before we can proceed, we (Paul's family) need an understanding of your thought process and/or reasoning on why you decided to visit Paul in this manner and why you did it without letting any of us know. Did you notify Paul's attorney? Was the Judge notified before your visit? Why was it "important to facilitate this quickly" and what does this have to do with the hearing?

Please respond as soon as possible so that we can move beyond this and have a discussion on what is best for Paul.

After sending this message, I noted that Paul's daughter, Allyne sent me an email at 1:17 in the morning. Understandably, she could not sleep either. Allyne loves her dad very much and gets very emotional, especially when she thinks someone is taking advantage of her father.

From: Allyne
To: Uncle Carl

I can't believe the people appointed by this corrupt court who were supposed to protect him also just took advantage of his disability and vulnerability! And we, as his family are supposed to be okay with this!!???

The reason they don't want to talk to us individually (without each other being on the phone call) is because they know this is WRONG! They completely deceived dad and went against what he specifically asked of this court appointed guardian! His own wishes and requests were overlooked and disregarded for the sake of his abuser's desire to see him! Are we supposed to sit back and watch my dad be victimized over and over again by these people who clearly don't have his best interest in mind??? And clearly Amanda doesn't understand the description of her job duties!!!

For example, suppose a child was victimized by a teacher who made sexual advances or something like that. And a year later that same child fell on the playground sustaining a head injury that resulted in amnesia. Would it be okay to allow that same teacher to be near her child as an experiment to see if the mere presence of the teacher/abuser was upsetting or pleasant????? That's exactly what they are doing to dad!!! Allowing his "abuser" (Sandy) to be near him without announcing who she really is, and then tricking him into being near her. Playing on his memory issues seems like a form of abuse and exploitation of its own! Again, I ask where is the actual protection for a disabled elderly person who has been taken advantage of in the state of Florida????

Later that day (Saturday), I sent Amanda's original email to Paul's attorney, Merideth Nagel, and asked if she knew anything about yesterday's arranged visit of Sandy:

From: Carl Baker
To: Merideth Nagel

Sent: Saturday, October 26, 2019 11:37:54 AM
Subject: Fwd: Baker Visit

Merideth,

FYI, since a permanent guardian has been appointed, I am no longer represented by Harry. (Note: My attorney for seeking guardianship of Paul was Harry Hackney.)

Did you receive a copy of this email from Amanda Ritter? Given the fact that we have a hearing on Sandy's petition for visitation on Friday, was the judge aware of this? Did Amanda let you know that she intended to revoke your instructions to the facility to not allow Sandy to visit Paul? Needless to say, Paul's daughter is very upset and none of us understand what is going on.

Thank you,
Carl Baker

Merideth replied to my email on Sunday afternoon.

From: Merideth Nagel
To: crbaker, Harry Hackney
Cc: amanda a Ritter, Mike Rogers, Cher Myers
Sent: Sunday, October 27, 2019 2:18:53 PM
Subject: RE: Baker Visit

Carl,

Thank you for the email. The law gives the guardian great discretion in deciding on the Ward's social environment, including who they may see, or not see. In this case both the parenting (sic) coordinator and the guardian agreed that a supervised visit would be in the Ward's best interests. Since the visit went well, if this issue goes to hearing on Friday the judge will rule that their decision was the right one. You would be unable to succeed in arguing that Ms. Ritter's decision should be overturned.

Paul is in good hands with Ms. Ritter. She is (and importantly also considered by judges to be) one of the best guardians in our circuit. She will not let Paul be taken advantage of, either emotionally or financially.

In order to conserve Paul's resources by avoiding what I believe would be a futile and unnecessary waste of fees, and considering his declining capacity, I do not believe that objecting to the guardian's decision about Mrs. Baker's visitation would be in his best interests. Therefore, I will defer to Ms. Ritter's judgment on these issues. I will however request agreement by the parties to remain as Mr. Baker's attorney, just in case I might be needed.

Again, he is in good hands with Ms. Ritter. I know that you feel strongly about Mrs. Baker, but so long as her visits make him happy, there is no reason to fight the issues. If you are concerned about her exercising some undue influence on Paul, you should not be. His daughter and son are his trustees, and can protect his finances, and his guardian will be sure to protect him, and keep him where he is happy and healthy.

Thank you,
Merideth C. Nagel, Esq.

Although Merideth has not spent a lot of time with Paul, she has always been protective of him as evidenced by the immediate safeguards that she put in place at Trinity Springs after Sandy tried to see him on August 28th. In fact, it was Merideth who suggested that I file criminal charges against Sandy for her abuse and exploitation of Paul. Merideth or a member of her firm have questioned Paul numerous times as to a visit from Sandy. Every time Paul has said that he wants nothing to do with her and he wants her out of his life. I do not understand what made Merideth completely reverse her earlier decisions and not continue to follow the wishes of her client. Although I am not sure, it appears to me that the Judge stated (or ordered) that she wanted visitation between Sandy and Paul and everyone complied. Unfortunately, this letter was the last time we heard a word from Merideth on this issue. Further, it is my opinion that Amanda did allow Sandy to "take advantage" of Paul, both emotionally and financially. Otherwise, she would not have walked of the door stealing much of Paul's property.

Besides Paul's family, Harry Hackney and Merideth are the only two other people who truly understood how abusive Sandy was to Paul and how she tried to exploit him. Since the Eldercaring Coordinator, Cher Meyers, was approved at the first hearing, she and Amanda were not present to hear my attorney's opening statement that outlined Sandy's abuse and exploitation of Paul. However, the judge heard the opening statement and evidently disregarded it and overtly pushed for Sandy to have visitation with Paul. In addition, I had sent documentation to both Cher and Amanda outlining Sandy's abuse and exploitation and they ignored it as well and set up the covert visit with Paul. If the Eldercaring Coordination Program is used in such a way that it prevents the Judge from hearing the facts of the case, and allows an abuser to meet with her victim, it should be eliminated immediately.

Amanda replied to Allyne's and my emails on Monday morning:

From: amanda a ritter
To: crbaker
Cc: Allyne Baker, Cher Myers, Mike Rogers, Pati Kersey, Merideth Nagel
Sent: Monday, October 28, 2019 9:31:35 AM
Subject: Re: Baker Visit

Good morning Allyne and Carl. In an October 10th email from the judicial assistant Misty Conner to myself, all attorney's and Cher's office, it was spelled out that the judge was looking for EVERY avenue between the Baker's to be explored before coming in front of her Friday. Cher and I are working hard now that I have my certified Letters of Guardianship to resolve some of these issues that have been drug out this year. In this email we were tasked by the judge (it actually said she was REQUIRING it) to explore visitation options. Cher and I came together as a united front on a very short time schedule to facilitate a very safe supervised visit. We had a very well devised plan and what we would do if there was push back from Paul or unexpected behavior from Sandy. There was absolutely not one moment of negativity or push back or bad behavior from either side.

(Note: This was a lie which will be explained later.) I made sure the Memory Care staff knew what was going on and they were informed to let me know right away if Paul's demeanor changed once we left from the visit. I also attended a workshop after and went back with a RN Care Manager that works with me to check on Paul again an hour or so later along with speaking to staff again. The reason you both were not informed was it was decided between Cher and I that we needed to see the total candid reaction from Paul to make sure he was not coached into his feelings (as this has been a well know allegation). I understand this is a very touchy and emotional subject and that was taken into consideration when making the decision to act on the visit right away without notice to all parties. So, I hope this answers the why would you do this question and we can move on to the how did it go question (which Cher and I were trying to facilitate a conference call sometime this afternoon to discuss with you, but if you would rather that by email also, just let us know) and move forward with making sure we are all making the right decisions for Paul. I have only Paul's best interests in mind and I will make sure that stays forefront in all decisions I make. It is important for him that he is just surrounded by people and situations that put a smile on his face and that he is not involved one bit in the battle that is taking place behind the scenes. I look forward to moving on from this and working with all parties to make sure that Paul is happy and taken care of.

Thank you,
Amanda Ritter

I am a bit uncertain what Amanda meant when she said, *"it was spelled out that the judge was looking for EVERY avenue between the Baker's to be explored before coming in front of her*

Friday." However, it seems reasonable to look at the October 10th email from the Judicial Assistant and see if we can relate it to the October 25th visit by Amanda, Cher, and Sandy.

Hello:

The Motion to Continue has been granted HOWEVER, the following is what Judge Morley is requiring at the next hearing:

1. Whether Mr. Baker's doctor will be willing to supervise a visit w/ his wife.
2. Whether his Pastor/Father/Rabbi will be willing to supervise a visit w/ his wife.
3. Any relatives/friends/including his brother that would be willing to supervise a visit w/ his wife.
4. She wants to hear from the Doctors who have examined Mr. Baker; and who have had interaction w/ his children and brother.
5. She has NOT made up her mind about visitation as of yet, however, there will be conditions/restrictions to any visitation that may happen so she is willing to hear evidence and suggestions that relate to what those conditions/restrictions may be.
6. Have all parties explored every avenue between the Bakers before the upcoming hearing?
7. Location for visit; maybe doctor's office/police department/church office/nursing room/restaurant/wife's home, etc.

**The Judge also wanted to let everyone know that October 11th was a date given at the last hearing and EVERYONE; including Cher, was present when this date was provided - not to mention I had sent previous emails regarding same. While she is unhappy to continue this hearing, she will under the above circumstances. She expects everyone to come to the next hearing FULLY PREPARED with her questions and concerns above addressed in detail. **

Neither Amanda nor Cher ever spoke to me, my wife Katherine or my brother Bruce or his wife on any of the above subjects. Further, it is my understanding that there was minimal conversation with Mark and Allyne on these issues. I have the following knowledge and comments on the items enumerated in this email from the court:

1. Merideth and Cher met with Dr. Winn, Paul's Psychiatrist, at the Veteran's Clinic in the Villages on October 10th. I was there but not present for that meeting. Doctor Winn later told me he would not agree to supervising a visit or testifying, because if he did, he could no longer treat Paul.

2. I know that no one spoke to any pastor in our church. However, we would strongly oppose Sandy's pastor supervising a visit.

3. Allyne told me that Amanda asked her who she would like to supervise the meeting between Sandy and her dad. She stated that she would like her Uncle Carl to be present and I agreed to do it. However, Amanda never spoke to me about it. Had she asked me, I would have told her that my wife Katherine, my brother Bruce, and our life-long friend Jack Warner all stated that they would supervise the visits also.

4. I know nothing about this. I do know that Dr. Winn has told Paul several times that he was fortunate to have strong support from his brothers and their families. (Paul told Doctor Winn that he liked living with his brother.)

5. Since the judge had not made up her mind yet on visitation, why did Amanda and Cher arrange a covert visit without notifying Paul's family? The one condition that we have always insisted on was that any meeting that Sandy has with Paul be monitored without exception.

6. The answer to this question is emphatically no. Obviously, most of Amanda's and Cher's time has been spent with Sandy, to include the time spent "coaching" her for this visit.

7. No one ever spoke to any member of our family about a location for visitation. The visit on October 25 was in Paul's bedroom which is certainly not acceptable. Outside the bedroom area at Trinity Springs is a large, bright sunroom with a table and chairs, which is ideal.

On Monday, October 28th, we coordinated a single response from the Baker family addressing the Friday visit with Sandy.

Amanda and Cher
The Baker family was surprised to learn of Sandy's visit with Paul

since we thought that was to be decided in court this Friday. But now that it has occurred, we just need to move on and continue to do what is best for Paul. There are, however, some points that need to be made and we also want to tell you what we observed after your visit.

Trinity Springs is Paul's home and sanctuary. It took him a while, but he felt safe there. He had been asked, one on one, by Merideth on numerous occasions whether he wanted to see Sandy. His response was always the same - he did not want to see her. When he first got to Trinity and there was the incident with Sandy, Paul was concerned and asked if she would be able to get into Trinity and see him without his permission. We and the Trinity staff assured him that he would not be forced to see anyone that he didn't want to. Over the ensuing weeks Paul has asked me on numerous occasions the same question. I repeatedly told him that his temporary guardian, Merideth, had made sure that Sandy could not get in to see him and Trinity Springs would not let her in if she tried.

We have always been up front with Paul even when our response to him was not what he wanted to hear. He became more concerned about Sandy once he learned that Sandy had petitioned the court for visitation. Paul knew the court date was close and he asked us if he would have to go to court. He was relieved that he did not have to and said again, that he did not want to see Sandy. He asked us many times if he would have to be alone with Sandy if the court ruled against him. I explained to him that Allyne and his present guardian (Amanda) had discussed this and if the court ruled that Sandy could visit him, Allyne and Amanda agreed that I would be there also.

I think it's important that you know what Paul told his family after your visit. He said three women came to see him and he did not know who they were. He said he was pulled away from the group of people he was with at the time. He said he was asked a lot of questions about whether he remembered "this or that." He said he did remember some of the things mentioned and that the woman questioning him remembered more than he did. She asked if he remembered that she was there at whatever she had questioned him about and he did not. He was confused by that. He said he did not understand who she was but that she told him she had been in love with him forever. He was confused and shocked by that and said his response was "Really?" He said she tried to kiss him. He also said all of the women were nice.

Obviously, we were not there, so only those present know what occurred. He had the items you left with him but did not know remember how they got there. He asked us if we knew where they came from. I then told him they came from his old house and that the woman who visited was Sandy and that she brought the items. At first, he did not believe me, but we showed him a picture of Sandy and he realized it was her. He then got upset and said, "they are playing games with my brain;" "That was like a performance;" "I can't live like this;" "I hate being tricked;" "Can't you do something about this?" "That's like someone doing something they know you don't want, without you knowing it."

The family's concern has always been that Paul be safe and his wishes honored. Our reason for wanting visits to be supervised was to prevent the abusive language, mocking and making fun of him that we have all seen and heard in the past. Since Paul left Sandy, he has continually stated that he wants nothing to do with Sandy, wants her to leave him alone, and wants a divorce. Even while they were still together there were continual threats of divorce. So even though Paul has a horrible disease, he has been noticeably clear and consistent concerning his desires. I say all of this so you can see the difficult position this puts his family in. He is begging us to fix this situation for him and telling us what he wants. We would support Paul in whatever he wanted and have always told him that. And specifically, since the visitation issue came up, we have told him that he needs to make his wishes known to all of you, not just us, and that if he wants to see Sandy, he has every right to do that and should say so. The pain and suffering the entire Baker family has been put through is something no one would want. We have gladly taken it all on only because of our love for Paul and knowing he needed protection.

    The safety Paul knew has deteriorated. Paul said that he now thinks that anyone can come to his room and he realizes he may not even know who they are. On Friday, he asked if he could come back to our house where he knew he was safe. We promised him that we would do everything in our power to make sure this does not happen again. Of course, we did not know at that time that the court and all the parties to the case, besides Paul and his family, were involved in a decision to make this visit happen. We can only assume that if Paul had been asked if he wanted to see Sandy before you brought her in, he would have again said no. Paul has Alzheimer's and he does not understand everything he hears, but that does not mean that you can't be honest and candid with him and try to help him understand what you are doing.

    Neither of you could possibly know Paul better than his family does since Paul has only seen you both twice. When the three of you came to Trinity Springs on Friday, Paul had no idea who any of you were. If you knew Paul you would have known that when he is nervous, or uncomfortable, or just doesn't know what to say, he always talks about his teenage years or his military service.

He frequently starts conversations with strangers that way. You previously indicated that most of the conversation during the visit was about those things. So perhaps you can now better understand why that would be the case.

Paul is almost always an incredibly happy person. Any of his doctors would tell you that. If you asked any of the staff at Trinity Springs to describe Paul, they would probably respond that Paul is always happy. Paul is a people person and loves to make others laugh and smile. His seeming happy during the visit likely had nothing to do with Sandy being there but rather enjoying the attention of three women. Had he known it was Sandy he was talking to my guess is that he probably would have acted much differently. You never got any "push back from Paul" because he did not know who she was.

We were fully anticipating that the court would allow some supervised visits from Sandy, but we did think that Paul's wishes would also be a determining factor, and we would have supported whatever decision Paul made. We would request that you be upfront with Paul and let him know who is visiting him. We would hope that you would also consider Paul's wishes and not force him into something he does not want to do. We would be pleased to work with you on developing guidelines to protect Paul during these supervised visits, if so desired.

Thank you,
The Baker Family

We realize that Amanda has total control over who visits Paul and she has even stated that to Allyne, which terrified Allyne, who perceived it as a threat. This made her overly cautious about how the family responded. Obviously, none of us want to be prevented from visiting Paul and if Amanda ever tried to do that, we would have to fight it in court. However, sometimes it is best "to get everything on the table" and have an open discussion about controversial issues. The above response did not include everything we wanted to say, so what follows is our putting "everything on the table" so there is a better understanding of why we think this entire episode is so horrific.

Paul said Sandy told him that she had loved him forever. If this is indeed what she said, it is a falsehood since she was still married when she met him three years ago.

Has anyone ever asked her what love even means to her?

- How do you counter this love with constant arguments about money?
- How about mocking your husband in front of family and friends?
- How about accusing a diagnosed Alzheimer's victim of using his disease to claim he forgot things?
- How about showing no relief when your husband with Alzheimer's returns home after being lost for hours (after one of your many arguments)? And your only concern is yourself and that you weren't notified soon enough that he was found, even though you made no attempt to find him and let two hours pass before you even let anyone know he was gone?
- How about not letting your spouse retrieve any of his belongings, even with a police escort, after realizing he no longer wants to be with you? And further keeping them for over 10

months only allowing him some clothes and toiletries through a mediator. Is that love?

It should be no surprise that this was not the relationship or marriage that we had hoped for Paul and certainly was not what he needed to comfort him through his final years with Alzheimer's.

Why are Amanda and Cher totally ignoring all the details of Paul's case? Sandy isolated Paul from his family in August 2018. Within hours of Paul leaving the marital home, Sandy tracked him down and threatened him with divorce, as usual. This time Paul responded that he too wanted a divorce and she appeared stunned that he had finally had enough. Sandy never tried to see Paul for months after he left her. Why would that be? Love? Who is fooling whom? While Sandy was isolating Paul with a passcode on his phone that he didn't know, we ran into the two of them at a restaurant. Paul agreed to meet with Carl but Sandy protested and ultimately prevented the meeting. Nothing like that happened after Paul left Sandy. She never asked us or came by the house to see Paul from January until March 20, 2019, when she had her attorney make a request to Paul's attorney for a visit. How strange is that?

There is really something wrong with everyone involved in this. Paul wanted out of his marriage, and still does, due to how he was treated and exploited. He did love Sandy, but it was not reciprocated. Everyone says they have Paul's best interests at heart. But who even knows Paul – or what his best interests are? We are supposed to believe that people that are court appointed and have spent really no time with Paul somehow understand who he is, while those that have known him for over 70 years are totally discounted. And to further convolute the matter an ex-wife of two years seems to be calling all the shots. Anyone could look at this and see how wrong it truly is.

Paul is a victim of his disease. He was then further victimized by Sandy, a repeat offender. And now he has been victimized by the governmental and judicial systems. Where is the justice for Paul? Does no one have a conscience? Paul, despite his disease is still a human being who has thoughts and feelings, who knows what he wants and his wishes should not be ignored. He deserves respect and should not be treated like a pawn who can be tricked into spending time with someone that he has emphatically said he doesn't want to see, simply because he no longer recognizes who they are. Obviously, knowing Paul's desire to have nothing to do with Sandy, the motivation for Amanda's and Cher's actions were certainly not in Paul's best interest. That means they were either acting in Sandy's best interest or as puppets for the court. Take your choice. When people in whatever capacity they serve must lie, or deceive, or hide what they are doing, there is something really wrong with the system. We can only hope that they would ask themselves how they would feel if someone treated them in like fashion. We do reap what we sow!

Informed Consent

It is my position that both Amanda Ritter and Cher Myers violated the guidelines for professional guardians as outlined in the Florida statutes. Note the below guidelines for informed consent.

(6)(a) "Decisions that Professional Guardians make on behalf of their Wards under guardianship shall be based on the principle of Informed Consent."

(d)(4) "Maximize the participation of Wards in understanding the facts and directing a decision, to the extent possible."

(d)(5) "Determine whether a Ward has previously stated preferences in regard to a decision of this nature."

When Paul's attorney, Merideth Nagel, asked Paul if he wanted to see Sandy, each and every time Paul responded that he did not want to see her, have anything to do with her and he wanted her out of his life.

(7)(d)(1) Professional Guardians should ask their Wards what they want."

Obviously, Amanda never asked Paul any questions since she and Cher planned a covert, unannounced visit with Sandy. Paul summarized it by saying, "I hate being tricked like this!" Paul still has his right to privacy which has also been violated. And now Paul is being exploited by his own guardian and the Eldercaring Coordinator.

What I also find troubling is Merideth Nagel, Paul's attorney, doing a complete 180 on Sandy visiting Paul. After asking Paul if he wanted to see Sandy several times and each time hearing his negative response, Merideth had Sandy barred from entering

Trinity Springs to visit Paul. Now she told me that she would not object to Sandy visiting Paul. Why the sudden change?

And finally, why was Judge Morley so adamant to quickly give Sandy visiting privileges with Paul, only to have her violate the court order shortly after her December visit? The entire episode makes no sense.

CHAPTER 58M-2
GUARDIANSHIP

(6) INFORMED CONSENT.

(a) Decisions that Professional Guardians make on behalf of their Wards under guardianship shall be based on the principle of Informed Consent.

(b) Informed Consent is a decision maker's agreement to a particular course of action based on a full disclosure of the facts needed to make the decision intelligently.

(c) To have Informed Consent, a decision maker must have adequate information on the issue, must be able to take voluntary action, and must not be coerced.

(d) In evaluating each requested decision, Professional Guardians shall do the following:

1. Have a clear understanding of the issue for which informed consent is being sought,

2. Have a clear understanding of the options, expected outcomes, risks and benefits of each alternative,

3. Determine the conditions that necessitate treatment or

action,

4. Maximize the participation of Wards in understanding the facts and directing a decision, to the extent possible,

5. Determine whether a Ward has previously stated preferences in regard to a decision of this nature,

6. Determine why this decision needs to be made now rather than later,

7. Determine what will happen if a decision is made to take no action,

8. Determine what the least restrictive alternative is for the situation; and,

9. Obtain written documentation of all reports relevant to each decision, if possible.

(7) STANDARDS FOR DECISION-MAKING.

(a) Professional Guardians shall assist and encourage Wards to participate in decisions, when possible.

(b) Professional Guardians shall, consistent with court orders and state statutes, exercise authority only as necessitated by the limitations of the Ward.

(c) Each decision made by a Professional Guardian shall be an informed decision based on the principle of Informed Consent as set forth in subsection (6).

(d) Professional Guardians shall identify and advocate for the goals, needs, and preferences of their Wards.

1. Professional Guardians shall ask their Wards what they want.

2. If a Ward has difficulty expressing what he or she wants, his

or her Professional Guardian shall, to the extent possible, help the Ward express his or her goals, needs, and preferences.

3. When a Ward, even with assistance, cannot express his or her goals and preferences, Professional Guardians shall seek input from others familiar with the Ward to determine what the Ward may have wanted.

4. To the extent that a Ward's goals and preferences have been made known to a Professional Guardian, the Professional Guardian shall honor those goals or preferences, except when following the Ward's goals and preferences would cause significant impairment to a Ward's physical, mental, or emotional health.

(e) Substituted Judgment.

1. Substituted Judgment is a principle of decision-making which requires the guardian to consider the decision their Ward would have made when the Ward had capacity and use that as the guiding force in any surrogate decision a guardian makes.

2. Substituted Judgment shall be used when making decisions on behalf of a ward except when following the Ward's wishes would cause significant impairment to a Ward's physical, mental, or emotional health, or when a Professional Guardian cannot establish a Ward's goals and preferences even with support.

(f) Best Interest.

1. Best Interest is the principle of decision-making that should be used only when a Ward has never had capacity, when a Ward's goals and preferences cannot be ascertained

even with support, or when following a Ward's wishes would cause significant impairment to a Ward's physical, mental, or emotional health or his or her property.
2. The Best Interest principle requires a guardian to consider the least restrictive course of action to provide for the needs of a Ward.
3. The Best Interest principle requires guardians to consider a Ward's past practice and evaluate evidence of his or her choices.
4. The Best Interest principle requires the course of action that maximizes what is best for a Ward and that includes consideration of the least intrusive, most normalizing, and least restrictive course of action possible given the needs of the Ward.

(8) LEAST RESTRICTIVE ALTERNATIVE.
(a) When making a decision, Professional Guardians shall carefully evaluate the ward's resources and the alternatives that are available and choose the one that best meets the personal and financial goals, needs, and preferences of Wards under their guardianship, while placing the least restrictions on their Wards' freedoms, rights, and ability to control their environments.
(b) Professional Guardians shall weigh the risks and benefits of each decision and develop a balance between maximizing the independence and self-determination of Wards and maintaining Wards' dignity, protection, and safety.
(c) Professional Guardians shall make individualized decisions. The least restrictive alternative for one Ward might

not be the least restrictive alternative for another Ward.

(d) The following guidelines apply in the determination of the least restrictive alternative:

1. Professional Guardians shall become familiar with the resources available for rights delegated to them including: options for residence, care, medical treatment, vocational training, and education for their wards.

2. Professional Guardians shall strive to know their Wards' goals and preferences.

3. Professional Guardians shall consider assessments of their Wards' needs as determined by specialists. This may include an independent assessment of a Ward's functional ability, health status, and care needs.

(9) SELF-DETERMINATION OF THE WARD.

(a) Professional Guardians shall provide Wards under their guardianship with every opportunity to exercise individual rights as they relate to the personal and financial needs of the Ward, as long as that exercise is consistent with court orders regarding the Ward's capacity.

(b) The Professional Guardian shall, whenever possible, seek to ensure that the Ward leads the planning process. If the Ward is unable to lead the process, the Professional Guardian shall, whenever possible, seek their participation.

(10) THE PROFESSIONAL GUARDIAN'S DUTIES REGARDING DIVERSITY AND PERSONAL PREFERENCES OF THE WARD.

Professional Guardians shall determine the extent to which Wards under guardianship identify with particular ethnic, religious, and cultural values. To determine these values, Professional Guardians shall consider the following:

(a) The Ward's attitudes regarding illness, pain, and suffering;

(b) The Ward's attitudes regarding death and dying;

(c) The Ward's views regarding quality of life issues;

(d) The Ward's views regarding societal roles and relationships; and,

(e) The Ward's attitudes regarding funeral and burial customs.

(11) CONFIDENTIALITY.

(a) Professional Guardians shall keep the affairs of Wards under guardianship confidential, unless otherwise provided by law or ordered by the Court.

(b) Professional Guardians shall respect Wards' privacy and dignity, especially when the disclosure of information is necessary.

(c) Disclosure of information shall be limited to what is necessary and relevant to the issue being addressed.

(d) Professional Guardians shall assist Wards in communicating with third parties unless the disclosure will substantially harm the Ward.

(12) DUTIES OF THE PROFESSIONAL GUARDIAN OF THE PERSON.

(a) Professional Guardians appointed guardians of the person shall have the following duties and obligations to Wards under guardianship, unless decision making authority has not been delegated to the Professional Guardian or the letters of guardianship provides otherwise:

1. To see that Wards are living in the most appropriate environment that addresses each Ward's goals, needs, and preferences subject to limitations of his or her financial resources and availability of government benefits,

   a. Professional Guardians must prioritize home or other community-based settings, when not inconsistent with a Ward's goals and preferences.

   b. Professional Guardians shall authorize moving Wards to a more restrictive environment only after evaluating other medical and health care options and making an independent determination that the move is the least restrictive alternative at the time, fulfills the current needs of a Ward, and serves the overall best interest of a Ward.

   c. Professional Guardians shall consider the proximity of the setting to those people and activities that are important to Wards when choosing a residential setting.

   d. When Professional Guardians consider placement of a Ward in a residential setting, the bases of the decision shall be to minimize the risk of significant impairment to a Ward's physical, mental, or emotional health, to obtain the most appropriate placement possible, and to secure the best treatment for the Ward consistent with Section 744.3215, F.S.

2. To ensure that provision is made for the support, care, comfort, health, and maintenance of Wards, subject to limitations of his or her financial resources and availability of government benefits,

3. To make reasonable efforts to secure for Wards medical, psychological, therapeutic, and social services, training, education, and social and vocational opportunities that are appropriate and that will maximize Wards' potential for self-reliance and independence, subject to limitations of his or her financial resources and availability of government benefits; and,

4. To report to the Office of Public and Professional Guardians, the Department of Children and Families' Adult Protective Services Unit and local law enforcement incidents of abuse, neglect and/or exploitation as defined by state statutes within a reasonable period of time. For purposes of this provision the phrase "reasonable period of time" shall mean the time period in which a reasonably prudent person, under the same or similar circumstances, would report incidents of abuse, neglect and/or exploitation to the Office of Public and Professional Guardians and other appropriate authorities.

(13) INITIAL AND ONGOING RESPONSIBILITIES OF THE PROFESSIONAL GUARDIAN OF THE PERSON.

(a) With the proper authority, Professional Guardians appointed guardian of the person shall take the following initial steps after appointment:

1. Professional Guardians shall address all issues of Wards under guardianship that require immediate action.

2. Professional Guardians shall meet with Wards as soon after the appointment as is feasible. At the first meeting, Professional Guardians shall:

a. Communicate to the Ward the role of the Professional Guardian,

b. Explain the rights retained by the Ward,

c. Assess the Ward's physical and social situation,

d. Assess the Ward's educational, vocational, and recreational needs,

e. Obtain the Ward's preferences,

f. Assess the support systems available to the Ward; and,

g. Attempt to gather any missing necessary information regarding the Ward.

3. After the first meeting with the Ward, the Professional Guardian shall notify relevant agencies and individuals of the appointment of a Professional Guardian, and shall complete the intake process by gathering information and ensuring that applicable evaluations are completed, if appropriate. The Professional Guardian shall:

a. Obtain a psychological evaluation, if appropriate.

b. Obtain an inventory of advance directives. Such statements of intent would include, but are not limited to, powers of attorney, living wills, organ donation statements, and statements by the person recorded in medical charts.

c. Establish contact and communicate with the Professional Guardian of the property and/or any other relevant fiduciary for the Ward.

Given everything that had taken place over the last four days, we had accepted the fact that the Judge was going to grant Sandy some sort of visiting privileges. We thought it was necessary to advise Paul what lies ahead and it would be better if he heard it from his family. Therefore, Bruce, Gail, Katherine, and I took Paul out to lunch on Monday (October 28, 2019) to have a talk with him. We told him that in all likelihood, the Court was going to allow Sandy to visit him. We also told him that it was solely his choice whether he wanted to see Sandy and we would fully support his choice. Once again, he told us he wanted nothing to do with her and he wanted her out of his life. We told him to think about it and again told him that it was his choice and it was fine with us if he wanted to see her.

The court hearing on Sandy's petition for visitation with Paul was held on Friday, November 1st.

I had hired my attorney, Harry Hackney, in February on a recommendation from Paul's attorney, Merideth Nagel, that I file a petition with the court to be Paul's guardian. I knew that Mark and Allyne were going to hire an attorney also and since the court appointed Amanda Ritter to be Paul's guardian, I saw no further need for an attorney. I had recommended that Mark and Allyne hire my attorney, Harry Hackney, since he was so familiar with the case. However, Mark and Allyne took Amanda Ritter's recommendation and hired Todd Mazenko.

I told Mark and Allyne that I would be available to testify at the hearing. I later learned that Merideth Nagel, Paul's attorney, stated that she was not going to make any presentation to the court on behalf of Paul and would support Amanda's recommendations. I then told Mark and Allyne that their attorney, Todd Mazenko, would have to put me on the stand to testify. However, they told me that their attorney was hired to deal with the trust only. Without the ability to take the stand, I saw no reason to attend the hearing.

(Note: I take full responsibility for this mistake. However, given the unusual circumstances that occurred, I am not certain that my testimony would have made any difference.)

Following the hearing, we learned that the judge granted unlimited visitation to Sandy with supervision by Sandy's minister and there would be no fee. I still do not understand why the judge chose Sandy's minister.

On the following Tuesday, before the court order was signed, Sandy, Sandy's sister, Sandy's minister, and Amanda visited Paul for about an hour. However, Paul was confused again as to who was there. He called me and told me four women from his high school class came to see him.

I told him that I was quite sure they were not from Troy High School and asked if he was sure it was not his wife, Sandy. He said he did not think so.

The following day, Bruce and I were running some errands and we stopped by Trinity Springs and confirmed who visited Paul. We told him exactly who was there and his response was, "I hate to be tricked like that."

One Thursday after completing an errand just a few blocks from Trinity Springs, I visited Paul bringing him the toothpaste he needed and a newly published book on the 10th Mountain Division, one of the units he commanded. He asked me if we could sit down and talk. He then asked me "if the bitch keeps coming to see him and tricking him by not telling him who she is, can she be arrested for harassment? (Note: He never calls Sandy by name and has for a long time referred to her as 'the bitch' when she comes up in a conversation.) I told him probably not and he should ask for the name of everyone that comes to see him.

On Sunday afternoon, Bruce and I planned to be at Trinity Springs with Paul to watch an NFL game. When I arrived, Paul told me about another strange visit he had on Saturday November 9th. From the description he gave me and the fact that they had a dog with them, I knew it was Paul's neighbors, Bill and Lillian. These are the same people who were mocking Paul in front of Allyne, Paul's daughter and made horrible comments about Katherine and me on Sandy's Facebook.

So, in addition to Sandy visiting Paul, it appears that Sandy is also sending her friends to visit Paul, even though they are not on the list of visitors allowed to see Paul. Paul told me that they stayed for "almost an hour." I went to the front desk and checked the visitor's log and found that Bill and Lil did sign in at 1:45 PM and out at 1:50 PM (which was not the time they left) and did not list who they were visiting. I spoke to the receptionist on the desk (who was a new employee) and she wrote down all the information. I was later told that the incident was recorded and it would not happen again.

Paul's daughter sent me a copy of the visitation order on Monday:

IN THE CIRCUIT COURT OF THE FIFTH JUDICIAL CIRCUIT IN AND

A Case Study Of Elder Abuse And Exploitation In Florida

FOR SUMTER COUNTY, FLORIDA
IN RE: GUARDIANSHIP OF: CASE NO.: 2019 MH 89
CASE NO.: 2019 GA 000158

JOHN PAUL BAKER   PROBATE DIVISION

ION Ward. _____/ ORDER ON PETITION FOR VISITATION THIS MATTER having come before the Court for consideration at hearing on November 1, 2019, before the Honorable Michelle T. Morley on Petitioner and wife of the Ward, Sandra Baker's Petition for Visitation. Petitioner, Sandra Baker, was present in Court and represented by counsel Cara C. Singeltary, Esq. Todd Mazenko, Esq., counsel specially appearing on behalf of the CoTrustees, Allyne C. Baker and Mark Baker, was present on behalf of his clients who were not present. Professional Guardian, Amanda Ritter, was present and represented by counsel Michael J. Rogers, Esq. The Ward, John Paul Baker, was not present but was represented by counsel, Merideth C. Nagel, Esq. who appeared telephonically. Eldercaring Coordinator, Cher Myers, and Petitioner's witness, Dr. Janice Gordon-Barnes, were also present. The Court reviewed the pleadings, considered argument of counsel, weighed the sworn testimony from Dr. Janice Gordon-Barnes and Cher Myers, and otherwise being fully advised of the premise, FINDS as follows:

    1. The parties agreed that Petitioner, Sandra Baker, should have visitation with the Ward/ her husband, John Paul Baker. No evidence was presented to convince the Court that Petitioner and the Ward should not have contact. The visit between Petitioner and the Ward on Friday, October 25, 2019, went very well and the parties appeared affectionate and happy to see each other despite the Ward's memory

issues.

2. Dr. Janice Gordon-Barnes, Reverend with Holy Trinity Episcopal Church in Fruitland Park, Florida, is willing and able to supervise visits between Petitioner and the Ward at the Ward's place of residence.

3. Petitioner is entitled to unlimited visitation with the Ward/her husband, who currently resides in a memory care facility, provided the visits are initially supervised by Dr. Gordon-Barnes or the guardian, depending on availability. It would be best for Sandra Baker's visits to be arranged so as not to coincide with the presence of the Ward's brothers, Carl Baker and Bruce Baker, or the Ward's children, Mark Baker and Allyne Baker.

4. Supervision is in order on a temporary basis for 3-4 weeks, with supervision tapering off in the third and fourth weeks. 5. The Ward's Guardian, Amanda Ritter, shall be notified by Dr. Gordon-Barnes in the event of any outburst or altercation during the visitation. WHEREFORE, IT IS ORDERED AND ADJUDGED as follows: 1. That the Petitioner, Sandra Baker, shall have unlimited visitation and/or contact with the Ward as often as can be arranged between Petitioner Sandra Baker, the Ward John Paul Baker, and Dr. Janice Gordon-Barnes or the guardian Amanda Ritter.

2. | 2. Initially the entirety of the visitation shall be supervised by Dr. Janice Gordon-Barnes or the guardian. However, so long as the visits remain positive, the supervision shall taper off at the discretion of Dr. Gordon-Barnes or other supervisor as the case may be. By way of example, if a visit is to be 3 hours long, the first 2 hours would be supervised with the 3rd hour unsupervised. Thereafter, the supervision could be reduced to the first hour being supervised with

the last two hours being unsupervised. After that, the visits would be unsupervised but Dr. Gordon Barnes or the guardian would remain nearby or outside, and ultimately there would be no supervision. It is intended that this transition would occur within 3-4 weeks. 3. In the event that Dr. Gordon-Barnes or another visit supervisor observes any outburst or altercation between Sandra Baker and Paul Baker during a visit the visit, shall immediate (sic) terminate and the Professional Guardian, Amanda Ritter, must be notified. DONE AND ORDERED in Chambers in Bushnell, Sumter County, Florida this November 7, 2019.
    Honorable Michelle T. Morley
    Circuit Court Judge

Note: Despite all the efforts of Judge Morley, Amanda and Cher to give Sandy visitation rights, Sandy violated the court order after only two supervised visits with Paul and her visitation was terminated.

If you refer to Amanda's October 25th email to me and Allyne, trying to justify her bringing Sandy to visit Paul (Page 303), I added emphasis to the phrase "at this time." In the next paragraph I wrote, "And to me, the last line indicates that they eventually plan to let Sandy visit Paul without one of them being present." It appears my assumption was correct.

There is another interesting twist to this case. Now if we look back even further at the Judge Morley's April 29th memo referring this case to eldercaring coordination, I find her words most interesting:

"This wife has not seen her husband since January. Brother took husband out of the house. They each want to be appointed the Ward's guardian. I found total incapacity today but in the midst of the negative opening statement I convinced them to go to eldercaring

coordination so I was unable to determine who should be appointed guardian. On a temporary basis, the court appointed lawyer for the Ward – Meredith Nagel – is the guardian. I hope the family can get in to see an EC (eldercaring coordinator) quickly so some form of visitation between husband and wife and an agreement on who will serve as guardian can be discussed. ...The brother is a retired Chief of Police. Ward is a retired Brigadier General. The wife (married in 2016 a few months after his Alzheimer's diagnosis) retired from GM but no indication what position she held."

The first two sentences tell me that the judge has no idea what the facts are in this case and immediately classifies Sandy as a victim. The second sentence is not true. After having a week to decide what he wanted to do, I visited Paul again and he immediately told me he wanted to leave Sandy and he asked if he could live with us. I said, "Of course you can." And Paul left voluntarily; I did not take him out of the house.

Again, I remind you that the "negative opening statement "the Judge is referring to is the opening statement of my attorney which briefly outlined the abuse and exploitation of Paul by Sandy. Sandy then took the stand and before another word was uttered, Paul's attorney, Merideth Nagel, asked to approach the bench. Within minutes, Sandy and I and our attorneys were all in the hallway discussing mediation (officially referred to as Eldercaring Coordination) to replace actual testimony in the court room. I was told earlier that this pilot study was Judge Morley's "pet project" and my attorney thought the Judge would push for this and that is exactly what she did. As a result of "convincing them to go to eldercaring coordination, (I) was unable to determine who should be appointed guardian." This is unbelievable. First, after hearing the opening statement, why wouldn't the judge want to hear from both sides so she would at least have a general understanding of the facts of the case. Was the eldercaring project created by her because she did not want to make those tough decisions?

The judge then stated that she hopes "the family can get in to see an EC (Coordinator) so some form of visitation between husband and wife and an agreement on who will serve as guardian can be discussed." If you review Chapter 11, you will see that Cher Myers, the eldercaring coordinator never really discussed visitation and she never discussed guardianship. Cher saw Paul at the initial interview on May 29th, at the VA Clinic on October 10th and then on October 25th when she and Amanda covertly snuck Sandy into the memory care unit to see Paul. Cher gave Sandy far more attention than she gave Paul, the true victim of this fiasco.

Paul called me at 3:18 PM on November 15th and told me that a woman who was "all dolled up" came into Trinity Springs and walked up to him when he was sitting with friends and asked if she could sit down with him. Although he thought it was Sandy, he was not sure; as a result, he told her he was busy with his friends. When she went to sit down with him, he got up went to his room and called me quite upset. He told me "I can't even live my life without that bitch harassing me." I told him to stay in his room and I would call the front desk and see who it was. I called Carol and she checked and it was Sandy. I told her that

Paul called me from his room all upset that she was there. Carol told me that they would ask her to leave.

I called Paul back at 3:30 PM and he was still upset. We talked for a short while and told me he could not live like this. He said, "I need to stand up like a man and tell her I want nothing to do with her and I want her out of my life." He told me he was going back to the living area to see if she left. I told him to go back to his room and call me if he has any more problems.

> *(Note: When we told Paul that the court had given Sandy permission to visit him, he became quite upset. We cautioned him then that he needed to control his anger when he saw her and not create a scene. He asked what he could do. I told him the same thing I have always told him. Walk away, go to your room and call me. That is exactly what Paul did.)*

Katherine was in the vicinity, so she went to Trinity Springs to check on Paul and see how he was after Sandy's unannounced visit.

Katherine summarized her visit as follows:

When I arrived, Carol was at the desk. She said that Sandy had been there and I asked if she was still there. When I signed in, I saw that Sandy and Sandy's minister, Dr. Barnes, had signed in at 3:00 and signed out at 3:50. I told Carol I was out and Carl had called me and asked me to stop by and make sure Paul was okay. She said that Carl had called because Paul was upset and that several of the staff went back to make sure everything was okay. She said that Sandy was just sitting quietly when she saw her. Later she told me Sandy was not around Paul but sitting separately from him.

When I saw Paul, he seemed very pleased to see me and asked me if I would sit with him. He was listening to music on the TV with Mercedes, Carol, and another woman I didn't know. I told him I heard he had a visitor. He said Sandy was there but he didn't want to see her. He said he called Carl and Sandy left. I don't know what really happened because he didn't seem to realize she had stayed there a while. I told him Carl had asked me to stop by since I was already out and just making sure he was okay. I told him that he was all we cared about and wanted to ensure that he was okay. After that we listened to music, he sang and we chatted with the other residents largely about the music. I asked if he was looking forward to seeing "The Sound of Music" and he was excited about that. When they called everyone to dinner, he asked if I wanted to stay for dinner and I told him I had to leave because we had plans. He walked with me as far as the dining area, told me he loved me, and said good-bye.

The next morning (Saturday) I went to Trinity Springs to pick up Paul for a day with his family. Paul, Bruce, Gail, Katherine and I had tickets to see "The Sound of Music" at the Sonnentag Theatre and planned to have dinner after the show. Theresa was at the desk and she told me that she went right down to the memory care unit yesterday after my call to check on Paul. Paul was in his room and Sandy and Dr. Barnes were sitting at a table in the open area. Theresa told Sandy that Paul's reaction was part of his disease and that may very well be different the next time she came for a visit.

When Paul and Sandy were fighting while they were married, I always told Paul to walk away to avoid a conflict and call me. In fact, I told Sandy to call me also and I would come to the house. I gave Paul the same advice for Trinity Springs. If you do not want to talk to Sandy or anyone else, go to your room and call me. That is exactly what Paul has done in the past and that is exactly what he did on Friday.

Apparently, Sandy believes that Paul did not talk to her on Friday because he did not recognize her. The opposite is true. Paul did not talk to Sandy because after two earlier visits, he did recognize her and as he has stated repeatedly to anyone who listens, he wants nothing to do with her and he wants her out of his life. That is exactly what he has told his attorney, Merideth Nagel, numerous times.

Even though Paul is a ward of the state, he still has free will and can choose who he does and who he does not want to talk to. No one wants any confrontation whatsoever and going to his room, his sanctuary, is certainly one way to prevent it. I have asked the Director of Trinity Springs (Mike) and Amanda, Paul's court appointed guardian, to give our family some guidance in this area because we will always comply with the court order, but we also have an obligation to protect Paul's life and liberty at the same time.

On November 18th, I received the following email from Amanda, Paul's guardian:

From: Amanda Ritter

To: Carl Baker
Cc: Cher Myers, Pati Kersey
Sent: Wednesday, November 20, 2019, 2:49:02 PM
Subject: Meeting with me (sic) and Cher

Good afternoon Carl. I was hoping you would have time to meet with myself and Cher Myers (Eldercaring Coordinator) on either December 4 or December 6 at 2pm. This meeting will be in reference to the court ordered visitation Sandy has with Paul. We can come to you if you are available. I look forward to your reply.
Thank you,

Amanda A. Ritter
Registered Professional Guardian
and VA Fiduciary

I was quite sure that Amanda wanted this meeting because Paul had refused to talk to Sandy on November 15 and she would be trying to hold me responsible for Paul's actions.

I responded to Amanda email on November 22nd:

Amanda
December 6th at 2:00 PM is fine for both Katherine and me.

Thank you.
Carl and Katherine

The meeting was scheduled for our home and since my brother Bruce and his wife, Gail were an integral part of Paul's well-being, they wanted to attend also.

What precipitated the meeting was Paul's refusal to speak to Sandy when she visited Trinity Springs on Friday, November 15th. Amanda had told Paul's daughter, Allyne, that she thought I had too much control over Paul and we thought that she may be considering either limiting or eliminating my visits to Paul. Fortunately, that was not the case.

At first, we discussed a few administrative matters regarding Paul's medical care. Amanda told us that she was writing the required annual plan for Paul and needed a list of all of Paul's doctors, the last appointment date and the next appointment date, which I did send her the following morning.

I opened the meeting stating that since Amanda asked for the meeting, she could start. However, I told them that we all hoped for an honest, open conversation so we could all be "on the same sheet of music" and do what is best for Paul. Both she and Cher agreed.

Amanda started by telling us that before she came to our house today, she stopped by Sandy's house and picked up several of Paul's jackets and brought them to Paul at Trinity Springs. We thanked her especially since Sandy had not let Paul have all his clothes from his home for close to a year now and the weather had turned cooler. Paul was wearing a jacket that I had provided him.

As stated multiple times, the family had made numerous requests to Cher Myers for the remainder of Paul's clothes, Paul's three pistols and Paul's personal items. For months, all we got from Cher was "lip service" (e.g., I am working on it.) and to date all Paul received is some of his clothes and toiletries which were delivered on July 3rd, 139 days after Paul left Sandy and the house he shared with her and moved in with us.

We told both of them that this has been going on too long. I told Cher in our first conversation on May 29, 2019, that I was genuinely concerned that Paul's three pistols were still in Sandy's possession and one of them was our dad's military pistol that he had for years and we wanted to pass down through our family. We also briefly discussed the potential danger of Sandy having possession of these weapons illegally while displaying signs of psychological problems.

I also stated that the "valued personal items" that Cher and Amanda told Sandy to bring on her surprise visit to Paul to "break the ice" were nothing but trinkets that meant truly little to Paul. There were two possible explanations for this: Sandy had no idea of what was important to Paul, her husband of two years, or she was playing a game to prove something. She had to know that Paul's military saber, the flag that draped our father's casket and Paul's license plate with, "Brigadier General Retired" (BG RET), were the things that meant a lot more to Paul than the items she chose. And my guess is this was just another act that showed us that she was in control and never really loved Paul.

Amanda said that Sandy had boxed a lot of Paul's personal items and stated that they are ready to be returned to Paul. After some discussion, it was decided that Amanda would hire a mover and have the boxes moved to our garage since Sandy does not want any of us in her house or on her property. It was agreed that the cost of moving these items from Sandy & Paul's home to

Carl and Katherine's home would be shared since Baker Family members and friends had offered to pick up these items at no cost, however, Sandy would not agree to that resolution. We did agree that any of Paul's furniture or other items that would enhance the sale of the home will remain until the house is sold.

Amanda told us that her main concern is what is best for Paul in terms of his health, his happiness, and his well-being. She said she is easy to work with and she realizes that Paul's relationship with his brother is very tight and it always will be. She also stated that right now Sandy is not going away since there is a court order giving her visitation rights with Paul. She also said there are allegations from Sandy that Paul has been manipulated by Carl. These allegations are totally without foundation, and we outlined all our efforts over the past few weeks to ensure that Paul made his own decisions regarding Sandy's visitations. Sandy making allegations that I am manipulating Paul is her cover for her own abuse and exploitation of Paul.

Bruce also responded to Sandy's outrageous allegation by giving an overview of why Paul and I were so close citing the fact that we graduated from college together, we went to basic training at the same time, we were commissioned as officers in the US Army together, we served in the same unit once in our military careers and Paul always came to either Bruce or me anytime he had a major decision to make or had a problem.

I asked Amanda and Cher if they had read all the information that I sent them documenting all of Sandy's abuse and exploitation of Paul. Cher stated immediately that Paul was a victim of domestic abuse. Dr. Phil McGraw, Clinical Psychologist, has often stated on his televison show that he would never put an abuser and the victim in the same room without their consent and someone to supervise the meeting. Yet Amanda and Cher had no problem putting Paul and Sandy in the same room!

Amanda said that all she wants is what is best for Paul and she was not trying to decipher the past and Sandy can no longer harm him or spend Paul's money. She went on to say that it was at her discretion to remove supervision from Sandy's visits with Paul but would not do so if she thought that it was unsafe.

I then asked Amanda about the current restrictions on Paul's visitors, sharing that Sandy's friends and neighbors are visiting Paul and he has no idea who they are. They are also the same people who have taken to Facebook and said some horrible things about Katherine and me "kidnapping" Paul. Amanda responded that she would not prevent "another loving person from visiting and making Paul happy."

This has been the problem throughout this entire case. No one, including the Judge, Paul's lawyer, the Eldercaring Coordinator, and the court appointed guardian wants to talk about all of Sandy's abuse and exploitation. When Harry Hackney, my attorney outlined it in his opening statement at the first hearing, Paul's attorney, Merideth Nagel made a motion to bring in an Eldercaring Coordinator to mediate an agreement in the case. All of this resulted in Sandy's abuse and exploitation of Paul being totally ignored.

That brought us to the next topic, the location of Sandy's visits. I stated that Sandy's visits with Paul should always be in an open space and never in his room. Amanda stated that Paul asked them to his room on the first visit because Sandy had some of Paul's items. I said that Paul's room is his sanctuary and he still has a right to privacy. I told Paul many times that if someone comes that he does not want to see, I do not want him creating a scene. The best solution is to go back to his room and that is exactly what he did the last time Sandy visited. We suggested that they meet in the room at the end of Paul's hallway to provide a quiet, semi-private place for their meetings.

It is important to note prior to this, I sat down with the Executive Director at Trinity Springs and repeated what I told Paul on how to avoid conflict. He stated that he agreed that is what Paul should do and emphasized that Paul is entitled to his privacy in his room.

Amanda told us that she had Paul examined by a psychiatrist that she had used in the past, and he had found that Paul was incapable of making any decisions. I find this somewhat strange because in an earlier conversation right after the examination, Amanda told me that the psychiatrist told her that Paul had no ill feelings against Sandy. I told her that Paul must have thought the doctor was referring to his first wife, Linda because Paul does have a good relationship with her and we have talked a lot about her lately since she had been quite ill.

> Note: I suggested that Sandy be examined by a psychiatrist as well, since we all agree that she has some mental health issues and, in my opinion, is a narcissistic sociopath. Amanda thought that was a good idea and stated she would schedule it. However, she never followed up on it and there was no examination of Sandy, despite her behavior. So instead, Amanda and Cher continued to fulfill the judge's wishes and pushed forward so that a mentally ill abuser could have visitation with our brother. This is a sad situation.

Amanda continued to explain that she had a noticeably short time frame to make Sandy's initial visit happen since she was tasked to get it done before the hearing on November 1st. I asked her if she was referring to the email from the Judge with the seven questions which she wanted researched prior to the hearing (see page 314). Amanda stated that she interpreted that email to make sure that Sandy could visit Paul and then she and Cher came up with their plan in response to that email.

Neither Amanda nor Cher ever spoke to the four of us about this even though the Judge asked, "Have all parties explored every avenue between the Bakers before the upcoming hearing?" They spent all their time coaching Sandy for her visit with Paul. The omission of the Baker family participation was evidently intentional and unethical.

I asked Amanda if she had notified Merideth Nagel, Paul's attorney, of her planned visit by Sandy. Amanda said that she did tell Merideth after the visit.

I than asked Amanda if she was familiar with the term informed consent which requires that Professional Guardians to "ask their Wards what they want." Cher responded that on the day of the visit (October 25th) at Trinity Springs, Amanda and Sandy stayed in the background while Cher approached Paul and told him that "his wife, Sandra Baker was here to see him." Paul asked if that was his first wife. And Cher responded that it was his present wife and Paul said that he would see her and then Amanda and Sandy came forward.

First of all, this does not at all comply with the principle of Informed Consent. Secondly, after seeing Paul's reaction to the mere mention of Sandy's name for the last 10 months, I have an exceedingly difficult time believing Cher's version of the story. Paul's recollection of this initial meeting with Sandy was entirely different, although we do recognize that his memory retention of recent events is sketchy at best.

Next, there was a lengthy conversation on how to best handle Sandy's next visit with Paul. Concerns regarding who should be there and how we approached Paul arose. I offered that perhaps I could help. Then both Amanda and Cher began reciting what I should say, what I can't say, how will Sandy react to my being there, what needs to be said to Paul so he will talk to Sandy and on and on. I sat back for a moment and realized the intensity of both Amanda and Cher. They were asking me to lie to my brother so that he would speak to Sandy. It appeared that both Amanda and Cher would do anything to please the Judge and were anticipating horrible consequences if Paul refused to speak to Sandy again. At this point, it became abundantly clear that Paul was no longer the primary concern here. The Judge was and evidently, Sandy was second.

Katherine saw the same thing and stated that any lies could very well effect Paul's trust in Carl. I suggested that Sandy bring Paul his BG RET license plate and I would tell Paul that Sandy was there to see him and she had the license plate for him. I will stay there with him and Sandy cannot harm him in any way. She wants to return it to him and he should thank her.

We all checked our calendars and decided that Amanda, Cher, Sandy, and I would meet at Trinity Springs on Wednesday, December 11, 2019, at 1:30 PM to visit Paul.

Quite candidly, I will be very surprised if Sandy agrees to this. And secondly, I do not know how we will handle this if Sandy does not have Paul's license plate. My second choice would be the flag that draped our father's coffin.

Sandy's Dec 11 Visit with Paul

I arrived at Trinity Springs at 1:26 PM. Amanda Ritter, Sandy, Sandy's sister, and Reverend Janice Gordon-Barnes were there. Cher arrived about 1:45 PM. I asked Sandy if she had Paul's license plate. She said angrily that she doesn't answer to me she answers to Amanda. Amanda told her that was not the right attitude if we are going to make any progress today. Sandy then told me she had the plate and wanted to know if I had her cell phone. I said, "no." Sandy stated that it was her phone. I replied," I hear you." There was no other conversation about the phone.

Sandy's sister who seemed like a very sensible person, stated that there was no reason for her to see Paul and said she would wait in the car. Cher and Amanda agreed.

Amanda, Cher and I went to visit Paul while Sandy and the reverend waited in the common area. Paul was in his room and asleep; I brought him to the sunroom at the end of the hallway where we sat down with Amanda and Cher.

I told Paul that Sandy was here to see him and she wants to correct a wrong and do the right thing by returning some personal property to him. I told him that I know this will mean a lot to him and I think it would be nice if he thanked her. He agreed and Cher went out and asked Sandy and the reverend to join us. I moved to a chair and that allowed Paul, Sandy, Amanda, and Cher to all sit together at the table.

When Sandy returned the license plate to Paul, you could see the joy in Paul's face and he let us know how happy he was to have this back. Sandy also returned a blanket from the Honor Flight, his coffee cup and a wooden Army seal to Paul. Additionally, she gave him a stuffed Santa Clause that sings HO, HO, HO. She reached into the large bag to give him something else, then stopped and said I do not think I will give him these now. At that time, I had no clue as to the other possessions of Paul she was withholding, nor did I know why she did not choose to give them to Paul. . However, nine days later, I would have the answer.

Paul went on to tell stories about the 10th Mountain Division which he confused with his time in being in the Adirondacks in New York several years ago and another story about meeting Celine Dion in Canada, which was not true.

Paul then sang, "You Lost That Loving Feeling" which is his favorite song. Sandy told Paul that he sang that song to her on her birthday and that it "melted her heart" and she would never forget it. That was a lie. The real reason why she will never forget it was that Paul sang that song at her birthday dinner in a restaurant and Sandy told all of us that she was extremely angry and embarrassed due to the words in the song.

Then the conversation went to songs by Elvis, Josh Groban, and the Eagles.

Reverend Gordon-Barnes then suggested that she bring communion to Paul some Sunday or perhaps they could pick

Paul up for church some Sunday. I told her that I would go with him and she stated that I was welcome also. Cher said it was too early in the process to discuss this.

Amanda then told everyone that she thought this meeting was a good start on working together to improve visitation. She stated there was no doubt that Paul and Carl had a remarkably close relationship and that Paul was much more comfortable with Carl being in the room. Amanda stated for now all visitations will include Carl and she and Cher will evaluate the progress as we move forward.

Note: The truth of the matter is that none of us want to see Paul leaving Trinity Springs with Sandy and given her past, I would strongly object to it.

The meeting ended after just less than 90 minutes. As we were leaving the room, Sandy asked Paul if she could help him move the returned items to his room. He did not answer her. Amanda then asked Paul if he wanted any help from Sandy taking the items to his room. Paul said, "No, Carl will help me." From the look on her face, you could tell this angered Sandy and she left the room. As we were walking out of the room, Sandy stopped Paul and said," You know that I love you." Paul responded, "Forever?" Sandy replied, "Yes, forever. Can I kiss you?" Paul and Sandy kissed goodbye.

When we were back in Paul's room, I started hanging the army plaque on his wall. I told Paul that he must have enjoyed his visit with Sandy since he kissed her. He responded, "Not really, I liked the one sitting next to me the best." *(He was referring to Cher.)* Needless to say, I was surprised at this.

I asked, "Then, why did you kiss Sandy?" He said, "I don't know." I asked him if he wanted to see Sandy again and he told me, "Not really." Paul was very confused by all of this.

As earlier promised, Cher came to our home at 4:15 PM and dropped off Paul's guns that Sandy has refused to return to Paul for nine months until now. The problem was that only two weapons were returned – the .38 Smith & Wesson 6-shot revolver and the Colt .32 caliber semi-automatic. The 9mm Glock semi-automatic pistol was still missing. However, some of the paperwork for the Glock was in the case. As is typical for Cher, she stated that instead of bringing this up with Sandy now and upsetting her, she would wait until after the holidays and see if it is in all the personal belongings that Sandy will be returning to Paul.

On December 20, 2019 at 11:19 AM, I received a call from Paul and he told me that a woman came to his room and had a long talk with him. I asked Paul if it was the nurse and he said he did not think so, but the woman knew a lot about him. I asked Paul if it was Sandy and he said it could have been her. I told him that I would check and call him back.

I called Trinity Springs and talked to Carol at the front desk. She confirmed it was Sandy and she was alone, unsupervised. She signed in at 10:07 AM and left at 11:20 AM. I told Carol that Sandy was not allowed to visit him without me or her minister being present. Carol apologized and said she had thought that the visiting restrictions had changed.

I immediately called Katherine who was shopping after she finished with her work at our church. She was at the Walmart located a block away from Trinity Springs and said she would go to Trinity Spring immediately to visit Paul and make sure everything was okay.

I then phoned Amanda Ritter at 11:30 AM. She told me that she would call Sandy as soon as she hung up from our call and get right back to me.

Amanda called back in less than 10 minutes and told me that Sandy did visit Paul and was in violation of the court order. She explained that Sandy called earlier and asked if Amanda could set up a visit with her and Paul before she left on Monday for the holidays. Amanda told her that we had all agreed that the next visit would be after the holidays and the time frame was too short to arrange for a visit before Monday. She said that Sandy "went off" and was not pleased that Amanda told her that I would be present during her visits. I told her that I was not happy that this visit was alone with Paul in his room. Amanda stated that she would report this to Judge Morley and schedule a hearing for Sandy. In addition, she suspended Sandy's ability to visit Paul, even with supervision until further notice.

Katherine came home with everything that Sandy had brought to Paul's room. Later that weekend, after reading everything she gave Paul and looking at the dirty, unwashed clothes that Sandy gave Paul, I became very concerned about her state of mind and Paul's safety. She just spent an hour alone with Paul in his room and anything could have happened.

Knowing that Sandy left The Villages early Monday morning to visit her family out of state, I waited until after Christmas and on December 26, 2019, I sent the following email to Amanda,

Paul's guardian, with copies to Cher and Paul's Attorney Merideth Nagel:

Amanda

During our meeting on December 6th, the six of us worked together to make Sandy's visit with Paul on December 11th not only possible, but comfortable for both of them, despite Sandy's initial show of anger towards me (which was quickly corrected by you). I think we are all in agreement that the visit went well.

However, Sandy's actions on December 20th cause me great concern for everyone's safety to include both you, Cher, Paul, and Sandy herself. Sandy knew the next visit to Paul was going to be scheduled after the holidays when she returned home. Yet she called you and requested (or demanded) a visit with Paul before she left town on Monday. I understand you told her the time frame to get everyone together was too short and she would have to wait until after the holidays.

So, what does Sandy do? She drives to Trinity Springs and tells Carol, the receptionist at the front desk, that she is there "to see her husband." Unfortunately, Carol had thought the rules for Sandy's visit had changed and she let her in. Sandy went directly to Paul's room and spent an hour with Paul behind a closed door without any supervision. Not only was this in violation of the court order and your instructions to her, but it is also exactly what we did not want.

Sandy will most likely tell you that she has every right to see "her husband" and does not think she did anything wrong. This type of conduct is truly characteristic of a sociopath which is exactly what she is. Sociopaths are manipulative, have a grandiose sense of self and entitlement, poor behavior control, impulsive behavior and a lack of remorse, shame, or guilt. These actions again show all of us that Sandy's mental state is anything but rational or stable. Sandy is heading down a road that does not have a good ending.

What Sandy brought with her to Trinity Springs may also be an indicator of her mental state. In addition to two cards, and numerous pictures of Paul and her together, she gave Paul a copy of their wedding vows, the original copy of their contract with the wedding planner with every "we" and "our" in the document circled, a copy of the receipt of payment to the Circuit Court for their marriage license and three soiled articles of Paul's clothing to include an old sweatshirt covered with paint, which I promptly threw in the garbage. The documents that she gave Paul will have no impact since Paul can no longer comprehend anything he reads.

According to Cher, Sandy still has one of Paul's weapons and possibly some pistols that belonged to her second husband, Ralph. Paul's entire family has been concerned about his safety because of the instability Sandy has demonstrated throughout their marriage. She had threatened to kill herself when Paul first left her and he told her he wanted a divorce. What you may not know is that Sandy told us that her sister committed suicide. With all her lies, I do not know if this is even true, but it would be best to take some precautionary steps now. The Baker Act was changed in 2018 to allow for the removal of firearms from a person who displays potentially risky behavior which could result in harm to themselves or others. Given Sandy's mental state, I recommend that you talk to the Judge about an intervention to help Sandy and possibly prevent a tragedy.

Thank you.

Carl

Later that day, Amanda did visit Trinity Springs to ensure the restrictions on Sandy were in place and she also visited with Paul to see how he was.

On the next day, December 27th, we received the following unexpected communication from the court:

VIA FLORIDA E-FILING PORTAL
Ms. Misty Conner
Judicial Assistant to the Honorable
Michelle T. Morley, Circuit Judge
215 E. McCollum Avenue, Room 266
Bushnell, FL 33513
RE: Proposed Order on Motion to Withdraw
Guardianship of John Paul Baker; Case No. 2019 GA 000158
Dear Ms. Conner,

Submitted herewith via the Florida E-Filing Portal is a proposed Order in "word" format Allowing Withdrawal of this office as Counsel for Petitioner, Sandra Baker, in the above referenced matter.

Should the proposed Order meet with the Court's approval, I would request that you enter the same and provide conformed copies to counsel for the parties and to Ms. Baker via the Efiling Portal. Thank you for your consideration and if I can be of any further assistance to the Court in any way, please do not hesitate to contact me.

IN THE CIRCUIT COURT OF THE FIFTH JUDICIAL CIRCUIT IN AND FOR SUMTER COUNTY, FLORIDA

IN RE: GUARDIANSHIP OF:
JOHN PAUL BAKER,
Ward.

------------------------~/

CASE NO.: 2019 MH 89
CASE NO.: 2019 GA 000158
PROBATE DIVISION

ORDER ALLOWING WITHDRAWAL AS COUNSEL FOR PETITIONER

THIS CAUSE having come before the Court to be heard upon the Motion to Withdraw as Counsel for the Petitioner, SANDRA BAKER, filed by Cara C. Singeltary, Attorney for Petitioner, and the Court having considered the Motion and being otherwise fully advised in the premises, it is hereby

ORDER and ADJUDGED that said Motion is hereby GRANTED. Cara C. Singeltary, Esq., and the HUNT LAW FIRM, P.A. are granted leave to withdraw as counsel of record and are relived of any further responsibility or liability in this case. Henceforth, all pleadings shall be sent to SANDRA BAKER at 3723 Mango Court, The Villages, FL 32163.

DONE AND ORDERED in Chambers, Bushnell, Sumter County, Florida this __ day of 20

THE HONORABLE MICHELLE MORLEY,

Circuit Judge

CERTIFICATE OF SERVICE

I HEREBY CERTIFY that a true and correct copy of the foregoing has been served via the Florida Court's ECF system on this _ day of , 20 __ to the following persons pursuant to Florida Rule of Judicial Administration 2.S16(b)(l): Cara C. Singeltary, Esq.

Hunt Law Firm, P.A., 601 S. 9th Street, Leesburg, FL 34748.

This is the second time that a law firm representing Sandy has filed a motion to withdraw from the case.

On January 9, 2020, Sandy texted the following note to Amanda Ritter, Paul's guardian:

"Paul's Belongings
I would like to get all of Paul's possessions out of here, since he is never coming back. Could you please tell me what the plans are to make that happen since he has been taken totally out of my life and this is uncomfortable for me to be reminded daily?"

This is typical for Sandy. She breaks the rules of the court order on visitation and is told she cannot visit Paul until further notice and she makes herself the victim. However, there is another possibility here.

Remember that Sandy told Amanda that having me present for all her visits with Paul was unacceptable to her. Then Sandy's attorney asks the court to withdraw as her attorney. Did Sandy visit Paul, in defiance of the court order, knowing that she would be prohibited from visiting Paul again? Did she actually want nothing to do with Paul any longer and this was her way out? Was all of this planned so she could save face and continue in her victim role? This type of behavior would be typical of a narcissistic sociopath.

Amanda added a comment to Sandy's text and forwarded it to Allyne and me:

"If I set up a mover to take your dads stuff to your uncles will the trust (Paul's) pay for it? Or would you rather me rent a U-Haul and the trust pay myself and someone I can get to help."

Allyne asked me how she should respond. I sent her the following email:

Allyne
First of all, Sandy should not be allowed to unilaterally determine what possessions are Paul's. Jack, Bruce, Kevin, and I have offered to use our SUV's and move all of Paul's possessions out of the house. Sandy does not want us to be in "her" home, but it is Paul's house too and Paul wants us to move his things and he could be with us as long as Amanda is there also. Another option is for you to go through the house when you are here to ensure that Paul receives everything that is rightfully his.
Let me know.
Carl

Allyne's attorney agreed to contact Sandy directly to try to facilitate some agreement to allow us to retrieve Paul's belongings. As expected, Sandy stated that she did not want me involved in this in any way. Since Bruce and I are the only two people who could identify Paul's property, I suggested that Bruce could go through the house with Allyne.

On Friday, January 10, 2020, Cher told Allyne that during Sandy's first visit, Paul was telling Sandy about this awful woman who was in his life and had done all these terrible things to him. Obviously, he didn't know he was speaking to Sandy. His Alzheimer's prevented him from identifying her by sight, but he remembered the abuse by Sandy. Cher also stated that she was surprised that Paul remembered these events so clearly.

What troubles me the most about the conversation is that this is the first time we heard that Paul told the story of how he was abused by Sandy to a woman he did not know was Sandy. Neither Cher nor Amanda ever mentioned that to anyone in our family and as far as I can tell, never put it in her report and never told the court. Nor did they acknowledge that Paul did not know that it was Sandy he was speaking to. In fact, Amanda wrote in her initial email that the surprise meeting that she and Cher orchestrated that there "was absolutely not one moment of negativity." Obviously, that was unequivocally a lie, not only to us, but the court as well.

On January 13th, Allyne texted me with the following message:

"It's confirmed...Cher and Amanda are going to Sandy's to get some of dad's stuff at 1:00pm on Friday. I am assuming they are going to confirm with you as well because they want to bring it to your house after that."

On January 14, 2020, I sent the following email to Amanda and Cher:
Amanda and Cher
I understand that you are picking up some of Paul's personal items on Friday. I will go with you since Paul and the entire family

want to make sure we get those items that mean so much to Paul and our family. For example, there are four or five copies of the book, Battling for Saipan, on the shelf in Paul's study. There is a chapter in the book about our father's heroism during the war with some pictures. These need to be picked up also.

It is unacceptable that you keep caving into Sandy's wishes. THIS IS PAUL'S HOUSE ALSO. She does not run the show — you do. What time do you want to meet me at the house? I can assure you that I have no intentions of confronting Sandy, or doing anything to disrupt this process. My concern is that we identify and receive ALL of Paul's cherished property, so this entire ordeal can finally reach closure. We can call the Sheriff's office and have a Deputy there to make sure there is no problem.

And by the way, I do not believe that Sandy cannot find Paul's Glock pistol.

Please reply as soon as possible and I will coordinate with the Sheriff's Office.

I received the following reply from Amanda:

I have a phone call in to my attorney. I will respond with my course of action allowable under the guardianship (my scope) after hearing from him.
Thank you,
Amanda Ritter

Cher's reply follows:

Carl, please understand our efforts to achieve goals set forth. Friday #1 to get as much of Paul's personal belongings as identified by Alene (sic) in a collaborative manner. We, Amanda and I, are coming in as neutral professionals! Your presence will not work and I am asking you to please stand down! Amanda and I have just been on the phone to determine whether we will have the sheriff's office at the residence at 1 PM on Friday to avoid any potential conflict. We understand Sandy may be in possession with a 9 mm Glock and having a deputy would be reassuring on that manner in the event we trigger her but also you would be a trigger as well let's don't make that happen

Cher Myers

Later in the day, Amanda sent me the following second email after speaking to her attorney:

"Good afternoon Carl. No one is caving into Sandy's wishes. Your attending the retrieval of Paul's stuff will only create conflict and Cher and I will not go if you are insisting on being there. My guardianship attorney has also agreed that you being there will not lend to a peaceful return of Paul's personal possessions.

I give you my word that we will load up as much as we can into our 2 SUV's over and beyond what we can pick through on the list we have been given by you and Allyne. I strive for the same thing you do in closure of this very stressful matter for your family and hope that you agree that using me as a neutral 3rd party will work to the benefit of causing the least amount of drama in this emotional time.

I have copied everyone you originally copied on this email reply as well as my attorney for transparency in the plan for retrieval of Paul's personal property on Friday."

Thank you,
Amanda A Ritter

Perhaps that is the problem. Everyone thinks they are a "neutral party" and none of them are advocating for Paul—the victim in all of this.

My wife, Katherine, has been an integral part of this entire fiasco from the beginning and her summary in relation to Paul retrieving his personal items says it all:

Since they both acknowledge that Sandy is unstable and unable to control herself, and they think she might be dangerous, why not tell her she has to leave the premises and let Paul go through the house and simply take what is solely his? How would that be substantially different than what they are allowing her to do? It is all truly insane.

As Paul's guardian, I thought Amanda was supposed to be solely interested in what is in the best interests of Paul and supposed to consider his wishes. There is no way that two strangers can walk into a marital property and discern what belonged to one of them versus the other one. There is also no way that Allyne in New York can make a list of everything that should be returned to Paul.

Given that Sandy has been shown to be an abusive, congenital liar who has tried to manipulate everyone involved, including the court, by perjuring herself numerous times, this seems incredulous. It is in Paul's best interests to have his belongings returned to him and/or his loved ones. I distinctly remember the family meeting we had with Paul and Sandy and Bruce and Gail, when Paul discussed his desire to make plans and set items aside to ensure that his children and grandchildren would receive many of his personal items that were important to him. Sandy very well knows that and yet has insisted for over a year to not even allow Paul into his own home. Sandy states, "she loves him forever" and violates a court order which she had to know would terminate her visitation rights. And all this has been ignored by the authorities that are supposed to protect vulnerable victims. Although Paul has Alzheimer's, he is still a human being and no one is willing to see him as such or treat him as such, except for his family. What a disgusting eye-opening experience this has been for us all. I would certainly have thought the State of Florida was better than this!

I wanted to make sure that Amanda and Cher had the serial number for Paul's missing weapon, so I sent this email on January 15th:

Amanda and Cher

FYI, Paul's weapon that is missing is a Glock 9mm, Model G19, Semi-automatic, Serial Number NLP120. It was in a Glock case with at least two magazines.

However, when Cher delivered the other gun case with the two other weapons, Some of the Glock paperwork was in that case. That leads me to believe the Glock is still there.

You have the Glock serial number to compare should you see another weapon.

Thanks.
Carl

On   On January 17, 2020, Amanda and Cher dropped off Paul's clothes, military uniforms and gear, military awards and plaques, boxes of personal items which included our father's personal items, military awards and honors, which were given to Paul after he died, hundreds of family pictures and much more. To give you a mental picture of the volume of the material that was delivered, it filled over one-half of one of my garages. **Understand, this was exactly one year and three days after Paul left Sandy.** No matter how you view this, it is totally unacceptable and I put the entire blame on the court and Paul's attorney.

This could have easily been accomplished by a court order instead of an inefficient, ineffective, costly, and useless pilot program called Eldercaring Coordination. I recommend that this program be immediately eliminated in abuse and exploitation cases.

I will be filing a complaint on Eldercaring Coordination with the Governor and Attorney General. If they do decide to retain it, for whatever reason, I would caution anyone from accepting this program as an alternative to a court hearing. Again, this was a horrible mistake to use an Eldercaring Coordinator in Paul's case.

I spent the next six hours on Friday and six additional hours on Saturday morning sorting through the boxes that Amanda and Cher delivered. Paul's first wife, Linda, his daughter, and granddaughter were visiting Paul and I wanted to have everything laid out so they could determine what they wanted to take back to New York. In one of the boxes was Paul's small safe that Paul and I could not locate in the house in 2017. The safe was locked and I did not have the combination and Paul had no idea what it was. There was definitely something in the safe.

Thinking it could possibly be the Glock 19 pistol, I waited to report the pistol missing until I opened the safe.

I was able to determine the manufacturer of the safe and the number for the key to bypass the combination. I went online and after receiving the completing the appropriate forms, I mailed a request for a duplicate key.

It took several weeks to receive the key, but I was finally able to open the safe and the Glock pistol was there. However, the gun case and both magazine clips were still missing.

Since the guardian, Amanda, and the Eldercaring Coordinator, Cher, complied with Sandy's wishes that neither Paul, nor any member of his family ever enter Paul's house again, it is impossible for us to know if all Paul's personal items have been returned. In fact, what we do know, is that they were not. Sandy still has all of Paul's golfing equipment, a Nativity set he purchased in Israel for $ 1,000, and the magazine clips for the Glock.

On February 13, 2020, Amanda sent me the following email:
"Sandy messaged me late last week and said she has another small box of stuff of Paul's she has come across. She said she would

like the picture book and picture of the two of them back in return. I looked all over Paul's room and they are not there. Are you positive they are not tucked somewhere in some of his things that you have?"

I responded,
"I still have boxes in the garage. I will go through them ASAP.
Since she is making an exchange, she can send Paul's golf clubs which are going to his son, the Nativity scene that he bought in Jerusalem which is going to his granddaughter and the two magazines to the Glock 19. Then as far as I am concerned, we are done."

It is important to note that Paul paid $1000 for the Nativity scene. Sandy told Katherine and me that she told Paul not to buy it. He told her he wanted it and got it for himself. Sandy added that Paul "paid way too much money for it."

We decided that I would leave the pictures Sandy wanted with the front desk at Trinity Springs on Wednesday, February 19th and Amanda wrote, "… and I will get them before going to retrieve what I can from Sandy's." My thought was that this should prove to be interesting.

On March 2, 2020. I sent an email to Amanda asking her if there is anything new on getting Paul's property from Sandy. This was her response:

"Good morning Carl. I have asked Sandy about the golf clubs, nativity scene and 2 magazines for the gun. She says the nativity set was purchased by them as a married couple, the golf clubs were given to Neal and Bill and she does not know where the magazines are just as she did not know where the gun was. I have copied Allyne and Mark on this reply as I have spoken with Allyne in the past about continuing to ask for misc personal items and Mark recently about the same topic. I believe they are both in agreement about me not going back to Sandy to ask for anything else. I am trying to be cautious of the money spent for my time and the non-response from Sandy about any more items.

I appreciate the excellent communication on Paul and his appointments."

This is typical of Amanda. Sandy fills her with a bunch of lies and for whatever reason, Amanda accepts her word and does not question her actions. The obvious question to Sandy should have been, "Sandy, what makes you think that you have the right to give away Paul's property." I have to wonder if Amanda realizes that she is Paul's guardian, not Sandy's.

I responded later that day with the following email to Amanda:

This is total bull from Sandy and you know it. When I was Paul's trustee, I strongly felt it was my obligation to protect Paul's assets and that is what I did. The only thing that has changed is that you, Mark and Allyne now have that responsibility. I was at an advantage since I had a long history with Paul and Sandy which gave me some insight as to what was going on there. Sandy has no right to give Paul's golf clubs (which he bought before they were married) to anyone. We have been asking for those clubs from Sandy since January 2019 when Paul was playing golf twice a week until he went to Trinity Springs. In fact, we have had him on the golf course twice in the last several months. Who are Neal and Bill? Once again, Paul's wishes have been completely ignored.

Further, Paul bought the Nativity scene in Israel (for around $1000). He was overly excited to show it to Katherine and me. As we were all looking at it, Sandy herself told us that she had tried to dissuade Paul from buying it as she thought it was over-priced. But he really wanted it and said it was his money and bought it anyway. She is clearly pulling the wool over your eyes again.

What Sandy is doing here is a crime. FYI, I have included a section of the Florida statute below:

812.014   Theft. —
(1)   A person commits theft if he or she knowingly obtains or uses, or endeavors to obtain or to use, the property
of another with intent to, either temporarily or permanently:
(a)   Deprive the other person of a right to the property or a benefit from the property.
(b)   Appropriate the property to his or her own use or to the use of any person not entitled to the use of the property.

It is grand theft of the third degree and a felony of the third degree, punishable as provided in s. 775.082, s. 775.083, or s. 775.084, if the property stolen is:
1.   Valued at $750 or more, but less than $5,000.

Mark is away, but I spoke with Allyne tonight and she sees no reason why Sandy should keep her father's possessions or be allowed to dispose of his clubs.

I think you need to reconsider your decision in this matter.

Thank you.
Carl

Amanda responded with the following email:

Carl,

I am not giving you a decision. I am working within the strict perimeters of my job. Allyne and Mark as trustees are directly paying my bill and I have been told to stop. My suggestion is you consult directly with both of them and come together as a unified front and get their attorneys advice on how to proceed and direct the guardianship as I can go back and forth for months between the parties, but will not do so without my attorney and the courts advice as that is who I work under. I respect Paul and his belongings but I have to be prudent in my handling of his business.

I immediately had several thoughts. Why is everyone in this case ignoring all of Sandy's illegal acts? Am I the only one that cares about the law? Secondly, was Amanda "prudent in the handling of his (Paul's) business when she spent her time picking up pictures and delivering them to Sandy without retrieving Paul's property.

It will be interesting to see how that is explained on her statement for payment of her time as Paul's guardian.

This time, I did not send a response to Amanda's email. Knowing that there were several pending matters which needed to be resolved which could result in Sandy being charged criminally, I decided to wait before taking any additional action. Several days later, I learned that abuse and exploitation charges were being forwarded to the Sumter County Sheriff's Office and the State Attorney.

On Wednesday, March 11, 2020, Amanda sent the following text to Sandy with a copy to Allyne:

"The accountant that is filing Paul's taxes needs to disclose your social security number on the return because you are married. Would you provide it to me?"

Sandy responded:

"It should be on Paul's last year tax return. Also last year there was no communication at all from them on who was doing what and I was audited of course with no changes to my refund. I want to make sure that because I wrote half the check to them for the property tax and they wrote the full amount from Paul's account they are not claiming all the property tax since they have proof for the whole amount and all I have is a duplicate check to them for half the amount.

I do not want to go through what I went through last year because of them."

Allyne replied to Amanda:

"You can relay to her that we will only be claiming/reporting the appropriate amounts for my dad. We are not crooked, and we do everything by the book and at the advice of our attorney and CPA. My uncle tried to communicate with her via email about taxes last year, so I am sure he has a record of that. *(Note: I do.)* And she did not respond, so that is why they filed for an extension because we didn't have all the accurate numbers. I'm not quite sure what audit she is talking about. I'm assuming the IRS would have audited my father as well since they are a 'married couple' in the eyes of the IRS. So maybe she should have communicated that to us. But I am guessing that's a line of bull. Dad got nothing in the mail from the IRS and we properly filed for an extension under the circumstances.

Does that mean she won't give Dad's accountant her SS #?"

Amanda tried one more time and Sandy replied a second time:

"Carl filed married separate last year as well as I. They filed last year without Communication so they had to have my social security number then. Where is Paul's last year's copy. I do not have it."

Amanda's final comment:

"I cannot get anywhere with her."

This is insane. Our brother Bruce was a tax examiner for NY State and has been doing taxes for years. So, he was the one trying to make sure Paul completed his taxes on time. We sent emails to Sandy and attempted to get Paul's SS statement, the one document we were missing. Sandy ignored our request, so I sent an email to Paul's attorney. That was ignored as well and I was told I should not have communicated with Paul's attorney.

Bruce filed an extension for Paul in hope that we would have the documents to file at a later date. Obviously, that did not happen and here we are a year later still trying to file Paul's 2018 federal taxes.

On May 20, 2020, another issue came to my attention which I found troubling. Evidently, Amanda told Allyne that the last time she was at Paul and Sandy's home, the golf cart was not there and she thought that Sandy may have sold it. The cart was both their property and each of them paid one-half of the amount. I believe the price was over $12,000.

Just to document our "unified front" that Amanda included in her earlier email, I sent the following email to Mark and Allyne on May 21st:

Mark and Allyne
Because none of us have been in Paul's house since August 2018, we have no idea what Sandy has taken from Paul. Before I file criminal charges against Sandy and put an end to this, I need some information from you so I can eliminate Amanda's comments that we are "not on the same page". Will both of you please send me an email answering the following questions:

    1. Did you tell or indicate to Sandy that Paul did not want his golf clubs (2 sets) and she could give them away?

    2. Did you tell Sandy that she could keep Paul's nativity set that he bought in Israel for about $1000?

    3. Did you tell Sandy, despite the fact that they each paid half for a new golf cart, she could keep it or sell it and not split the proceeds

with Paul?

Should the criminal justice system refuse to criminally charge Sandy, we should talk to Paul's attorney about filing a civil suit to include forcing the sale of the home.

Once I get your answers to these questions, I will keep you up to date on this and any response from the Governor or Attorney General.

Thank you.

Mark's response:

Simple answers:

No, I did not tell or indicate to Sandy that we did not want Dad's golf clubs back or she could give them away, as I have had no contact with Sandy since Dad left her of his own will.

No, I did not tell Sandy she can keep Dad's Nativity set, as I have had no contact with Sandy since Dad left her of his own will.

No, I did not tell Sandy she could have or sell Dad's golf cart, as I have not had contact with Sandy since Dad left her of his own will.

Having said that after Amanda went and tried to get this stuff and Sandy refused, I did tell Amanda to stop pursuing. I did this for the sole reason that I did not want to keep allowing Dad to get billed for something Amanda clearly couldn't achieve, and Sandy already gave the golf clubs away at that time we were told. I did say to Amanda, that it wasn't Sandy's right to give the clubs away, even though I didn't want them.

But I will tell you that Allyne and I felt the golf cart is a true material possession of value and Dad needed to be compensated for that, or we would have happily taken it.

We feel that we have been constantly fighting to get at

least some of Dad's possessions back and weighing what is most important, which is not right.

-Mark

Allyne's response:

Uncle Carl,

I too have never spoken to Sandy since dad left their house of his own free will.

I would never indicate to anyone that any of dad's belongings should have been left in Sandy's possession.

As Mark indicated, we were having such a struggle even getting his essentials (clothing, and such). And my focus was on his sentimental belongings that could not be replaced. (Military memorabilia, and photos, etc.)

None of this should have gone the way it has! It's as if dad's rights have been taken away because of his diagnosis! It is disgusting, especially when he has such a supportive family continually trying to protect him, and yet we keep hitting roadblocks!

It is obscene that this has been allowed! And Dad should be compensated for everything that we can prove was rightfully his. It's not in our nature to turn a blind eye to any of this just because she is going to fight. We can fight for what's right!

Allyne

On the next day, everything changed again. Allyne called me and told me that there was an offer on the home and that the golf cart was back in the garage. Allyne questioned Amanda about the golf cart and found out that Sandy was "hiding" it in a neighbor's garage and had told Amanda that she no longer had it. When the buyer wanted the golf cart included in the sale, Sandy refused because her and Paul's names were on the cart.

(Note: They are decals and easily removed.)

The contract was signed and the closing scheduled for July 14, 2020.

(Note: No matter what Sandy decided on the golf cart, one-half the value goes to Paul's trust.)

In early June 2020, Amanda sent her first bill to Allyne for review at the same time she submitted it to the court for approval. The court did approve Amanda's bill as written and the bill as submitted follows:

After reviewing the bill, I had several concerns and sent the following email to Amanda on June 8th:

Billing for John Paul Baker

DATE	MILES	DESCRIPTION OF SERVICE	MILEAGE	TIME	CHARGE
8/8/2019		Initial phone call with Harry Hackney on history of case; email cliffs notes to Mike Rogers and ask for representation.		0.80	60.00
8/9/2019		Phone call with Mike on case.		0.30	22.50
8/19/2019		Phone call and email with M. Nagel. Re: case history and placement.		1.00	75.00
8/21/2019		Phone call with Carl Baker re: placement and email re: the same.		0.20	15.00
8/22/2019		Multiple emails from Carl with pages of history. Print and review.		1.00	$ 75.00
8/22/2019	22	Update application and take to attorney office and get Oath signed and notarized.	12.76	1.00	75.00
8/22/2019		Forward my attorney's office everything I have currently on the case.		0.20	15.00
		Call from Sandie Baker. Just got home from 10 days away and would like an update on her			

Date	Description			
8/26/2019	husband.		0.20	15.00
8/26/2019	Travel and tour facilities for Paul. Brookdale, Trinity Springs, Village Veranda, The Willows, Sumter 36 Place. Compile email with my recommendation	20.88	4.00	300.00
8/27/2019	Email for update on my letters of guardianship. Call with Carl re: 1823		0.20	15.00
8/28/2019	Help facilitate fee to hold room so that furniture can be delivered and room can be set up. Email my attorney about possible visitation hearing date		0.20	15.00
8/29/2019	Call from Cara Singletary; Trinity Springs, and Sandie Baker re: Sandie at facility. Multiple calls, texts and emails.		1.00	75.00
8/30/2019	Multiple calls and emails re: jt stipulation		0.30	$ 22.50
9/4/2019	Meet with Paul at Trinity. Clean and well groomed. Lacking in appropriate boundaries as he like to touch and hug. Pleasantly confused; alert to self only. (Travel time and mileage split with another 14 client)	8.76	1.50	$ 112.50
9/4/2019	Meeting with my attorney regarding difficult 22 decisions I need to make in this case.	12.76	1.50	$ 112.50
9/6/2019	Email regarding need to establish bond prior to letters being entered. Fill out bond application and forward to Jurisco.		0.50	37.50
9/8/2019	Multiple emails from family regarding their opinion on the guardianship. Forward to my attorney.		0.10	7.50
9/9/2019	Call from Angela at Trinity. Needs medication refill. Forward what is needed to Carl		0.10	7.50
	Follow-up email to Carl requesting medication list, physician list and medical notes. Discuss the neuropsychologist evaluating Paul and request a			

Date	Description	Hours	Amount
9/9/2019	copy of his Medicare card.	0.20	15.00
9/9/2019		0.10	7.50
9/9/2019	Email from Carl regarding Paul's guns to Cher and I Phone call with Allyne, Carl and Katherine responding to the emails from family and the role of a guardian.	1.00	75.00
9/15/2019	Forward service plan to Merideth Nagel to sign for Trinity	0.10	7.50
9/16/2019	Texts from Allyne regarding personal property and forward to my attorney along with reply on whether I will have authority or trust.	0.40	$ 30.00
9/16/2019	Phone call Carl Baker. Why have I not been appointed and how can they help. Texts with Sandie re: the same	0.10	7.50
9/16/2019	Sandie Baker call. She is back from vacation and wants to know if I am the guardian.	0.10	7.50
9/17/2019	Call from Angelina at Trinity. Who is providing the medications. Need refill on a med but it is too early to refill on insurance. Need to pay for 2 week supply. Forward to Carl.	0.10	7.50
9/19/2019	Email notice of hearing.	0.10	7.50
9/20/2019	Received large pack of paperwork in the mail from Carl with Paul's medical information. Go over.	0.50	$ 37.50
9/22/2019	Set up Neuropsychologist to see Paul. Send him all records by fax. Discuss history over the phone.	1.00	$ 75.00
9/24/2019	Phone call with Carl Baker who wants me to notify him when I get court papers. Phone call with Dr. Mavrides about his assessment	0.50	37.50
	Multiple emails with Merideth re: Mavrides		

Date	Description		Miles	Hours	Amount
9/24/2019	assessment and visitation			0.30	22.50
9/26/2019	Phone call and follow-up email from Carl Baker			0.50	$ 37.50
9/27/2019	Ask Sandie for the 2018 Social Security Statement. She doesn't have it. Many texts with her grievances			0.20	15.00
9/28/2019	Travel to Trinity on a Saturday to meet Allyne Baker who is here visiting her dad- 22		12.76	1.50	$ 112.50
9/30/2019	Email and phone call with Merideth; Mike; and Cher			0.30	$ 22.50
10/1/2019	Phone call with Cher regarding case.			0.20	15.00
10/7/2019	Mult emails with Harry and Mike			0.30	22.50
10/8/2019	Call with my attorney regarding visitation and Elder Care Coordinator			0.20	15.00
10/8/2019	Email with copy of petition for reimbursement to Sandie			0.10	7.50
10/9/2019	Phone call with Cher			0.30	$ 22.50
10/9/2019	Call with Sandie Baker			0.30	$ 22.50
10/15/2019	Take original bond to court house for filing to facilitate LOGs. No one in clerks office has my letters. They assume they are still with judge or JA. Email my attorney to follow-up. 34	$	19.72	1.50	112.50
10/16/2019	Meet at Sandie Baker's home with Cher (Elder caring Coordinator) Neighbor and friend from up north were also in attendance. Discuss history from her point of view and goals. Includes travel time. 20	$	11.60	2.80	210.00
10/17/2019	Mult emails from Carl and reply			0.20	15.00
10/21/2019	Email from the JA that my letters are signed			0.10	7.50

Date	Description			
10/22/2019	Email from Cher re: guns and personal items		0.10	7.50
10/23/2019	Call with Mike on case and plan. Waiting for call with Merideth and Cher. Call Cher's office again and set phone call form tomorrow		0.30	$ 22.50
10/24/2019	Phone call with Elder Care Coordinator		0.50	37.50
10/24/2019	Travel to Sumter County Courthouse to get certified copies of my Letters of Guardianship. Call Trinity Springs. Travel to Trinity to show them certified copy and to speak with staff about Paul. Discuss 34 dynamics of visitation.	19.72	2.50	$ 187.50
10/25/2019	Email my attorney about visit this afternoon		0.10	7.50
10/25/2019	Meeting/Visitation at Trinity set by Eldercare Coordinator. Cher myself, Sandie, and Paul Baker present. (No Mileage or travel time as I was originally there on other business)- Includes F/U call with Cher		2.00	150.00
10/28/2019	Scheduled Phone conf. with Mike and Merideth. Merideth did not answer		0.20	15.00
10/28/2019	Phone calls with Allyne and Mark, email from Carl all regarding visit.		1.00	75.00
10/30/2019	Meeting with Mike re: joint stip and hearing back 22 from Cara and Sandie.	12.76	1.00	75.00
11/1/2019	34 Travel to and attend hearing for visitation	19.72	2.00	$ 150.00
11/5/2019	Travel to Meeting at facility with Sandie; Janice, myself and Paul. Court ordered supervised 28 visitation.	16.24	2.50	187.50
11/11/2019	Forward LOGs to Allyne at her request and email		0.10	7.50

Date	Description			
11/12/2019	Emails from Mike and Todd re: CPA		0.10	7.50
11/13/2019	Provide Trinity with visitation order.		0.10	7.50
11/15/2019	Voicemails from Sandie and Janice; Call back regarding super./ised visit today. Asked Janice to put it in writing for my notes.		0.10	7.50
11/18/2019	Call with Jennifer the ARNP regarding ulcer on foot and records.		0.10	7.50
11/18/2019	Phone call and email with Mark and Mike re: car		0.50	37.50
11/19/2019	Chers office called to set up teleconf.		0.10	$ 7.50
11/20/2019	Call with Cher.		0.50	37.50
11/22/2019	Email to set up meeting with Carl		0.10	$ 7.50
12/2/2019	Go over and sign petaton to terminate lease and send to attorney to file.		0.20	15.00
12/4/2019	Email form Mike and call with Cara		0.60	45.00
12/5/2019	Call with Sandie Baker regarding property taxes and meeting with her tomorrow.		0.20	$ 15.00
12/6/2019	Travel to meeting at Carl Baker's home with Cher 24 and Myself.	13.92	3.50	262.50
12/6/2019	Travel to Sandie Bakers home to pick up check for half of the property taxes to mail to Allyne. Travel to post office to priority mail check and let Allyne 22 know.	$ 12.76	1.50	$ 112.50
12/9/2019	Call with Cara Singletary		0.50	$ 37.50
12/11/2019	Travel to supervised visit at Trinity with Paul, Carl, 28 Sandie, myself and Cher.	16.24	2.50	$ 187.50
12/12/2019	Call with Cher Myers		0.30	$ 22.50
	Email Mike and let him know Sandie turned in car			

A Case Study Of Elder Abuse And Exploitation In Florida

12/12/2019	yesterday.	0.10	$	7.50
12/13/2019	Complete initial plan of person and forward to attorneys office for filing	1.00		75.00
12/16/2019	Email to Allyne to get needed info for the initial inventory and reply's	0.20	$	15.00
12/18/2019	Sign and return inventory to attorney and ask about the need for a bond as I am not in control of assets and it creates an expense that isn't needed for the future. Sign and return petaton to waive bond.	0.30		22.50
12/18/2019	Email from Sandy	0.10	$	7.50
12/20/2019	Call form Carl Baker	0.20		15.00
12/20/2019	Time spent notifying all parties of visitation that did not mirror the court order. Halt further visitation. Communication with Sandy.	0.50	$	37.50
12/26/2019	Long email from Carl and reply from Merideth	0.20		15.00
1/6/2020	Phone calls, emails and texts re: checks and amounts.	0.30		22.50
1/7/2020	Sign petition to waive annual accountings and return to attorney	0.20		15.00
1/9/2019	Email form Sandie re: getting Paul's personal items out of the home	0.10		7.50
1/10/2020	Call from Sandie Baker. She is unsure where my hostility is coming from and would like to speak about recent changes. I request we speak via email or text so I have a record.	0.10	$	7.50
1/10/2020	Call with Cher Myers.	0.50	$	37.50
1/14/2020	Call with Cher and Carl and email to attorney	0.50		37.50

Carl R. Baker

Date	Description			
1/15/2020	F/U with appt with VA today		0.10	7.50
1/17/2020	Travel to Sandie Bakers home to pick up Paul 28 Bakers belongings and take to Carl Bakers home.	$ 16.10	4.00	300.00
1/23/2020	Call from Susan with Home Health. Told her to call facility to schedule PT.		0.10	7.50
1/29/2020	Call with Kim at DCF. Explained to her I have no first hand knowledge of any accusations as I came into case after they were made.		0.30	22.50
1/29/2020	Phone call and multiple faxes with CPA		0.50	37.50
1/30/2020	Dermatology appt		0.10	7.50
2/3/2020	Emails with Mike re: Judge Morley		0.20	15.00
2/7/2020	Call from Bridget from Trinity and their bill. Give her Allyne's info.		0.10	7.50
2/7/2020	Visit at facility. Go over resident service plan with DON. Correct some of his tasks that require greater help. Visit with Paul. He is in very good spirits. No medication changes (Split travel time and mileage 14 with another client)	8.05	1.50	112.50
2/7/2020	Call with Mike re: email form Todd about Eldercare Coor.		0.30	22.50
2/11/2020	Visit facility with Carrie Wood, RN and Paul. (Split 14 travel time and mileage with another client)	8.05	1.50	112.50
2/18/2020	Call with Allyne, Carl and Carrie; mult emails		0.80	60.00
2/20/2020	Travel to facility to see Paul and check on all recent medical notes in chart. Get requested pics by 28 Sandy and take to her home and drop off	$ 16.10	2.00	150.00
2/21/2020	Email with Allyne and Mark and reply's		0.20	15.00

Date	Description			
2/25/2020	Email with Allyne and Mark and Todd		0.10	7.50
2/25/2020	Voicemail from Sandy on house. Email her and advise her she needs to work with the trustees and their attorney on the house		0.10	7.50
2/28/2020	Medical Update		0.10	7.50
3/6/2020	Call with Allyne and Mark		0.50	37.50
3/10/2020	Travel to facility to see Paul and to check on his chart and room. Discuss with the front desk and ED about visitation restrictions. They currently do not have a plan in place. (mileage and travel time 14 shared with another client)	8.05	1.50	112.50
3/11/2020	Call with CPA and correspond with Sandie, Allyne and Mark		0.50	37.50
3/13/2020	Email from Trinity on visitation restrictions.		0.10	$ 7.50
3/23/2020	Receive 2018 and 2019 tax returns in the mail. Review and make copies of both. Email Allyne and Mark. Sign and mail 2018 and forward 2019 along 4 with invoices to Allyne. Travel to post office.	2.30	1.00	75.00
3/24/2020	Call with Mark		0.40	30.00
3/24/2020	Teleconf with facility on update with Paul. Let them know Allyne would be calling and having them help Paul talk on the phone.		0.30	$ 22.50
3/30/2020	Compile billing and check all notes. Go back over history of case and clean up filings. Forward to attorney.		1.00 $	75.00

Total Billing for
August 2019 through March 31, 2020

71.90 Hours @ $75.00 Per Hour	$	5,392.50
362 Miles @ 0.58 Per Mile		209.96
102 Miles @ 0.575 Per Mile	$	58.65
Reimb. Postage and certified copy		22.75

TOTAL   5,683.86

We are in the process of reviewing the bill that you sent and have several requests for information.

1. Would you please send us a copy of the Doctor Mavrides' assessment. You can send it to my email. It is the only document we are missing from Paul's medical folder.

2. On your October 15th visit with Sandy, we noticed that you stated, "a neighbor and friend from up north were also in attendance." Please furnish us with the names and why it was necessary for them to be a part of the conversation.

Thank you.
Carl

Note: We saw no reason for a neighbor and friend to be present for the Conversation with Sandy.

Amanda responded immediately with the following email:

Hi. Sure I can send Allyne, Mark and your selfA (sic) copy of Dr. Mavrides's report. As far as the specifics on names on my billing I'm not sure what the relevance is to us moving forward so I'm not going to address that question. When I put together my bill I sent a copy to Allyne and let her know that in some instances I was being vague as I didn't think that me divulging any more information would work for the greater good of the peace that we have come to. I hope you are all doing well.

Thank you,
Amanda Ritter

Note: This is one of the reasons why I would never be able to recommend Amanda as a guardian. Based on this and other responses, it is evident that Amanda has forgotten that she is Paul's guardian, not Sandy's. Amanda told us that she had seen a man in Sandy's house on several occasions. I think it was the man who has stayed over with Sandy several times and the one who we believe was guiding her through the exploitation of Paul. If this is true, he has committed a crime also. That is the relevance of my request. Evidently, no one cares about the law!

I replied with the following email the following morning (June 9, 2020):

Amanda
I don't understand the lack of transparency and why your being open about the details of your charges would somehow be deleterious to anyone's peace. It is natural and normal for anyone to want to understand the bills they are being requested to pay. Please reconsider your response.
Carl

Amanda's response:

Good morning. What I do not understand is the relevance of this information. I feel like it is a waste of time money and effort that we are even discussing this by email. These were random people that were there to support Sandi but had no relevance to the situation.

Thank you,
Amanda Ritter
A short time later, Amanda sent another email:

Good morning Allyne, Mark and Carl. Here is the Dr. Mavrides report. As far as the names of the 2 ladies, I don't even have them in my notes. It was the neighbor who also went to the court hearing I was at with her and a childhood friend. I did not share any personal information with them.

Note: I do not believe that Amanda did not discuss personal business with these two women present. This was the meeting to coach Sandy on the "secret meeting" with Paul. My wife's immediate response was, "If no personal info was shared, what did they discuss...the weather?" There is no way that personal information was not discussed, just look at the bill. In my opinion, this was just another lie by Amanda.

Since Amanda is Paul's guardian, I do not understand why Paul must pay every time Sandy calls Amanda. There is a mediator, Cher Myers, who is paid by me, Paul, and Sandy. Why doesn't Amanda refer Sandy to Cher when she calls on an issue and let Cher bill for the conversation rather than putting it all on Paul's bill. As many times as Paul has told everyone that he wants nothing to do with Sandy and wants her out of his life, the court, Amanda, and Cher continue to push Sandy on Paul. Why?

As an example, look at the following dates on Amanda's bill:
08/26/19 - Call from Sandy.
08/28/19 - Sandy tries to force her way into Trinity Springs.
09/16/19 - Call from Sandy.
10/15/19 - Amanda coaches Sandy for a visit with Paul that he does not want.
10/25/19 - Sandy's secret visit to Paul.
12/20/19 - Sandy's visit to Paul in violation of the court order.

01/09/20 – Call from Sandy.
02/25/20 – Call from Sandy.

The amount Amanda billed for these events total $525.00. So, the exploitation and abuse of Paul continues and to add insult to injury, he is paying for it. How could any normal, caring person look at this situation and conclude that "the system is not broken?

Allyne discussed all of this with her attorney. He told her that it would cost more in attorney fees than the reduction in the bill. Allyne paid the bill in full.

Note: Allyne and Mark's attorney was recommended by Amanda and Amanda's attorney was Judge Morley's former law partner. I saw this as a problem and suggested that they hire Harry Hackney who was familiar with the case. Thinking that this may upset Amanda, Mark and Allyne went ahead and hired the attorney Amanda recommended. As you will see, this excuse for not doing what is right because of the additional attorney fee costs, will surface again. Who is on Paul's side in this fiasco?

On June 28, 2020, Sandy posted the following on her Facebook:

"Today Paul and I have been married 4 years. I will always adore this kind, sweet, loving man who brought joy and happiness into my life. The picture here was when we were in Hawaii two years ago and we packed more fun and adventure into our time together that was stolen from us way to early. Paul may you know the truth when you get to heaven. I will carry those fond memories in my heart and nobody can steal them from me."

Katherine commented last week that Sandy would post something on her Facebook on their fourth anniversary, so we were expecting this. This is just another example of Sandy's sociopathic behavior where she always presents herself as the victim. Truth be known, Paul's doctor told Sandy that Paul should not be traveling, but Sandy again disregarded the doctor's order and took Paul to Hawaii. Despite Paul's Alzheimer's, he does know the truth and that is why he left Sandy 18 months ago and is seeking a divorce.

On Tuesday, July 6, 2020, there was a sign on Hillsboro Trail for a garage sale on 3723 Mango Court which is Paul's and Sandy' house. No one in Paul's family was notified of the garage sale. Given Sandy's previous larcenies of Paul's non-marital personal property, it will be interesting to see if any of the proceeds from the sale of Paul's personal items are given to Allyne to deposit in Paul's trust account.

(Note: Paul's trust never received a dime from the sale of the golf cart or from the sale all of Paul's premarital property which was protected by the Antenuptial Agreement which they both signed. This is a grand larceny by Sandy in the amount of thousands of dollars.)

On the evening of July 7, 2020, I received the following email from Paul's daughter, Allyne:

"Uncle Carl,
Spoke to Amanda today. She was calling to let us know the underwriter for the title company was trying to say that we needed

an order from the court for the sale of dad's house to go forward. She says that it's not necessary. Her Atty called the underwriter also to say it's not necessary, but the title company is insisting. Hoping to get this straightened out with our own Atty tomorrow.

But on another note, Amanda said that was all she was calling for and "everything is great with your dad". I didn't question her as I am confused about that statement. Either she has no clue what she's talking about (which would mean she's not really in tune with who she is responsible for as their "guardian") or she's blatantly lying to us! I'm not sure which is worse! But with all that has gone on this week with Dad, for her to say everything is great with him, that is completely inaccurate at the very least!

I'll keep you posted on the title company tomorrow."

Note: On July 5th, Paul became very confused and went to the wrong room to go to bed. When the nurse told Paul that it was not his room, he thought they had changed his room and became upset, kicking the door. They finally got him in his own room, and I called Paul to calm him down. While I was on the phone with him, he told me there was a lot of water on the floor in his room. I told him that I would take care of it and call him back later. I immediately called the memory care nurse and she stated she would check on him. I tried to call Paul back, but he did not answer. Over an hour later, at 10:45 PM, the nurse called me told me that Paul is really confused and left the water running in the kitchen sink and had flooded his room. The next morning, I got another call from a visiting nurse telling me that Paul was totally confused and had dressed this morning with three multiple layers of clothes and he was ignoring his personal hygiene. This was quite a change in Paul's behavior, so I spoke to the Executive Director at Trinity Springs who increased Paul's daily supervision and ran some medical tests to see if they could determine the cause for Paul's increased confusion. As I have always done, I relayed this information to Mark and Allyne. That is the reason she sent the above email commenting on Amanda's statement that "everything is great with your dad."

On July 12, 2020, two days before the closing on Paul's and Sandy's house, the title company wanted an order from the court approving the sale. Although the attorneys did not think this was necessary, on July 13th, Amanda's attorney, Michael Rodgers, drafted a petition for Amanda, Paul's guardian, to sign and notarize. The problem was that Amanda never read the order and the order had Sandra Baker listed as the current trustee of Paul's trust instead of Paul's daughter, Allyne Baker. Mike Rogers did correct the petition to the court before the closing, but they told Allyne it was going to take a couple of weeks for the judge to sign the petition. The buyers did not want to wait and backed out of the contract. Clearly, the sale was lost because of errors by Amanda and her attorney. That is the second time a contract did not result in the sale of the house.

On July 14th, we learned that Sandy had already moved out of the home and the home was vacant. Evidently, Sandy had turned the appliances off, and neglected to empty the ice maker which resulted in the realtor discovering water on the floor in the kitchen from all the ice in the freezer melting.

Allyne consulted her Attorney, Todd Mazenko and he advised her to have the locks changed immediately. On July 16th, Allyne sent the following email asking for some help:

Uncle Carl - Can you please check Dad's house to make sure all is okay? This has all been advised by our attorney and the locksmith has all info he should need. If the neighbors start any trouble, our attorney said to videotape the encounter and call the police. They have no rights to that house. And we are not preventing Sandy from having access, she can contact our attorney if she is in the area to have a key as she is still half owner of the property. We are only preventing the neighbors (Bill and Lil) as our attorney says they are a liability. We asked Amanda Ritter to be present and she declined. I'll forward you that exchange.

Thanks. Allyne

The locksmith was going to be at the house at 1:00 PM on the 16th. Based on the entries on Sandy's Facebook, we knew the next-door neighbors could be a problem, so both Bruce and I went to the house to meet with the locksmith.

Once the locksmith arrived and started to change the locks, Bill and Lil, the next-door neighbors, came running over screaming obscenities at all of us. "Get the [expletive] off this property. There is a court order and you are not allowed be on this property! Get the [expletive] out of here, you are not allowed on this property. You rotten [expletive], you ruined Paul's life and broke up a happy marriage." I replied: "That's not true and some day you will learn what really happened." He replied, "I know the truth you [expletive]."

Note: Interestingly, there is no court order that forbids anyone from being on this property. This was most likely another lie by Sandy, which they accepted as truth. In fact, as neighbors, they had no standing to tell us to leave. They were extremely angry, threatening and out of control. The obscenities that came out of their mouths were unbelievable.

We calmly explained that we are Paul's brothers and have every right to be there at Allyne's (Paul's daughter) request since she lives in upstate New York. Lil said that we were lying. She started screaming for her husband, Bill, and screamed at the neighbors to call the police. She ran back to the house for a moment presumably to find her husband Bill who went in the house and returned a minute later stating that she had Allyne on the phone, and Allyne did not give us permission to be there, which we immediately knew was a lie.

Then they started yelling at the locksmith. He told them he had paperwork from the trustee of the property authorizing the work. The neighbors continued their ranting and raving and it was getting more bizarre. It also became very apparent that we were never going to have a rational discussion with Bill and Lil. The locksmith said "these people" are nuts, and returned to his truck and called 911, the Sumter County Sheriff's Office.

While waiting in the road for the Sheriff Deputy to arrive, both Bill and Lil continued to scream at us saying things like "You're both murderers, you killed your brother." "I hope you rot in Hell." Bill then looked at my twin brother, Bruce and said, "Who the hell are you?" Bruce told him he was Paul's brother. Bill replied, "Oh Yeah. You're the one who hates your brother, well he hated you also. You wrecked his life and took him away from the only happiness he had!" To avoid any further conflict, we got in our car and rolled up the windows until the Deputies arrived.

When the two Deputies arrived, we explained the situation to them and showed them all the paperwork from Allyne and her attorney. The Deputy called the real estate agent and spoke with her for about 10 minutes. One Deputy then went over to Bill and Lil, who were continuing to yell out all types of accusations.

Several minutes later, the Deputy came back over and told the locksmith to go ahead and proceed with changing the locks. After the locks was changed, we thanked the locksmith and Deputies, and left the area. While we were there, the locksmith was the only one who entered the house.

Shortly after we left, Allyne told us that evidently Lil called Sandy and Sandy also called the Sheriff's Office. Sandy then called Allyne's lawyer crying and yelling and claiming that Mark (Paul's son) was breaking into her home on Mango Court. Sandy further stated that she is now homeless and cannot afford an attorney because her husband's children took all her money.

Quite evidently, lying is like breathing for Sandy. This is typical of Sandy. She is attempting to make herself the victim again. No one has taken any of Sandy's money, yet she has stolen much of Paul's nonmarital assets, which rightfully belong to Paul. Further, Bruce and I recovered the money she tried to steal from Paul's trust account. In fact, earlier financial records showed that Sandy had over $200,000 in her own accounts.

Additionally, we could not understand why the neighbors were calling us "murderers". Paul is still alive. Perhaps Sandy told them Paul had died to cover the embarrassing fact that the court revoked her visiting privileges.

Note: This may not be as far-fetched as it first sounds and perhaps more diabolical. Today is July 1, 2021. Paul and Sandy's 5th anniversary would have been June 28th. This is the first time Sandy has not placed something on her Facebook for her anniversary emphasizing her "victim" status. As I have said all along, I certainly recommend that Sandy seek mental health treatment.

On Wednesday, July 22, 2020, Allyne sent me the following text message:

"Sandy just tried to cancel the homeowner's insurance. They called me at work and told me they would not cancel it without ALL signatures and a closing statement. Can you believe her? Why would she do that when she is half owner?"

I called Allyne and we discussed this. We agreed that it makes no sense. She is still responsible for her half of the bills for the house. Additionally, Sandy is now stating that she will not sign an extension for the realtor to continue listing the property. Obviously, she has some serious mental issues and is in need of professional help.

Later that day, Sandy did finally sign the extension for the sale of the home.

Following are the July 24th text messages between Sandy and Amanda and Amanda and Allyne:

Sandy to Amanda
Could you please tell me if Allyne took over the SECO, VCDD, bug exterminator and lawn guy that I am paying for? Carl lied to the police that they took over the insurance and that is why the locks were changed. I can't afford the utilities now and since they feel they own the house now by not informing me about anything, I am going to shut off electric and call VCDD and explain the situation. I am paying for everything here and not living in it just so I don't lose this house. I literally am broke since they drove me to this. Carl must be so happy now. He said he would ruin me.

A Case Study Of Elder Abuse And Exploitation In Florida

The realtor said they don't want to get involved. How convenient.

Note: Once again Sandy is lying again about my telling the police "that they took over the insurance and that is why the locks were changed." The locks were changed on July 16th. Allyne did not notify me that Sandy tried to cancel the insurance until July 22nd. Sandy is such a pathetic liar; she can't even keep her dates straight. Further, I have never told Sandy that I "would ruin" her.

Amanda to Sandy
I will forward this to Allyne and Mark. I have no idea.

Sandy to Amanda
I just had a Villages realtor call me and said he has a buyer for the house, but because Homerun Realty has it, he will not get a commission because he is not MLS. That is why I wanted a Villages realtor to take over the realtor wants to talk to you so you can talk some sense into the Bakers. I am so sick of this as I am sure you are too.

Note: From the beginning, Sandy refused to use the Village realtor that the Bakers recommended and had used in multiple successful sales.

Mark to Amanda
Oh, poor Sandy.
Her plans to drain my father of all his money failed so she doesn't have the cash she counted on.

Amanda to Mark and Allyne
I am on the verge of blocking her number.

Amanda to Mark and Allyne

Yes, that was my conversation with her on Tuesday after she left me an exceptionally long voicemail about not wanting to sign with the old realtor. *I did not even involve you guys.* I called her and told her the realtor has enough skin in the game and they want to get the house sold and it would be ludicrous to switch to another real estate agent. So, I was hoping that would appease her for a while I just can't deal with her anymore.

Allyne to Amanda

That's probably a good idea to block her. These communications are pointless. She needs to get her own "counsel". That's how things work. And I thought she turned the electricity back on. Do we need to turn it on in Dad's name so we don't have a bigger issue? But it's all going to get worked out in closing. Whoever is paying will be reimbursed the other half at closing. It's not rocket science.

Amanda to Allyne

The communication is pointless and I can't charge your dad for pointless communication and I am not going to waste anymore of my free time on her. I just wanted you guys to know what was going on.

Allyne to Amanda

Let's also remember Sandy chose the realtor. And now we are just trying to keep it consistent. She is mentally ill. I'm convinced.

Amanda to Allyne

I just called Sandy and told her to send me the bills and I will work on changing then into Paul's name Monday morning. and to not shut anything off and she agreed. I will have a few hours on Monday to sit down and change the bills into your dad's name.

Allyne to Amanda
And Amanda. Todd said they should be in the name of his trust since that is how the house is deeded and it's not his residence. Thank you for changing that.

Amanda to Allyne
She is a crying lunatic right now. I guess she is closing on another house today and can't afford bills at both places out of pocket and I told her I didn't need to get into any of that. I was just trying to handle business and I hung up.

Sure. The problem is you try to call and put them in the name of the trust they want to talk to me as Guardian so it sounds like this is something we both need to do. What a pain in the ass.

Allyne to Amanda
See... more lies come out. She claimed she was homeless and broke. But just closed on another home. She's a compulsive liar. Sorry. I'll be available if you need me.

Amanda to Allyne
Don't be sorry. We will get it done. I don't have time until Monday. I have a full afternoon today.

Allyne to Amanda
OK. I am available Monday.

On July 27, 2020, Allyne was attempting to get all the bills sent to her and make sure the house was being cared for properly. The following were the text messages from that day:

Amanda to Sandy
Allyne says she is getting a new lawn care company and we can cancel Lawnscapes.

Note from Allyne: "we". " Amanda definitely acts like she's on "team Sandy". If she was really Dad's guardian and looking out for his best interests then what is this..."

Note: Amanda has acted as Sandy's guardian so many times throughout this entire case, we feel that she cannot be trusted.

Sandy to Amanda
I am sick about this. Chris is doing all my neighbors because of Paul and he does such a good job. He is a trustworthy family man who is just trying to make a living for his family. Chris loved Paul and they had such a good relationship. What is wrong with his kids? I am in total disagreement with this! I am paying half in the long run and this is affecting a good friend who help (sic) me with the sprinkler system and plant advice. I refuse to pay half if they do this to him.

Mark to Amanda
It is just business We are not cruel at all. Personal feelings have nothing to do with this. We are just doing a job as trustees. Sandy can keep her opinions to herself. Her character is the one that will be questioned on her reckoning day. If she wants a say tell her to pay the

bills. But she doesn't and this is why we are taking over expenses. #byesandy

Sandy called Mark and Allyne's attorney asking for a key because the real estate agent won't deal with her. Mark responded to his attorney.

Mark to Todd Mazenko (Attorney)
I think she wants a key. She has been asking the real estate agent for one. They don't want to deal (with her), so I suggest they direct her to our attorney. You don't need to speak to her. We will take this as her request.

We will get her a key as soon as we get around to making a copy and finding her new address, say maybe in four weeks. We sat without a key for over a year and couldn't get on site. We are taking over all bills, so I am not exactly in a rush to get her a key. She moved out of state as well.

Maybe she should obtain counsel if she needs something.

On July 30th, Allyne received an email from her attorney stating that Sandy Baker called and wanted a key to the house. She stated that she owns half the house and has the right to a key. She lives out of state but would not give an address and said "she is homeless. Instead, she gave a P. O. Box in Wildwood without a Zip Code. She was told to contact her attorney and stated, "she can't afford an attorney because she's homeless."

Several days prior, Amanda told Allyne that Sandy just

closed on a new home. The purchase has been confirmed from her Facebook and Sandy now lives in Bossier City, Louisiana. Regardless, there was no way Allyne was going to mail a key to a P. O. Box in Wildwood when Sandy no longer resides in Florida.

Anyone who reviews what has taken place in the last ten days can gain some insight of the Baker family frustrations trying to work with Sandy, who we believe has mental problems. She buys a new home at the same time she's crying on the phone claiming she is "homeless." Time and time again, I have recommended that Sandy seek some form of mental health treatment. Both Cher and Amanda have stated that Sandy has problems. If the probate court was not so broken and, in such disarray, perhaps the judge could have taken the time to learn what was going on in her case and possibly prevented this entire fiasco from happening by ordering that Sandy receive treatment.

On August 7, 2020, we verified that Sandy had illegally taken, sold, or disposed of most of Paul's pre-marital furniture, wall hangings, tools, and personal property. In addition, she has taken possession of property that they each paid one-half of the initial cost—e.g., golf cart, furniture, rugs, lighting fixtures and more. All in all, Sandy has taken property that was rightfully Paul's and worth thousands of dollars. We have documentation and/or receipts for all of this. Again, Paul is the victim of another crime. I had earlier told Amanda that we needed to make sure this did not happen. At that time, Amanda told me that the golf cart was being stored in a neighbor's garage which made absolutely no sense. I thought all along that she would take everything of value that she could, and I was right.

I sent the following email to Amanda and Merideth on August 9th to document the theft and seek their recommendations to remedy the situation:

To: Amanda and Merideth:

Several days ago, we verified that Sandy has taken everything from the house on Mango Court except a couch, an electric fireplace and two lanai chairs. This means that Sandy has taken, sold, or disposed of all of Paul's pre-marital furniture, wall hangings, tools, and some personal property. In addition, she has taken possession of property that they each paid one-half of the initial cost - e.g., golf cart, furniture, rugs, lighting fixtures and more. All in all, Sandy has taken property that was rightfully his which has a minimum value in the amount of $12,000. (Half the value of the golf cart alone is over $4,000). I have documentation and/or receipts for all of this and can furnish photos if needed. Paul is again the victim of Sandy's abuse and exploitation and she needs to be held accountable.

We all know that Paul has no need for any of his property, but that certainly does not allow Sandy to take it all. Hopefully, you (perhaps with some help from the court) can arrange for the value of the property that Sandy has taken, be reimbursed from the proceeds of the sale of the house and deposited into Paul's trust account.

Thank you.

Merideth immediately replied that she is following up with Amanda on this.

On September 14, 2020, I sent a follow-up email to Amanda

and Merideth:

> From: Carl Baker
> To: Amanda Ritter, Merideth Nagel
> Sent: Monday, September 14, 2020 1:14:01 PM
> Subject: Fwd: Property Sandy has Taken from Paul
>
> Any progress on this?
>
> Thank you.

I received the following two replies within a few hours:

Carl,
   Thank you for reaching out; however, the Guardian has approved the distribution of Carl's (sic) assets, based on her evaluation of his best interests. Recall that she has to keep in mind his best interests, and not those of his beneficiaries and/or family members.
   I am satisfied with her position on this issue.

Merideth

I do not understand Meredith's response, especially as his attorney. How is it in Paul's best interest to have Sandy take his assets? And secondly, the Antenuptial Agreement is noticeably clear and states that these assets "remain the sole and exclusive and separate property" of Paul.

Good afternoon Carl. I did receive the prior email and had a phone conference with Mark and Allyne. Personal property was dealt with in a way that they were satisfied with as Paul's trustees because to fight getting anything back besides the list of items that Cher and I were given would cost more money than the items are worth. This decision was also supported by both my attorney Mike Rogers and their attorney Todd Mazenko.

Thank you,
Amanda Ritter
Professional Guardian and VA Fiduciary

Let me put this in the proper prospective. In 2014, Paul knew he had Alzheimer's and while his mind was still clear, he decided how he wanted his assets distributed. He took every legal precaution to make sure his wishes were followed and established a will and a trust. He also purchased a life insurance policy for $100,000 which he left to his daughter, Allyne, since she was a single mother. Prior to his marriage to Sandy, Paul again took legal action to protect his assets and he and Sandy decided that both their individual pre-marriage assets would remain with each individual. In simple terms, what was his would remain his, and what was hers would remain hers. And they legally documented the agreement by creating individual trusts and individual trust accounts and they signed an antenuptial agreement stating their intentions. Further, at the family meeting on October 20, 2017, Paul again stated he wanted to set aside his personal property for his children and grandchildren. All of us, including Sandy, agreed and stated we would take care of it.

Obviously, Sandy did not like this agreement and the quest

for Paul's premarital assets began. Now she believed that what is hers is hers and what is Paul's is hers also. To obtain her goals, Sandy's abuse and exploitation of Paul increased dramatically.

When Paul left Sandy and moved to our home, Sandy refused to allow Paul into their house and would not let him have more than a few articles of clothing. When Amanda and Cher came into the picture, the first request to each of them was to get a court order and recover Paul's property. It was months before he received any additional clothing and a year before he received the remainder. Paul was forced to spend several hundred dollars to buy clothes even though he had a closet full of clothes. Sandy had garage sales and either sold or gave away most of Paul's personal property to include his furniture, electronics, golf clubs and tools in violation of their agreement. Paul and Sandy split the cost of a new golf cart, some light fixtures, a rug and more. Sandy either took that property or sold it and kept all the money as well. A conservative estimate of the value of this property is more than $12,000. In addition, Sandy took Paul's safe which he has had for years and we have no idea what was in the safe.

What I find extremely troubling is that the court, Amanda, Cher and Merideth ignored all the legal documents and did nothing to stop this or correct it. How anyone could believe that this was "in Paul's best interest" is beyond me. So, Paul, a ward of the State, becomes a victim again, but this time Sandy has evidently been sanctioned by the State of Florida to steal Paul's property. Paul considered himself separated from Sandy. He very much wanted a divorce and met with a divorce attorney. But he could not take any action once Sandy petitioned the court to have him declared incapacitated. Thereafter, only his guardian could file such action. She knew that was what Paul wanted and she talked about it, but normal separation and divorce protocols were ignored due to his illness and Sandy's lies.

Again, Paul's family is hearing that same excuse that the cost (attorney fees) to return to Paul the property he rightfully owns, outweigh the value of the property. Mark had told me earlier that he was concerned that it would not be worth going after the property that Sandy had stolen. I told him that I felt someone needs to hold Sandy accountable and that I would handle it and if there was any cost to the trust, I would pay it.

However, I did not believe that the cost would be over $12,000 and this, in my opinion, was a cover for Amanda's poor decision.

My complaint is that Sandy takes Paul's personal property and the golf cart and other property that Paul paid one-half of, committing another crime that the State ignores. Further, this was not unexpected. Amanda would not allow any member of the Baker family in the house, thereby allowing Sandy to decide what she did or did not want without any regard to ownership or fairness. No matter how you look at it, this is a larceny, and certainly was not in Paul's best interest. Taking the easier solution to a problem is not always the right solution.

In addition, what I see here is that Sandy's abuse and exploitation of Paul continues with the endorsement of the court. If the benefit did not outweigh Paul's legal costs of taking possession of his own property, Amanda's, Merideth's, and the court's actions, coupled with their total lack of doing what is best for Paul, put everyone in this position and created the circumstances that allowed Sandy to steal Paul's property without being held accountable. This is insane.

    I go back to my original premise: The court should have never made Paul a ward of the state when there was a loving family willing and able to care for Paul. The court based all its decisions on what they label as "a family disagreement" when, in fact, Sandy was abusing and exploiting Paul. In reality, Amanda was the court appointed guardian, but I was the one who took care of Paul. I took care of all his need and supplies; I took him to all his medical appointments; and when Paul was upset or getting angry, the staff always called me and I would either speak to Paul by phone or drive to Trinity Springs.

    With all that has happened in this case, can anyone honestly believe that this entire system is not horribly broken and mismanaged?

    There was finally another offer on the house and the closing was scheduled for December 16, 2020. In another attempt to hold Sandy accountable for the grand larceny of Paul's property, on December 2nd, I sent the following email to Mark and Allyne who are the trustees for Paul's trust account:

Mark and Allyne,

    I understand the closing on the house is December 16th. After the house closes, you need to be prepared for an accurate distribution of the funds to your dad's trust and Sandy's trust. FYI, I have listed some concerns that may help you fairly divide the proceeds.

    1. There are house expenses that Allyne has paid and Sandy's half

should be deducted from her part of the proceeds and deposited in Paul's trust.

2. I have most of the records for their home improvements and they each paid one-half. In some cases, Sandy paid the contractor with her check and then took half the cost from Paul's checking account. Do not let her tell you that she paid the entire cost. If she submits anything in writing to you, send it to me and I will give you the documentation for Paul's payments. Any home improvements or routine expenses that she claims after Paul left the home on January 14, 2019, are Sandy's full responsibility.

3. When Sandy moved to Louisiana, she illegal took some of Paul's property. She has taken possession of property that they each paid one-half of the initial cost - e.g., golf cart, furniture, rugs, lighting fixtures and more. Additionally, she took all your dad's furniture, furnishings, and some personal property which he purchased long before they were married. All in all, Sandy has taken property that was not hers which has a minimum value in the amount of $12,000.00. (Half the value of the golf cart alone is over $4,000). This would be a good time to hold Sandy accountable for this larceny. Talk to your trust attorney about this. This is rightfully your dad's money and I do not see any reason why this should be ignored. I have documentation and/or receipts for all of this and can furnish photos if needed.

Let me know if you have any questions or if you need any help with this.

In a telephone conversation later in the day, Allyne told me that her attorney (Todd) stated that Florida law permits Sandy to take whatever property she wants from the house because it is marital property unless it is property covered by a prenuptial. Fortunately, Paul and Sandy did sign an Antenuptial Agreement which prohibits Sandy from taking any of Paul's property covered by the agreement. I sent a copy to Allyne to give to her attorney and I am awaiting his response.

A week later, Allyne told me that she did send the Antenuptial Agreement to her Attorney (Todd Mazenko) for him to review and take appropriate action against Sandy. We were not seeking any criminal action, just reimbursement from Sandy for a fair value of the property she had stolen from Paul, which could be deducted from her half of the funds from the sale of the home. However, now Todd was stating that the only way to hold Sandy accountable was to file for a divorce from Sandy and request the family court for reimbursement. It is difficult for me to believe that this is the only remedy for Sandy's actions. And yet again, Paul is being abused by the system and no one really cares. It is also difficult for me to believe that anyone in the Florida state government truly understands what actually happens in this process or procedure, or whatever you call it. And if they are aware of the problems, why do they fail to correct them?

Just when you think you have heard it all, another unbelievable incident appears. On October 6, 2020, Amanda's attorney, Michael Rogers, Judge Morley's former law partner, submitted a bill of $1,796.90 to be paid from Paul's trust.

To fully understand the bill, Allyne sent the following email to her attorney:

Todd: I would like you to request an itemized statement of Mr. Roger's billable hours. We should be certain that my father is not being charged for the time spent by Mr. Rogers and/or his paralegal to correct and resubmit their own ill-prepared petition to the court (where they had names mixed up) regarding the guardianship granting approval of the sale of my father's house. I certainly believe that would be inappropriate. Not to mention, Mr. Roger's insistence that the petition was not needed in the first place, when indeed it was necessary is ultimately the cause of the sale of my father's house falling through. His inadequate preparedness has cost my father enough with the loss of that sale.

Todd responded:

Allyne: Mike Roger's itemized billing ledger is attached to the Petition. I just reviewed it. I don't see anything that appears to be excessive or out of the ordinary. It looks like the ledger also complies with the Court's previous Order. Please let me know if there is anything in particular that concerns you.

Allyne did have some legitimate concerns and replied:

Todd: What concerns me is making sure we are doing right by my dad. It is my brother's and my obligation to protect my father's best intertest. Mark and I, with your help, are however, the only ones in this situation who are actually protecting his rights by protecting his life savings. So, I will be reasonable and I understand that contesting this would most likely cost my father more money than it would save him. But it is a hard pill to swallow. Why would my father be responsible to pay Mike Rogers for the time he spent to correct his own egregious error? How unprofessional! I sometimes just feel the need to make it known that this entire guardianship arrangement has been nothing but a financial detriment to my father. This guardianship is only necessary because of Sandy and yet this manipulative scam artist continues to navigate through this process without having her own representation. To make matters worse, my father is being billed for all the conversations she chooses to have with all attorneys whenever she pleases. That makes it seem like she is still being allowed to exploit my father even though we managed to get him to a safe living facility. It's just so upsetting! What purpose does Meredith serve? Shouldn't she be questioning these things since she is still listed on these documents as "Dad's attorney"? I'm assuming the court will expect my father to pay her fees at some point to which I will have to question FOR WHAT??

In addition, Allyne was told that since the court approved the bill, her contesting the bill or her refusing to pay it in full could result in her being removed as trustee for her father's trust and the result would be everything would go to Amanda to handle. This is crazy and another attempt to cover their questionable conduct and abuse of Paul.

The PETITION FOR ORDER AUTHORIZING PAYMENT OF ATTORNEY FEES AND COSTS AND THE AFFIDAVIT OF ATTORNEY'S FEES AND COSTS FOLLOW:

A Case Study Of Elder Abuse And Exploitation In Florida

Filing # 132874269 E-Filed 08/17/2021 05:04:17 PM

IN THE CIRCUIT COURT OF THE FIFTH
JUDICIAL CIRCUIT IN AND FOR SUMTER
COUNTY, FLORIDA

CASE NO. 2019-GA-000158

In Re: Guardianship of

John Paul Baker,

    Incapacitated.
_____/

PETITION FOR ORDER AUTHORIZING PAYMENT OF ATTORNEY'S FEES AND COSTS

Petitioner, Michael J. Rogers, alleges:

1. Petitioner is engaged in the practice of law in Lake County and elsewhere in the State of Florida, and is a member in good standing of the Florida Bar.

2. *Amanda A. Ritter* is the duly appointed and acting Plenary Guardian of Person and Property of the Ward, *John Paul Baker.*

3. Petitioner has rendered services and advanced costs on behalf of the Plenary Guardian of Person and Property from October 19, 2020 through August 16, 2021, as more fully described and set forth in the Affidavit of Attorney's Fees and Costs attached hereto. Petitioner has not received compensation for said services rendered and costs advanced.

4. Based upon the criteria established by Section 744.108(2) of the Florida Guardianship Law, petitioner believes that a reasonable fee for the services performed and costs expended by petitioner during that period of time is $1,868.70.

5. Petitioner is asking the court to direct compensation to him in the amount of $1,850.00 for 9.50 of professional services rendered as follows: $300.00 per hour for 4.50 hours of attorney time; and $100.00 per hour for 5.00 hours of paralegal time.

6. Petitioner is asking the court to direct reimbursement to him in the amount of $18.70 for costs advanced on behalf of the Plenary Guardian of Person and Property.

7. Since the initiation of this guardianship, Petitioner has received a total of $11,020.00 as compensation for in excess of 41.80 hours of services rendered; and a total of $52.75 as reimbursement of costs advanced on behalf of the Plenary Guardian of Person and Property.

8. The time expended, fees incurred and costs advanced referenced in paragraph seven above do not include the time expended nor the fees and costs for which this petition is based.

WHEREFORE, Petitioner requests that an order be entered allowing petitioner a reasonable fee for services rendered and directing reimbursement of costs advanced on behalf of the Plenary Guardian of Person and Property; and further directing the Guardian of The Property to pay those fees and costs from the assets of the estate of the Ward.

Under penalties of perjury, I declare that I have read the foregoing and that the facts alleged are true to the best of my knowledge and belief.

I HEREBY CERTIFY that a true and correct copy of the foregoing has been furnished by e-service, via Florida Courts E-filing Portal, this 17th day of August, 2021, to:

Merideth C. Nagel, MERIDETH NAGEL, P.A., service@mnagellaw.com, Merideth.Nagel@mnagellaw.com, Joshua.Rosenberg@mnagellaw.com;

Amanda A. Ritter, amanda.a.ritter@gmail.com

Allyn Baker, abaker@powers-santola.com

Mark Baker, mebaker@coolins.com

Sandra Baker, rasanmi@aol.com

Michael J. Rogers, Esquire
Florida Bar No. 0009441
GAYLORD & ROGERS, LLC
Post Office Drawer 2047
Eustis, Florida 32727-2047
Telephone: (352) 483-4888
Facsimile: (352) 483-0732
E-Service: lisa@gaylordrogers.com
betty@gaylordrogers.com

A Case Study Of Elder Abuse And Exploitation In Florida

IN THE CIRCUIT COURT OF THE FIFTH
JUDICIAL CIRCUIT IN AND FOR SUMTER
COUNTY, FLORIDA

CASE NO. 2019-GA-000158

In Re: Guardianship of

John Paul Baker,

  Incapacitated.
_____/

AFFIDAVIT OF ATTORNEY'S FEES AND COSTS

The undersigned hereby swears that he has rendered services and advanced costs on behalf of the Plenary Guardian of Person and Property in the above-styled cause as follows:

SEE ATTACHED EXHIBIT "A"

FURTHER AFFIANT SAYETH NOT.

             /s/ Michael J. Rogers
             Michael J. Rogers, Esquire
             Florida Bar No. 0009441
             GAYLORD & ROGERS, LLC
             Post Office Drawer 2047
             Eustis, Florida 32727-2047
             Telephone: (352) 483-4888
             Facsimile: (352) 483-0732
             E-Service: lisa@gaylordrogers.com
                    betty@gaylordrogers.com

State of **Florida**
County of **Lake**

  The foregoing instrument was sworn and subscribed to before me by means of physical presence this _17th_ day of _August_, 2021, by **Michael J. Rogers**, who is personally known to me or who has produced a Florida Driver's License as identification.

             /s/ Lisa H. Oaks
                      , Notary Public

          Stamp/Seal: LISA H. OAKS
                  MY COMMISSION # GG 141477
                  EXPIRES: September 10, 2021
                  Bonded Thru Notary Public Underwriters

Carl R. Baker

Gaylord & Rogers, L.L.C.
804 North Bay Street
Post Office Drawer 2047
Eustis, FL 32727-2047

Ph:352-483-4888   Fax:352-483-0732

Guardianship of John Baker
c/o Amanda A. Ritter, Guardian
Post Office Box 895159
Leesburg, Florida 34789

August 16, 2021

		File #:	19-0189
Attention:		Inv #:	23889

RE: Guardianship of John Paul Baker

DATE	DESCRIPTION	HOURS	RATE	AMOUNT
Oct-19-20	Receipt and review of executed Order Authorizing Payment of Attorney's Fees and Costs (MJR).	0.10	$300.00	30.00
	Draft e-mail correspondence to client providing copy of signed Order Authorizing Payment of Attorney's Fees and Costs.	0.10	$100.00	10.00
Oct-27-20	Correspondence to client providing Annual Plan and Physician's Report forms.	0.40	$100.00	40.00
Oct-28-20	Draft Petition for Order Authorizing Payment of Compensation, Expenses, and Reimbursement of Guardian. Draft proposed Order Authorizing Payment of Compensation, Expenses, and Reimbursement of Guardian. Correspondence to Court regarding proposed Order.	1.00	$100.00	100.00
Nov-04-20	Receipt and review of e-mail from Amanda regarding new contract on house and need to file petition for authority to execute and sell Wards interest as guardian. Draft reply regarding same.	0.20	$300.00	60.00
	Receipt and review of e-mail from Amanda Ritter requesting Petition for Authorization to Sell Ward's Interest in Real Property, and attaching a Residential Contract for Sale and Purchase.	0.20	$300.00	60.00

Invoice #:	23889	Page 2		August 16, 2021	
		Revised Petition for Authorization to Convey Ward's Interest in Real Property and revised Order. Revised Consents (3).	0.20	$300.00	60.00
		E-mailed Consents to interested parties.	0.10	$100.00	10.00
Nov-05-20		Receipt and review of e-mail from Debbie with Todd Mazenko's office attaching signed Consent to Convey Ward's Real Property signed by Todd Mazenko on behalf of Allyne Baker and Mark Baker, Co-Trustees.	0.10	$300.00	30.00
		Receipt and review of signed, original Petition for Authorization to Convey Ward's Interest in Real Property signed by Amanda Ritter.	0.10	$300.00	30.00
Nov-16-20		Draft correspondence to clerk regarding proposed Order authorizing Guardian to Convey Ward's Interest in Real Property.	0.20	$100.00	20.00
		Receipt and review of signed, original Consent to Convey Ward's Real Property received from Sandra Baker.	0.10	$300.00	30.00
Nov-17-20		Draft e-mail correspondence to Judicial Assistant forwarding cover letter and proposed Order authorizing Guardian to Convey Ward's Interest in Real Property for Judge Morley's consideration.	0.10	$100.00	10.00
Nov-19-20		Draft e-mail correspondence to client providing copy of signed Order Authorizing Guardian to Convey Ward's Interest in Real Property.	0.10	$100.00	10.00
Nov-23-20		Receipt and review of executed Order Authorizing Guardian to Convey Ward's Interest in Real Property.	0.10	$300.00	30.00
Dec-09-20		Receipt and review of e-mail from closing agent, Belinda Stephenson, confirming that her office will prepare deed for Amanda's signature.	0.10	$300.00	30.00
Feb-17-21		Receipt and review of Annual Plan with Physicians report signed by Amanda.	0.20	$300.00	60.00
Feb-18-21		Receipt and review of e-mail from Amanda Ritter attaching Annual Guardianship Plan and Physician's Report.	0.10	$300.00	30.00

Carl R. Baker

Invoice #:	23889	Page 3			August 16, 2021
		Prepare Notice of Confidential Information as to Annual Plan and Physician's Report.	0.10	$100.00	10.00
Feb-22-21		Draft proposed Order Approving Annual Plan. Correspondence to Court regarding proposed order.	0.40	$100.00	40.00
Apr-22-21		Receipt and review of Report of Clerk regarding delinquent guardianship report (Annual Accounting for 10/21/19 through 10/31/20).	0.10	$300.00	30.00
Apr-28-21		Receipt and review of e-mail from Amanda suggesting seeking discharge of guardian of property. Draft reply regarding same. Follow up telephone call with Amanda regarding same and confirming e-mail with BAR and Amanda.	0.20	$300.00	60.00
Apr-29-21		Review file and docket. Draft Response to Report of Clerk Regarding Delinquent Guardianship Report, accounting.	0.40	$100.00	40.00
May-07-21		Receipt and review of e-mail from Amanda Ritter attaching copy of signed Response to Clerk.	0.10	$300.00	30.00
May-11-21		Draft e-mail correspondence to client providing copy of signed Response to Report of Clerk.	0.10	$100.00	10.00
Jul-01-21		Receipt and review of e-mail from Amanda regarding declining condition of Mr. Baker and request for DNR. Draft reply regarding same.	0.20	$300.00	60.00
Jul-08-21		Receipt and review of e-mail from Amanda Ritter attaching copy of Living Will.	0.10	$300.00	30.00
Jul-30-21		Receipt and review of e-mail from Amanda Ritter regarding DNR with attached letters from doctors.	0.20	$300.00	60.00
Aug-02-21		Receipt and review of e-mail from Amanda regarding status of DNR Petition and frustration of Mr. Baker's children in same.	0.10	$300.00	30.00
		E-mail exchanges with Judicial Assistant; e-mail exchanges with Guardian.	0.10	$100.00	10.00
Aug-03-21		Office conference with Amanda to review and sign Petition to Execute DNR.	0.20	$300.00	60.00

IN THE CIRCUIT COURT OF THE FIFTH
JUDICIAL CIRCUIT IN AND FOR SUMTER
COUNTY, FLORIDA

CASE NO. 2019-GA-000158

In Re: Guardianship of

John Paul Baker,

Incapacitated.

_____/

AFFIDAVIT OF ATTORNEY'S FEES AND COSTS

The undersigned hereby swears that he has rendered services and advanced costs on behalf of the Plenary Guardian of Person and Property in the above-styled cause as follows:

SEE ATTACHED EXHIBIT "A"

FURTHER AFFIANT SAYETH NOT.

_____
Michael J. Rogers, Esquire
Florida Bar No. 0009441
GAYLORD & ROGERS, LLC
Post Office Drawer 2047
Eustis, Florida 32727-2047
Telephone: (352) 483-4888
Facsimile: (352) 483-0732
E-Service: lisa@gaylordrogers.com
betty@gaylordrogers.com

State of **Florida**
County of **Lake**

The foregoing instrument was sworn and subscribed to before me by means of physical presence this ___17th___ day of ___August___, 2021, by **Michael J. Rogers**, who is personally known to me or who has produced a Florida Driver's License as identification.

_____, Notary Public

Stamp/Seal:

LISA H. OAKS
MY COMMISSION # GG 141477
EXPIRES: September 10, 2021
Bonded Thru Notary Public Underwriters

Carl R. Baker

8. The time expended, fees incurred and costs advanced referenced in paragraph seven above do not include the time expended nor the fees and costs for which this petition is based.

WHEREFORE, Petitioner requests that an order be entered allowing petitioner a reasonable fee for services rendered and directing reimbursement of costs advanced on behalf of the Plenary Guardian of Person and Property; and further directing the Guardian of The Property to pay those fees and costs from the assets of the estate of the Ward.

Under penalties of perjury, I declare that I have read the foregoing and that the facts alleged are true to the best of my knowledge and belief.

I HEREBY CERTIFY that a true and correct copy of the foregoing has been furnished by e-service, via Florida Courts E-filing Portal, this __17th__ day of __August__, 2021, to:

Merideth C. Nagel, MERIDETH NAGEL, P.A., service@mnagellaw.com, Merideth.Nagel@mnagellaw.com, Joshua.Rosenberg@mnagellaw.com;

Amanda A. Ritter, amanda.a.ritter@gmail.com

Allyn Baker, abaker@powers-santola.com

Mark Baker, mebaker@coolins.com

Sandra Baker, rasanmi@aol.com

_____
Michael J. Rogers, Esquire
Florida Bar No. 0009441
GAYLORD & ROGERS, LLC
Post Office Drawer 2047
Eustis, Florida 32727-2047
Telephone: (352) 483-4888
Facsimile: (352) 483-0732
E-Service: lisa@gaylordrogers.com
betty@gaylordrogers.com

An analysis of the bill submitted by Attorney Michael J. Rodgers identifies three areas of concern:

The first is that Mr. Rogers evidently spoke to Sandy Baker, who he does not represent, answered her questions regarding the sale of the house and charged Paul's trust $120.00. How does he justify charging Paul for helping his abusive wife and why should Paul have to pay it?

Secondly, it appears that Amanda gave her attorney all the correspondence regarding the bills that were submitted by Cher which were inaccurate and charged both Paul and me for meetings that never took place or that neither of us were aware of. Cher eventually reduced the bill by $393.77 and the bill was paid in full. Michael Rogers was not the attorney for Cher Myers. Yet, because we requested a correction in Cher's original bill, Amanda's attorney charged Paul $300.00 for legal services to review these bills. Why? When you reference the earlier stated professional violations of Amanda and Cher, this entire episode does not pass the smell test and certainly does not justify taking more money from Paul's trust.

And finally, there is the aforementioned mistake made by Michael Rogers in drafting a required court order to complete the sale of the house. Attorney Rogers' mistake was overlooked by Amanda and resulted in the house not selling, which resulted in additional expenses to Paul's trust. Attorney Mike Rogers charged Paul $470.00 for that fiasco to include legal fees for correcting his own mistake. Unbelievable!

So, in summary, the victimization of Paul by the State of Florida continues. Most of these people who are lining their pockets from the probate court system, will claim the system is not broken. I adamantly disagree!!

In talking to Allyne, Paul's daughter, during the first week in March of 2021, I learned that Sandy was still calling Amada Ritter, Paul's court appointed guardian, several times a week. Why? I told Allyne to make sure that Amanda was not charging Paul's trust for these calls.

To further complicate the matter, on March 22, 2021, I received the following email from Amanda:

From: amanda a. ritter
To: crbaker
Date: Monday, 22 March 2021 4:19 PM EDT
Subject: More old military items

Good afternoon. Prior to Sandy moving she met me so she could give me a Publix bag full of more military items that were Paul's. The bag was sitting in my office and I was getting things sorted and found it there. I never went through it. It is at Trinity Springs at the receptionist desk for you to pick up the next time you are there.

Thank you,
Amanda Ritter
Professional Guardian and VA Fiduciary

I responded immediately after I read it:

From: crbaker
To: amanda a. ritter
Date: Monday, 22 March 2021 4:55 PM EDT

Subject: Re: More old military items

I will pick them up on Wednesday morning when I visit Paul. Thanks.

Let me see if I have this correct. Sandy left the Mango Court home in mid-July 2020. So sometime before she left, Sandy gave Amanda a Publix bag full of old military items to give to Paul. Eight months later, Amanda discovered the bag while "getting things sorted" in her office. Really? She did drop it off at Trinity Springs for me to pick up and give it to Paul; I did pick up the bag on Wednesday when I visited Paul.

> Truth is ever to be found in simplicity, and not in the multiplicity and confusion of things."
> —*Sir Isaac Newton*

CHAPTER 14

Resolution or Turmoil

There are several events that occurred during this case that I find troubling and inexcusable that should not and will not be ignored. Mistakes can happen, but what is outlined below is far more serious than a simple mistake.

I first reported the criminal complaint on Sandy to the Florida Department of Law Enforcement (FDLE) on October 5, 2018. They had the case for three months and never initiated an investigation. I ended up filing another criminal complaint with the Sumter County Sheriff's Office and from what I know and what is in the report, there was not much of an investigation. The crime I reported was exploitation, which is a Class 1 felony, yet there were no interviews of Paul or any member of the Baker family and the detective called Sandy on the phone rather than conducting a face-to-face interview/interrogation. No wonder she refused to speak with him. In fact, I do not have any indication that the detective ever left his office. It appears he completed the entire investigation on his computer and by phone. I hope that is not a permissible practice in the Sheriff's Office.

The initial elder abuse investigation against Sandy, by the Department of Children and Families, was closed with no continued supervision or criminal referrals. I could not see how the investigator could come to that conclusion and a supervisor would approve it. I filed a complaint and a second thorough investigation resulted in two criminal referrals against Sandy for inadequate supervision and exploitation. I sent an email to Amanda to advise her of the criminal referrals:

From: "crbaker"
To: "amanda a ritter"
Sent: Tuesday, March 24, 2020 4:00:16 PM
Subject: Fwd: Criminal Referrals - CONFIDENTIAL

Amanda
Several months ago, I appealed the finding of the Florida Department of Families and Children (Elder Abuse) on Sandy's abuse of Paul. I just confirmed that the Exploitation and Inadequate

Supervision charges have been verified and have been referred to the Sumter County Sheriff's Office and the State Attorney's office for follow up.

Please let me know if you hear anything on this and I will keep you posted if I receive any additional information.

I never heard one word from Amanda about the criminal referrals.

Right from the beginning, I could tell that State Attorney Brad King (the prosecutor) was not going to prosecute this case. He started off by stating that Sandy's actions were civil and not criminal. That changed to his office declaring that the homestead provision made Sandy's actions legal. This was not true since both Paul and Sandy waived their homestead rights in their Antenuptial Agreement. And despite the new findings and criminal referrals by the Department of Children and Families, Brad King again refused to prosecute Sandy. Two things trouble me greatly: the first, based on years of experience, is that I strongly believe that a jury would convict Sandy on the indisputable evidence that DCF and I have documented; and secondly, the reasons that Mr. King recited for not prosecuting were, in my opinion and my attorney's opinion, not legally correct. The Attorney General stated the State Attorney is an elected official and she had no authority to resolve it.

The Eldercare Coordination Program was a total waste of time and money and should have never been recommended by the Judge. It certainly did not help Paul and it cost the Baker family thousands of dollars for nothing. In fact, many of the state guidelines of conduct for the coordinator were ignored or violated.

And finally, has one person involved in this fiasco ever gone to Judge Morley to request a court order to force Sandy to act like a reasonable human being? Quite candidly, I am not sure that Judge Morley had any idea what was going on in her case. Did Merideth, Amanda or Cher keep her up to date? And if anyone claims that she had been updated, why did she not take some corrective action? I have said it before and I will repeat it again. The Florida probate court system is broken and it desperately needs to be fixed!

There was only one more avenue to pursue in our attempt to correct this horrible bureaucratic failure. Following is the certified letter that I sent to Governor Ron DeSantis and Attorney General Ashley Moody on April 22, 2020:

Dear Governor DeSantis and Attorney General Moody:
Having served in law enforcement for over 40 years, it is unfortunate that I need to send you this letter. I have exhausted all other avenues, and this is my last resort in the hope of finding some justice for my brother, Paul and our family.

I began my career as a Trooper in the New York State Police, working myself up through the ranks in the uniform force and the Bureau of Criminal Investigation. I retired in 1990 as a Deputy Superintendent (Colonel) and moved to Virginia to take the position of Director of the Bureau of Criminal Investigation (Lt. Colonel) in the Virginia State Police. Two years later, the Governor appointed me to Superintendent (Colonel) of the Virginia State Police. In 1994, when George Allen was elected Governor, he appointed me to serve

A Case Study Of Elder Abuse And Exploitation In Florida

on his Cabinet as the Deputy Secretary of Public Safety overseeing the operations of 11 agencies to include the State Police and National Guard. I served my last 11 years in public service as Chief of Police in Chesterfield County (Virginia) overseeing a department of 600 employees. I retired in 2007 and started my own company, Public Safety Consulting and was a partner in another consulting firm, Decide Smart. I tell you this to emphasize the vast experience I have in criminal investigations.

After what Paul and our family experienced over the last several years, we have an overwhelming concern for seniors in Florida, especially the most vulnerable ones. Also, very disturbing is the tens of thousands of dollars that have been unnecessarily expended to try and protect my brother from an abusive/exploitive wife while the systems in Florida have done nothing but further victimize him. I would not have thought that what our family witnessed over the last three years was even possible if I had not experienced it myself. This has indeed been an eye-opening experience and a nightmare for Paul and those who love him.

My brother, J. Paul Baker, retired from the US Army as a Brigadier General after 32 years of service. He was exposed to Agent Orange while serving in Viet Nam and has had numerous medical problems later in life. He now has a pacemaker, he was diagnosed with Alzheimer's dementia in 2015, and today, he is in a memory care facility. Most recently, he was diagnosed with breast cancer and had a mastectomy of the left breast several weeks ago.

I will try to provide a brief chronological overview of our involvement in the Florida system and then explain the problems we encountered in detail by agency.

Paul had a short-term, late-life marriage in 2016 to Sandy

Kaniewski. Sandy began isolating Paul from his family in August of 2018 after numerous attempts by her to take over his nonmarital assets were prevented by us. Previously, Paul and I communicated almost every day and played golf together twice a week. We were concerned for Paul's safety so our first efforts were to have the Sheriff's Office perform wellness checks on Paul. When $220,000 was removed from his trust account, I filed a complaint with the Elder Abuse Hotline. In January of 2019, I finally managed to talk to Paul for the first time in four months. The following week, Paul told me he wanted out of his marriage and moved out of their home and came to live with us. His wife then initiated court action to have Paul declared incompetent and force him to return to her. The court appointed Merideth Nagel as Paul's attorney. In our initial meeting with Merideth Nagel, she suggested that I file a criminal complaint against Sandy, which I did — FDLE first and secondly to the Sumter County Sheriff's Office.

Before any testimony was given in the initial probate court hearing, an Eldercare Coordinator was interjected into the process resulting in more problems than solutions. As a result of Sandy's petition, Paul was declared incapacitated and a professional guardian was appointed. During the entire process, not once did the court or anyone, other than my attorney, address the abuse or exploitation by Sandy.

What you are about to read may seem unbelievable, but unfortunately it is true and accurate. I have documented every event and all correspondence with all those involved to include the state and county agencies that were an integral part of the case. I am certain that you will find it rather shocking. I was especially disappointed in the actions of Florida's criminal justice agencies.

Their customer service is unbelievably poor. I am sending this to you because I have the highest respect for both of you and am certain that you would want to be aware of how your constituents are treated and hopefully make changes that would prevent another family from experiencing what we went through.

The enclosures with this letter will give you a better understanding of our experiences over the last several years. It is certainly not complete. I apologize for the length of the enclosures but understanding the events that led to where we are today is important.

Quite candidly, I could not believe that I found so many failures in a system that should be protecting senior citizens, especially in Florida with such a large and growing senior population. The State has a population approaching 20 million with 23% being age 60 or over. That makes the senior population at about 4.6 million and projected to double by 2030.

Following is a partial list of the problems that we (the Baker family) encountered from the initial abuse and exploitation through the court case and criminal complaint. What you are about to read is only a summary of what took place. I do have much more if needed.

Florida Department of Law Enforcement (FDLE)
Concern:

When I was told to file a criminal complaint by my brother's attorney, I immediately called FDLE based on my years of experience working in state investigation bureaus in New York and Virginia. However, FDLE failed to initiate a criminal investigation. In summary, I filed my initial criminal complaint with FDLE on October 15th, 2018. Approximately one month later, on November 13th, I received a call from Special Agent Schrenker who told me that FDLE would adopt the case and a Special Agent that handles investigations in Sumter County would be calling me. Exactly one month later, on December 13th, Special Agent Schrenker forwarded my case to the Brooksville Field Office for evaluation and follow up. I have no idea why it took a month to forward the case file to the Field Office. I also did not understand why I never heard another word from FDLE. On January 15th, 2019, exactly three months after my initial call to report Sandy's abuse and exploitation, it became obvious to me that there was no investigation by FDLE, so I called Special Agent Schrenker and asked him to close the case.

Enclosure 1:
Letter of Complaint to Commissioner Richard L. Swearingen dated December 9, 2019, and response dated December 23, 2019.

Florida Department of Children and Families
Concern:

The first investigation was incomplete with no criminal referrals. I appealed their findings and the second investigation was thorough with criminal referrals for exploitation and inadequate supervision.

Enclosure 2:
Florida Abuse Hotline Fax Transmittal Form Dated November 01, 2018.
Letter of Complaint to Secretary Chad Poppell Dated

December 20, 2019.

Transcript of telephone message I received from Sheri Peterson on January 22, 2019.

Copy of Confidential Investigative Summary (updated) showing findings verified for maltreatment/exploitation and inadequate supervision against Sandra.

My understanding is that these two charges were referred to the Sumter County Sheriff's Office and the State Attorney on March 3, 2020.

Given all my attempts to contact Sheri Peterson (a letter and seven phone calls), it is very difficult for me to believe that she never was notified that I called or received my letter until I sent a complaint to the Secretary. In any case, another investigator was assigned to review the case.

We would like to commend Investigator Kimberly Mummey for her effort and taking the time to do a thorough investigation.

State Attorney's Office

Concern:
Failure to prosecute and incomplete understanding of the case (Antenuptial Agreement - homestead waiver).

Enclosure 3:
Timeline on Sandy's Quest to Take Paul's money.
Letter to State Attorney Brad King dated July 17, 2019.
Memorandum dated August 16, 2019, from Erik Rauba to his supervisor, Mark Simpson, which was emailed to me. (Note: This memo was largely inaccurate and a gross incompetent portrayal of

the facts surrounding this case.)

My reply memorandum to State Attorney Brad King dated September 19, 2019.

Spread Sheet on the changes to Paul's trust.

Because of the new criminal referral by the Florida Department of Children and Families, I sent the following email to Brad King:

From: "crbaker"
To: "BKING"
Sent: Wednesday, April 8, 2020 9:43:40 AM
Subject: Update on Criminal Referral - Sandra Kaniewski S-2019-16863

Mr. King:
Several months ago, I appealed the finding of the Florida Department of Families and Children (Elder Abuse) on Sandy's abuse of Paul and they assigned another investigator to look at the case. Several weeks ago, I confirmed that the exploitation and inadequate supervision charges have been verified and were sent to the Sumter County Sheriff's Office and the State Attorney's Office for follow up on or about March 3rd. I have a copy of the DFC report. Detective Cohen has not yet received the referral.

I am checking to see if you have received this recent referral. If not, I will send a copy to both of you.

Thank you.
Carl Baker

From: "BKING"
To: "crbaker"
Cc: "Mark Simpson"
Sent: Thursday, April 9, 2020 9:06:30 AM
Subject: RE: Update on Criminal Referral - Sandra Kaniewski S-2019-16863

"Regardless of a new or amended finding by DCF, our position still remains as stated in the memo sent to you on 08/26/2019 which is attached. I understand that you do not agree, but your disagreement will not change the decision."

That is an interesting response by Mr. King. Most likely, he had not read the updated report and, obviously, it makes no difference as he is not going to prosecute this case.

Given all the mistakes in the State Attorney's memorandum which were overlooked in two reviews (by Simpson and King), their failure to realize the homestead exemption was waived (which negates one of their main reasons for not prosecuting) and their disregard of the "endeavoring to obtain or use" wording in the statute, I really question the professionalism of this office.

From the very beginning of the investigation, both Detective Cohen and Erik Rauba were indicating to me that they were not going to prosecute this case. From all the cases I have had in my career, I never encountered so much negativity at the investigative stage of a case. In my experiences, if the prosecutor did not think they had everything needed to prosecute, he or she would specifically tell me what was lacking and I would continue the investigation to try and obtain the needed information. We worked as a team. I never saw any of that team work here. Instead of being treated as a complainant who was concerned about my brother's well-being, they acted like they never had any intention of prosecuting this case and hoped I would just go away.

Further, the criticism for returning Paul's trust to the original 2014 language was unwarranted. Any loving family would have done the same.

In my many years of criminal investigation experience, this is the worst prosecutor's office I have ever worked with. First, they never returned my calls. Once, Erik Rauba called me and I missed the call. I did return the call shortly afterwards, but never got another call from him. Customer service is obviously not a high priority at the State Attorney's Office.

I am really looking for your help here. The exploitation statute appears to be a perfect fit given Sandy's actions and conduct. I am requesting your legal opinion on Sandy's waiving of the homestead, property, estate, and other rights, which means she is not entitled to a life estate in the home.

If you also feel that Paul's wife should not be charged under this statute, can you recommend another charge? To let a person like Sandy, walk away without being held accountable is unacceptable to me and hopefully to you as well. Without prosecution, the law is just words on a page in a book that sits on a shelf.

Eldercare Coordination Program

Concern:

This was an inappropriate application of the Eldercare Coordination Program and a total waste of time and money. First, this was not a family dispute but a crime. You cannot mediate criminal conduct. Secondly, we were charged thousands of dollars to mediate the rightful return of Paul's personal property, that should have been accomplished by a simple court order. And finally, by having secret meetings with Sandy and covertly bringing Sandy to visit Paul against his and his family's wishes, prior to a scheduled court hearing on visitation, the Eldercare Coordinator and guardian violated the standards of conduct outlined in the statutes.

Enclosure 4:
Email to Cher Myers, Eldercaring Coordinator dated April 6, 2020.

Even though I took the time to send documents outlining Sandy's abuse to everyone involved in the case, it was ignored. No one, not the Judge, not Paul's lawyer, not the Eldercaring Coordinator, not the guardian, no one wants to talk about all of Sandy's abuse and exploitation. When Harry Hackney, my attorney, outlined the abuse by Sandy in his opening statement at the first hearing, Paul's attorney, Merideth Nagel made a motion to bring in an Eldercaring Coordinator to mediate an agreement in the case. I was not familiar with this program, but everyone was telling me this was Judge Morley's "pet pilot program" and it would keep Paul out of the courtroom. With mixed feelings, I agreed to give mediation a chance. I had high hopes that the mediation would work. However, it turned out to be one of the worst decisions I have ever made. The email (Enclosure 4) gives you an idea what took place and the problems we encountered. The bottom line is that Paul and I paid thousands of dollars to have some of Paul clothes and personal items returned to him, which could have been easily accomplished with a simple court order. You need to take a hard look at this program and I have much more information and documentation should you need it.

There is no hidden agenda here. Paul's entire family came together to ensure that the remainder of Paul's life would be the best it could possibly be. We would do whatever needed to be done to protect Paul. We really tried to work with Sandy by constantly offering our assistance, scheduling family meetings and taking care of Paul when she was away, which was frequent. Unfortunately, it became evident that Sandy did not have the same agenda.

By documenting all that has happened over the last several years, it is our hope and desire that your review of this case will improve a system which is horribly broken and just may prevent someone else from making the same mistakes we made. In many ways, this case could serve as a guide should another family have the unfortunate experience of ending up in probate court. One would have to wonder how many similar cases there are that are buried in the bureaucratic files in Florida and across this country. And the second question that comes to mind is how many of these type cases are never reported, in part because of the system itself and the expense.

The Baker family has lived this nightmare for several years now. My wife and I took care of Paul for months until it was time for him to move to a memory care facility. This fiasco has already cost the Baker family close to $30,000.00 and I expect in the end, it will be over $60,000.00 and this does not include memory care and medical costs. If nothing else, just for a minute, ponder this, which is our main concern. If this one evil person can cause so much havoc on two different families (Baker and Kaniewski) and not be held accountable for her actions, it allows her criminal behavior to continue. I want to do everything within my power to help see that this broken system is fixed.

I realize that this is a lot of information to wade through and want you to know that I will be available by phone or email should you have any questions or need additional information. We do have other concerns and would like to meet with you or a member of your staff to discuss this further. We would be willing to drive to Tallahassee if that would help.

The Villages is a wonderful place to live and a showcase for Florida's retirement living. Most of us feel safe and protected here. However, there are improvements that can be made. I hope you can understand why I felt obligated to let you know about our experience with the probate court and criminal justice process. From what I know about your administration, I trust that corrective action will be taken so nothing like this can happen again.

Thank you for your service and may God continue to bless you both.

Respectfully,
Carl R. Baker

Several days after I mailed the letters to the Governor and the Attorney General, the following article was posted on *Village-News. com*:

Retiring state attorney will be remembered for cases not pursued in The Villages

Longtime State Attorney Brad King has announced his retirement and he will likely be remembered in The Villages for the ones who got away.

King, a former Marion County sheriff's deputy who was first elected in 1988 to serve as chief prosecutor for Sumter, Lake, Marion, Hernando and Citrus counties, made the announcement on Friday. He has indicated he will leave office by Dec. 31. King said he wanted to spend more time with family.

The Republican had pre-filed to run for another term, but then he had a change of heart.

King quietly greased the path for his successor, his office's executive director William McDonald Gladson, to take over the reins. Gladson was the only candidate to qualify for state attorney for the Fifth Judicial Circuit by Friday's deadline. That means Gladson will automatically be elected and will take office in January.

In The Villages, King will be remembered for two prominent cases he chose not to vigorously pursue:

• Last year, a man who left a woman to die in The Villages after she fell in 2017 from his golf cart at Brownwood, walked out of a courtroom virtually unpunished thanks to a decision by King's office. Timothy Jacob Foxworth on May 20 pleaded no contest to two misdemeanor charges in connection with the July 16, 2017 incident which claimed the life of 51-year-old Shelly Osterhout. The sentence enraged her family, including her father, who wrote a letter to the court in which he decried the prosecutor's office's fear of the Foxworth family's "deep pockets."

• In 2018, Villagers were stunned when King's office announced two suspects would not be prosecuted in the 2016 beating death of 26-year-old Austin Stevens at Spanish Springs Town Square. A document from the prosecutor's office indicated that it has been determined that Stevens was the "initial aggressor" on the night of June 5, 2016. The original police report said teens who had been in a minivan that had passed by Stevens' workplace had been taunting the McCall's Tavern employees. Stevens went to the corner at TooJay's to confront the teens. The original report said one of them ran up behind Stevens and punched Stevens on the side of his head, causing Stevens to fall to the ground and strike the back of his head on the concrete. While on the ground and unresponsive, another teen kicked Stevens in the face, the original report said. Stevens was airlifted to Ocala Regional Medical Center, where he died of injuries suffered during the beating.

(04/27/20 The Village News.com)

The first response I received from my letter to the Governor and Attorney General was a phone call on May 29th, from the Office of Professional Guardians of the Department of Elder Affairs. They requested the following information which was sent to them on June 3rd:

• A copy of the updated investigative report from the Department of Children and Families with verified findings of exploitation and inadequate supervision against Paul's wife, Sandra Baker.

- A copy of my email to Paul's guardian, Amanda Ritter updating her on the criminal case and the verified findings of exploitation and inadequate supervision against Sandy.
- Copies of all my correspondence with Amanda Ritter regarding Sandy's unannounced (covert) visit to Paul which was arranged by Amanda and Cher Myers without any notification to the Baker family.
- Information on Sandy's secret meeting with Paul and the violation of guardian standards and correspondence concerning the return of Paul's property.

On June 15, 2020, I received the following letter from the Department of Elder Affairs:

Re: Complaint 2020-097

Dear Mr. Baker:
The Office of Public and Professional Guardians (OPPG), within the Department of Elder Affairs, has the statutory duty to have oversight of professional guardians and investigate legally sufficient complaints about professional guardians pursuant to Section 744.2001, Florida Statutes.

The OPPG has reviewed your complaint pertaining to the conduct of Amanda Ritter and finds that the allegations within your complaint are legally insufficient, in that they fail to state ultimate facts that would lead to a conclusion that the guardian violated the Florida Guardianship Law or OPPG Standards of Practice for Professional Guardians. Therefore, the OPPG is unable to pursue any investigation or disciplinary action against the guardian and has closed your complaint.

Please contact the OPPG at (855) 305-3030 if you have any questions.

Sincerely,
Chante' Jones

This letter certainly was not specific as to why my complaint was "legally insufficient", so on June 22nd, I mailed a letter to Elder Affairs for clarification:

Dear Director Jones:
Thank you for your letter dated June 11, 2020, regarding Complaint 2020-097.

For your information, in my letters to the Governor and Attorney General dated April 22, 2020, my primary concern was the lack of prosecution for the exploitation of my brother, John Paul Baker and I was surprised that your office asked for additional information on Paul's guardian. I did send your office four emails explaining the situation.

Now that I have your response, I am asking for some clarification, so I have a better understanding of the process. I do not understand what you mean by stating that "...the allegations within your complaint are legally insufficient."

How were they legally insufficient? Does that mean you need additional information from me? If so, I would certainly provide that to you. Does it mean that you do not believe what I stated was true? If so, I would like a chance to respond. If you feel that Amanda followed the principle of Informed Consent and did not ignore my brother's previous stated preference to not see his wife, I would like to know how you arrived at that conclusion.

I thank you and would appreciate any information that you can provide me so I can better understand your decision.

Sincerely,
Carl R. Baker
cc: Governor Ron DeSantis
   Attorney General Ashley Moody

On July 23rd, I received the following reply from Executive Director Jones:

Mr. Baker

This letter is in response to your additional communication to the Office of Public and Professional Guardians on Tuesday, June 30, 2020, via mail regarding complaint # 2020-097.

Per Section 744.2004, Florida Statutes, "A complaint is legally sufficient if it contains ultimate facts that show a violation of a standard of practice by a professional guardian has occurred."

Upon review of court files, we determined that your complaint was legally insufficient due to the following factors:

- There is a court order dated Thursday, November 7, 2019, that granted supervised visitation to Sandra Baker.
- The court order further states that "No evidence was presented to convince the Court that Petitioner and the Ward should not have

contact.

- The court order goes on to say, "The Petitioner Sandra Baker, shall have unlimited visitation and/or contact with the Ward as often as can be arranged."

In summary, as the visit was approved by the court, your allegation was determined to not be legally sufficient.

If you feel that someone is in immediate danger, please contact your local law enforcement. If you suspect, have seen, or know of abuse or exploitation, please also contact the Florida Abuse Hotline at 1-800-96-ABUSE (1-800-962-2873).

Chante' Jones, Esq.
Executive Director
Office of Public and Professional Guardians

This letter makes no sense to me and certainly did not address my concerns. In my opinion, this letter was nothing but a "typical attempted whitewash" in the hope that I would just go away and another indication that the State of Florida truly does not care about the senior population.

The event that resulted in my complaint took place on October 25, 2019, two weeks before the November 7th court order. My letter to Governor DeSantis and Attorney General Moody clearly stated that the guardian, Amanda Ritter and the Eldercaring Coordinator, Cher Myers, by having secret meetings with Sandy and covertly bringing Sandy to visit Paul against his and his family's wishes, prior to a scheduled court hearing on visitation, violated the standards of conduct outlined in the statutes. Further, Paul started the visitation by telling the story of how he was abused by his wife, Sandy to a woman he did not know was Sandy. Initially, neither Cher nor Amanda ever mentioned that to anyone in our family and as far as I can tell, never put it in their report and never told the court. Nor did they acknowledge that Paul did not know that it was Sandy he was speaking to. In fact, Amanda wrote in her initial email that the surprise meeting that she and Cher orchestrated, that there "was absolutely not one moment of negativity." That was a lie. And covertly bringing an abusive wife to visit Paul, is simply elder abuse by two people the court appointed to safeguard him.

After all the work the court, Amanda and Cher did to give Sandy visitation rights to Paul, against his and his family's wishes, six weeks later, Sandy violated the court order and her visitation rights were terminated. This is what happens when the court thinks the government can take better care of the ward, rather than a loving family. And they think the system is not broken and evidently, will go to extremes to keep it intact. This should be totally unacceptable by anyone's standards and is usually an indication of incompetence, corruption, poor leadership, or a combination of all three.

Neither Governor DeSantis nor Attorney General Moody responded to my letter. I waited two and half months and then sent follow-up certified letters to both of them on July 8th:

Dear Governor DeSantis:
Two and one-half months ago (April 22nd), I sent a 10-page letter to you and Attorney General Moody outlining my disappointment

and concerns regarding the criminal exploitation and abuse of my brother, John Paul Baker.

To date, I have not received a response from your office or AG Moody's office or any acknowledgement that you are reviewing my concerns. The only letter I did receive was from the Department of Elder Affairs regarding Paul's guardian and I did respond to the Executive Director, with a copy to you and AG Moody, asking for some clarification.

The main concern of my original letter was the lack of prosecution of Sandra Baker for exploitation and abuse and the numerous mistakes made by state agencies that resulted in no one being held accountable.

From my own involvement and interactions and discussions with other professionals and practitioners, it has become apparent that the entire process governing abused and exploited seniors is horribly broken. I voiced my concerns to you in hope that my family's experience would serve as an impetus for a substantive discussion and needed changes and improvements for all Floridians. I am extremely disappointed that to date, my concerns seem to have fallen on deaf ears.

I am respectfully awaiting a reply or a confirmation that someone is reviewing my concerns. As stated in my previous letter, I am available to discuss this entire matter and will travel to Tallahassee if necessary.

Thank you,
/signed/

Dear Attorney General Moody:
Two and one-half months ago (April 22nd), I sent a 10-page

letter to you and Governor DeSantis, outlining my disappointment and concerns regarding the criminal exploitation and abuse of my brother, John Paul Baker.

To date, I have not received a response from your office or the Governor's office or any acknowledgement that you are reviewing my concerns. The only letter I did receive was from the Department of Elder Affairs regarding Paul's guardian and I did respond to the Executive Director, with a copy to you, asking for some clarification.

The main concern of my original letter to you was the lack of prosecution of Sandra Baker for exploitation and abuse and the numerous mistakes made by state agencies that resulted in no one being held accountable. In that letter, I also asked for some clarification from your Office on the exploitation statute and the State Attorney's refusal to prosecute based on the homestead rights, which were waived in an antenuptial agreement. Further, the State Attorney also based his decision on a memorandum written by his staff which was inaccurate and a gross incompetent portrayal of the facts of the case.

I am respectfully awaiting a reply or a confirmation that someone is reviewing my concerns. As stated in my previous letter, I am available to discuss this entire matter and will travel to Tallahassee if necessary.

Thank you,
/signed/

When I was serving on Governor Allen's Cabinet in Virginia, every letter to the Governor was logged in and assigned to a staff member to draft a response for the Governor's review, which had to be completed by a certain date. I assure you, in a relatively short time, a response to the citizen's letter was in the mail. It is called "good customer service," and obvious is certainly lacking in Governor DeSantis' administration. The number of unanswered letters, emails, and phone calls that I initiated to the Florida state government, seeking help and justice for Sandy's exploitation and abuse of my brother Paul, is quite astonishing and unacceptable by anyone's standards.

On Friday, July 17, almost three months after I sent my letter, I received an email reply from the Attorney General's Office:

Dear Mr. Baker,
The Florida Office of the Attorney General is in receipt of your correspondence dated April 22, 2020 and your follow up correspondence dated July 8, 2020, requesting a response from our office regarding your concerns regarding a lack of prosecution in the criminal case involving your brother, John Paul Baker. The Office is also in possession of a letter copy dated June 22, 2020, addressed to the Office of Public and Professional Guardians.

First, I would like to express my sincere thanks to you for your extensive service protecting and serving in your role of prior law enforcement, as well as to your brother for his 32 years of service in the U.S. Army. I have great admiration and respect for those who serve in the military and in law enforcement for risking their lives daily in order to preserve our rights, safety, and freedom.

Further, I would like to take a moment to convey how sorry I am to hear about your family's difficulties surrounding your brother's health, as well as the criminal and legal problems surrounding Paul's marriage. The investigation and prosecution of potential violations of criminal law, such as those alleged in your complaint, are under the jurisdiction of the local police or sheriff and elected state attorney for the county and judicial circuit in which the criminal activity is believed to have occurred. These authorities operate independently and are not part of the Attorney General's Office. You may wish to follow up directly with the state attorney's office in your circuit with respect to your specific concerns regarding the review of a criminal case.

Regarding the concerns you expressed pertaining to the Department of Children and Families, you may choose to make a report or file a complaint with the Office of Inspector General online at:

Office of Inspector General
1317 Winewood Blvd, Bldg 5, 2nd Floor
Tallahassee, FL 32399
Web Form: https://www.myflfamilies.com/admin/ig/rptfraud1.shtml
Telephone: (850) 488-1225
Fax: (850) 488-1428

For complaints or concerns regarding court appointed public or professional guardians, please follow-up directly with the Office of Public and Professional Guardians at:

Office of Public & Professional Guardians
Florida Department of Elder Affairs
Toll-free Complaint Line: (855) 305-3030
Website: http://elderaffairs.state.fl.us/doea/spgo.php

With respect to your request for a legal opinion regarding the applicability of state statute to the conduct of any individual or agency, Section 16.01(3), Florida Statutes does not authorize the Attorney General to render opinions to private individuals or entities. An Attorney General Opinion cannot and will not be issued in this matter.

If you require legal guidance or assistance, please consult with an attorney. If you need help finding an attorney, The Florida Bar offers a Lawyer Referral Service toll-free at (800) 342-8011 or online at https://lrs.floridabar.org/.

Thank you for contacting the Florida Office of the Attorney General regarding your concerns. I hope the provided information and resources prove helpful.

Sincerely,
Angelique Witmer
Office of the Attorney General
State of Florida

Evidently, in Florida, when there is a disagreement between the State Attorney and a citizen in the application of a statute, the only way to resolve it is by filing a lawsuit. I never thought it would come to this and I never wanted to or considered suing the State of Florida, but if there is no other way to change this horrible process, I may have to consider it.

It is now December 2020, eight months after my original letter to Governor DeSantis and five and a half months after my follow-up letter to him. I still have not received a reply. I find this totally unacceptable and disgraceful that Governor DeSantis (and his staff) can totally ignore and disregard any letter of complaint from any citizen of Florida. Perhaps a lawsuit is necessary and, unless I see something more positive from the State, I will be consulting with an attorney.

As a final attempt to see if I can get any assistance or comment from the State of Florida, on December 21, 2020, I delivered the following letter to The Villages office of State Representative Brett Hage:

> December 21, 2020
> Representative Brett T. Hage
> 916 Avenida Central
> The Villages, Florida 32159-5704
> Dear Representative Hage:
> Since you represent The Villages and are a member of both the Children, Families and Seniors Committee and the Criminal Justice and Public Safety Committee, I am advising you what I and others consider an unbelievable injustice which is devasting to us and potentially all seniors in the Villages and Sumter County.
> I am enclosing copies of certified letters that I sent to Governor Ron DeSantis and Attorney General Ashley Moody. AG Moody did respond to my letter, Governor DeSantis did not. I sent a second certified letter to the Governor and still have not received a response.
> When you read the letters and attachments, you should have a fair understanding of the problems that our family encountered and the nightmare our family has been through in a system that is horribly broken. I have over 400 pages of documentation outlining every aspect of this case, should you need any additional information.
> Once you review the case, I would appreciate a response outlining your recommendations, so other victims and families will not have to

suffer through any similar experience.
Thank you.

The signed letter also included all the enclosures that I had previous sent to the Governor and the Attorney General.

"Hope springs eternal." We will see!

It is now February 22, 2021, which is two months since Representative Hage received my letter and I have not yet had a response from him. Evidently, Florida state officials do not feel they have an obligation to respond to their constituents. To follow up, I sent the following second letter to his office in the Villages:

February 22, 2021
Representative Brett T. Hage
916 Avenida Central
The Villages, Florida 32159-5704

Dear Representative Hage:
Two months ago, I hand delivered the attached letter to your office. To date, I have not received a reply from you.

This letter is to respectfully request when I can expect the courtesy of a reply. If no reply is coming, I would appreciate knowing that as well.
Thank you.
Carl R. Baker

On February 26th, I received the following email from

Representative Hage's office:

Good morning Mr. Baker,
Please see the attached to include what our office has on file for you. The letters and attachments were not present. Please call our office so we can help you and find out what you are needing assistance with. We will look forward to hearing from you. Thank you.
Sincerely,
Nancy K. Bowers

I immediately called Nancy and she requested that I send her some documents regarding outlining my concerns with Paul's case. I emailed twelve documents to her including my letter to the Governor, the Attorney General, Secretary Poppell and the State Attorney (prosecutor). I also sent her the timeline for the entire saga.

In a subsequent telephone conversation, Nancy told me that Representative Hage was working with Judge Morley on a bill that would establish a Eldercaring Coordinator statute. I did tell Nancy that I was not an advocate of the program and it was a huge mistake in Paul's case. However, I agreed to review the bill and forward my comments to her.

On March 7th, I sent the following email to Representative Hage's office with an attached summary of Amanda's, Cher's and Sandy's October 25, 2019 covert visit to Paul:

Nancy
Thank you again for the update. I have reviewed HB 441 in detail

and offer the following comments:

I do believe that sometimes there is a need for mediation for families to resolve their differences during a very difficult time. A brochure explaining the program would be beneficial in helping the parties make that decision.

However, eldercaring should not be used when there is evidence of criminal conduct by one of the parties nor should the court be allowed to appoint an eldercaring coordinator without the agreement of the parties to the action.

Lines 161 - 167 revised:
  (a) Upon agreement of the parties to the action, the court may appoint an eldercaring coordinator and refer the parties to eldercaring coordination to assist in the resolution of disputes concerning the care and safety of the elder who is the subject of an action.
  (b) The court shall not refer a party who has a history of domestic violence or exploitation of an elderly person...

In my brother's case, a motion was made in court and I had no idea what was happening. In a ten-minute conversation in the hall outside the courtroom, my attorney told me this was the judge's "pet project" and it was a mediation process outside the courtroom, to resolve conflict and save attorney fees. Hearing that this program would also eliminate the need for my brother to testify and see Sandy in the courtroom, I agreed to the eldercaring coordinator and had high hopes for a resolution. In retrospect, eldercaring coordination was a huge mistake.

In the Bill, lines 176 -188, the court shall consider whether a party has committed exploitation or domestic abuse. This is absolutely necessary. In Paul's case, the elephant in the room, Sandy's abuse and exploitation, was known by the judge, Paul's attorney, the eldercaring coordinator and the guardian. Yet during the entire process, Sandy's criminal acts were totally ignored. Then the guardian and eldercaring coordinator covertly arranged a meeting with Paul and his abusive wife without notifying Paul or any member of his family in violation of their own standards. Furthermore, this was orchestrated prior to a scheduled hearing to determine these same visitation issues. The judge had laid out specific items to be considered and addressed in that hearing and told both the eldercaring coordinator and the guardian to consult with us on these items. They never spoke to us about them and we did not see the request from the judge until after the covert visit and hearing. So, I would caution that just because mediation/eldercaring is provided under this legislation, that does not mean that it will be competently and legally carried out unless there is also accountability imposed for irresponsible behavior. To date, there has been none.

The attachment to this email and the original letter that I delivered to your office fully explains the frustrations the Baker family has experienced with how the Florida State government has handled this case. Despite all my efforts, I still have many concerns regarding Florida's lack of response to elder abuse and exploitation. However, I do appreciate your following up on my letter to Representative Hage and will be available for further discussion.

Warm regards,
Carl

Florida House Bill 441 was amended, passed and will take effect July 1, 2021. As a follow-up, I sent the following email to Representative Brett Hage's office:

Nancy

I just wanted to thank you and Representative Hage for the recent success in the legislative session. Although my experience with Eldercaring Coordination was not good, there is language in HB 441 that will hopefully improve it for future probate court cases.

To be specific, Section 1 (1) (a) which states " that the elder is still entitled to the dignity of having his voice heard" is absolutely necessary. Unfortunately, my brother was denied that opportunity several times.

Lines 201-220 begin by stating, "The court shall consider whether a party has committed an act of exploitation of an elderly or disabled adult or domestic violence..." Again, this was ignored by the court throughout my brother's case.

In summary, despite all the letters with documentation that I have sent to state agencies and government officials, from the Governor on down, your office is the only one that made any effort to improve what I believe is a horribly "broken system" that must be corrected.

Thank you!
Carl R. Baker

As this case study comes to its completion, the story continues. Now that you know the truth, I have some questions for the reader:

Do you think, John Paul Baker, a highly decorated veteran with thirty-two years of military service was treated honestly, properly and with dignity throughout this ordeal?

Since you have now reviewed all the major events of this story, and have read the responses, or the lack thereof, from our Florida government officials, what do you think?

- Do you believe that all the actions of the government employees and the court personnel were legal, ethical and in Paul's best interest?
- Why did Paul's guardian and Eldercaring Coordinator spend more time with Sandy than they spent with Paul?
- Why wasn't Paul's personal property returned to him in accordance with his trust and Antenuptial Agreement? Why did the court (guardian) let Sandy take it? Was it because he has Alzheimer's and wouldn't know the difference?
- After reviewing the guardian statutes, do you see any justifiable reason for the court not appointing a Baker family member as guardian?
- Can you now understand why so many people think the entire probate process is broken?
- And finally, would you want you and your loved one to have an experience anything close to what the Baker family experienced?

In this case, there is only one last step that must be taken:

"The Office of the Chief Inspector General was created in Section 14.32, Florida Statutes, effective October 1, 1994. This office has the responsibility for promoting accountability, integrity, and efficiency in state government. The Chief Inspector General has responsibility for monitoring the activities of the Offices of Inspectors General in the state agencies that are under the jurisdiction of the Governor. The Chief Inspector General also serves in accordance with 20.055, Florida Statutes, as the agency Inspector General for the Office of the Governor. The Chief Inspector General reports directly to the Governor both administratively and functionally.

Within the Office of Chief Inspector General, there are two distinct functions: audits and investigations.

The audit function is an independent, objective assurance and consulting activity designed to add value and improve the Office of the Governor's operations or operations funded by the Office of the Governor. In carrying out the audit responsibilities, the Chief Inspector General reviews and evaluates internal controls to ensure fiscal accountability of the agency. Audits are conducted in accordance with professional auditing standards.

In carrying out the investigative duties, the Chief Inspector General initiates, conducts, supervises, and coordinates investigations designed to detect, deter, prevent, and eradicate fraud, waste, mismanagement, misconduct, and other abuses in government."

Once completed, I will be sending a copy of this case study to the Office of the Chief Inspector General which will serve as an official complaint as to how the State of Florida treated Paul.

Looking at the entire history of this case, I may not receive a response, but I will request one. In any case, they will be unable to claim they were never notified.

Carl R. Baker
1816 Wading Heron Way
The Villages, Florida 32163-2150
August 12, 2021

Chief Inspector General Melinda M. Miguel
Executive Office of the Governor
The Capitol, Suite 1902
Tallahassee, FL 32399-0001
RE: A CASE STUDY OF ELDER ABUSE AND EXPLOITATION IN FLORIDA (Formal Complaint)

Dear Inspector General Miguel:

My brother, J. Paul Baker, retired from the US Army as a Brigadier General after 32 years of service. He was exposed to Agent Orange while serving in Viet Nam and has had numerous medical problems later in life. He now has a pacemaker, he was diagnosed with Alzheimer's dementia in 2015, breast cancer in 2020, and today, he is in a hospice memory care facility and not expected to live much longer.

After what Paul and our family experienced over the last several years, we have an overwhelming concern for seniors in Florida, especially the most vulnerable ones. Also, very disturbing is the tens of thousands of dollars that have been unnecessarily expended to try and protect my brother from an abusive/exploitative wife while the systems in Florida have done nothing but further victimize him. I would not have thought what our family witnessed over the last four years was even possible if I had not experienced it myself. This has indeed been an eye-opening experience and a nightmare for Paul and those who love him.

Every aspect of this case has been carefully and fully documented in the enclosed study. Quite candidly, I could not believe that I found so many failures in a system that should be protecting senior citizens, especially in Florida with such a large and growing senior population. The State has a population approaching 20 million with 23% being age 60 or over. That makes the senior population at about 4.6 million and projected to double by 2030.

The study will outline the problems, misdeeds and violations of statutes and standards of the Department of Law Enforcement (FDLE), the Department of Children and Families, the State Attorney's Office, the Sumter County Circuit Court, the Eldercare program and the court appointed guardian. However, on the other hand, some of the Florida State employees that I encountered were true professionals who provided great customer service and I commend them by name in the study.

I support Governor DeSantis and like what he is doing. However, I have a concern that he is not getting the support he needs from his staff. As you will see in the study, I sent two letters to the Governor which went unanswered.

Based on my 40 years of working in both state and local government, I know Florida needs to make some substantial improvements in elder abuse enforcement. My hope is this case study serves as a catalyst to make those positive changes so another family will not have to experience the frustration and inequities that we endured.

I realize that this is a lot to read, but please review it thoroughly to get an accurate picture of what is occurring in Florida's probate cases. I look forward to your response.

Respectfully,

Carl R. Baker

I received the following email response on August 14, 2021.

A Case Study Of Elder Abuse And Exploitation In Florida

STATE OF FLORIDA
Office of the Governor
THE CAPITOL
TALLAHASSEE, FLORIDA 32399-0001

www.flgov.com
850-717-9418

RON DESANTIS
GOVERNOR

August 13, 2021

Mr. Carl Baker
crbaker501@centurylink.net

RE: Chief Inspector General Correspondence # 2020-05-29-0015

Dear Mr. Baker:

    The Office of the Chief Inspector General received your correspondence on August 13, 2021, in which you expressed concerns about the court appointed guardian, the State Attorney's Office, the Sumter County Circuit Court, the Department of Children and Families, the Florida Department of Law Enforcement, and the Eldercare program.

    Please be advised that this office does not have jurisdiction over professional guardians; however, you may wish to contact the Circuit Judge who appointed the professional guardian. Information regarding the Judges in the Fifth Judicial Circuit at https://www.circuit5.org/courts-judges/. You may also wish to contact the Office of Public & Professional Guardians. You may find their information online at https://elderaffairs.org/programs-services/office-of-public-professional-guardians-oppg/.

    Please understand that State Attorneys operate independently of the Governor's office. As elected officials, State Attorneys answer to the voters of their individual jurisdictions. Those who believe elected officials have used their office for private gain should contact the Florida Commission on Ethics by calling (850) 488-7864, or by writing to the following address:

Florida Commission on Ethics
Post Office Drawer 15709
Tallahassee, FL 32317-5709

    Additionally, please be advised that this office does not have jurisdiction over court matters. You may wish to speak to an attorney who can advise you of any civil remedies that may be available to you. The Florida Bar offers a Lawyer Referral Service which you may contact by calling toll-free at (800) 342-8011 or by submitting a request online at https://lrs.floridabar.org/. Additionally, Florida Legal Services, Inc. provides pro-bono legal services to those who qualify. You may contact Florida Legal Services, Inc. by calling (407) 801-4350, by faxing (407) 505-7327, or by writing to the following address:

Florida Legal Services
P.O. Box 533986
Orlando, FL 32853

    After having had the opportunity to review your correspondence, by copy of this letter, we are referring your complaint to the Inspector Generals for the Department of Children and Families, the Florida Department of law Enforcement and the Department of Elderly Affairs for review and action deemed appropriate.

Interesting response. I am not sure how the IG will respond to the allegations that I have documented. Time will tell and their response will guide my next action.

On August 23, 2021, I received the following email from Taroub J. Faraj, Inspector General, the Department of Elder Affairs:

Dear Mr. Baker:

The Department of Elder Affairs (DOEA), Office of Inspector General (OIG) is in receipt of your correspondence with the Office of the Chief Inspector General on August 13, 2021, regarding the guardianship of your brother, Paul Baker.

The DOEA OIG does not have purview over matters of public/professional guardians, those of the Office of Public and Professional Guardians (OPPG) housed within DOEA, or their determinations on whether complaints have legal sufficiency to proceed with an investigation.

Your correspondence has been forwarded by the OIG to OPPG for their review. If you have any further questions regarding your brother's guardianship, please refer them to OPPG by either calling (850) 414-2381 or via email at OPPGcomplaints@elderaffairs.org

I hope that I am not getting "the run around" on this. I filed the entire complaint with the Chief Inspector General since an earlier response I received from the Department of Elder Affairs did not answer my concerns and was not acceptable.

On August 31, 2021, there was an article in *The Villages Daily Sun* stating that Governor and Mrs. DeSantis would be having a meeting in The Villages to answer questions from the public.

Also, there was a form available on-line to submit a question. I submitted the following question:

> "Governor and Mrs. DeSantis:
> We have the upmost respect for the job you are doing and fully support you. I have personally sent you two letters on an elder abuse case that unfortunately went unanswered. Most recently, I sent a 400+ page report to your Chief Inspector General. I am awaiting a reply. If you are not familiar with this case, please review it. You will be shocked and terribly disappointed how the State of Florida treated my brother, a 32-year Army veteran, throughout this ordeal. I would very much like to get this resolved so no other families have to experience such a lack of concern. I would very much appreciate you getting in touch with me.
> Respectively,
> Carl R. Baker
>
> *(Note: I included my email address to facilitate their response.)*

Again, I do not have a response, but to be fair, it has only been a little over a week. However, it certainly would be difficult for the Governor to say he did not receive it.

It is now the end of September, 2021, so it is probably safe to say that my correspondence to Governor DeSantis was ignored again. That makes it three times the Governor has not responded to my correspondence.

However, I did receive the following letter from the Department of Elder Affairs dated September 7, 2021:

Carl R. Baker

Ron DeSantis
Governor

Richard Prudom
Secretary

September 7, 2021

Carl Baker
1816 Wading Heron Way
The Villages, FL 32163

Re: OPPG Complaint 2021-139

Dear Carl Baker:

The Office of Public and Professional Guardians (OPPG), within the Department of Elder Affairs, has the statutory duty to have oversight of professional guardians and investigate legally sufficient complaints about professional guardians pursuant to Section 744.2001, Florida Statutes.

The OPPG has reviewed your complaint and finds that the allegations within your complaint are legally insufficient, in that they fail to state ultimate facts that would lead to a conclusion that the guardian violated the Florida Guardianship Law or OPPG Standards of Practice for Professional Guardians. Therefore, the OPPG is unable to pursue any investigation or disciplinary action against the guardian and has closed your complaint.

Please contact the OPPG via phone at (855) 305-3030 or via email at OPPGcomplaints@elderaffairs.org if you have any questions.

Sincerely,

Chante' Jones

Chante' Jones, Esq.
Executive Director
Office of Public and Professional Guardians

4040 Esplanade Way, Tallahassee, FL 32399-7000
Phone: (850) 414-2381 | TDD: (850) 414-2001
visit us at: elderaffairs.org

This is the exact same form letter that I received from Executive Director Jones on June 15, 2020. At that time, I sent another letter to Director Jones asking for an explanation of "legally insufficient." Her response stated, " Per Section 744.2004, Florida Statutes, "A complaint is legally sufficient if it contains ultimate facts that show a violation of a standard of practice by a professional guardian has occurred."

If you review the earlier correspondence that I sent to the Governor, I listed and documented several violations that Paul's guardian, Amanda Ritter, committed, yet they were ignored again. I concluded that the Department of Elder Affairs has no credibility whatsoever and for the Chief Inspector General to allow this response on elder abuse should be unacceptable by anyone's standards. It was clearly a "whitewash." I was hoping that if Governor DeSantis truly understood what was taking place in his administration, he would be shocked and certainly correct it. I was wrong. It appears to me that the Governor has no idea how his staff handles elder abuse and exploitation cases in Florida and it is obvious, he doesn't really care.

On September 30, Team DeSantis emailed me a political survey and left a space for comments. I thought that if I responded, perhaps someone just might send my comments to Governor DeSantis. So, I sent the following reply:

My wife and I fully supported and donated money to help elect him as Governor. However, I have sent two certified letters and an email to Governor DeSantis regarding the abuse and exploitation of my brother, a retired Army Colonel with 32 years of service who now is in hospice and most likely in his final days. I have never received a response from Governor DeSantis. In August, I sent a 400+ page report to the Chief Inspector General with documentation of the failures of the State of Florida regarding my brother's case and how he was mistreated. To date, I have not received an answer from the IG in response to my concerns.

All this does not reflect favorably on Governor DeSantis and I certainly do not want this to harm his career. My goal in all of this is to repair a broken system in hope that other seniors in Florida will not have to experience what our family went through. I cannot be sure that the Governor's staff ever actually gave my correspondence to him to read.

I am sending this email as another attempt to make sure Governor DeSantis knows what is going on in his administration. Anything you can do to help me would be appreciated.

Thank you,
Carl R. Baker

As of October 12, 2021, I have still not heard a word from Governor DeSantis. Today also marks two months from the time I submitted my letter and 400+ page report to the Chief Inspector General. Since the matter appears to be still pending, I sent the following letter:

Dear Inspector General Miguel:
Two months ago, I sent you the above complaint. To date, I have received the following correspondence from the State of Florida regarding this complaint:

On August 13th, I received an email acknowledgement that your office had received the complaint and case study that I mailed to you.

On August 23rd, I received an email from Taroub J. Faraj, the Inspector General of the Department of Elder Affairs stating that the Office of Public and Professional Guardians(OPPG) was reviewing my complaint.

On September 7th, Chante' Jones, the Executive Director of the Office of Public and Professional Guardians, sent me a form letter regarding my complaint stating that my complaint was "legally insufficient." This is the exact same letter that I received from Executive Director Jones on June 15, 2020. At that time, I sent a reply letter to Director Jones asking for an explanation of "legally insufficient." Her response stated, " Per Section 744.2004, Florida Statutes, "A complaint is legally sufficient if it contains ultimate facts that show a violation of a standard of practice by a professional guardian has occurred."

What I do not understand is how any discerning person who reads the documentation of the lies and the violations of standards of practice outlined in this case study, could possibly draw the conclusion that this complaint was not "legally sufficient."

I have two questions for you:1. Will I receive a comprehensive reply from your office regarding all my concerns outlined in the original August 12th complaint?

2. Do you and Governor DeSantis agree with the conclusions of Director Jones regarding the conduct of the guardian?

Respectfully,
Carl R. Baker

In early December, I received a survey from the Republican Party of Florida which included a form letter from Governor Ron DeSantis. I filled in the survey and since there was a space for comments, I wrote the following:

"I have supported Gov DeSantis, but I have problem with his Administration. I have sent two letters and an email to him and did not receive a reply. I filed a complaint with the Inspector General and followed it up with two letters and have not received a reply. I would like to speak to the Governor about Florida's unfair treatment of my brother, an Army veteran who served for 32 years and retired as a Colonel. Five minutes of his time is all I am requesting. Thank you. "
Carl R. Baker (Cell Phone number included.)

Quite candidly, I would be shocked if he called me, but thought I would make one last attempt.

It is now December 15th and over two months have passed since I sent the second letter to Inspector General Miguel. I have yet to receive a reply. This is unacceptable. Two letters, an email and a note to Governor DeSantis and two letters to the Inspector General have gone unanswered. The only conclusion that can be drawn is obvious. Governor DeSantis is not interested nor does he care that his Administration ignores citizen complaints involving cases of elder abuse and exploitation. To claim he knew nothing about this complaint is likewise unacceptable since the primary concern of government is to protect and serve its citizens. This serves as the truth that the system is broken and the DeSantis Administration really does not care about elder abuse and actually permits further abuse of the victims by the State of Florida.

Words cannot express the disappointment that our family has experienced during this entire case. Paul is now oblivious to all that is taking place and is most likely in his final days. May our Lord bring him home gently.

"I will tell you what justice is. Justice is the law. And the law is man's feeble attempt to set down the principles of decency. And decency is not a deal. It isn't an angle or a contract or a hustle. Decency is what your grandmother taught you.
It's in your bones."
—*"The Bonfire of the Vanities"*

CHAPTER 15

Postscript

On February 14, 2020, I took Paul to see his dermatologist for a checkup. I made the appointment because he had a growth on his chest which was bleeding from his nipple. This is not the first time he had this problem. In June of 2019, he had a biopsy for a growth at the same spot, and it came back negative for cancer.

This time, Paul's biopsy came back positive for breast cancer.

Results:
CUTANEOUS ADENOCARCINOMA, ULCERATED
Comment: If the tumor is a primary, it has mixed features of porocarcinoma and syringold carcinoma. Immunostaining is pending. Distinction from a cutaneous metastatic breast carcinoma would be difficult, as they would have virtually the same routine histopathology. Clinical pathologic correlation required, and perhaps consultation with oncology.

Paul spent a year in Vietnam in 1970–71. Since he was an artillery forward observer, he spent most of his time on the battlefield and he did have exposure to Agent Orange. This type of cancer is rare, but I have spoken to several male veterans that have experienced Agent Orange exposure and were later diagnosed with breast cancer.

On February 18, 2020, Paul was referred to the Florida Cancer Research Institute for additional testing. On February 20th, he had a full body PET scan, which confirmed that he had breast cancer. Fortunately, the cancer had spread to only several lymph nodes. The operation on April 2nd, was a success and at the follow-up visit in June with his oncologist, it was determined that Paul would not need chemotherapy or radiation.

Several months later in July, Paul tested positive for COVID-19. The poor guy cannot seem to catch a break. With all the precautions and isolation, we had not spent any real time with Paul in months. We call him daily, but Paul is starting to have a difficult time with the phone and forgets to hang it up. I did take him to his doctor appointments occasionally, but now, all his appointments have been cancelled due to COVID-19. However, in November Paul broke a tooth at the gum line, and I did take him to a doctor for oral surgery. Eventually, we were able to visit Paul with an appointment, but in December 2020, Trinity Springs had another COVID -19 case and we were no longer able to visit him for several weeks.

After 32 years of military service, it breaks our hearts to see the abuse Paul has had to endure. As family, we all pray that somehow, someway, we can make the remainder of his life here on earth, somewhat better.

Sadly, in January and February of 2021, Paul's mental state and health began declining rapidly. He went from walking to shuffling and then to a wheelchair. He was sent to the hospital twice for an infection and swelling in his lower body. He was in the hospital for 5 days, and on February 11, Paul was placed in hospice at Trinity Springs. He can no longer walk or feed himself. We pray that our Lord gently brings him home.

Trinity Springs required 24-hour care for Paul at the cost of $18,000 per month. Heretofore, the staff at TS would advise me if Paul needed anything and I would purchase it and bring it to Paul the next day. Paul's court appointed guardian, for whatever reason, resurfaced and began purchasing supplies for Paul. When she purchased twin sheets for his hospital bed, a staff member at Trinity told me that she told Amanda she did not need to buy sheets since they were furnished by hospice. Amanda replied, "That's OK. Paul has a lot of money." And again, I must question the court's decision to not appoint a family member as Paul's guardian.

In July of 2021, another COVID case at Trinity Springs again prevented visits with Paul for several weeks. Ever since then, there have been additional COVID cases which have limited our visits with Paul. I do try and call him every day, but it gets increasingly more difficult to talk to him with his declining mental state.

On November 16, 2021, Allyne received the following early morning text message from Amanda Ritter, Paul's court appointed guardian and sent it to all of us:

"Good morning. I just got a call from the hospice nurse. He is under the impression that your dad is beginning the actively dying process. I am so sorry that I'm telling you this in a text but I want you to have the information and I know that you're both probably working as Allyne you did not answer your phone. He is doing chain stroke respirations and his breathing is stopping for about 2 to 5 seconds every once in a while. The nurse said of course he is not God but in his experience he only gives him at the very most a very few days. Are you both OK if I call the companion company to have them put 24 hour care back in so that we have eyes on him and that he is not alone. I'm sure you are I just wanted to OK this prior to making the call. I'm also going to forward you the hospice nurse that I just spoke to Tony. His hours are only 8 AM to 5 PM we will be notified by the facility or after hours if anything happens during those times. He said you're more than welcome to call him and get this information straight from him I gave him the authority to give either of you any information you needed. He said that your dad is not in any distress."

I was surprised since I had just visited Paul the day before, and I saw no change. I immediately sent an email to family:

To: Bruce, Lynn, Carol, Allyne:
"Just so you know, I visited Paul yesterday at noon. The only change that I saw was I thought he had a fever which I reported to the nurse. Otherwise, I saw no change, but at this point things can change rapidly. He was eating and talked and laughed some. Katherine and I will visit him again tomorrow."
Carl

The next morning, Allyne sent everyone an update on her Dad:

"I just spoke with Tony (hospice nurse) again. He called when he was with dad. He said his breathing is normal today. He will visit again tomorrow to check him and if his breathing is normal, he will take him off 'the transition' list and go back to weekly visits instead of daily. He apologized for the alarm, but explained he placed Dad in that status due to his observations and his training."

On November 28, 2021, Allyne received the following text from Amanda, Paul's guardian:

"I hope you both had a good Thanksgiving. Just got a call from the emergency on call hospice nurse. Your dad had a vomiting episode today. There was concern he may of had a stroke but she said besides very slight drooping on one side of his face there are no other signs. She said it's very similar to the episode he had a few months ago.

She's putting him on an all liquid diet for 24 hours and some anti-nausea meds. She said it's hard to tell if it was something he ate, he may have a virus, or it may be the start of transitioning. I told her we did not want to jump to any conclusions as we had an episode about a week ago where there was a false report. So my opinion is we just stay in close contact this week and see how he recovers. Have a great night."

Allyne commented:

"I never know what to think. It's so hard when she has proven to not be trusted, yet we are stuck with her.

She and I bumped heads again a few weeks ago over banking matters. I wasn't happy with her lack of attention to what we think was fraud on his account. The bank wouldn't talk to me even though I write the checks and Mark and I are trustees. So when I told her that it was unacceptable what she hadn't done yet, she threatened to quit and told me in a very aggressive tone, and with a bit of gloating ... 'if I thought I could do a better job then go ahead and try, but there's a BIG road block in your way by the name of Sandy!!!'

She was mad that I asked for a BANKING POA. I told her it was time! There were things that needed to be handled like this and I thought it was wasteful to be forcing my father to pay her when it was an issue that Mark and I were perfectly capable of handling. She refuses to give that to us.

I just hate this situation. It's entirely mentally exhausting!"

Personally, I do not understand why Amanda continues to communicate with Sandy. However, you look at it, Sandy deserted

A Case Study Of Elder Abuse And Exploitation In Florida

Paul and moved to Louisiana when she realized that she was not getting any of Paul's trust funds. And on the way out the door, she took thousands of dollars of Paul's property.

I also had two reports that Paul was unable to hold down his food and he was put on a liquid diet. We realize that this in not uncommon for Alzheimer patients. Paul's overall health continues to decline, but somehow, he recovered and for now is back on solid food.

Just to give you an idea of the costs, should you ever be forced into a guardianship case in probate court, I have listed the approximate costs to the Baker family through December 31, 2021. Note that the below list includes memory care, but does not include Paul's medical or personal costs:

Trinity Springs ($4900/mo.)	$ 132,300
24 Hour Nursing Care ($18,000+/mo.)[1]	199,000
Attorney Fees	58,177
Court Ordered Medical Evaluations	1,285
Court Appointed Guardian[2]	5,704
Eldercaring Coordinator	5,094
Miscellaneous	2,985
TOTAL	**$ 404,545**

1 After several months, the 24-hour nursing care was cut to 12 and then 8 hours a day which lowered the cost.

2 I took Paul to all his doctor appointments which saved guardian costs. I expect another guardian invoice shortly.

In addition to the above costs, Sandy took property from Paul in violation of the Antenuptial Agreement, to include his personal items, furniture and wall decorations and sold many other items, including the golf cart. Sandy kept all the proceeds from the sale, which, in my opinion after reviewing the statutes, is grand larceny. Again, the State of Florida did nothing.

And finally, I have always believed that you need to fight for what is right and you may have to fight to be heard. Even if the other side does not share your beliefs or really care what you think, there is a much larger issue here. You fight in the hope that this will not happen to someone else and the abuse will stop and the cycle will end. For me, to do nothing and remain silent is unacceptable. Silence in the face of injustice only enables it to repeat itself causing additional pain and suffering to others.

The probate court system, the State Attorney's Office and relevant state agencies in Florida, need a complete review. They are horribly broken, in disarray, and unfortunately, ready to claim their next victim. What is shocking to me is how little the Florida government officials, at all levels, including the Governor's Office, really care.

I am not sure what the problem is with the system. Are they overworked or understaffed? Do they not care? Are they incompetent or lazy? Do they not know how to do their jobs? Are they biased? Are they corrupt? Are they operating without administrative oversight? Or is it a combination of all the above?

Despite all our efforts and the numerous pages documenting Sandy's abuse and exploitation of Paul, the Court, somehow in its mind, justified placing Paul's guardianship in the hands of a stranger rather than a loving, caring family. After reading this case, I think you will agree that to overtly state that doing this "was in Paul's best interest" was absolutely not true.

In all likelihood, I can probably predict what lies ahead. Sandy will continue the lies and will continue to play the victim.

"The law of the Lord is perfect" (Psalm 19:7); the law of man is not. When you have seen justice abused and misrepresented and despite your efforts, and your government does not seem to care, where do you go?
You go to the Lord who is the only true court of appeal. And all of Paul's family and friends are continuing to pray for justice.

> "We are never defeated unless we give up on God."
> *— Ronald Reagan*

APPENDIX A

Complete Timeline
2014 - 2021

February 8, 2014
Sandy involved in a personal injury autoaccident with husband Ralph.

August 18, 2014
John Paul Baker trust created.

August 2014
Paul started dating Sandy while her husband Ralph was still alive. Takes Paul to her timeshare in Naples for 3 days.

September 2014
Paul and Sandy continue to date, and Paul hid the fact that he frequently stayed overnight with Sandy.

October 10, 2014
Sandy's husband, Ralph died. Paul attended Ralph's memorial

services with Sandy and "helped her spread Ralph's ashes." Ralph's family was not happy.

May 2015
Allyne (Paul's daughter) was not happy that Paul was going to sell his home and buy a home together with Sandy. The first time Sandy met Allyne (May 2015), Sandy stated that Paul needed to be in a facility sometime soon and suggested that Allyne fly down in the fall and plan something with Bruce, Carl and her to get Paul to agree to go into a facility. {Note – This would be after Paul and Sandy bought the house together, but before they were married.}

Oct 2015
Paul and Sandy completed the sale of both their homes and bought one home together on November 6th.

Nov 2015
Paul was clinically diagnosed with Alzheimer's Dementia. Paul had been showing signs of dementia for at least four years.

Dec 2015
Paul and Sandy moved into their newly purchased home at 3723 Mango Court, each paying half.

Dec 2015
Bruce (our brother) suggested that they open a joint checking account for shared expenses and each deposit the same amount of money in each month. They both said it was a good idea, but it was never done. After questioning Paul on this several times, he finally admitted that Sandy did not want to do it. Consequently, there was never any documentation, and obviously no proof that

Sandy ever paid her fair share of these expenses. In Paul's confused state, especially pertaining to numbers and money, it was evident that he was paying significantly more than half of the shared costs.

June 15, 2016
Paul updated his trust to reflect the new home and his marriage to Sandy. Sandy updated her trust also. They both named their children as beneficiaries as had previously been the case. They also signed antenuptial agreement on June 17th.

June 28, 2016
Paul and Sandy were married. No one from the Baker family was invited.

July 11, 2016
Paul asked Carl how he could leave his military pension to Sandy. Carl told him he could not change the retirement option he originally chose and, therefore, could not do it.

February 11, 2017
Sandy went out of town alone and left Paul without some of his medicine. Carl took Paul to Walgreen's and picked up his medicine.

February 17-21, 2017
Sandy went to Las Vegas alone without giving anyone her flight schedule or hotel reservations.

February 23, 2017
Carl went with Paul and Sandy to Paul's appointment with his Alzheimer's doctor. The doctor stated that Paul should not be left alone.

March 2017

Paul called Carl and stated that Sandy told him he needed to start taking his money from his IRA. Carl told him that he handles Paul's finances and Paul does not have an IRA. Evidently, Sandy did not believe Carl, and had Paul call Bruce and ask him about the IRA. Bruce always did Paul's taxes and he also told Paul that he did not have an IRA. About 10 days later, Paul called Carl again and with Sandy standing right next to him, said "Sandy says I have an IRA." Carl replied, "Sandy is wrong. You do not have an IRA." Sandy immediately shouted, "I want to know where your f---king money is." The phone then went dead. Obviously, they were having an argument.

{Note: This is interesting for several reasons. Sandy has a long-term friend who lost his wife and frequently visits Sandy and Paul. Paul told me he is a CPA and he has offered to do their taxes. I believe that Sandy is getting direction from him, to what extent, I do not know. When talking to Ralph's daughter, Christine, she brought him up stating she believes this man is Sandy's next target.}

April 24 ,2017

While working over at Paul's house, Paul told me that Sandy has had a difficult life and that he wants to do something for her. I told him he should buy her a nice gift. He told me wanted to give her one of his pensions. Again, I told him that was not possible. I suggested that he put her on his Tri-Care (military health insurance). He later did get her health insurance.

June 2017

According to Paul's financial adviser in Albany, New York, Paul called him and told him he wanted to change the beneficiary on his $100,000 life insurance policy from his daughter, Allyne, to his wife, Sandra. The adviser reminded Paul that he started this policy years ago because Allyne was a single mother and he (Paul) wanted to make sure that Allyne would be financially set and wanted to make sure he left something extra for Allyne. The adviser could hear a woman in the background telling Paul what to say. Paul again stated that he wanted the policy changed. The financial adviser told Paul that since he had Alzheimer's, Paul should talk this over with his family. The woman (Sandy) told Paul to just tell him to mail them the change of beneficiary forms, which Paul did. The adviser later told me he knew exactly what was going on. Sandy wanted the change and Paul was not sure, so the agent never sent the change of beneficiary forms. The agent made the right choice.

Note: It is unfortunate the lawyer who later changed Paul's trust twice, after Sandy isolated him from his family, was not as perceptive as his financial adviser.

June 30, 2017
Paul and Sandy were scheduled to come to Carl's and Katherine's house for dinner. They did not show. When we called to see where they were, Sandy said she forgot and they currently had company at their home.

{Note: Typical of Sandy. Another example of her showing that she is in control.}

October 20, 2017
Family meeting to discuss Paul's condition. Sandy promised she would not schedule any more travel for Paul per the doctor's orders. {However, she continued to ignore the doctor's orders.} She also promised to buy an erasable white board to write down where she goes, since Paul is left alone so often and forgets where she went

and when she will be home. {It was months before she actually followed through with this.} We all offered to assist Sandy by taking Paul so she could have more time for herself.

November 6, 2017
Paul and Sandy travel to Israel returning home on November 5th.

November 26, 2017
Sandy wants to buy a larger home supposedly to use up Paul's trust assets (over $250,000 in cash) so his assets will not be taken to pay for his medical care. I told Paul that his monthly pension amount would more than cover the cost and his current home was over 2000 square feet for 2 people and he did not need a larger home. He agreed, which upset Sandy.

December 18, 2017
Paul wanted to send both his children $10,000 as a gift. He had told me several times before that he wanted to do this while he was still alive. Sandy stopped him. {Note: He did finally send the gifts to his children in July 2018 and Sandy went ballistic. Within a month, she tried to change Paul's trust.}

April 12, 2018
Paul and Sandy had another fight. Paul left the house and went out for lunch. He got lost trying to find his way home. He called Carl and Katherine and they found him in Clermont and brought him home. Sandy went off on Carl and Katherine and made herself the victim again.

May 1, 2018
Sandy and Paul took their 2016 Buick Enclave to the dealership for

service. Sandy talked Paul into leasing a new 2018 Buick Enclave for her to drive at a cost of $28,784. {Note: Paul did not drive since he got lost on April 12th.}

May 19, 2018
Paul and Sandy went to Hawaii for 18 days disregarding the doctor's orders that Paul needed routine and should not travel.

June 2018
Sandy started her search for a memory care facility for Paul. I told her I thought that she was premature and that we agreed that was a decision we would make collectively. As usual, Sandy took offense to my statement saying, "I'm his wife!" The trust includes both Paul's brothers in that decision.

July 7, 2018
Paul was scammed out of money by a landscaper and when I brought it to his attention, he asked me to completely take over his finances since he trusted me more than he trusted Sandy.

Aug 11, 2018
Family dinner at Carl and Katherine's home. MarkAndrea, Allyne, and Paul's grandchildren came to Florida to see Paul. Sandy immediately brought up the trust and stated she was going to the attorney to see what changes should be made. Both Mark and Allyne told her they saw no reason to change Paul's trust. Sandy disregarded their wishes and made anappointment with the trust attorney.

August 15, 2018
Meeting with Attorney Sham Shanawany (Millhorn & Shanawany) and Paul and Sandy Baker. Paul asked Carl to attend with him

and Sandy got extremely upset. In the end, there were no changes to Paul's trusts at this time.

August 22, 2018
Paul and Sandy had a fight and Paul left his house and started to walk to Carl's home. Sandy called and Carl picked up Paul and he had dinner with Carl and Katherine. After dinner, Carl drove Paul home. The next day, Sandy isolated Paul from Carl, Katherine, Bruce and Gail and there was no real conversation with Paul until January 2019.

September 6, 2018
Carl mailed Paul's checkbook and checks to him by registered mail because Sandy was using two different numbered check series and too many checks made out to "cash" to feel comfortable about responsibly handling Paul's finances.

September 20, 2018
Sandy changes Paul's trust making her successor trustee, power of attorney and reducing Allyne's distribution from 65% to 15%.

September 21, 2018
Paul and Sandy went to the BB&T Bank in The Villages. $220,000 was removed from Paul's checking account. {Note: We did not know until January of 2019 that Sandy had changed Paul's trust theday before on September 20, 2018 and a second time on December 3, 2018.}

October 8, 2018
Carl filed an elder abuse complaint with the Florida Department of Children and Families.

October 15, 2018
Carl filed a criminal complaint with the Florida Department of Law Enforcement (FDLE)against Sandy for abuse and exploitation of Paul.

November 9, 2018
Carl and Katherine run into Paul and Sandy Carrabba's restaurant. The next day we go to a show at the Ocala Civic Theater with Bruce and Gail and see Paul and Sandy again.

November 17, 2018
Paul attended the Villages' Honor Flight. Sandy did not want Bruce and Carl to attend. Carl did send a "Welcome Home letter.

December 3, 2018
Sandy has Paul's trust changed again. We have no idea why she made these changes.

December 13, 2018
Sandy had Paul turn in his license since she would not let him drive the new Buick Enclave.

January 7, 2019
Carl stopped by Paul's home and knocked on the door. To his surprise, this time Paul answered. Sandy was not at home. Paul broke down and cried and said he was sick of being alone. After a 30-minute conversation, Paul told Carl to leave because he was scared Sandy would be home shortly. He asked Carl to stay in contact with him.

January 9, 2019
Carl sent a confidential letter to Paul telling him that he filed a

criminal complaint against Sandy. {Note: Allyne was on the phone with her dad when Sandy opened the letter. Paul never saw it.}

January 14, 2019
Hoping that Sandy was again playing golf, Carl and Katherine drove to Paul's house and rang the doorbell. Paul came to the doo and within minutes stated he wanted to leave Sandy. They drove Paul back to their house. Sandy called the Sheriff and told them Carland Katherine had kidnapped Paul. The Deputy spoke to Paul and determined that he left of his own free will because he wanted to get away from Sandy. The complaint was closed as unfounded.

January 15, 2019
After three months, FDLE had done nothing on the criminal complaint and Carl asked thatthe case be closed. The case was given to the Sumter County Sheriff's Office for investigation on March 25th – Detective Jeff Cohen.

January 31, 2019
Sandy filed a petition with the court to determine incapacity asking that Paul be returned to live with her.

February 5, 2019
The court issued an order appointingMerideth C. Nagel, Esq. as attorney and Elisor for Paul. The court also issued an order naming the examining committee to determine incapacity.

February 27, 2019
Upon a recommendation from Paul'sattorney, Carl hired an attorney (Harry Hackney and filed petition with the courtto be Paul's guardian.

March 6, 2019
Sandy's attorneys filed a petition with the court to be released from representing Sandy.

March 18, 2019
Sandy initiates a welfare check on Paul through the SCSO. The Deputy checked Paul and saw no problem.

March 20, 2019
Presumably, Sandy filed an elder abuse complaint against Carl and Katherine. Investigation wasclosed as unfounded. Sandy continues herharassment.

March 28, 2019
Sandy filed a second petition with thecourt to determine incapacity and be named as Paul's guardian.

April 29, 2019
Court hearing on Sandy's petition for incapacity. After opening statements, Paul's attorney made a motion to defer thetestimony and use an EldercaringCoordinator to mediate the case.

May 15, 2019
Carl and Katherine completed a fiveweek Alzheimer's caregiver training course.

May 29, 2019
Paul and Carl had their initial meeting with Cher Myers, the Eldercaring Coordinator.

May 30, 2019
Letter of complaint from Sandy's attorney (Hunt Law Firm) for

filing criminal charges against Sandy and more.

June 17, 2019
Meeting with Detective Cohen the State Attorney's Office.

July 3, 2019
Cher (Pati) dropped some of Paul's clothes and Personal items at Carl's home (6 monthsafter Paul left Sandy.)

July 17, 2019
Appeal mailed to SA Brad King to reconsidercriminal charges against Sandy.

August 9, 2019
Family dinner at Carl and Katherine's home. Bruce, Gail, Paul, Allyne, Andrea and all of Paul's grandchildren were there.

August 28, 2019
While Paul and Carl are at Trinity Springs discussing Paul's move, Sandy shows upand demands to see Paul. That was not allowed and Paul's attorney blocked all future visits from Sandy.

September 3, 2019
Paul moved to the memory care unit at Trinity Springs.

September 30, 2019
Mailed Bar complaint against Michael Hollander.

October 4, 2019
Judge Morley stated that Amanda A. Ritter is qualified and appointed plenary guardian of the person and property of John Paul Baker.

October 10, 2019
Paul had appointment with Dr. Winn at the VA Clinic. Both Merideth and Cher were present and had a private meeting with the Doctor.

October 22, 2019
Carl, Katherine, Bruce, and Gail took Paul to lunch to discuss Sandy's request (petition) to visit him. Paul was adamant that he did not want to see her or have anything to do with her.

October 25, 2019
Amanda and Cher took Sandy to see Paul without Paul's approval and without our knowledge. This violated a number of the standards that guide their conduct.

November 1, 2019
Court hearing on Sandy's petition to visit Paul. The court granted her request, but required supervision.

November 5, 2019
Sandy, Sandy's sister, Sandy's minister and Amanda visited Paul at Trinity Springs. Paul told me later that afternoon that "four girls from his high school" came to visit him.

December 6, 2019
Meeting with Amanda, Cher, Bruce, Gail, Katherine and Carl to discuss Sandy's future visits with Paul.

December 11, 2019
Amanda, Cher, Carl, Sandy, and Sandy's minister visited Paul.

December 20, 2019
Sandy visited Paul alone without Amanda's approval in violation of

the court order. Sandy is now barred from visiting Paul.

December 27, 2019
Sandy's attorneys petitioned the court to be released from representing Sandy. Sandy's first law firm did the same.

January 17, 2020
Amanda and Cher brought most of Paul's clothing and some personal property to Carl'shouse. This is over a year after Paul left Sandy.

February 12, 2020
Paul diagnosed with breast cancer, possibly from exposure to Agent Orange in Viet Nam.

April 2, 2020
Paul had surgery for breast cancer. Everything went well.

April 22, 2020
Letters sent to Governor DeSantis and Attorney General Moody requesting a review of case.

July 14, 2020
Paul and Sandy's house did not close and the seller cancelled the contract. It is the second time this occurred and the blame clearly rests with Paul's guardian and attorney who made an error on a court document. Sandy had left the house vacant and moved to Bossier City, Louisiana.

July 20, 2020
Paul tested positive with the COVID-19 virus.

August 7, 2020
It was verified that Sandy illegally had taken, sold,or disposed of

most of Paul's pre-marital furniture, wall hangings, light fixtures, tools, and personal property. The Antenuptial Agreement states that these assets "remain the sole and exclusive and separate property" of Paul. In addition, she took possession of property that they each paid one-half of the initial cost - e.g., golf cart, furniture, rugs, lighting fixtures and more.

December 21, 2020
Letter sent to State Representative Brett T. Hage.

December 30, 2020
Paul and Sandy's house sold.

February 12, 2021
After 6 days in the hospital, Paul was placed in hospice at Trinity Springs.

February 22, 2021
Since I did not receive a reply from my first letter to Representative Hage, I sent a second letter to his office.

February 26, 2021
I received an email from Representative Hage's office which began a discussion on Paul's case and other issues.

March 7, 2021
I sent a reply email to Representative Hage's office after reviewing House Bill 441 (Eldercaring Coordination) and outlining my concerns and included a summary of our experience with Eldercaring.

July 1, 2021
House Bill 441 passed in April and will take effect July 1. The Bill

states, "The court will consider whether a party has committed an act of exploitation of an elderly or disabled adult or domestic violence..."

August 10, 2021

I personally delivered a copy of this case study to Representative Hage's office and mailed a copy to the Office of the Chief Inspector General.

December 15, 2021

I never received a response to four communications I sent to Governor DeSantis or two letters to the Inspector General.

APPENDIX B

Paul's Trusts
2014 – 2018

APPENDIX B

	THE JOHN PAUL BAKER TRUSTS				
DATE	8/18/2014	6/15/2016	9/20/2018	12/3/2018	1/23/2019
Decision Maker	Paul Baker	Paul Baker	Sandra Baker	Sandra Baker	Paul/Carl Baker
Successor Trustees	Allyne Baker Carl Baker Bruce Baker	Carl Baker Bruce Baker	Sandra Baker	Sandra Baker	Mark Baker Allyne Baker
Power of Attorney	Allyne Baker Carl Baker Bruce Baker	Carl Baker Bruce Baker	Sandra Baker [1]	Sandra Baker	Carl Baker [2] Bruce Baker
Health Care Surrogates	Allyne Baker Carl Baker Bruce Baker	Sandra Baker Carl Baker Bruce Baker	Sandra Baker Mark Baker	Sandra Baker Mark Baker	Mark Baker [3] Allyne Baker Carl Baker Bruce Baker
Distribution	Allyne Baker 65% Mark Baker 35%	Allyne Baker 65% Mark Baker 35%	Allyne Baker 15% [4] Mark Baker 50% Kaila Baker 35% (grand daughter)	Allyne Baker 50% Mark Baker 50%	Allyne Baker 65% Mark Baker 35%
Residence	Allyne Baker	Sandra must sell home within 12 months of Paul's death. Paul's half of sale proceeds go to Paul's Trust account	Sandra may utilize [5] home as long as she chooses (lives). Paul's half of sale proceeds go to Mark and Allyne	Sandra may utilize home as long as she chooses (lives). Paul's half of sale proceeds go to Mark and Allyne	Sandra must sell home [6] within 12 months of Paul's death. Paul's half of sale proceeds go to Paul's Trust account

Footnotes

1 This would have given Sandra complete control of Paul's trust funds as soon as he was ruled incapacitated. This has been her plan right from the beginning. She could have spent it any way she saw fit, believing there would be no guardian and she had sole power of attorney. This is criminal exploitation.

Note: In Paul's trusts (prior to the September 20, 2018, trust which was created by Sandra), all of Paul's residue of his estate would be distributed to Mark Baker and Allyne Baker, in accordance with the provisions of the trust. When Sandra changed Paul's trust on September 20, 2018, she also had Paul change his Last Will and Testament to state that if the Trust Agreement is not in existence on the date of his death, he gives, devises and bequeaths all tangible property and all of the residue of his estate to Sandra if she survives him. Clearly there would be no need for such a change unless she intended to have Paul revoke his trust. This has been Sandra's goal from the beginning and is a textbook case of exploitation, which is why she started isolating Paul from his family in August 2018 - one month before she had Paul change his trust documents.

2 Paul is unsure if he will stay in Florida or return to New York where his children and grandchildren live. For convenience sake, Carl and Bruce Baker would only have power of attorney as long as Paul is in Florida. The plan was to change the power of attorney to Mark and Allyne Baker if or when Paul moves back to New York.

3 The attorney suggested that all four of us be health care surrogates to cover both Florida and New York.

4 Sandra disliked Carl, Bruce and Allyne because she knew they stood in her way to gain control of Paul's trust funds. The change in distribution for Allyne from 65% to 15% was the result of Sandra's hatred and jealousy of Allyne and her need to demonstrate that she was in control of Paul.

5 Another example of criminal exploitation. The statute includes "the intent to temporarily deprive the use of funds, assets, or property..."

6 The Antenuptial Agreement signed by Paul and Sandra on 6-17-16 also states that upon the death of either party, the survivor shall have up to twelve months to either sell the residence or to buy-out the other spouse's interest. If sold, the proceeds shall be divided equally between Paul's trust and Sandra's trust.

APPENDIX C

Antenuptial Agreement

Carl R. Baker

ANTENUPTIAL AGREEMENT

THIS ANTENUPTIAL AGREEMENT entered into by and between JOHN PAUL BAKER (hereinafter referred to as "Husband") and SANDRA J. KANIEWSKI (hereinafter referred to as "Wife").

WITNESSETH:

WHEREAS the parties hereto intend to enter into marriage, each to the other, and both parties have in his or her own right certain real and/or personal property at the time of their intended marriage; and

WHEREAS the parties desire to make reasonable and sufficient provisions in release and in full satisfaction of all rights which they have or could acquire, by reason of their marriage, in and to the property which the parties now individually own or may hereafter individually acquire, to settle all questions of property and financial responsibility between them, and to otherwise fix their rights in and to all their property; and

WHEREAS the parties acknowledge that each Party prior to their marriage to one another has accumulated assets and wealth and the parties further acknowledge that it is their intention that such assets and wealth of each Party shall remain the sole and exclusive and separate property of such Party except as otherwise provided herein; and

WHEREAS each Party intends that his/her separate property shall inure to the sole and exclusive benefit of himself/herself while the Parties are married or in the event of the dissolution of the Parties' marriage, or to his/her own beneficiaries in the event of the death of said Party except as otherwise expressly provided herein by said Party; and

WHEREAS each Party acknowledges that they have provided a fair and reasonable disclosure of their earnings, property and financial obligations to the other as more fully set forth on attached Schedule A and Schedule B; and

WHEREAS the Parties are desirous of settling their property rights, and it is the desire of both parties to finally and for all time settle, adjust, compromise and determine the respective property rights of each party against the other by reason of their impending marriage, all dower, curtesy, and homestead rights and all other rights existing between the parties growing out of their impending marriage relationship, whether arising by statute or by common law; and

WHEREAS it is expressly understood and agreed that this Agreement shall not be construed as a consent by either party to a separation, nor a condonation by either party of any conduct of the other, nor, except as in this Agreement otherwise provided, as a waiver by either party of any right or cause of action arising by reason of the conduct of the other. Nevertheless, it is understood that each party hereto hereby reserves all such rights as he or she may have to commence and consummate proceedings in any court of competent jurisdiction with respect to an action for divorce should the impending marriage fail; and

WHEREAS the Parties each acknowledge and represent that this Agreement has been executed by each of them free from fraud, undue influence or economic, physical or emotional duress of any kind whatsoever exerted by the other or by any persons and that the Parties each have entered into this

Agreement freely and voluntarily and that no one has caused them to enter into this Agreement through coercion, force, pressure or undue influence.

NOW THEREFORE, in consideration of the marriage and the mutual promises and benefits accruing to the parties hereto, the parties agree as follows:

1. **Consideration.**

The parties to this Agreement acknowledge that the provisions of this Agreement, and their marriage to each other, are the considerations for the Agreement and are sufficient consideration to support the Agreement. The parties love each other dearly and it is their intention to make their marriage last until death do them part. However, it is their mutual conviction that this Agreement is in their own best interests and entered into with the desire that it will strengthen their marriage and keep them together as Husband and Wife forever.

2. **Property/Financial Disclosure.**

The parties acknowledge that disclosure of JOHN PAUL BAKER'S income and his separate property, real or personal, owned by him at the time of execution of this Agreement is set forth on Schedule A, incorporated by reference and attached herein, and that disclosure of SANDRA J. KANIEWSKI'S income and her separate property, real or personal, owned by her at the time of execution of this Agreement is set forth on Schedule B, incorporated by reference and attached herein. Further, to facilitate full and fair disclosure of any income, expenses, assets and liabilities of each party prior to their marriage not otherwise contained in Schedule A or Schedule B to this Agreement, JOHN PAUL BAKER and SANDRA J. KANIEWSKI acknowledge they each have been provided Family Law Financial Affidavit forms by MILLHORN ELDER LAW PLANNING GROUP and have been advised to exchange the information contained therein (Present Gross Monthly Income and Deductions; Average Monthly Expenses; and Assets and Liabilities) prior to their marriage. JOHN PAUL BAKER and SANDRA J. KANIEWSKI signify that they understand and agree to waive financial disclosures beyond the information contained in Schedule A and Schedule B to this Agreement by initialing below:

JOHN PAUL BAKER'S INITIALS _____   SANDRA J. KANIEWSKI'S INITIALS _____

3. **JOHN PAUL BAKER'S Separate Property.**

All of the tangible and intangible real and personal property now owned or hereafter acquired by JOHN PAUL BAKER, in his individual name, shall remain his sole and separate property through the marriage and shall forever remain non-marital property, except as set forth herein (specifically noting that the Marital Home is discussed in Paragraph 11 of this Agreement, and the provisions of that Paragraph control the treatment of the Marital Home), and SANDRA J. KANIEWSKI shall not have any right, title interest, lien or claim under the present or future laws of the State of Florida, or any other jurisdiction, in or to any of JOHN PAUL BAKER'S separate property. The Parties acknowledge and agree that during the marriage, SANDRA J. KANIEWSKI may devote considerable personal time, skill, service, industry and effort and money to the investment and management of JOHN PAUL BAKER'S separate property and the income therefrom. Any such monetary or non-monetary contribution whether such contribution produces increased value, dividends, rents, interests, profits, appreciation, or other forms of income shall not cause any change of characterization of such property, and such property shall remain JOHN PAUL BAKER'S separate property and shall not create any interest subject to equitable distribution, a community property interest, community property income, community property assets, or a claim to an equitable lien. Such contributions by SANDRA J. KANIEWSKI shall not create any other claim, right, lien or interest whatsoever in favor of SANDRA J. KANIEWSKI in or to JOHN PAUL BAKER'S separate property.

    A) All of JOHN PAUL BAKER'S separate property shall be free from any claim or demand by SANDRA J. KANIEWSKI at any time during the marriage or in the event of separation or marital dissolution. JOHN PAUL BAKER shall be free to sell, use, transfer, exchange, abandon, lease, consume, expend, assign, create a security interest in, mortgage, encumber, dispose of or otherwise control or manage his separate property as if unmarried.

    B) Except as otherwise set forth herein, the following events shall not, under any circumstances, be evidence of any intention by either Party of any agreement between the Parties to change their separate property into marital property:

    a) any oral statements by either Party;

    b) any written statement by either Party other than an express written Agreement, which has been notarized and which specifically expresses the Parties' mutual intent to change specifically enumerated separate property into marital property;

    c) the filing of joint tax returns;

    d) the designation of one Party by the other as a beneficiary of his or her estate or trust under the terms of any contractual asset including, but not limited to, any life insurance policy, any survivor annuity or other lifetime or death benefit under any pension, profit sharing or other employee benefit plan or retirement plan;

    e) any monetary or non-monetary payment or contribution from the separate property of either Party toward the separate property of the other Party or toward obligations including, but not limited to, mortgage or deed of trust payments, real property taxes, home owners association or condominium fees or other like fees, income taxes, repairs, maintenance or capital improvements with respect to any real property which is separate property of the other Party or real property which is titled in the sole name of the other Party (or in the joint names of the other Party and one or more third Parties);or

    f) the occupation or use by one Party of any real property which is separate property of the other Party or real property which is titled in the sole name of the other Party (or in the joint names of the other Party and one or more third Parties).

4. **SANDRA J. KANIEWSKI'S Separate Property.**
All of the tangible and intangible real and personal property now owned or hereafter acquired by SANDRA J. KANIEWSKI, in her individual name, shall remain her sole and separate property through the marriage and shall forever remain non-marital property, except as set forth herein, and JOHN PAUL

BAKER shall not have any right, title interest, lien or claim under the present or future laws of the State of Florida, or any other jurisdiction, in or to any of SANDRA J. KANIEWSKI'S separate property. The Parties acknowledge and agree that during the marriage, JOHN PAUL BAKER may devote considerable personal time, skill, service, industry and effort and money to the investment and management of SANDRA J. KANIEWSKI'S separate property and the income therefrom. Any such monetary or non-monetary contribution whether such contribution produces increased value, dividends, rents, interests, profits, appreciation, or other forms of income shall not cause any change of characterization of such property, and such property shall remain SANDRA J. KANIEWSKI'S separate property and shall not create any interest subject to equitable distribution, a community property interest, community property income, community property assets, or a claim to an equitable lien. Such contributions by JOHN PAUL BAKER shall not create any other claim, right, lien or interest whatsoever in favor of JOHN PAUL BAKER in or to SANDRA J. KANIEWSKI'S separate property.

A)   All of SANDRA J. KANIEWSKI'S separate property shall be free from any claim or demand by JOHN PAUL BAKER at any time during the marriage or in the event of separation or marital dissolution. SANDRA J. KANIEWSKI shall be free to sell, use, transfer, exchange, abandon, lease, consume, expend, assign, create a security interest in, mortgage, encumber, dispose of or otherwise control or manage her separate property as if unmarried.

B)   Except as otherwise set forth herein, the following events shall not, under any circumstances, be evidence of any intention by either Party of any agreement between the Parties to change their separate property into marital property:

    a)   any oral statements by either Party;

    b)   any written statement by either Party other than an express written Agreement, which has been notarized and which specifically expresses the Parties' mutual intent to change specifically enumerated separate property into marital property;

    c)   the filing of joint tax returns;

    d)   the designation of one Party by the other as a beneficiary of his or her estate or trust under the terms of any contractual asset including, but not limited to, any life insurance policy, any survivor annuity or other lifetime or death benefit under any pension, profit sharing or other employee benefit plan or retirement plan;

    e)   any monetary or non-monetary payment or contribution from the separate property of either Party toward the separate property of the other Party or toward obligations including, but not limited to, mortgage or deed of trust payments, real property taxes, home owners association or condominium fees or other like fees, income taxes, repairs, maintenance or capital improvements with respect to any real property which is separate property of the other Party or real property which is titled in the sole name of the other Party (or in the joint names of the other Party and one or more third Parties); or

    f)   the occupation or use by one Party of any real property which is separate property of the other Party or real property which is titled in the sole name of the other Party (or in the joint names of the other Party and one or more third Parties).

5. **Property Acquired During Marriage.**

Except for property which constitutes Separate Property under Paragraph 3 and subparts and Paragraph 4 and subparts hereinabove and for property which constitutes the Marital Home under Paragraph 11, all property acquired during the marriage shall be owned as follows irrespective of monetary or non-monetary contributions made by either Party:

    A) If there is written evidence of who holds title to certain property, including but not limited to a deed, automobile title, DMV title, or bank, brokerage and trust account signature card or other account agreement, then such property shall be owned in accordance with such written evidence. The Parties may also choose to enter into a written agreement (which must be executed with the same formality as this Agreement) which may adjust the percentage of ownership in any property according to percentage of down payment made, the percentage of mortgage to be paid, the percentage of repairs to be made, or according to any other method of determining percentage as the Parties may agree; in addition, said written agreement may set forth the respective liabilities of the Parties for the amount of down payment, monthly mortgage payments, household expenses, repairs, or any and all other type of liability for the property, as the Parties may agree. If the property is jointly titled in the name of the Parties and the title does not specify otherwise and there is no written agreement (which must be executed with the same formality as this Agreement) to the contrary, the property shall be owned equally by the Parties. If the property is titled in the sole name of one of the Parties, the property shall be owned solely by the Party in whose name the property is titled.

    B) If there is no written evidence of who holds title to certain property then such other property shall be equally owned by the Parties, provided, however, that any tangible personal property brought into the marriage by either of the Parties shall remain the separate property of the Party bringing the property into the marriage.

    C) Each Party shall be free to title any property acquired by him or her (other than property titled jointly in the names of the Parties) in his or her sole name (or jointly in his or her name and the name of one or more third Parties) and such property so titled shall be owned solely by the Party who is the named titled holder and shall not be subject to claims of the other Party of any nature, type or kind whatsoever.

6. **Gifts to Each Other.**

Neither Party shall have any obligation to make inter vivos or testamentary gifts, transfers, conveyances, devises or bequests of property to the other, except as otherwise provided in this Agreement, and each Party specifically agrees that no promises have been made by either of them regarding any such inter vivos or testamentary gifts, transfers, conveyances, devises or bequests of property other than set forth in this Agreement. However, the Parties do not intend by this Agreement to restrict their respective rights to make or to receive any inter vivos or testamentary gifts, transfers, conveyances, devises or bequests to or from the other Party. Nothing in this Agreement shall preclude either Party from designating the other Party as a beneficiary under any insurance policy, pension, profit sharing or other employee benefit plan or retirement plan, and this Agreement shall not operate as a waiver of either Party's right to take by reason of such designation whether such designation was made prior to or subsequent to the date of this Agreement. Further, nothing in this Agreement shall preclude either Party from taking property from the other by reason of the titling of such property as joint tenants with right of survivorship, or as tenants by the entireties, regardless of the date of the creation of the tenancy, and nothing in this Agreement shall preclude either Party from serving as the other Party's personal representative or trustee if such other Party is expressly named to serve as such Party's personal representative or trustee under the terms of his or her will or trust agreement executed after the date of execution of this Agreement.

7. **Pre-Marital Debt.**

The Parties represent and acknowledge to each other that whatever debts they had at the time of entry into the marriage have been disclosed to each other prior to entering into this Agreement. Any separate, pre-marital debt of the Parties, including but not limited to credit card debt incurred prior to the marriage, shall be their sole and exclusive obligation and they shall not call upon the other Party to satisfy same or pay for same in any manner.

8. **Financial Arrangements during the Marriage.**

Except as otherwise set forth in this Agreement, the Parties specifically make no delineation as to the precise use of their income during the marriage, other than to state their general intention that their incomes shall be used for their mutual benefit for the purposes of maintaining a lifestyle upon which the Parties mutually agree. It is not the present expectation of either Party to seek to have the other Party utilize pre-marital assets in order to pay their expenses, including but not limited to individual medical and dental expenses, whether normally incurred or incurred as a result of catastrophic illness. With the exception of this Agreement between the Parties, the income of each of the Parties shall be used as each so determines free from any claim of the other Party.

9. **Community Property.**

The Parties agree that in the event that at any time during their marriage they should become residents of a community property state, under the laws of which JOHN PAUL BAKER and SANDRA J. KANIEWSKI acquire property interests in the community, or any other statute under the laws of which property interests are different from property interests of JOHN PAUL BAKER and SANDRA J. KANIEWSKI under the laws of the State of Florida, their property interests shall nevertheless remain the same as they would have been under the terms and provisions of this Agreement construed in accordance with the laws of the State of Florida as if the Parties remained residents of the State of Florida.

The Parties hereto agree that they and their respective executors, administrators, personal representatives, heirs-at-law, devisees, legatees, distributes, trustees, beneficiaries, successors and assigns or other transferees, will each make, execute, acknowledge and deliver any and all deeds and other instruments which shall be necessary or desirable to transfer any right, title or interest in any property or estate of the other which they or their respective estates may acquire by virtue of any community property laws or other laws of inheritance or ownership of property which would change the disposition otherwise determined by the State of Florida to the person who would otherwise be entitled thereto by virtue of State of Florida law.

10. **Insurance Coverage.**

Neither Party agrees at this time to provide any health, medical, disability, life insurance, or any other type of insurance coverage for or on behalf of the other. The Parties agree that any Insurance Policy now titled in JOHN PAUL BAKER'S sole name shall remain his sole and separate property; and that any Insurance Policy now titled in SANDRA J. KANIEWSKI'S sole name shall remain her sole and separate property; ownership in each instance to be free from any claim or right on the part of the other.

11. **The Marital Home.**

The Parties acknowledge that upon their marriage they intend to reside at 3723 Mango Court, The Villages, Florida 32163 ("the marital home"), this property being equally owned by JOHN PAUL BAKER and SANDRA J. KANIEWSKI as tenants-in-common. The parties' use of this residence or any other separately-owned residence as the parties' marital home shall in no way confer/convey or transmute the character of this property to marital property from the sole and separate property of the individual who owned the property prior to the marriage, even if the marital home is later titled in joint names. The party who supplied the funds for the property's purchase shall be deemed the sole owner of the home, unless a subsequent amendment to this Agreement states otherwise. If another residence is purchased during the marriage and subsequently used as the marital home, ownership of that residence will be based pro rata on the contribution of each of the parties to the purchase of and payments for that residence.

Upon the death of JOHN PAUL BAKER or SANDRA J. KANIEWSKI, then upon that event, JOHN PAUL BAKER and SANDRA J. KANIEWSKI agree that the survivor of JOHN PAUL BAKER or SANDRA J. KANIEWSKI shall have up to twelve (12) months from the date of the death of JOHN PAUL BAKER or SANDRA J. KANIEWSKI to either sell the residence and property, or to buy-out the other spouse's interest in the residence and property. In the event the residence and property is sold, then the net proceeds from the sale of the residence and property shall be divided equally between the surviving spouse and the deceased spouse's revocable trust.

12. **Vehicles.**

The Parties agree that the automobile now titled in JOHN PAUL BAKER'S sole name shall remain his sole and separate property; and that the automobile now titled in SANDRA J. KANIEWSKI'S sole name shall remain her sole and separate property; ownership in each instance to be free from any claim or right on the part of the other. Each agrees to hold the other harmless as to the operation, maintenance and all financial responsibilities arising out of the ownership of said vehicles, including any property tax for or liens thereon.

13. **Individual Retirement Accounts.**

The Parties agree that any Retirement Accounts now titled in JOHN PAUL BAKER'S sole name shall remain his sole and separate property; and that any Retirement Accounts now titled in SANDRA J. KANIEWSKI'S sole name shall remain her sole and separate property; ownership in each instance to be free from any claim or right on the part of the other.

14. **Support.**

JOHN PAUL BAKER and SANDRA J. KANIEWSKI hereby expressly waive and release any and all rights that they may have to receive or claim support and maintenance, spousal support, or alimony from one another, and to that end, each party agrees that they will at no time hereafter seek or ask, in any manner, any monies of any nature from one another except as set forth in this Agreement. Further, the parties warrant and agree that in the event of separation and/or if divorce proceedings are instituted by either of them, neither party shall, in such proceedings, make demand for alimony or support and maintenance from the other except as provided in this Agreement. To that end, JOHN PAUL BAKER and SANDRA J. KANIEWSKI expressly waive the right to receive alimony in any form from the other at any time (temporary, permanent, lump sum or rehabilitative), and further each party expressly waives any and all right, entitlement, interest, or claim for alimony in any form from the other now or at any time in the future except as set forth in this Agreement.

15. **Encumbrances or Disposition of Property.**

Each Party retains the management and control of his or her sole and separate property and may encumber, sell or dispose of this property without the consent of the other party. Each Party shall execute any instrument necessary to effectuate this paragraph promptly at the request of the other party (provided that no personal liability is incurred by the non-encumbering party). If either Party does not join in or execute an instrument as required by this paragraph, the other party may sue for specific performance or for damages regardless of the doctrine of spousal immunity, and the defaulting party shall be responsible for the other party's costs, expenses and attorney's fees. This paragraph shall not require a party to execute a Promissory Note or other evidence of debt, provided that a Party may be required to execute a mortgage, deed of trust, or similar instrument encumbering property on which the Parties reside (provided that no personal liability shall arise or be attributable to the unencumbering party). Execution of an instrument shall not give the Party executing it any right or interest in the property of the party requesting the execution.

16. **Disposition of Property Upon Death of a Party.**

Each Party consents that the estate of the other may be disposed of by a Will, Codicil or other testamentary devise, or a Will substitute, to the devisees of the other party as if the marriage had not taken place, or in the absence of a Will or its substitute, that the estate of each Party shall descend to the heirs of that Party as if the marriage had not taken place. In either event, the estate shall be free of any claim or demand of inheritance, dower, courtesy, family allowance, exempt property, the elective share or any spousal claim or other claim given by law, irrespective of the marriage and any law to the contrary.

    A) Each Party to this Agreement hereby expressly waives any and all rights, including the above-referenced rights in and to the other party's estate, specifically including any share that they might, by law, have the option of electing to take in case of the death of the other spouse.

    B) Neither Party intends by this Agreement to limit or restrict the right to give or receive a testamentary gift from the other. Either of the Parties may elect to make a gift to the other by Will without invalidating this paragraph, and may thereafter change or eliminate the gift by a Codicil or other Will without in any way affecting the continued effectiveness of this Agreement.

17. **Mutual Cooperation.**

The Parties agree and covenant that they will make, execute and deliver the writings and instruments necessary to effectuate the provisions of this Agreement and to carry out the true intent and purpose of the parties.

18. **Waiver of Homestead, Property, Estate and Other Rights.**

Each Party waives all rights in the property and/or estate of the other, to include but not be limited to the rights to elective share, intestate share, homestead property, exempt property and family allowance, and releases any claim, demand, right or interest that may be acquired as a result of the marriage in and to any real property of the other because of the homestead property provision of the Florida Constitution, or any Florida Statute as it relates to the descent of the property as homestead.

19. **Income Taxes; Tax Planning.**

The Parties shall file annually any required income tax returns, federal, state or otherwise, either jointly or separately, as determined by agreement between them each period. If separate returns are filed, each Party shall pay his or her own income tax, and any interest or penalties thereon. If a return is filed jointly, each Party shall contribute his or her proportionate share of the tax, and any interest and penalty thereon, based upon their respective taxable incomes. Each Party agrees to elect to "split" any gifts made by the other, if requested, so as to qualify the gifts for the annual exclusion from taxable gifts for federal gift tax purposes under Subtitle B of the Federal Code, and to sign and file any gift tax return in order to effectuate the election of the split gift.

20. **Marriage, Dissolution or Separation.**

This Agreement shall be construed as the Settlement Agreement in the event of a separation or Dissolution of Marriage of the parties hereto, and shall not be subject to modification by Final Judgment of Dissolution of Marriage, or any subsequent Order or Decree of the court having jurisdiction thereof. This Agreement shall govern all of the rights to property, alimony, temporary support, permanent support, lump sum alimony, rehabilitative alimony, property settlement or costs or attorney's fees upon a separation or dissolution of the marriage of the parties. In the event the parties separate or file for a Dissolution of Marriage, the property acquired by the parties during the marriage which is held as tenants in common shall be divided according to the fractional ownership of each party; property held as a tenancy by the entireties shall be equally divided between the two parties. In the event several parcels of real property are owned by the parties, and the parties do not want to divide ownership of properties, the parties may mutually agree among themselves as to which parcels of real property each party desires to have, and Quit-Claim Deeds shall be executed between the parties to effect ownership in the respective parties in accordance with such agreement. Each party releases all claims or demands that either of them may acquire because of the marriage or because of their relationship prior to marriage.

21. **Release.**

Except as otherwise provided in this Agreement, each Party releases all claims or demands in the property or estate of the other, however and whenever acquired, including acquisitions in the future. If a Party becomes the owner of or acquires the right to an asset during the marriage from any source other than the party's spouse, then that asset shall remain free from all claims, demands, inheritances, rights or suits of the other party or their estate.

22. **Debts.**

Neither Party shall assume or become responsible for the payment of any pre-existing debts or obligations of the other Party because of the marriage. Neither Party shall do anything that would cause the debt or obligation of one of them to be a claim, demand, lien or encumbrance against the property of the other without the other party's written consent. If a debt or obligation of one Party is asserted as a claim or demand against the other without such written consent, the party who is responsible for the debt or obligation shall indemnify the other party from the claim or demand, including the indemnified Party's costs, expenses and attorney's fees.

23. **Counsel.**

The Parties acknowledge that each has been advised not to enter into this Agreement without the advice of separate, independent legal counsel, and if either Party signs this Agreement without the advice of separate, independent counsel he or she does so freely, voluntarily and with full knowledge of his or her respective individual rights and obligations under this Agreement or arising because of the contemplated marriage between the Parties, and the extent to which that party's legal rights are affected by this Agreement. This Agreement was drafted at the specific request and by the mutual consent of both JOHN PAUL BAKER and SANDRA J. KANIEWSKI, jointly, by MILLHORN ELDER LAW PLANNING GROUP, following full disclosure that independent counsel was available to each party, and MILLHORN ELDER LAW PLANNING GROUP was retained for the sole purpose of assisting JOHN PAUL BAKER and SANDRA J. KANIEWSKI in drafting an Agreement crafted jointly by JOHN PAUL BAKER and SANDRA J. KANIEWSKI. JOHN PAUL BAKER and SANDRA J. KANIEWSKI signify that they understand and agree to MILLHORN ELDER LAW PLANNING GROUP drafting this Agreement at the specific request and by the mutual consent of both Parties, jointly, by initialing below:

JOHN PAUL BAKER'S INITIALS _____   SANDRA J. KANIEWSKI'S INITIALS _____

24. **Entire Agreement.**

The Parties have incorporated in this Agreement their entire understanding. No oral statements or prior written matter extrinsic to this Agreement shall have any force or effect. The Parties are not relying upon any representations other than those expressly set forth in this Agreement. The Parties warrant there have been no promises, representations, warranties or undertakings by either Party to the other, oral or written, of any character or nature, except as set forth herein.

25. **Costs of Enforcement.**

The Parties agree that any costs, including but not limited to counsel fees, court costs, investigation fees and travel expenses, incurred by a Party in the successful enforcement of any of the covenants or provisions of this Agreement, whether through litigation or other action necessary to compel compliance herewith, shall be borne by the defaulting party. Any such costs incurred by a party in the successful defense to any action for enforcement of any of the covenants or provisions of this Agreement shall be borne by the party seeking to enforce compliance.

26. **Captions; Gender; Number.**

The paragraph and subparagraph headings in this Agreement are inserted for convenience only and are not a substantive part of this Agreement. Reference to any gender includes either masculine or feminine, as appropriate, and reference to any number includes both singular and plural where the context permits or requires.

27. **Prior Agreements Invalidated.**

The Parties, in consideration of the covenants herein contained, hereby cancel, annul and invalidate any and all prior pre-nuptial or any other agreements made by them.

28. **Governing Law.**

This Agreement shall be governed by the laws of the State of Florida unless both Parties agree otherwise in writing.

29. **Modification and Waiver.**

A modification or waiver of any of the provisions of this Agreement shall be effective only if made in writing and executed with the same formality of this Agreement. The failure of either Party to insist upon strict performance of any of the provisions of this Agreement shall not be construed as a waiver of any subsequent default of the same or similar nature.

30. **Benefit.**

This Agreement shall be binding upon and inure to the benefit of the Parties hereto, their estates, their heirs, legal representatives, Personal Representatives, successors and assigns.

31. **Effective Date.**

This Agreement shall be effective upon the date last signed by a Party.

[THIS SPACE HAS BEEN INTENTIONALLY LEFT BLANK]
[THIS DOCUMENT CONTINUES ON THE NEXT PAGE]

IN WITNESS WHEREOF, the parties hereto have signed, sealed and acknowledged this Antenuptial Agreement this 17 day of June, 2016, in the presence of:

_____
WITNESS #1, Sign Name

Kimberly R. Hess
WITNESS #1, Print Name

_____
WITNESS #2, Sign Name

Karon Hamilton
WITNESS #2, Print Name

_____
JOHN PAUL BAKER, Husband

_____
SANDRA J. KANIEWSKI, Wife

STATE OF Florida
COUNTY OF Sumter

The foregoing instrument was acknowledged and subscribed before me by JOHN PAUL BAKER, ____ who is personally known to me or ✓ who has produced a Florida Driver's License as identification, and SANDRA J. KANIEWSKI, ____ who is personally known to me or ✓ who has produced an Florida License as identification, and sworn to and subscribed before me by the witnesses, Kimberly R. Hess, _____, who is personally known to me, and Karon Hamilton, _____, who is personally known to me, and subscribed by me in the presence of the Grantors and the subscribing witnesses.

WITNESS my hand and official Seal in the County and State last aforesaid this 17 day of June, 2016.

{Notary Seal}

MARIE VARNER
MY COMMISSION # FF 917160
EXPIRES: September 10, 2019
Bonded Thru Notary Public Underwriters

_____
NOTARY PUBLIC, State of Florida